W9-AEA-975

THE GUINNESS BOOK OF

MUSIC

THE GUINNESS BOOK OF
MUSIC

GUINNESS BOOKS

Editor: Beatrice Frei
Art Editor: David Roberts
Illustrations and Diagrams: Peter Harris

First published in 1976
Second edition 1981
Third edition 1986

Published in Great Britain by Guinness Superlatives Ltd,
33 London Road, Enfield, Middlesex, England.

Typeset in Bembo
by DP Press Ltd, Sevenoaks, Kent
Printed and bound in Great Britain by
Butler & Tanner Ltd, Frome, Somerset

British Library Cataloguing in Publication Data

Dearling, Robert
The Guinness book of music.—3rd ed.
1. Music—History and criticism
I. Title II. Dearling, Celia
780′.9 ML160

ISBN 0–85112–460–7 (cased edition)

Cover design: David Roberts/Artwork: Peter Harris

Introduction

When *The Guinness Book of Music Facts and Feats* was first published in 1976 the emphasis was on the superlatives of music in the grand Guinness tradition: firsts, biggests, smallests, and other extremes of the subject. In addition to updating and correcting data given in the first edition, and expanding some categories while reducing others, the second edition (1981) introduced much new information gleaned from valuable correspondence from readers the world over and from further extensive study of the musical sources then available.

In the year of this second edition, the 20-volume *New Grove Dictionary of Music and Musicians* was published. It released a flood of information hitherto dammed up in theses and dissertations inaccessible to the general reader, as well as stimulating a great amount of original research by specialists in many subjects and many nations. The authors of this third edition of *The Guinness Book of Music* have checked many sources, but where information conflicts they have allowed *New Grove* to be the arbiter.

In preparing the present book some basic material has been retained (updated as necessary) in order to give perspective to the rest, but the bulk of the book concentrates on the stranger aspects of music: superlatives still, but sometimes only in their unique oddity. No apology is offered for presenting apparently insane facts alongside apparently sensible ones, even if it may seem that the world of music is peopled by thieves, lunatics, egocentric maniacs, mad inventors and charlatans determined to be the first to achieve some bizarre and worthless 'record'.

Some subjects have run their course and do not lend themselves to further development; others have received due attention, not only in Guinness publications but also elsewhere, and need no further exposure. Nevertheless, the scope of this book is even wider than before in that artists, previously excluded, now find a place; but the artists chosen are amongst the more colourful of the species, i.e. opera singers. Thieving composers who appropriate their colleagues' music with or without a by-your-leave are unmasked, and in the section called 'A Galaxy of Instruments' the authors list and describe many of the less-common Western instruments and some of the more interesting ethnic examples. Previous editions gave special attention to lute and bagpipe; in this edition it is the turn of the clarinet and drum families, both of which have interesting and involved histories. The final section lifts the lid off some of the stranger aspects of modern music.

Since the first edition appeared the authors have been fortunate in receiving many letters of encouragement. We are grateful to the large number of institutions and individuals who have assisted in bringing this mass of material together to make what we hope is a readable, entertaining and useful book. Many credits appear in their appropriate places; we assure those kind correspondents not mentioned that failure to make specific acknowledgement of their valuable assistance in no way implies a lack of appreciation.

In order to be of maximum help to the reader, this edition's index is widened to include subjects as well as people, and instruments are incorporated. To make room for what we think is a substantial gain in accessibility of information, some minor figures have been omitted. However, the expanded entries for subjects and major figures are designed to lead the reader to the topics of specific interest in this endlessly fascinating subject of music.

Robert and Celia Dearling,
Lincolnshire, England

Contents

Contents

I
Today's Orchestra

After centuries of change and development today's orchestra has arrived at a point at which it is a well-balanced, well-integrated unit capable of producing telling sounds whether playing alone or with soloists or choir. Yet each instrument has its own clear identity and its own history. We have tried to trace the origin of each, its acceptance into so-called 'serious' or 'art' music (which usually followed a long period of use as a folk instrument), its first use in the orchestra, its first concerto, and its first appearance in a symphony.

Grouping is by the traditional method: woodwind, brass, strings, percussion. The construction and working of instruments is left to more detailed textbooks, but a table of extreme upper and lower notes should help to place each instrument into its orchestral context.

Woodwind

Piccolo
It: *flauto piccolo, ottavino*
Fr: *petite flûte*
Ger: *kleine Flöte*

Today's piccolo, the highest-pitched woodwind instrument, is made of wood or metal or a combination of these. It plays an octave above the flute.

Highly-pitched flutes existed in prehistoric times, but as an instrument with close family ties with the flute it was not developed until the early 18th century, and then probably only because the flute makers, in order to compete with the recorder family, needed a flute to parallel the range of the sopranino recorder. Handel appears to have been the first to specify *flauto piccolo* (in *Water Music*, 1717). Vivaldi's three concerti, RV 443–445, usually played today on piccolo, were in fact written for *flautino*, the Italian term for flageolet, or sopranino recorder, and other 18th-century examples (for sixth-flute, octave-flute, etc.) were doubtless all written for types of recorder.

Metal piccolo, the highest voice in the modern woodwind section. (Photo: Les Prudden)

However, piccolo players in search of a true piccolo concerto are satisfied by Valentino Bucchi's work of 1973. Arcady Dubensky, the Russian violinist, wrote a *Capriccio* for solo piccolo in 1948, and there is a sonata for piccolo and piano (1956) by the Dutchman Ton Bruynèl.

Beethoven was the first to call for the instrument in a symphony: in the finale of the Fifth it is joined by double bassoon and trombones in a thrilling expansion and enrichment of symphonic resources.

Flute

It: *flauto (traverso)*
Fr: *flûte (traversière)*
Ger: *Flöte, Querflöte, Traversflöte*

The reedless flute (from Latin *flatus* = 'breath' or 'blowing') of wood or bone has a venerable history. It is no etymological accident that the Latin word *tibia* means both 'flute' and 'shin-bone'. An end-blown variety dates from Paleolithic times (long flutes have been found in early Egyptian sites of before 3300 BC) and led ultimately to the recorder family, but the side-blown flute ('cross-flute', 'traverse flute', 'transverse flute') occurs at least as early as the 9th century BC in China and may have existed earlier still in central Asia. After the Romans, the flute was forgotten until it re-emerged in Germany in the 10th century, having drifted across from Byzantium. It spread as a folk instrument, finally entering the orchestra in 1681 in Lully's ballet *Triomphe d'amour*. The first published works playable on the flute appeared during the 1690s, but other instruments were given as alternatives: the relative newcomer to art music was not yet quite accepted. The massive popularity of the flute began in 1702 with what is possibly the first publication to specify the flute without alternatives: Michel de la Barre's *Pièces pour la flûte traversière avec la basse-continue*.

The first flute 'concerti' are the seven Sonatas for flute and strings of 1725 by Alessandro Scarlatti, and the first concerti, so called, are Vivaldi's six of Op 10, published *c.*1729–30. The latter were, however, mostly if not completely arranged from chamber works, and it is doubtful whether Vivaldi did the arranging. The first symphonies to include flutes (two of them in two works) are A. Scarlatti's *12 Sinfonie di Concerti grosso*, begun in 1715.

Perhaps the instrument's popularity is now in better proportion than it was during the flute-crazed 18th century, when flute sonatas and concerti were produced in floods. J.J. Quantz wrote 312 concerti for his employer, King Frederick the Great, and the good king himself, not satisfied with Quantz's sonata total of at least 204, wrote 120 of his own. But flute mania persists still: Henry Brant wrote his *Angels and Devils* (1931) for flute solo accompanied by an orchestra of three piccolos, five flutes and two alto flutes; and in 1970 the Hungarian Zsolt Durkó composed a concerto for 12 flutes and orchestra.

The **flûte d'amour** and the **alto flute**, pitched respectively a minor third and a fourth below the flute, both arose during the 18th century and have been used occasionally since then for special effects in the orchestra. A concerto for flûte d'amour by J.M. Molter exists in the Karlsruhe Landesbibliothek (Mus Hs 307) and was composed possibly around 1750. The name 'bass flute', sometimes applied incorrectly to the alto flute, should be reserved for an instrument pitched an octave below the flute; it achieved a certain currency among Italian operatic composers early this century.

Oboe

It: *oboe*
Fr: *hautbois*
Ger: *Hoboe, Oboe*

A double-reed conical-bore instrument which, although regarded as a woodwind instrument and often constructed of hardwood, may today also be made of plastic or other synthetic material, or even of metal. Its history is somewhat obscure but seems to be involved with the shawm family, from which the 'hautbois' developed in France during the Middle Ages. The name comes from the French meaning 'high-' or 'loud-wood'. Its first orchestral use was in a ballet with music by Lully, *L'amore malade*, given in Paris in January 1657. As the oboe's popularity grew, especially in England, French players were imported to play the 'hoboy' or 'hautboy', these names sometimes preceded by the word 'French'. Henry Purcell (1659–95) did much to establish the instrument in English orchestral music; meanwhile, Torelli in Bologna was the first to use the oboe in works called 'symphony', e.g. Giegling 31, written before 1700. The first true oboe concerto was by Domenico Marcheselli, published in 1708.

The **oboe d'amore**, an alto instrument pitched in A, was first used by Bach and may have been developed at his instigation. Its use outside Bach's circle is extremely rare, Richard Strauss's *Symphonia Domestica* (1904) being the

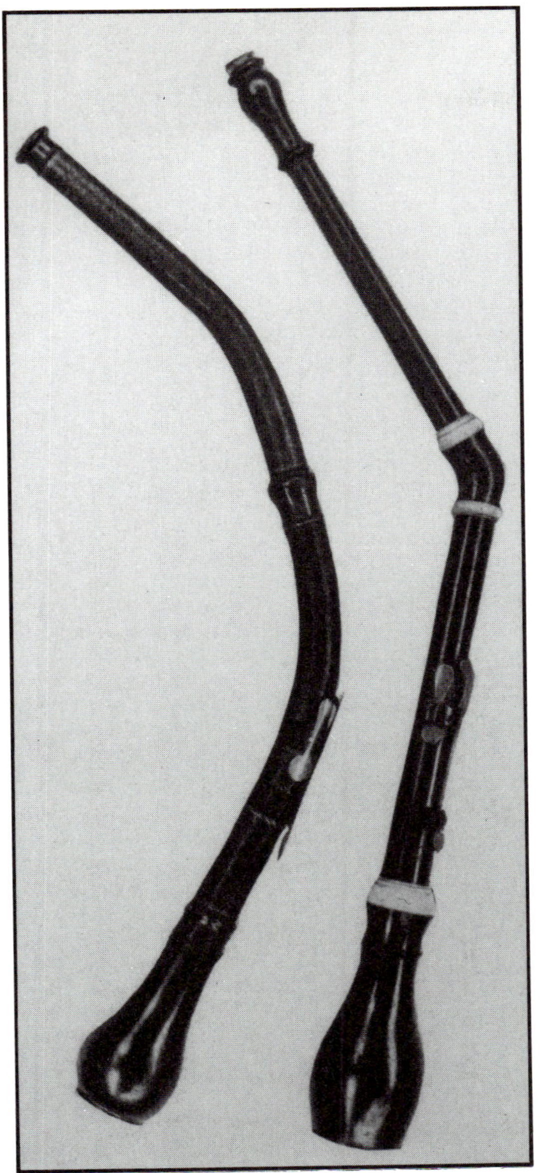

Cors anglais: far left Bimboni, Florence, c.1790; far right Milhouse, London, c.1800. Left: oboe and English horn. (Boosey & Hawkes Ltd)

most notable example. Less familiar, and rather odder, is the Concerto (1971) by Edward Bogusławski for oboe, oboe d'amore, musette and orchestra.

Known in Italian as *corno inglese*, in French as *cor anglais*, and in German as *Englisches Horn*, the **tenor oboe**'s name has been attributed to its early use by Purcell (thus, an instrument first used by an Englishman) and to its bent, or angled, shape. The origin of the component 'horn' is a complete mystery, however. The name *cor anglais* first arose in Vienna in the 1760s, and the instrument itself occurs in Haydn's Divertimento in F (Hob II:16), composed at Lukavec, near Pilsen, in Bohemia, in 1760, and in his Symphony No 22 in E flat, 'The Philosopher' (1764), composed in Eisenstadt, now in Austria. Doubtless it had been used before this in music now either lost or not yet recovered. Later it became known in chamber music, e.g. by Mozart (Adagio in C, K 580A, for cor anglais, violin, viola and cello, 1789) and by Michael Haydn (Quartet in C, Perger 115, for cor anglais, violin, cello and bass, 1795). Cor anglais concerti are rare: Paganini's of *c.*1805 is lost, leaving Donizetti's Concertino of 1817 as the earliest in existence. In 1949 the German composer Siegfried Borris also wrote a Cor Anglais Concertino.

The **oboe da caccia** is a mirage. Once thought to be a type of cor anglais, the term refers merely to a servant who played oboe at hunting parties.

The **baritone-** or **bass-oboe** sounds an octave below the standard soprano oboe and appeared probably before 1750, but in today's orchestra its part is taken by the Heckelphone, invented in 1903 by Wilhelm Heckel of Bierbach-am-Rhein, and first specified by Richard Strauss in his opera *Salome* (1905).

At the very bottom of the oboe range comes the **contrabass oboe**, invented by one Delusse in the 18th century. It is difficult to imagine what advantage this has over the bassoon in the same range; indeed, when it was first introduced at the Paris Opéra in 1784 it was played by a bassoonist.

Clarinet

It: *clarinetto*
Fr: *clarinette*
Ger: *Klarinette*

The clarinet is a single-reed instrument of mainly cylindrical bore, the youngest member of the orchestral woodwind (with the exception of the saxophone, which, although usually grouped with the woodwind, is made of metal). If all the members of the clarinet family are taken into account (see p 13), it is the instrument with the widest range of all. Early this century a performance of Mozart's Symphony No 40 in G minor was given at the Brussels Conservatory with all parts played in their correct registers by clarinets. Since then, a further extension has been made at the very bottom of the range with the invention of the somewhat superfluous, and perhaps unplayable, sub-contrabass clarinet.

Single-reed instruments were slow to enter the orchestra because traditionally they were regarded as folk instruments, suitable for dancing to but out of place in art music. Many folk instruments are still loosely termed 'clarinets', among them certain multiple-pipe examples with chanters or drone pipes that are in effect bagpipes without bags; and Dr Hans Hickmann, during his studies of early Egyptian musical instruments, called a single-reed pipe a clarinet, for want of its real name. Some ethnic examples are noted on pp 14–15, but the list makes no claim of completeness.

The clarinet was invented during the last decade of the 17th century by the firm of J.C. Denner (1655–1707) of Nuremberg, it being a development of the recorder and shawm families. The reported action of Denner was that he 'improved the shawm and invented the clarinet', which does *not* mean that the clarinet is merely an improved shawm, with the shawm becoming obsolete, for the Denner firm continued to make shawms for many years, calling them by their relatively new French derivative *chalumeau* (see p 42). It would appear that the newly-invented clarinet was meant to occupy a range higher than the rather low-pitched shawm; only when the shawm finally became obsolete later in the 18th century was the clarinet family extended downwards to fill the gap.

Nuremberg in the late 17th century at about the time the clarinet was being developed there. (Mary Evans Picture Library)

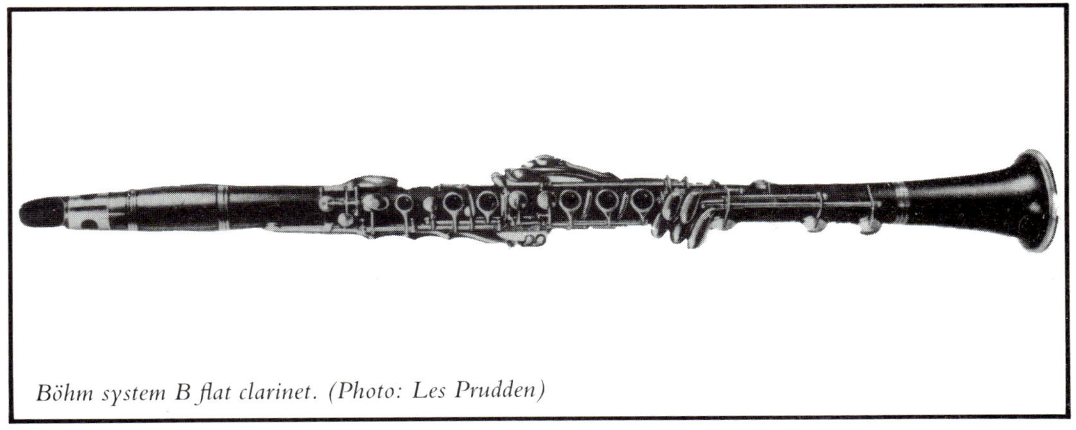

Böhm system B flat clarinet. (Photo: Les Prudden)

The Clarinet Family

Obsolete instruments are marked with an asterisk.

Octave	★clarinet in C, mid-19th century Italian
	★clarinet in B flat, 19th century military
	★clarinet in A, early 19th century
	clarinet in A flat, early 19th century (= clarinetto sestino, used in military and Balkan folk bands)
	★clarinet in G, late 18th century
Sopranino	clarinet in F, late 18th century, mainly military
	★clarinet in E, late 18th century
	clarinet in E flat, late 18th century, military and orchestral
	clarinet in D, early 18th century
Soprano	clarinet in C, early 18th century
	★clarinet in B, late 18th century
	clarinet in B flat, early 18th century } the standard 20th century orchestral clarinets
	clarinet in A, 18th century } the standard 20th century orchestral clarinets
Basset-horns and **alto clarinets**	★basset-horn in G, late 18th century
	basset-horn in F, late 18th century
	★basset-horn in D, late 18th century
	★*clarinette d'amour* in D, known only from a 1772 reference (see p 15)
	★*clarinette d'amour* in A flat, *c.*1760
	clarinette d'amour in G, *c.*1760
	★clarinet in G, *c.*1789 (today termed 'basset clarinet')
	★clarinet in F, early 19th century (called 'tenor clarinet'; replaced by the basset-horn in E flat)
	clarinet in E flat, 19th century (called 'tenor clarinet'; used chiefly in military bands)
Baritone/ bass	★bass clarinet in C, late 18th century
	bass clarinet in B flat, 1793
	bass clarinet in A, late 19th century
	contrabasset-horn in G
	contrabasset-horn in F
	contrabasset-horn in E flat
Contrabass	★contrabass clarinet in E flat, 19th century
	★contrabass clarinet in C, 19th century
	contrabass clarinet in B flat, *c.*1840
	pedal clarinet in B flat, 1889
Subcontrabass	sub-contrabass clarinet in B flat, *c.*1930

Although Denner invented the clarinet before the turn of the century, it was not until 1710 that the actual name appeared in the Nuremberg archives; by what name Denner called his clarinets when he first sold them is not clear. 'Clarinet' means literally 'little clarino', since the tone of early examples was similar to that of the trumpet. At first, clarinets were often pitched in the trumpet keys of C and D. Vivaldi used clarinets in his oratorio *Juditha Triumphans*, and *Airs à deux clarinettes ou chalumeaux* by J-P. Dreux were published in Amsterdam; both works appeared in 1716, so the clarinet was already widespread in Europe within two decades of its invention. Handel's *Riccardo Primo* of 1726–7 contains two clarinet parts written for August Freudenthal and Franz Rosenberg; three undated clarinet concerti were composed by Vivaldi (died 1741) and a Mr Charles played a (solo?) clarinet concerto in Dublin in 1742, possibly an arrangement (from recorder? oboe?). A symphony including two clarinets by Johann Daniel Berlin (1714–87), working in Trondheim, is dated 'possibly after 1750' and may therefore antedate the symphonies by Jan Stamic given in 1753 at the Concert Spirituel in Paris in which clarinets replace oboe parts; three such works were published by Bayard in Paris in 1755–60. Valentin Roeser produced the first clarinet instruction book in Paris in1764.

Modern clarinets are pitched in A and B flat. Higher-pitched instruments in most keys have been made in the past and, after a period of relative neglect, are beginning to appear in modern scores. The most important and frequently used of these is the high clarinet in E flat, which first occurred in opera orchestras in the late 18th century; it was used tellingly by Berlioz in his *Symphonie Fantastique* (1830) and appears in scores by Stravinsky, Richard Strauss, Ravel, Mahler and many others. Low-pitched clarinets have also appeared, some dating perhaps from as early as 1800.

Although a woodwind instrument, various materials have been used in its construction. Mouthpieces of ebonite are preferred (but wood, metal — including gold and aluminium — ivory, glass and plastics have been used), and the body might be of boxwood, cocuswood from Jamaica or Cuba, African blackwood (much favoured) and brass or silver. Ivory was popular two centuries ago; ebonite and perspex have also been used, while metals are favoured for the larger clarinets

Types of Clarinet

As mentioned above, instruments of clarinet type, and others loosely called clarinets, are widespread as folk instruments throughout the world. A small ethnic selection has been included here (indicated +), but the main purpose of this list is to show its wide range of names and types as used in art music.

Alboquea+
A Basque instrument, its reed enclosed by a resonator.

Argul+
A Near East clarinet with two pipes of unequal length.

Bass clarinet
(see p 13) First documented in Paris in 1772; however, Rendell suggests that a German three-keyed instrument may date from 1750 or earlier. Much used in military bands, many models were doubled upon themselves like a bassoon to facilitate portability. A strange instrument made in Italy by Papalini about 1810 solves the portability problem by forming the tube into a series of compact 's'-bends. It was pitched in C and was made of two lengths of pearwood hollowed out and glued. After many attempts to build a successful bass clarinet, Adolphe Sax's straight model of 1836, designed, it appears, without relying on previous models, made its début in the same year in Act 5 of Meyerbeer's opera *Les Huguenots* and has remained basically unchanged ever since. Important parts for the bass clarinet have been written by Neukomm, Wagner, Liszt, Janáček, Bantock, Richard Strauss, Shostakovich and many others.

Basse guerrière
A 13-keyed bass clarinet made in 1807 by Dumas of Sommières.

Basse-orgue
A bass clarinet doubled like a bassoon, made by Sautermeister, Lyons, in 1812.

Basset-horn (see p 13)
Also known as the tenor clarinet. The origin of the basset-horn is attributed to the instrument-making firm of A. and M. Mayrhofer of Passau, Bavaria, about 1770. The name derives from a German diminutive of 'bass' and its semi-circular shape which resembles an ancient hunting horn (later models were angled rather than curved, and a number of strangely contorted designs have been built in order to bring the keys of a long instrument within easier reach of the player). The first composer to use the instrument extensively was Mozart who, from about 1781, wrote a series of chamber, vocal and orchestral works exploiting its subtly different qualities. Its first concerto is now thought to be Mozart's A major work, K 622,

written originally for an instrument now called the 'basset clarinet' in G (later the pitch was standardized at F), which extended four semitones below the standard clarinet. Isolated works for basset-horn exist by Beethoven and Mendelssohn, and a basset-horn concerto in F by Alessandro Rolla in manuscript at Einsiedeln, Switzerland, bears the date 24 April 1829, although internal evidence suggests a considerably earlier date.

Bathyphone
A double-bass clarinet in C made for military use by W.F. Wieprecht in 1839.

Brelka+
A Slav instrument, its reeds enclosed by a resonator.

Clarinette a doppio tonalità
An attempt by a Milanese firm to produce a combination clarinet capable of playing in two keys.

Clarinette basse recourbée a pavilion de cuivre
A modified version of Adolphe Sax's bass clarinet, made for military use.

Clarinette-bourdon
A B flat double bass clarinet invented by Sax in about 1840.

Clarinette-con-rabasse
A brass E flat instrument made by Sax about 1843, sounding an octave below the alto clarinet and designed for military use.

Clarinette d'amour
(It: *clarinetto d'amore*; Ger: *Liebesklarinette*; Eng: = French name)
This first appeared in the mid-18th century, sometimes pitched in G, less often in A flat or F. It was a straight instrument with a pear-shaped bell and may have been the origin of the basset-horn. J.C. Bach in *Temistocle* (London, 1772) called for two *clarinettes d'amour* in D, a pitch otherwise unknown for this instrument. Perhaps Bach meant the basset-horn in D. (See Chart)

Clarinetto sestino
A high-pitched clarinet in A flat designed in South Germany about 1839 for military use. It is often used with brilliant virtuosity in Balkan folk-bands.

Clarione
Italian for bass clarinet. The word appeared as early as 1720, indicating at that time probably a larger clarinet than the earliest models, i.e. an instrument more nearly approaching the length of the modern clarinet.

Combination clarinet
A general term for the various attempts to build a clarinet which combines the two differently-pitched instruments in A and B flat.

Contrabass clarinet
An instrument pitched in C, E flat or B flat whose tube can measure up to 10ft (3m) in length, sounding an octave below the bass clarinet. A model made by Richard Kohl in 1898 is reported to have had a tube length of 16ft (4.87m), but no example is known to have survived. The contrabass clarinet was first used in d'Indy's *Fervaal* (1897). (See Chart)

Contrabasset-horn
A 19-keyed instrument built by G. Streitwolf of Göttingen in 1829, pitched in F or E flat and sounding an octave below the basset-horn.

Contre-basse guerrière
A double-bass clarinet invented by Dumas, Sommières, in 1807.

Erkencho+
South American native clarinet.

Glicibarifono
A bass clarinet made by Catterini of Padua in about 1838. Its parallel tubes were bored in a single block of boxwood.

Hornpipe+
An English instrument of the 15th–18th centuries made in one- or two-pipe versions of bone or elderwood. At the lower end was fixed a cowhorn with a serrated edge.

Launedda+
A Sicilian instrument consisting of three separate pipes of uneven length.

Mullerphone
A bassoon-shaped bass clarinet made by J. Muller of Lyons in 1846.

Pedal clarinet
A 13-keyed double-bass clarinet for orchestral use, made in 1889 by Fontaine-Besson of Paris.

Pibgorn+
Welsh equivalent of the hornpipe, qv.

Pungi+
An Indian folk instrument, similar to the hornpipe but with a chanter. It possibly originated in the China of extreme antiquity.

Sextklarinette
German for *clarinetto sestino*.

Stock-and-horn+
A Scottish instrument very similar to the hornpipe.

Sub-contrabass clarinet
A monster instrument, sounding an octave below the contrabass clarinet, built by Houvanaghel in France, *c.*1930. (See Chart)

Zummarah+
A folk-instrument of the Near East consisting of two pipes of uneven length.

Bassoon
It: *fagotto*
Fr: *basson*
Ger: *Fagott*

A double-reed instrument of conical bore: lowest of the standard orchestral wind group. Usually constructed of maple, the bassoon's total bore length of 100in (254cm) requires that it be doubled back on itself and held by a seated player at an angle across his body. The name comes from It: *bassone* = 'big bass', and 'bassoon' is the form used in England since the time of Purcell.

Several instruments have contributed to the name and development of the bassoon, each with its own history. The French *fagot* ('faggot' = a bundle of sticks, an image suggested by an instrument folded many times upon itself; more recently and less endearingly called 'sausage bassoon') was known in the 14th century; its abbreviation *fag* is still commonly used in the universal musical language based on Italian. **Dulcian** is the name of a primitive one-piece bassoon from about the mid-16th century whose tone was considered 'sweet' (Latin: *dulc*; cf. 'dulcet') in comparison with the higher wind instruments; while the same instrument was known in England as the curtal or curtall (Latin: *curtus* = an instrument 'shortened' by being folded). The bass shawm was called 'pommer' or similar, probably a name of onomatopoeic origin.

From its inception the bassoon, by whatever name, was accepted as an important foundation in the wind group, and its use, whether specified in the score or not, was standard in the bassline of the orchestra until Beethoven's time. Five differently-pitched dulcians were used in Heinrich's Schütz's *Psalm XXIV* of 1624, but its first sonatas (with treble instrument and continuo) date from three years earlier: Dario Castello's *Sonate concertante*. The very first bassoon solo was a *Fantasia* (1638) by Selma y Salaverde; the instrument appeared in the opera house first in 1668 in Cesti's *Il pomo d'oro*; and it received its first concerto by at least 1730, when Boismortier's Op 26 was published. However, one or more of Vivaldi's 38 bassoon concerti may antedate this. Best known, of course, is Mozart's in B flat, K 191, of 1774.

Johann Ernst Galliard wrote a so-called 'sonata' for 24 bassoons and four double bassoons which was performed at Lincoln's Inn Fields Theatre, London, in 1745, a remarkable work that easily out-bassoons Corrette's Concerto *Le Phénix* (*c.*1738), for four bassoons and continuo. Concerti continue to be written, e.g. Helmut Eder's of 1968; and improvements to the instrument continue to be made. Giles Brindley invented the 'logical bassoon' in 1967. It has a square bore, two folds, electrically operated pads and a heated wire to dispel condensation.

The five-membered family of dulcians has been pared down to a two-member family of bassoons — at least as far as common usage goes. Below the bassoon lies the **double bassoon** (It: *contrafagotto;* Fr: *contre basson*; Ger: *Kontrafagott*) which developed in parallel with the standard bassoon. Handel used it for special effects in operas and oratorios, as did Haydn in *The Creation* (1798), and Beethoven introduced it into the symphony orchestra in his Fifth Symphony (1805). Henk Badings wrote a concerto for bassoon and double bassoon in 1964 and Ruth Gipps's *Leviathan*, Op 59 (1969) is scored for double bassoon and chamber orchestra.

Smaller bassoons have had intermittent exposure since an otherwise unknown composer called J.G.M. Frost wrote a wind parthia in the mid-18th century for two *fagotti-octavo* (pitched an octave higher than the normal bassoon) and two *fagotti-quarto* (= the **tenoroon**, pitched in F); generally, though, they can do little that is not done better by cor anglais, clarinet or saxophone.

Saxophone
It: *sassofono*
Fr: *Saxophone*
Ger: *Saxophon*

The saxophone is a 'woodwind' instrument made of brass. This anomaly is accounted for by the following reasoning: with its reed mouthpiece, keys rather than valves, overall shape akin to the bass clarinet, playing position similar to that of the bassoon, and the nature of its voice, it is far nearer to the woodwind family than to other instruments made of brass.

The basic design was invented about 1840 by Adolphe Sax and patented in Paris in 1846. There is no evidence that Sax drew upon any of the earlier instruments which have been suggested as 'forerunners' of the saxophone, e.g. the alto bassoon or certain clarinets, even though, as a woodwind player himself, doubtless he was familiar with them. Its single-reed conical-bore design is now applied to a wide range of models for both orchestral and military use, and saxophone bands are self-sufficient in popular and jazz groups.

Its first serious use occurred in Jean-Georges Kastner's biblical opera *The Last King of Judah*, performed in Paris on 1 December 1844 (i.e.

substantially before the instrument was even patented), and it remained a mainly French operatic instrument for most of the 19th century, although it was heard in England at one of Jullien's concerts in 1850. Its first solo use was in Debussy's *Rhapsody* (1903); its first symphony, in which it appeared in strength, was Richard Strauss's *Symphonia Domestica* (1904), where four are required, together with a bass saxophone; and its first true concerto appears to be Josef Holbrooke's of 1928. Sandór Jemnitz composed a duet sonata in 1934 for the unique combination of saxophone and banjo, and Toshiro Mayuzumi's *Tone Pleromas 55* (1955) is scored for five saxophones, piano and musical saw.

BRASS

Trumpet
It: *tromba*
Fr: *trompette*
Ger: *Trompete*

The man who picked up a conch shell or a discarded animal horn with a broken tip and blew through it to make a noise was the first person to invent the trumpet. He used it to signal to fellow members of his tribe or to terrify strangers, and versions of the trumpet have been used for both purposes ever since. Ancient trumpets were made of horn, wood, silver, bronze or other metals and were simply cylindrical or conical tubes with flared ends which produced piercing, braying noises. Today's trumpets are made of brass, have three of four valves, and do not suffer from the severely restricted range common to all simple tube-like instruments. In 1796 the Austrian maker Anton Weidinger built a keyed trumpet capable of playing a chromatic scale, and Haydn and Hummel composed concerti for it. The valve trumpet appeared in about 1816 and was apparently first used in Berlioz's Overture *Les francs-juges* in 1826.

The early histories of trumpet and horn are inextricably mixed (see below) but, regardless of sound and pitch, it is the shape that most easily distinguishes them. In about 1400 the straight (and sometimes very long) horn/trumpet was bent into an 's'-shape, then into the flattened loop familiar today, while the horn became hoop-shaped. Trumpets were prominent in ceremonial and church occasions, invariably accompanied by drums in the earliest 'orchestras', and formed the backbone of musical groups at court. Fantini's sonatas for trumpet and continuo date from 1638, and by

Polish military trumpeter and drummer, 16th century. Trumpets and drums were inseparable in military and orchestral music until at least the start of the 19th century. (National Museum, Cracow)

1665 trumpets were playing concerti — Cazzati's concerto-like 'sonatas' date from that year — and the composers of San Petronio Cathedral, Bologna, led by Giuseppe Torelli, wrote many spectacular trumpet works with oboes and string band before 1700. These sonatas, concerti and symphonies showed the brilliant *clarino* technique of the skilful players, a skill which lasted until about 1750 when, for a reason perhaps connected with the increasing sophistication of orchestral music for other instruments that tended to highlight the trumpet's tonal limitations, it faded. Trumpets (always with drums) continued to be used in the symphony orchestra, but in colouristic and emphatic roles rather than as virtuoso soloists.

Trumpets have existed, and continue to be built, in a wide range of sizes. The largest is probably the bass trumpet built in the 1860s by C.W. Moritz to Wagner's specification for *The Ring* (see also below, under tuba); the smallest, the tiny piccolo B flat trumpet made in Italy *c.*1960, measures just over 1ft (30cm) from mouthpiece to bell, although, of course, the folded tube is much longer.

Tibetan monks playing ceremonial trumpets and shanai on the roof of Gundeling monastery. (Popperfoto)

Horn
It: *corno*
Fr: *cor*
Ger: *Horn*

There is no more complicated and confusing topic in music than the horn. Nomenclature, technique, use, history and repertoire all lay traps for the organologist, and no two authorities agree on some aspects of the subject. For instance, can the small helical pipes of Lower Egypt before the First Dynasty be classed as horns or trumpets?

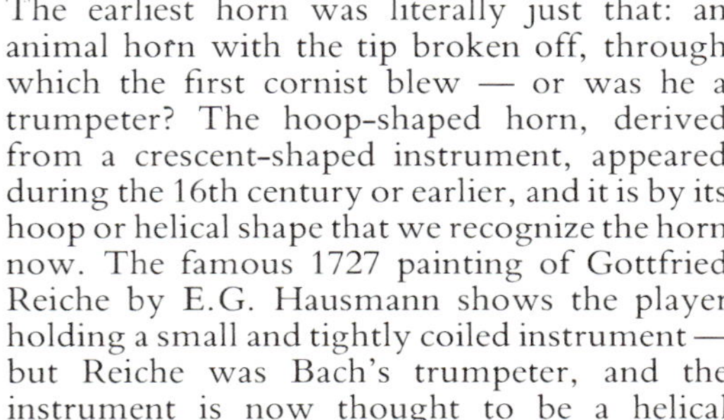

The earliest horn was literally just that: an animal horn with the tip broken off, through which the first cornist blew — or was he a trumpeter? The hoop-shaped horn, derived from a crescent-shaped instrument, appeared during the 16th century or earlier, and it is by its hoop or helical shape that we recognize the horn now. The famous 1727 painting of Gottfried Reiche by E.G. Hausmann shows the player holding a small and tightly coiled instrument — but Reiche was Bach's trumpeter, and the instrument is now thought to be a helical

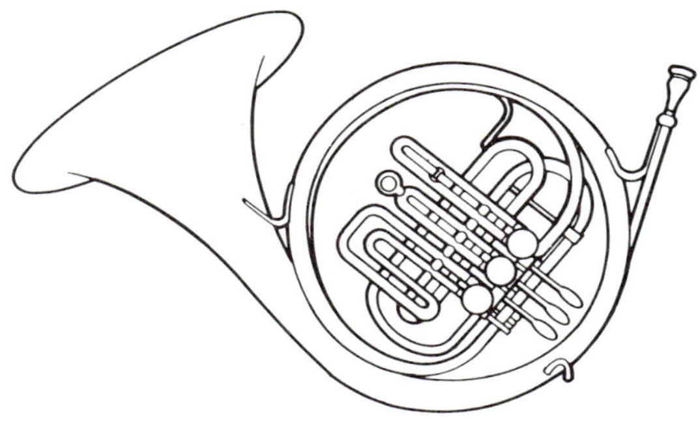

French horn.

trumpet! Both horn and trumpet have been used in the hunting field (where the French, bless them, called the hunting horn *tromp*), as military signalling instruments and as 'posthorns' on 18th-century carriages, so usage offers no clarification, and two illustrations in *New Grove* serve only to confuse matters further: in Vol 19, p 215 (article: Trumpet), 'Trumpets of animal horn' in a miniature from AD 1007–14 appear to be virtually identical to the 'Arctuate hunting horn' in a 14th-century miniature (Vol 8, p 702, article: Horn), except that the latter is rather more curved.

The tube length of the instrument does nothing to aid identification either, for trumpets and horns in C might be the same length in the 18th century, and the Russian horns bands employ one straight instrument per note, the length being from a few inches to enormous instruments requiring stands to support them.

Taking refuge from hunters and soldiers, the horn entered the opera house in 1639 in Venice in Cavalli's *Le nozze di Teti e di Peleo* but seems to have retained only a tenuous hold. Cavalli's instruments were probably tightly-coiled helical horns; the large and slender hoop-shaped horns worn over the shoulders of French huntsmen seem to have appeared some time during the 17th century, and it is these that gave rise to the name 'french horn', used incorrectly and increasingly rarely for today's orchestral horn.

Limitations of the horn, which could play in only the key in which it was built, were eased around 1703 by the introduction of 'crooks': short loops inserted between mouthpiece and instrument that changed the basic length; but a change of key still required a change of crook. From *c.*1750 the crooks were slotted into the body of the horn.

Polish wine cup of the late 12th century bearing a bas-relief of soldiers blowing what appear to be battle or signal horns. (National Museum, Cracow)

The first symphony to employ horns in non-solo roles was by Torelli (Giegling 37), composed before 1700, but the horn was not used regularly in symphony orchestras until the mid-18th century.

Vivaldi's undated concerti RV 538 and 539 for two horns, or Bach's *Brandenburg Concerto* No 1 in F, BWV 1046 (before 1721) may mark the first occurrence of horns as concerto soloists. At first, evidently, they were reluctant to play singly. The first concerti for *one* solo horn are probably the five of Hasse's Op 4 (published in London in 1742), but Mattheson reports that a blind travelling horn player in Hamburg in 1713 'produced more tones than an organ but with less mathematical precision'. This indicates not only the possibility of a solo horn concerto as early as 1713 (perhaps Telemann's lone horn concerto in D was available by then), but also the possibility of hand-stopping (i.e. squeezing the notes with the hand in the bell to produce notes not normally obtainable on the horn) by this date, a technique usually attributed to A.J. Hampel of Dresden some 45 years later.

Attempts to make the horn 'omnitonic' (i.e. to play any note in any key at will) brought some strange inventions: the models with various alternative air channels, slides and valves were almost unremarkable compared to Duport's instrument built in Paris in about 1815, for it had no fewer than eight mouthpieces. The first successful piston valved horn was made by Heinrich Stölzel and Friedrich Blühmel of Silesia in about 1815 and patented in 1818. The double horn was mooted in 1865 by Gautrot, a design which has been perfected in the modern F/B flat double horn with four rotary valves.

Trombone
It/Fr: *trombone*
Ger: *Posaune*

In the 14th century a trumpet with a slide was developed from the Roman *buccina* and was called 'trombone' (Italian for 'large trumpet'). The French seized upon its spectacular action and called it *saqueboute* ('pull-push'), from which the English word 'sackbut' was derived. From early on it was built in many sizes, and its solemn tones made it most suitable for use in church. The first symphonies known to employ the trombone were those of Torelli and his colleagues at Bologna before 1700, where it was used in the bassline as a matter of course; doubtless orchestral works elsewhere were similarly enriched, but those at Bologna actually carried the title 'sinfonia'. In the early years of the 18th century the chamber symphony dispensed with trombones, and often with brass and woodwind altogether. Beethoven's famous use of them in the finale of his Fifth Symphony (1805) is antedated by the Symphony in D (*c.*1773) by Joseph Starzer, the scoring of which includes alto, tenor and bass trombones; and Leopold Hofmann's *Symphonia Pastorella* of 1766 (or earlier) includes two trombones in all three movements: they play an elaborate duet in the Andante.

Concerti for trombone are uncommon: Wagenseil's in E flat, *c.*1760?, seems to be the earliest. One Bachschmidt (1705/9–*c.*1780) was the first trombone virtuoso, but since few works have survived from his period (there are examples by Michael Haydn and Albrechtsberger) we may speculate that he was forced to travel widely so that his small repertoire might be spread amongst the greatest number of listeners. Ian Parrott, the English composer, contributed a concerto in 1967, and Nielsen's Flute Concerto (1926) is notable for its elaborate trombone part.

British composer Derek Bourgeois (b. 1941), composer of a Concerto for Bass Tuba and orchestra. (The Composer)

Tuba
It/Fr: *tuba*
Ger: *Basstuba*

Not connected in any way other than name with the Roman brass trumpet, the orchestral tuba in F was built by Johann Gottfried Moritz in 1829 at the instigation of a Prussian bandmaster, and was patented on 12 September 1835. Attempts had been made to produce an extra-low instrument to give the brass a firm foundation, but the contrabass ophicleide ('keyed serpent') and large trombones were all in one way or another deficient. Berlioz was the first to use the tuba, replacing the ophicleide part in his *Symphonie Fantastique* (1830) with tuba and thereafter regularly employing it. Its first concerto was premièred on 13 June 1954 at London's Royal Festival Hall, when Philip Catelinet played Vaughan Williams's concerto written for a London Symphony Orchestra Jubilee concert. Sir John Barbirolli conducted. Derek Bourgeois's Bass Tuba Concerto dates from 1972.

Another English composer, John White, wrote a Symphony for organ and six tubas in 1967; the following year he contributed a work lasting 3½h entitled *Machine for Cello and Tuba*. In the Hoffnung Music Festival Concert held in the Royal Festival Hall on 13 November 1956, Chopin's A minor Mazurka Op 68/2 was played by Gerard Hoffnung himself and members of the Morley College Symphony Orchestra in an arrangement by Daniel Abrams — for tour tubas!

But England has not been the only country to give solo opportunities to the portliest of instruments. The American Walter Sinclair Hartley composed a Tuba Sonata, Op 76, in 1967; while mention should be made of the contribution of George Kleinsinger. In 1944 he wrote the music for Paul Tripp's children's story *Tubby the Tuba* (and its sequel *Tubby at the Circus*), the hero, of course, being played by the tuba. The memorable narrator was Danny Kaye.

The modern tuba has a conical bore, six (or seven) valves, and much elliptical pipework terminating in a large flared bell. The tenor and bass tubas equate approximately with the ranges of cello and double bass respectively, and the contrabass tuba, introduced in 1845, is pitched in either C or B flat. Varieties of tuba include **bombardon**, a band version of the tuba in F, and **euphonium**, a tenor tuba in B flat. The **Sousaphone** and **helicon** are circular instruments suitable for marching, their coils worn round the player's body and their bells rearing over his head. The **Wagner tuba** was required by that composer to fill in the gap between horns and trombones; some were made, possibly by C.W. Moritz of Berlin, during the 1850s. Wagner tubas are pitched in B flat and F and may be distinguished visually in the orchestra by their gracefully angled bells. In addition to Wagner, the instruments have been called for by Bruckner, Stravinsky, Richard Strauss and less familiar composers such as Rautavaara, who uses four in his Symphony No 3, Op 20 (1961).

Monster 'subcontrabass tubas' such as Adolphe Sax's **saxhorn-bourdon** of 1851 and Besson's **Trombotonar** have been made, the latter standing some 10ft (3m) tall, but they have met with opposition both from players and those responsible for storing and transporting orchestral instruments, not to mention the rare audiences who have heard them.

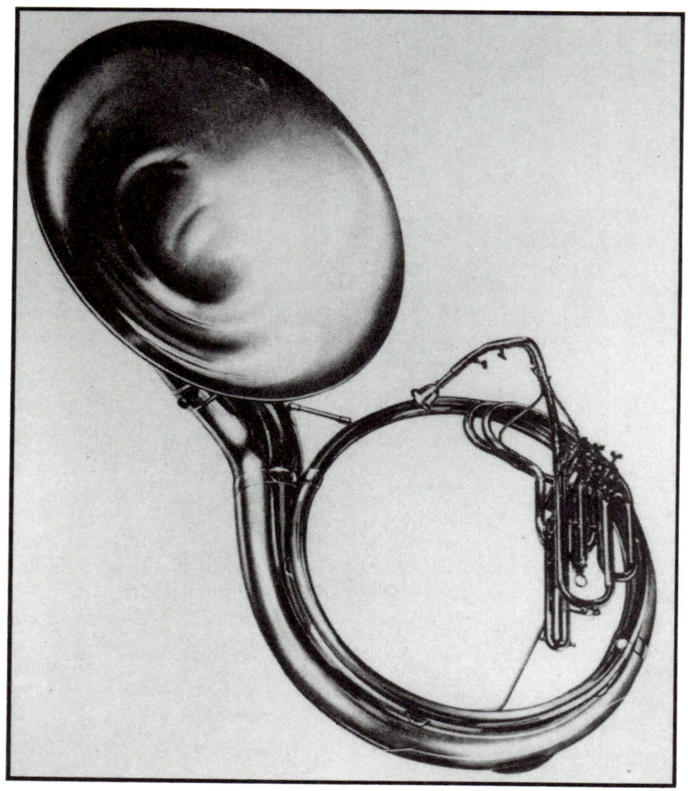

Sousaphone. The earliest models, as specified in 1892 by John Philip Sousa, the 'March King', had upward-facing bells and were known amongst marching bands as 'rain-catchers'. The forward-facing models soon replaced them. (Photo: Les Prudden)

NAMES AND FREQUENCIES OF NOTES

The system used is the standard one based on the piano keyboard for easy reference, taking the note C at 251.6cps as 'middle C'. In this system the octave running from middle C to the B above serves as a reference upon which upper and lower octaves depend. The C above middle C is noted as C′ (i.e. the first C above middle C), the next as C″, and so on. Octaves below middle C are noted as C, to B, and C,, to B,, and so on.

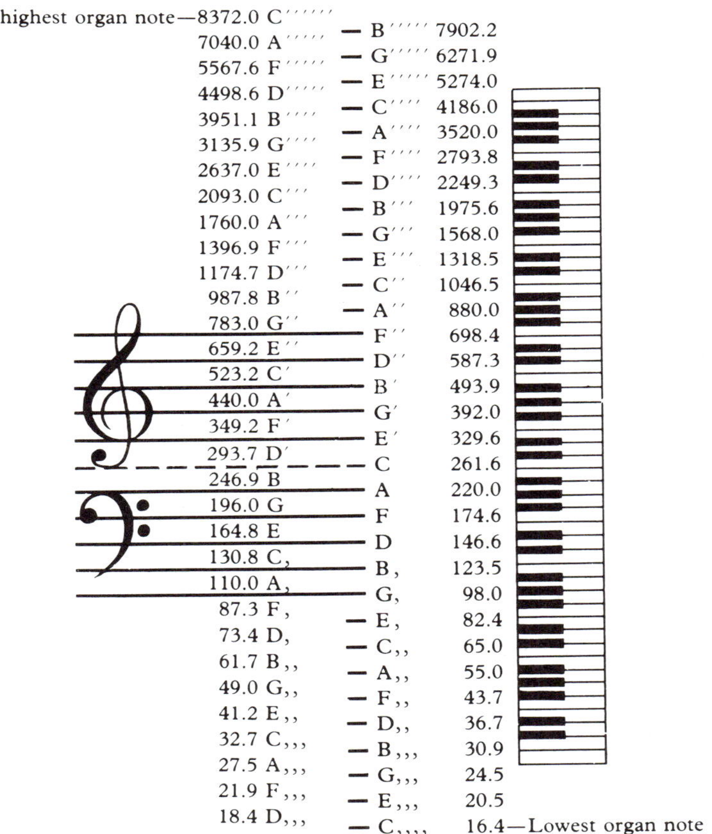

STRINGS

Violin

It: *violino*
Fr: *violon*
Ger: *Violine, Geige* (Old German for 'rebec')

The violin and one of its first famous builders seem to have appeared almost simultaneously. Andrea Amati, who founded the Cremona violin-making school, was born perhaps as early as 1500 — certainly no later than 1511 — and the violin in its modern form, but with only three strings, came into existence *c.*1505, also in northern Italy. Its ultimate ancestor is the lyre, which developed into the *crwth*, a Welsh bowed lyre, during the first century BC (and itself survived for 2000 years), which in turn evolved into the viol family. The immediate ancestor of the violin is the *lyra da braccio*, a bowed lyre held up by the arm.

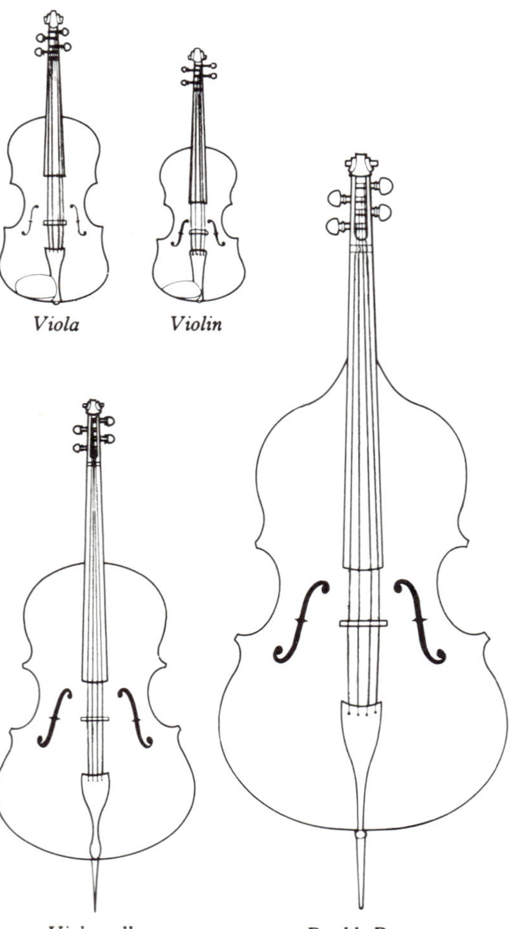

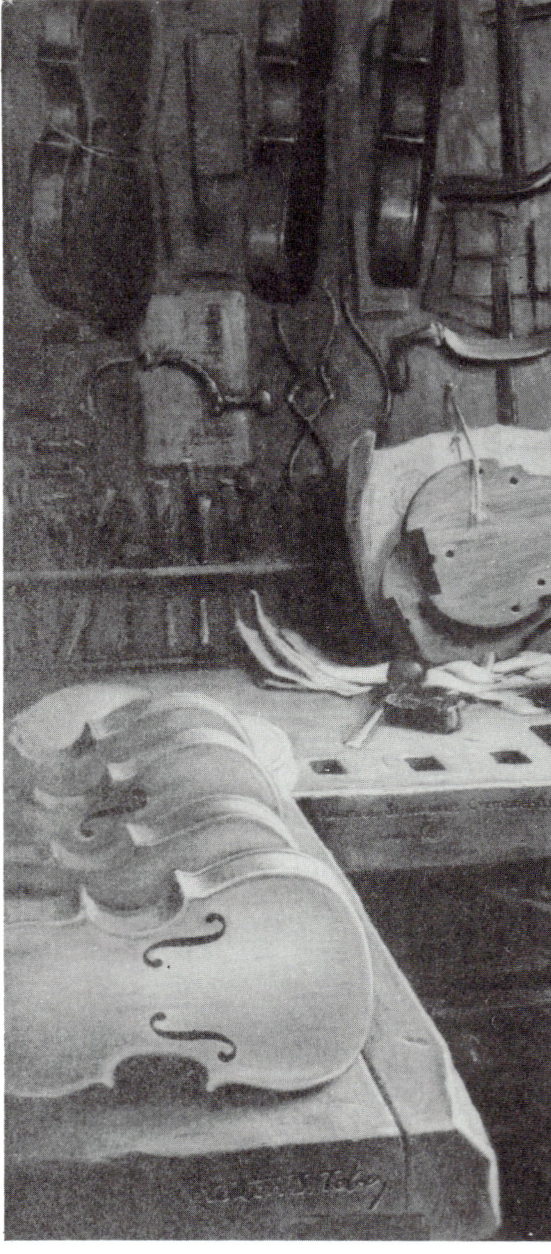

The very name 'violin' suggests joyousness, for its Latin ancestor is *vitulari* ('to skip like a calf'). The word then descended through Latin *vitula* (the root of 'fiddle') and Middle English 'viel', to 'viol', the diminutive of which is 'violin' = a small viol. Contrary to traditional belief, 'violin' is not a diminutive of viola.

Viols and violins co-existed for some two

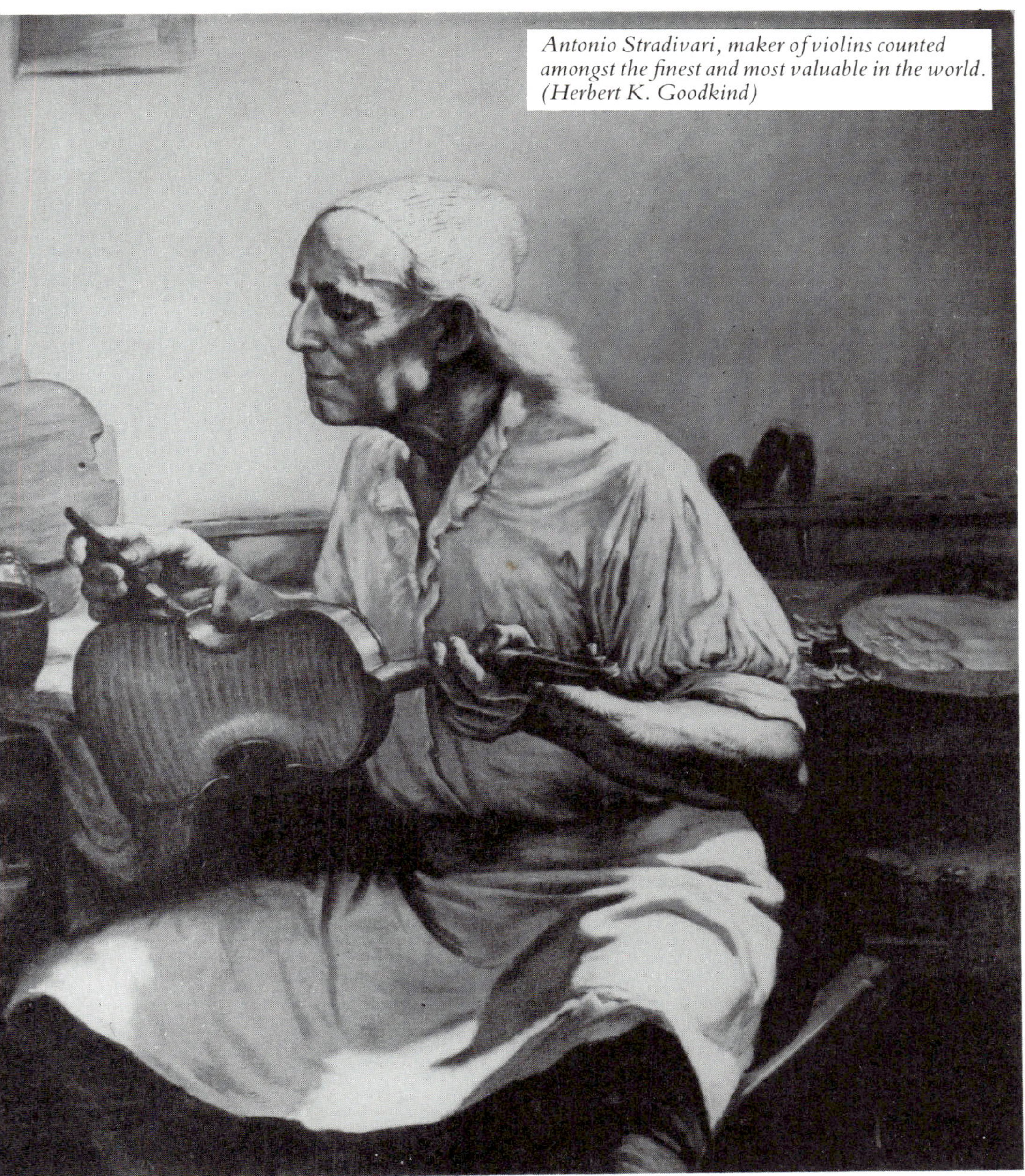

Antonio Stradivari, maker of violins counted amongst the finest and most valuable in the world. (Herbert K. Goodkind)

centuries before the latter conquered in about 1550, after which the violin was accepted as the mainstay of instrumental groups for frivolous sports like dancing, and as a support for vocal music. During the 17th century the violin attained respectability with the honour of its very own sonatas: first by G.B. Cima in 1610 (with violone), then in 1620 by Marini (with continuo, i.e. keyboard *and* violone), and finally in duet with *chitarrone* (lute continuo) in 1622 by Salomone Rossi, but it was not totally freed of accompaniment in art music until Biber's Passacaglia of *c.*1675. A solo violin occurs in some slow movements of Torelli's trumpet concertos of *c.*1690–5, and the violin achieves its first solo concerto in the same composer's Op 6, published in 1698. Passages for two solo violins occur concomitantly. By the beginning of the

■ *Some 700 of the 1116 violins by Stradivarius (1644–1737) have survived. His Alard violin was confirmed by Jacques Francais to have been sold in 1981 by private treaty by W.E. Hill for $1.2 million (then £600 000) to a Singaporean.* ■

18th century, therefore, the violin was established in all the solo, concertante and orchestral genres in which it was to play so strong a part for the next two centuries and beyond.

Stradivarius violin (1707) called 'Cathédrale' by a previous owner, Jean Baptiste Cartier, pupil of Viotti. The violin was sold for £396 000 at Sotheby's in November 1984. (Sotheby's.)

A small violin, the **violino piccolo**, appears in Monteverdi's *Orfeo* (1607); it sounds an octave above the violin. Bach's *violino piccolo* as used in the *Brandenburg* Concerto No 1 is tuned a third above normal.

Viola

It: *viola*
Fr: *alto*
Ger: *Bratsche*

Development of the lower instruments in the violin family — viola and cello — took place within a short time of that of the violin itself, although precise details are doubtful. In any case, viola and cello were both well established by 1535, the viola as the alto or tenor voice to the violin's treble. The word viola was the general term for any bowed instrument around 1500; with the appearance of the alto-tenor violin apparently the makers were at a loss as to what to call it, so they took the old word as a useful and fortuitous augmentative of 'violin'.

A Maggini viola, sold at Christie's for £129 000 in November 1984. (Christie, Manson & Woods Ltd)

In comparison with the violin, cello, and even the double bass, the viola is a Cinderella as far as solo works are concerned. Telemann's Concerto in G, dating probably from before 1721, is so isolated and early that one suspects it may be the surviving version of a work originally for another instrument. Not until Karl Stamitz (1745–1801) did the viola receive support from a virtuoso willing and able to write and perform concerti for it (he composed three or four in the early 1770s), although Michael Haydn wrote a concerto in C, Perger 55, for viola and keyboard in about 1761. Mozart's great *Sinfonia Concertante* in E flat for violin and viola, K 364, dates from 1779 (Mozart himself played the viola). Although the viola's appearance in the symphony parallels that of the violin and cello, Berlioz looked kindly on it and gave it an important part (written for Paganini) in his Symphony Op 16 (1834) titled *Harold in Italy*, and now and again the viola has been placed in unexpected prominence in works that omitted violins from the string group (see p 200). Works such as Walton's Concerto (1929, revised 1961) have served the instrument well during the present century, and Benjamin James Dale's *Introduction and Andante* (1911) places six violas in the spotlight unaccompanied.

Cello

(accepted English abbreviation for the Italian name)
It: *violoncello*
Fr: *violoncelle*
Ger: *Violoncello*

This instrument existed (as 'bass-violin' or some such description) for about a century and a half before it was given a name. It came into being soon after the violin (see above) and was described in 1529 as a three-string violin, but the word 'violoncello' was invented in the mid-17th century to mean a 'small violone', the violone being the name of the lowest of the viol

■ *The highest ever auction price for a violoncello is £275 000 at Sotheby's London in April 1984 for a Stradivari made, according to the label, in '168★'.* ■

family. The present four-string tuning was established by 1532. Five-string models have occasionally appeared: Bach's Suite No 6, BWV 1012, calls for a five-string cello.

The cello was a subservient member of the violin family for half a century or so until cello players sought some of the glory by writing solo works for their instrument, the first being Domenico Gabrieli, nicknamed in the tortuous Bolognese dialect 'Mingàn dal viulunzaal' ('Domenico of the violoncello'), whose *Ricercare* for cello and continuo date from *c*.1675, while another Bolognese, Giovanni Battista Degli Antoni, who also built cellos, wrote a similarly titled and scored work for his Op 1 in 1687. By 1700 the cello was appearing in Corelli's *Concerti Grossi* (published in 1715 but written many years earlier) as a solo foil to the two solo violins, and the first cello concerti

The 'Bonjour' Stradivarius violoncello made, according to the label, in '168', which sold for £275 000 at Sotheby's in April 1984. (Sotheby's)*

came in 1701: Giuseppe Maria Jaccini's *Concerti per Camera*, Op 4.

Thereafter, cello concerti became popular, Vivaldi alone contributing 27, plus another for two cellos, a line which has continued through C.P.E. Bach, Boccherini, Haydn, Schumann, Dvořák, Elgar and Shostakovich, to mention only a few of the best known. Cello groups such as that of the Berlin Philharmonic Orchestra have prospered and attracted specially composed works, for instance Helmut Eder's *Melodia-Ritmica* of 1974.

In 1764 Wagenseil composed six sonatas for three cellos and double bass which include the rare direction *ondeggiando*, indicating an increase and decrease in bow pressure without a bow change, thus producing a periodic swelling and diminishing of tone. These sonatas were published by Doblinger, Vienna, in 1979.

Double bass
It: *contrabass*
Fr: *contre basse*
Ger: *Kontrabass*

The double bass is the only member of the modern string family with sloping shoulders. This tells us that it was taken over more or less unchanged from the viol family, and its name 'violone' ('big viol') persisted until the late 18th century. Its function was to 'double' the 'bass' (i.e. cello) line and support the keyboard player's left-hand part. This lowest member of the violins was considered unworthy of a solo until Haydn, newly arrived at Prince Esterházy's court in 1761, found a bassist called Johann Georg Schwenda for whom he wrote a concerto (now lost) and important solo parts in the symphonies Nos 6–8 (1761), 31 and 72 (1763–5). Vaňhal's Concerto in E (*c.*1765) is the earliest extant double bass concerto; Rodney Slatford, the English bass virtuoso, knows of more than 200 others. Probably the earliest bass virtuoso was Caspar Bohrer (1744–1809) who was also a trumpeter (apparently a living could not be made out of bass playing in those days: Haydn's bassist Schwenda was actually employed as a bassoonist), but the most famous was undoubtedly Domenico Dragonetti (1763–1846), the Venetian-born player and composer. The most spectacular works for the instrument are a fugue for four double basses (1939) by Dubensky, and a *Quadrat* (1969) for the same group by Apergis. Franz Anton Hoffmeister wrote a quartet for double bass with string trio early in the 19th century, while the present century has seen the appearance of several works for the instrument, including sonatas by Farkas and Kardos, a duo for two double basses by Sydeman, and a concerto by Reginald Barrett Ayres.

The lumbering grandeur of large stringed instruments has caught the imagination of both makers and composers over the years. An enormous bass viol 13ft (4m) high was built by J.B. Vuillaume of Paris in 1849. Its three strings were tuned from the lower end of the instrument and stopping was effected either by hand (if the player had sufficient reach) or by pedals. Berlioz was enthusiastic, but Karl Geiringer, who heard it played in the 1940s, said that its tone was unexpectedly weak. A double bass 14ft (4.26m) high was built in 1924 by Arthur K. Ferris in Ironia, New Jersey. Its soundbox was 8ft (2.43m) across and it weighed 11.6cwt (599kg). Other huge string basses have been reported, but the largest of all would appear to be that built in 1889 by one John Goyers: his 'Grand Bass' stood 15ft (4.75m) high.

Apart from bowing and plucking it, what else can one do with a double bass? David Bedford, in a piece written in 1977, asks that it should be strummed with a guitar plectrum. Not to be outdone, the guitarist in the same work plays *his* instrument with a double bass bow.

How High? How Low?

Many authorities, from Berlioz onward, have given the absolute ranges for orchestral instruments; no two authorities agree. Our table gives what is believed to be the upper and lower extremes obtainable by professional players. The purity and quality of extreme upper notes on bowed stringed instruments depend upon the skill of the players, and may be several notes higher than those shown for viola, cello and double bass. The usual extreme upper violin note is B''' (1975.6cps), but an extension up to F'''' (2793.8cps) is not unusual today. Tchaikovsky's Violin Concerto requires the soloist to reach A'''' (3520cps), but in bar six of the finale (*Passacaglia*) of his Violin Concerto Op 15 of 1939, Benjamin Britten calls for B'''' (3951.1cps) from the soloist.

In modern scores timpani are notated in the bass clef at actual pitch, the tuning being indicated at the start of a piece; tuning changes during a work are indicated by a direction in the score, e.g. *change C to C#*, or *muta C in C#*.

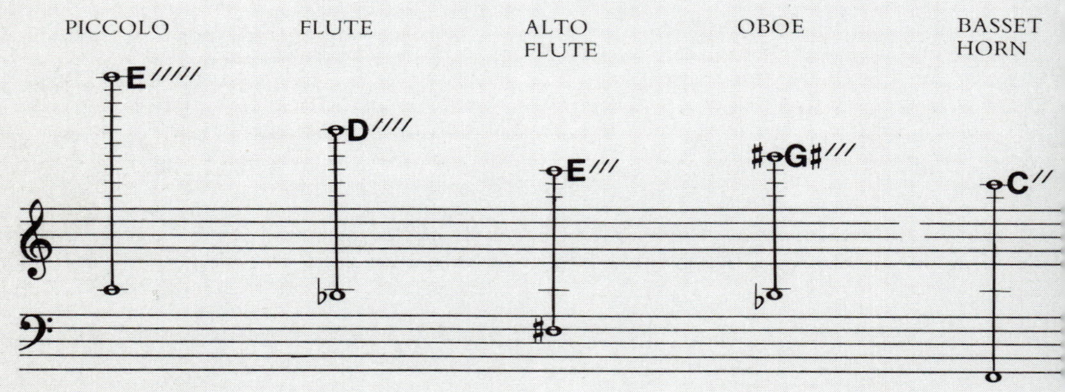

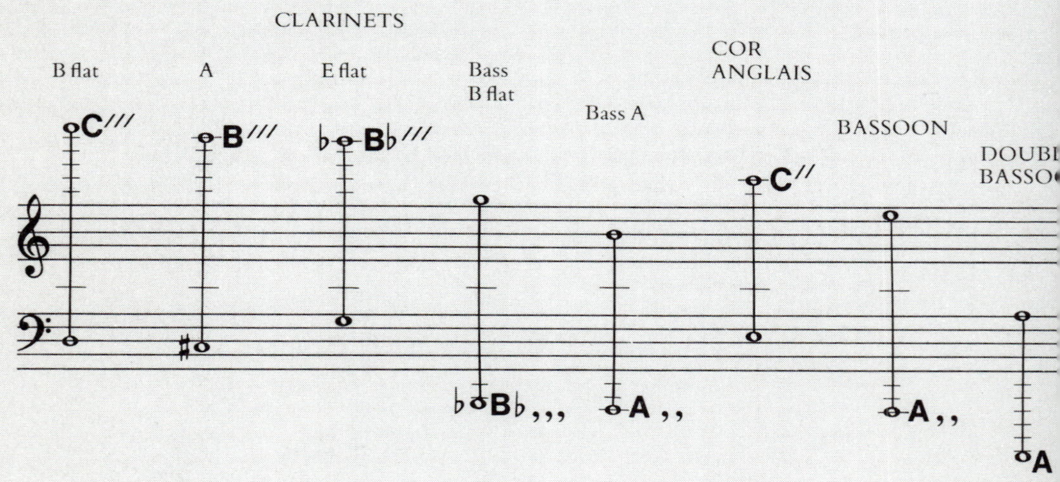

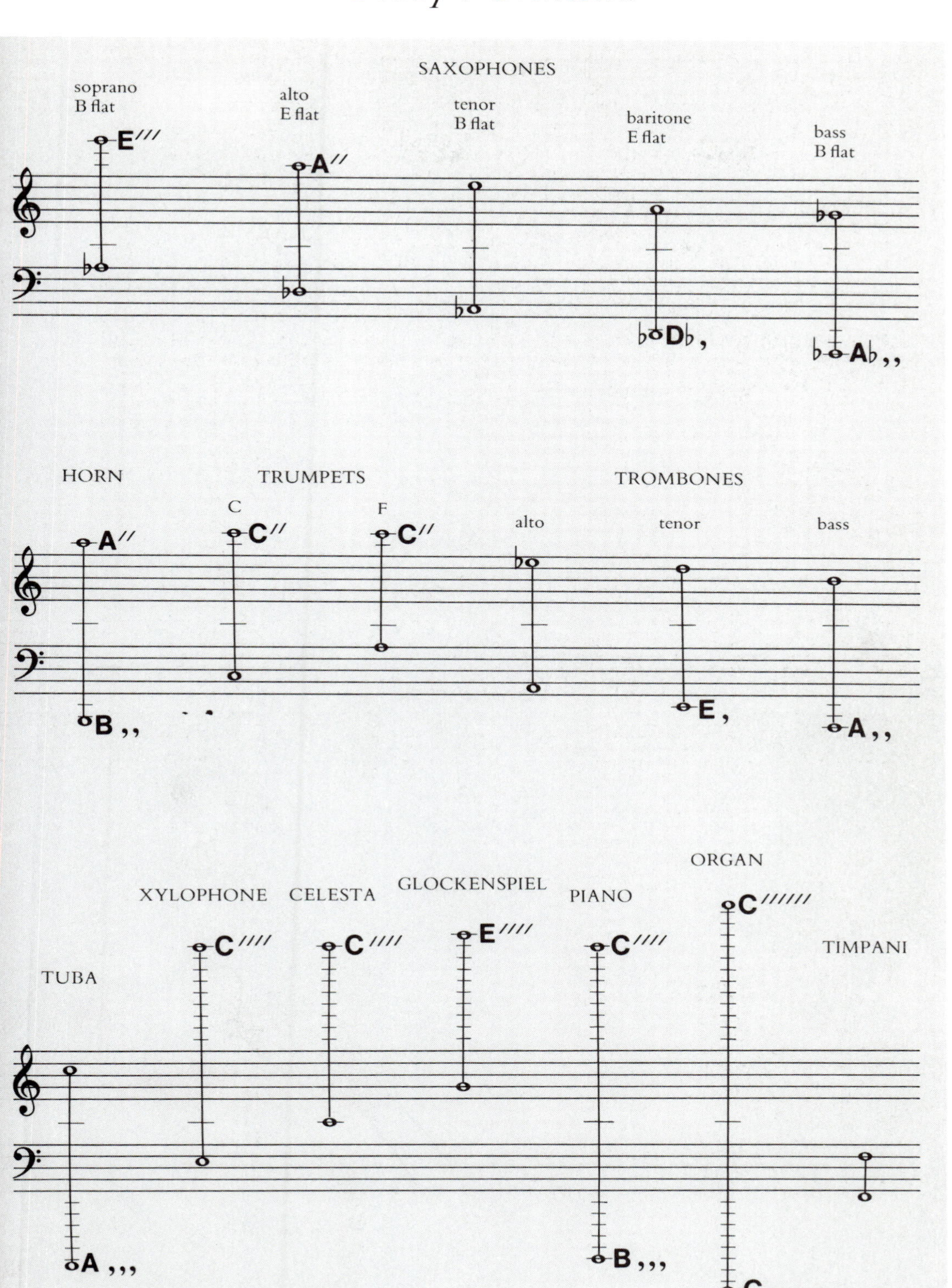
SAXOPHONES
soprano
B flat
E'''
alto
E flat
A''
tenor
B flat
baritone
E flat
D♭,
bass
B flat
A♭,,
HORN
A''
B,,
TRUMPETS
C
C''
F
C''
TROMBONES
alto
tenor
E,
bass
A,,
TUBA
A,,,
XYLOPHONE
C''''
CELESTA
C''''
GLOCKENSPIEL
E''''
PIANO
C''''
B,,,
ORGAN
C''''''
C,,,,
TIMPANI

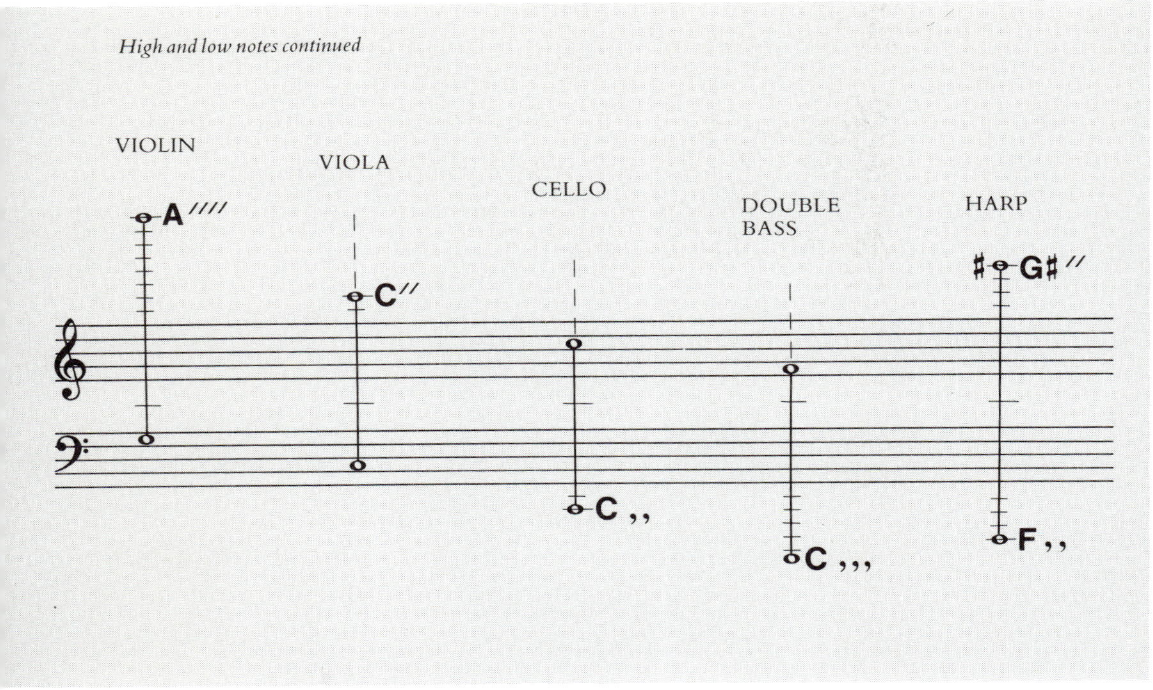

High and low notes continued

VIOLIN A''''

VIOLA C''

CELLO C,,

DOUBLE BASS C,,,

HARP G♯'' F,,

The Ecclesfield School rings the changes for the record books with a 56 hours 3 minutes marathon. (Dave Muscroft)

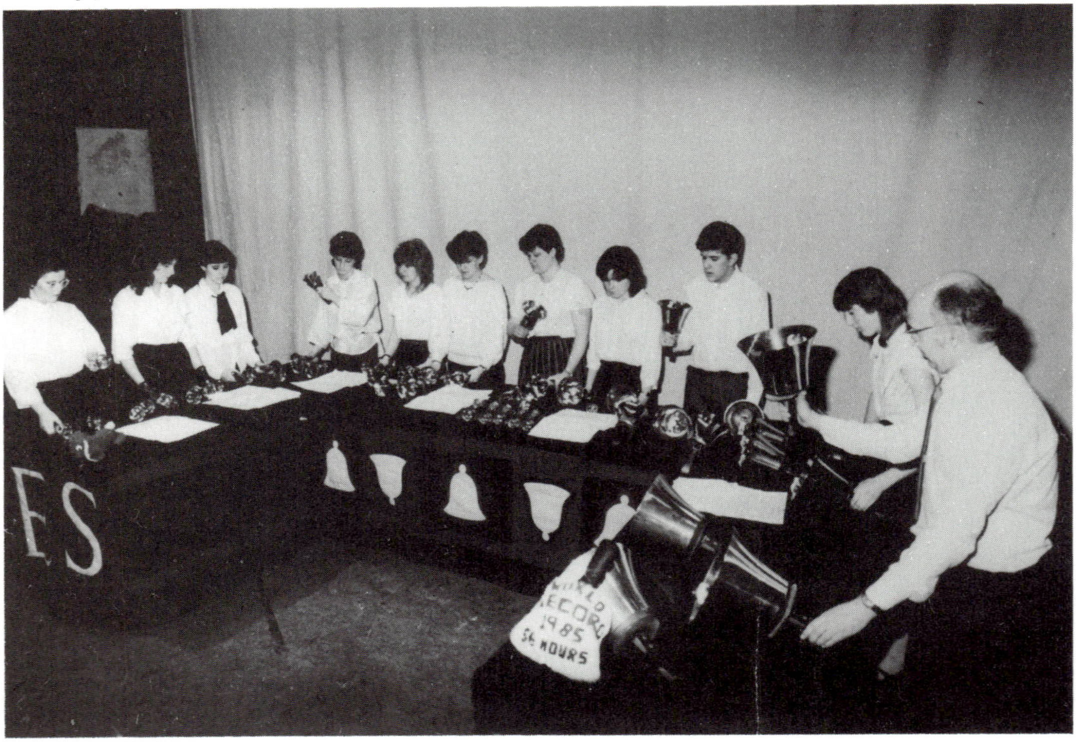

PERCUSSION

The percussion section has far more members than any other in the orchestra. In the following list only the most frequently encountered members are given. There is simply no room to detail all the variations of them, nor the various whips, whistles, sirens, tea-trays, aircraft engines, panes of glass and so on which the concert-goer may encounter, especially in works by modern composers. If an object, no matter how apparently mute, can be induced to 'speak', someone, somewhere, has put it into a score, and in all probability it will be relegated to the 'kitchen department' of the orchestra.

Anvil The sound of a struck anvil as a musical effect has been known at least since 1528 and it has been used intermittently since 1825 (Auber's opera *Le Maçon*). Wagner called for 18 anvils in *Das Rheingold*. Sometimes a real anvil is used, but the substitute of metal bars on a frame is more convenient.

Bass drum
It: *gran casa*
Fr: *grosse caisse*
Ger: *grosse Trommel*

This deepest of the conventional orchestral drums was formerly single-headed (gong drum) but is now more usually two-headed for greater power and resonance. It stands at least 2ft 6in (76cm) in diameter and is played, usually, with felt-headed sticks. The drum's origin lies in Eastern and Middle Eastern models of extreme antiquity, existing in central Asia before 3500 BC, but its Western use occurred, like that of cymbals and triangle, only during the 18th century as Turkish military instruments became popular for their exotic effects. Apparently its very first use was in Domenico Freschi's opera *Berenice vendicativa*, produced in Venice in 1680, and its first orchestral use outside the opera house was in Gottfried Finger's *Concerto alla Turchesa* (*c*.1715–25?).

Rameau's use of *tambour voilé* in his *Ouverture* to the *ballet heroique* called *Zaïs* (1748) has been taken to mean bass drum in a recording by one famous conductor, but this should surely be interpreted as 'veiled' or 'covered' drum, or draped timpano; however, the use of a single timpano is possibly unique, and its very daring contribution (it begins the *ouverture* solo for two slow bars) marks Rameau as a distinctly forward-looking composer. George Glantz's *Turkish* Symphony (1774) is the bass drum's first symphonic appearance; since then it has claimed the attention of countless composers. Shostakovich uses the instrument in possibly a unique way: as an accompaniment to the soloist's cadenza in the first movement of his Cello Concerto No 2 (1966), the part consisting of eight *ff* secco strokes and five *mf* strokes.

Bells (tubular, etc) Bells have been used musically since at least *c*.3500 BC in Egypt. Today's orchestral instruments consist of a series of metal tubes hung from a frame and struck near the top edge with a covered mallet. Bells were first required in art music in a funeral cantata by G.M. Hoffmann (*c*.1730); he probably envisaged the organ's bell effects. Dalayrac, on the other hand, may have expected real bells for his opera *Camille* (1791). The more reliable and controllable tubular bells were first used in Sullivan's *Golden Legend* (1890), but the unforgettable bells in Tchaikovsky's *1812* Overture were originally intended to be those of the city of Moscow. Real church bells (and a cannon!) were used in Pleyel's *La Révolution du Dix Août 1792 ou Le Tocsin Allégorique*, a revolutionary hymn for large orchestra and voices, first performed in Strasbourg cathedral on that date. Pleyel chose his bells from the 900 collected in Strasbourg when discarded by places of worship in the Bas-Rhin area.

Castanets Made of chestnut wood and usually considered essentially Spanish (castaña = chestnut in Spanish), castanets were known to the Egyptians by 730 BC, and an earlier form from *c*.2000 BC, described as 'boot-shaped', were probably made from some kind of gourd. When heard in the orchestra a sophisticated playing method is used: they are fastened to a stick and shaken like a rattle, or mounted by elastic to a board and operated by the fingers. The traditional way of playing by Spanish dancers is much more difficult to learn.

Celesta A keyboard instrument similar to a small piano, the hammers of which strike metal plates rather than strings. It was invented by Auguste Mustel in 1880 and first used that year by Widor in his ballet *Der Korrigane*.

Chinese blocks Actually used by the Chinese, these oblong blocks of hardwood with one or two slits are hit with wooden sticks. Gershwin was the first to use them in the orchestra, in his Piano Concerto (1925). Temple blocks are similar, but being skull shaped and hollow they are more resonant. Walton used them in *Façade* (1923).

The jingle of bells in the rain as Morris dancers practise their traditional dance. (BBC Hulton Picture Library)

Cymbals
It: *piatti, cinelli*
Fr: *cymbales*
Ger: *Becken*

The word 'cymbal' (from Gk: *kymbos* = cup), and similar spellings, has been used for instruments as dissimilar as little bells and the organ, taking in psaltery and harpsichord on the way. Here we are discussing the modern orchestral cymbals, comprising two metal plates, and their ancestors. Their origin is totally lost: references occur from at least 1000 BC. It is quite possible that they have existed from the time man first learnt to work metal (*c.*2500 BC), even if only as the impromptu banging together of two metal dishes. They have existed in numerous configurations (deep bowl to almost flat plates, small finger cymbals less than 3in (7cm) in diameter to monstrous ear-splitters some 40in (100cm) across).

The cymbal, like the triangle and bass drum, developed in both Turkish and Western military music alike but whereas the playing method of the triangle is limited, that of the cymbal is extremely varied. The usual 'clash' is obtained by sweeping the two plates against each other in a vertical or horizontal motion for a loud sound (two players may be employed for special clashes), while quieter effects are produced by lightly touching the plates together edge to edge, brushing or rattling them, or simply drawing them apart. When suspended they may be played with hard or soft sticks, scratched with the fingernails or scraped with a violin bow to make them howl in apparent agony. Jazz and dance bands often mount two cymbals horizontally ('high-hat') and operate them with a foot lever or, when mounted singly, they may be struck with a drumstick, stroked with wire brushes, etc.

Glockenspiel A German word meaning 'bell-play'. In the 18th century this meant a structure of small bells struck by hammers operated from a keyboard, a development of a Roman instrument of the 4th century. Handel used the glockenspiel in his oratorio *Saul* (1739) and elsewhere. The modern instrument consists of flat horizontal metal plates struck by hand-held hammers. It was introduced *c.*1850 and first played in Adam's opera *Si J'étais Roi* (1852). Perhaps the glockenspiel's only concerto is S. Strohbach's (1959), in which it joins two flutes and a string orchestra.

Gong (Tam tam) It is easy to see that the word 'gong' is onomatopoeic. It comes from Java, an island near the centre of a vast archipelago comprising Indonesia, an area in which the gong is extremely prevalent, existing there in many sizes since the 3rd or 2nd century BC. It may have been introduced to Indonesia from Asia; it is said to have entered China from Hsi Yu, a country then lying between Tibet and Burma, but it is generally thought of as a traditional Chinese instrument due to the use of the Chinese name 'Tam tam', also onomatopoeic.

The gong attained popularity in the West first in France during revolutionary times: Gossec used it in 1791 in his *Funeral March on the Death of Mirabeau*, in which it is struck with the traditional soft-headed stick. Since then, other playing methods have been devised: it may be struck or stroked with a metal beater, energized with a violin bow, laid horizontally so that it fails to 'ring' when struck, or lowered into and raised from a bowl of water, a procedure which results in a downward and upward glissando. It has even been spun freely on a wooden surface (the orchestra platform) and allowed gradually to sink to rest, a fascinating or excruciating effect depending upon your point of view and proximity to the action.

Kettledrums
It: *timpani*
Fr: *timbales*
Ger: *Pauken*

'Kettledrum' is an obsolescent name for the modern orchestral timpani, used in groups or two or more. The name derives from the kettle-size and kettle-shape of native African and Arabian instruments, while the Italian word (singular: *timpano*) has been used in England since 1660, when many other musical terms were exchanged for the Italian equivalents. The kettledrum, which probably originated in the ancient orient, came to Western Europe via the Balkans and Russia and was first used in the orchestra in 1565, where two drums were called for in the intermedia *Psyche ed Amore* by an unknown composer. In 1607 Monteverdi required them in his opera *Orfeo*, Lully called for *tymbales* in his opera *Thésée* (1675), and their first symphonic appearance was in Torelli's Symphony in C, Giegling 33, before 1700. The first 'timpani concerto', paradoxically, is a symphony: J.W. Hertel's Symphony in D of *c.*1748 includes eight obligato timpani in its scoring and features a cadenza for the single drummer. Word comes from Eastern Europe of a timpani concerto by Jiří Družecký (1745–1819), but the earliest confirmed concerto — called thus — is that by Julius Tausch, composed about 1870. A recent concerto by Scott Lyell Cresswell (b. 1944) proves that interest persists in the genre.

Marimba and Vibraphone Imported from Latin America, the original marimba was a species of xylophone developed in Africa in which calabash resonators amplify the sound of metal, stone or wooden plates. Today's orchestral marimba replaces the gourds with metal tubes, and the plates ('bars') are invariably made of wood. Percy Grainger was the first to use the marimba (in his suite *In A Nutshell*, before 1914). Marimba concerti have been composed by Paul Creston (1940), Mario Kuri-

Aldana (with wind orchestra, 1962), Akira Miyoshi (1969) and others, and the related vibraphone (with rotating flaps at the tops of the tubes to modify the resonances) joins the marimba in Milhaud's Concerto (1947) and in Oliver Nelson's concerto for xylophone, marimba, vibraphone and wind; and the vibraphone (without marimba) joins recorder, strings and celesta in Vagn Holmboe's Concerto. The first symphony to include a marimba is Karl Amadeus Hartmann's Eighth (1962). The vibraphone occurs first in Milhaud's incidental music *L'annonce faite à Marie*, Op 117 (1932); its first symphonic appearance was in Britten's *Spring Symphony* (1949).

Rattle One of the most primitive of all instruments. In its least sophisticated form it consisted of a skull, human or animal, filled with loose teeth or pebbles. Rattles and scrapers had magical significance for early man and they remain standard equipment of tribal witch-doctors. Lepers were compelled to sound rattles as a warning of approach, and rattles warned of gas attack during World War I. Its orchestral use, therefore, usually conveys some bizarre or portentous effect; it was first called for, apparently, in Varèse's *Ionisation* (1921).

Side drum or Snare drum

It: *tamburo militare*
Fr: *tambour militaire, caisse claire*
Ger: *kleine Trommel*

The modern orchestral side drum comprises a two-headed cylindrical drum with snares (wires) across the lower head. The snares may be released from contact by a lever. The drum is mounted at an angle and played with two sticks. When used for military purposes it is slung against the player's side (hence its name). The modern instrument is shallower (5–8in; 12–20cm) and of much smaller diameter (*c.* 15in; 38cm) than hitherto; indeed its size and proportions have varied considerably in the past. It first came to Europe during the crusades as a military instrument (tabor) but was slow to enter the orchestra.

Apparently its first 'serious' score was Handel's *Musick for the Royal Fireworks* (1749), where the open-air occasion paralleled military practice. Marais is said to have used the side drum as early as 1706. The multi-movement symphony/overture to Grétry's opera *Le Magnifique* (1773) is the first symphony to employ the side drum, but its most spectacular symphonic use is in Nielsen's Symphony No 5 (1922), in which it plays a prominent part as a representation of evil forces, at one point directed to improvise 'as if at all costs to stop the progress of the orchestra'. Nielsen used the instrument again as a prominent foil to the soloist in his Clarinet Concerto (1928); but the first real side drum concerto appeared in 1958: Rolf Liebermann's *Geigy Festival Concerto* for Basler Trommel (a deep military snare drum).

Tam tam — see gong

Temple blocks — see Chinese blocks

Timpani — see Kettledrums

Triangle

It: *triangolo*
Fr: *triangle*
Ger: *Triangel*

The triangle is the smallest member of the orchestra, but since it involves striking a metal object with a metal striker, its tone is not surprisingly the most piercing. It is descended from the Egyptian sistrum which carried metal plates or rings on its metal rungs and gave a sharp jingling sound when shaken.

When first mentioned in the 10th century, the triangle was not necessarily triangular: it may have been trapezoidal (i.e. with four non-parallel sides) or of three unequal sides, and until the 19th century it usually sported metal rings on its lowest bar. Turkish military bands used it, and it was acquaintance with these bands that brought the instrument to prominence in Western Europe. In 1680 it was used together with other 'Turkish' instruments in Strungk's opera *Esther* and Freschi's opera *Berenice Vendicativa*. Orchestral inventories list it in Hamburg in 1710 and Dresden in 1717, but the earliest known purely orchestral score to include it was Georg Glantz's *Turkish* Symphony in 1774. Then, in 1798 and 1800, Clementi published waltzes for piano accompanied by triangle and tamborine (Opp 38 and 39). Thinking better of it, he later republished them for piano and flute.

No concerto, we believe, has been written for solo triangle, but Paganini used it prominently in his Violin Concerto No 2 (1826), again in No 4 (1830), and Liszt did likewise in his Piano Concerto No 1 (1853). Boieldieu, in *Le Calife de Bagdad* (1800), called for high- and low-pitched triangles, and tuned triangles have existed, but by far the commonest sound is the high and indefinitely pitched jingle.

Example of an early folk xylophone.

Vibraphone — see marimba

Wind Machine Not so much a musical instrument as a sound-effect machine, this consists of a silk or canvas cloth on a barrel which rubs on strips of pasteboard when rotated. Alternatively, the blades of an electric fan are replaced by strips of cane. The wind machine wandered into the orchestra from the theatre in 1897, when Richard Strauss used it in *Don Quixote*.

Xylophone The name (Gk: *xylon* = 'wood'; *phone* = 'sound') describes the tone: a number of wooden bars on a frame are struck with wooden mallets. Its earliest ancestor is the two-bar signalling device of early man, but by the 14th century in Java and Mali the number of bars had increased sufficiently for complicated rhythmic tunes to be played by executants holding two mallets in each hand. Its first Western mention (as *hültze glechter*) occurs in 1511, Hans Holbein pictured a xylophone played by a skeleton in 1523–5, and Mersenne illustrated a keyboard version in 1636–7.

Although known to Mendelssohn and other composers of his time, the xylophone's first use in 'art' music would appear to be in J.G. Kastner's odd *Livre-Partition* (an essay followed by a work for chorus and orchestra) entitled *Les danses des morts* in 1852. Saint-Saëns continued Holbein's and Kastner's macabre theme in *Danse Macabre* (1874). The instrument's first symphonic role was in Mahler's 6th Symphony (1904), and in 1961 Istvan Láng wrote a concerto for xylophone.

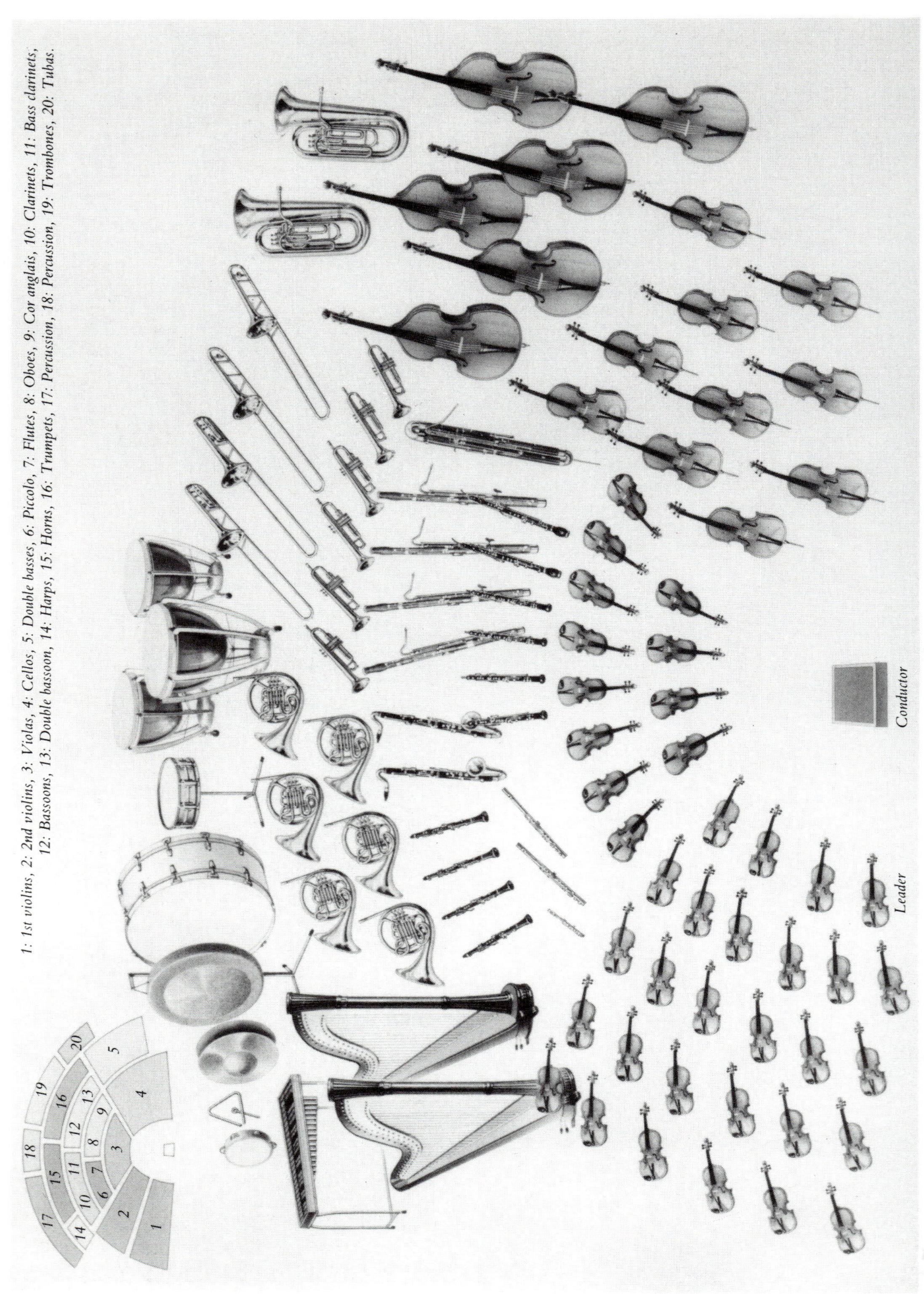

THE STANDARD DISPOSITION OF A MODERN SYMPHONY ORCHESTRA

(Photo © Marshall Cavendish Ltd; Artwork; Brian Delf)

II

A Galaxy of Instruments

In earlier editions of the *Guinness Book of Music* we illustrated early man's struggle to produce musical sounds from the objects he found about him: ringing stones, conch shells, reeds, hollow logs, and so on. We categorized these and later instruments according to the system invented by Curt Sachs in *The History of Musical Instruments*, in which they are grouped according to how the air is made to vibrate and by the method and materials of construction.

For the present book we have devised an alphabetical list of the better-known non-orchestral instruments and some of the stranger and more endearing inventions of musical man, and have included a list of drums from all eras and areas. Man's ingenuity and persistence emerge in a favourable light: some of the difficulties he has endured in order to wrest sounds that other people actually find enjoyable from his unlikely materials prove how potent a driving force is the desire to make music.

Ala Bohemica, left, pictured in the Velislav bible, 1340. The other instruments are, from left, cetera, fiddle and psaltery. (Prague University Library)

Some Non-Orchestral Instruments

Aeolian harp A rectangular frame across which are stretched a number of strings all tuned to the same note. This device, named after the wind god Aeolus, is stood in a breeze and the strings vibrate in the passage of air. As the strength of the wind increases, overtones emerge from some of the strings to combine with the basic notes to produce a weird, unearthly, disembodied sound. This type of instrument existed at the dawn of history: King David is said to have owned one. During the 19th century the instrument was fitted with a keyboard which controlled shutters to direct the wind on to certain strings at will, the strings by now being tuned to various notes. The indefinite attack of the notes make the aeolian harp unsuitable for serious music but it remains a curiosity of considerable charm.

Ala Bohemica (Bohemian wing) A 14th-century stringed instrument of the psaltery type consisting of a flat, hollow, bird-wing-shaped table with two round sounding-holes, at one end of which is what looks like half a wheel standing upright. The strings run the length of the table, some of them raised to pass through holes in the semi-wheel. (See dulcimer)

Alphorn A long wooden horn used for signalling in the Alps. Its first reference dates from the 15th century although it is undoubtedly of prehistoric origin. Best known for its use in Alpine districts, it is nevertheless widespread in Europe.

■ *The world's longest alphorn was made by Peter Wutherich in Boise, Idaho in 1984. From lip to tip it measures 78ft 9½in (24m) and its sound takes 73.01 milliseconds to emerge from the bowl after entry from the mouthpiece.* ■

Rossini imitated the call of the alphorn in his *William Tell* Overture (1829), but Leopold Mozart actually wrote a *Sinfonia Pastorale* in G (alternatively attributed to Hofstetter) for *corno pastoriccio* (i.e. alphorn) with strings. At a Hoffnung Festival Concert in London's Royal Festival Hall on 13 November 1956, Dennis Brain played the finale of this symphony, using an ordinary garden hosepipe fitted with a horn mouthpiece. F. Farkas wrote a *Concertino rustico* for alphorn and strings in 1977, and a *Petite Suite Alpestre* for solo alphorn the year before.

Anata A primitive Peruvian wooden flute with mouthpiece. The Peruvians use a similar word, antaras, to denote the five- or six-tube cane panpipes.

Apunga A horn made from an elephant's tusk, its sound resembling the trumpeting made naturally by that animal. Imported into Europe, intricately carved and called 'oliphant' in the 10th century, the ivory horn became a status symbol amongst the well-off; carried into battle it was a fearsome adversary.

Balalaika and domra The balalaika is a stringed instrument allied to the lute and the guitar which was widespread as a folk instrument in Europe from about the 17th century. The triangular balalaika, together with its larger and rounder relative the domra, were modernized about 100 years ago, and the improved form is now considered to be the national instrument of Russia. It is made in six sizes: piccolo, primo, secunda, viola, bass and contrabass; the domra family is similarly constituted. Concerti for domra and balalaika respectively have been written by Shushakov and Budashkin.

Baryton A six-stringed bass gamba invented perhaps as long ago as the beginning of the 17th century. Six bowed strings were not enough for its inventor, however, for running behind them he put perhaps as many as 40 sympathetic strings which hummed along with the played strings. These sympathetic strings could also be plucked through a hole in the back of the fingerboard, a startling effect for audiences to whom the actions of the baryton player were invisible.

The earliest surviving music for baryton is Johann Georg Krause's nine *Partien* of 1703, but Prince Nikolaus Esterházy favoured it and his long-suffering servant Haydn provided him with no less than 12 divertimenti, 2 concerti, 24 duos and 125 trios for baryton. There is, however, no truth in the story that Haydn invented the alternative name by which the baryton is sometimes known: *lyra bastarda*. A small 20th-century revival of interest in the instrument is evident in the appearance of expert players who have recorded some of Haydn's trios, and in the existence of a *Concerto all'Antica* (1955) for baryton and strings by F. Farkas (who prudently gave the soloist an option: '. . . or viola da gamba'.)

Birimbao Argentinian Jew's harp.

Black pudding A less than flattering name in the North of England for the serpent.

Bladder-pipe A perhaps very ancient but certainly medieval wind instrument which uses an animal bladder as an air reservoir between the player's lips and the reed or reeds. No original example survives, but the sound it made probably resembled that of the bagpipes, particularly since some early pictures of the bladder pipe show it as possessing a second, drone, pipe. Modern examples using a (perhaps more hygienic) rubber balloon are widespread in Europe.

Bottle The humble glass bottle, from aspirin to demijohn size, has been commandeered for jazz use and, together with jug-thumpers, bottle-blowers give impromptu performances to anyone who will listen. Tuned bottles were blown in a performance of the Andante of Haydn's 'Surprise' Symphony in the Hoffnung Music Festival Concert in London on 13 November 1956, perhaps the first 'serious' use of the instrument. Since then bottles have been used in *Arcana 19* (1962) by the Japanese composer Kuniharu Akiyama. In the **bouteillophone** the bottles are struck (gently) with hard beaters: Satie called for the instrument in his Ballet *Parade* in 1916. It is sometimes called *beautyphone*, a name thought to derive more from its French name (*bouteillophone*) than from its sound.

Brake drum Literally a car part, giving off a characterful ringing sound when suspended and struck. Its sonority is much admired by avant-garde composers.

Buccina A Roman trumpet with a slide, from which the trombone developed. In Sicily the non-slide trumpet was called *busine*.

Bull-roarer This appropriately-named instrument has not changed in thousands of years. Its eerie hum, growl or roar has been used to frighten away women from ceremonies taboo to them, to invoke magic powers and to stampede cattle. Its Greek name was *rombos*; it is also known by such enchanting names as 'swish', 'thunderstick', 'hummer-buzzer', 'whirling-stick' and 'bummer'.

Whether working from cave-paintings or the latest model off some Aboriginal Australian bull-roarer production line, even the most inexpert handy-person could make such an instrument. A flat piece of wood anything from 6in (15cm) long is smoothed, its edges bevelled and rounded off, one long edge serrated, and a design carved on one or both of its flat sides. The ends are then tapered in both planes, a hole is drilled near one end and a piece of cord is inserted and fastened securely. Holding the end of the cord, the thing is whirled round one's head. Pitch and volume depend on size of blade, length of wood and the vigour with which the player whirls.

Primitive people all over the world have used the bull-roarer, and its size, shape and decorations are subject to endless variation. Its best-known association today is with the Aboriginal tribes of Northern Australia where it is still usually made of wood, although bone, stone and even iron have been used. Composers have risked its use in the orchestra, for example John Antill in his ballet *Corroboree* (1946), while Henry Cowell, confident of a large room and an adventurous audience, called for three thundersticks and the ultra-civilized group of two violins, viola and two cellos in his *Ensemble* (1924).

Carillon Originally devised as a civic time signal that played tunes in the Low Countries in the 16th century, it consists of many bells fastened to a framework, their clappers operated from a keyboard in a lower room, or below the tower in which the bells are housed. The bells may range in weight from 22lb (10kg) (with a diameter of 8in, 20cm) to over 18 tons/tonnes (with a diameter of more than 10ft, 3m). Their use in the orchestra, therefore, becomes a problem, and one suspects that the bells called for by Handel in *Acis e Galatea* (1718) and elsewhere were a rather more compact

■ *The largest carillon (minimum of 23 bells) in the world is the Laura Spelman Rockefeller Memorial carillon in Riverside Church, New York City, USA with 74 bells weighing 102 tons. The bourdon, giving the note lower C, weighs 40 926lb (18 563kg). This 18.27 ton bell, cast in England, with a diameter of 10ft 2in (3.09m) is the largest tuned bell in the world.*

The heaviest carillon in Great Britain is in St Nicholas Church, Aberdeen, Scotland. It consists of 48 bells, the total weight of which is 25 tons 8cwt 2qrs 13lb (25 838kg). The bourdon bell weighs 4 tons 9cwt 3qrs 26lb (4571kg) and is the note G sharp. ■

Eighteenth-century Chinese pavilion. (Photo: Les Prudden)

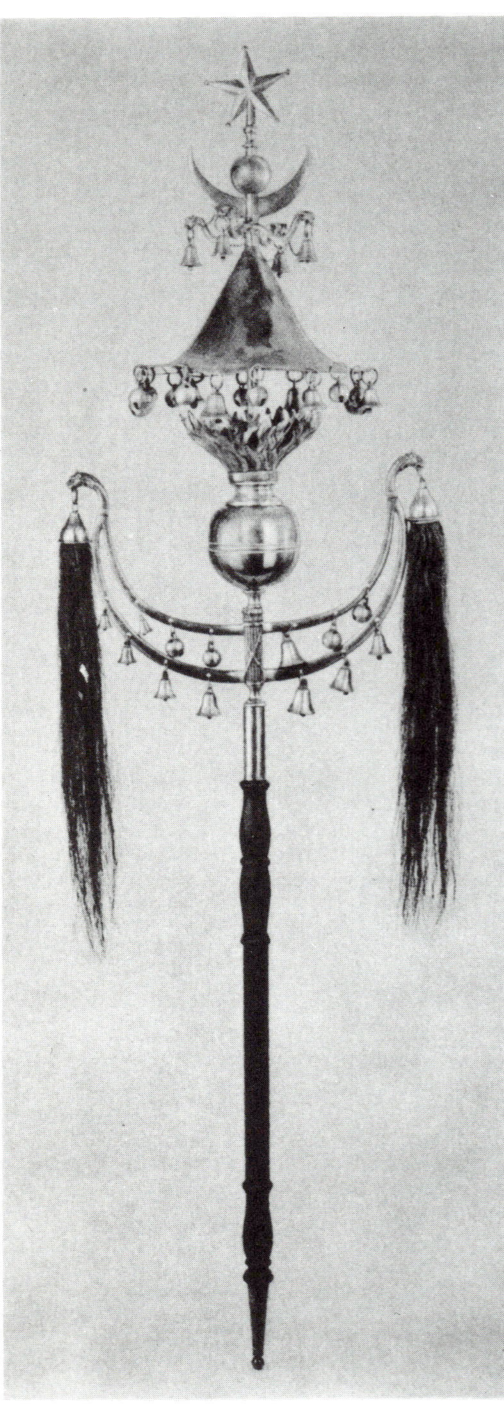

instrument in which metal plates are struck with hammers. Confusion with an orchestral instrument is encouraged by the existence for the carillon of an alternative name: glockenspiel.

Chacocra A straight trumpet used in Jewish ceremonies during the first century AD and probably long before.

Chalumeau in French, *salmoè* in Italian, *shalmey* or *shawm* in English. This is a single-reed instrument which may have contributed to the development of the clarinet (see p 12). The name itself (from Latin *calamus* or *calamellus* = reed) is most confusing, for it seems that shawms were known, as such, in England and Germany from the Middle Ages (they were probably introduced from the Far East), but the French version of the name was not used until shortly before 1700. Denner, who invented the clarinet in Nuremberg, is said also to have 'improved' the chalumeau, apparently taking that French word (meaning a double-reed bagpipe chanter) to be the equivalent of English shawm and German *Schalmei*. In general terms, the shawm existed until *c*.1700; it was then 'improved' to become the chalumeau which enjoyed a further half-century or so of popularity until being finally succeeded by the clarinet, which developed from the shawm (possibly with recorder influence) around 1700.

In 1704 J-P. Dreux published his *Fanfares pour deux chalumeaux ou deux trompettes & continuo*, and M.A. Ziani included chalumeaux in his opera *Caio Popilio* in Vienna. In less than thirty years four sizes had evolved: treble, alto, tenor, bass. Graupner composed concerti and chamber works for chalumeaux, and Vivaldi's Concerto in C, RV 558, includes two *salmoè*.

Charango A small Chilean double-strung guitar made from an armadillo shell.

Chinese pavilion, bell tree, Turkish crescent, jingling johnny, and probably as many other names, have been given to the military percussion instrument comprising a vertical pole upon which are fixed small bells and button bells on crescent-shaped cross pieces. Usually featured are two coloured horsetail plumes for decoration, and the head of the pole is invariably crowned with a regimental emblem or patriotic insignia. When carried on the march the johnny jingles, and its contribution to the band may be intensified by bouncing the pole up and down and/or twisting it on its axis. Military bands have used the instrument since at least the 16th century.

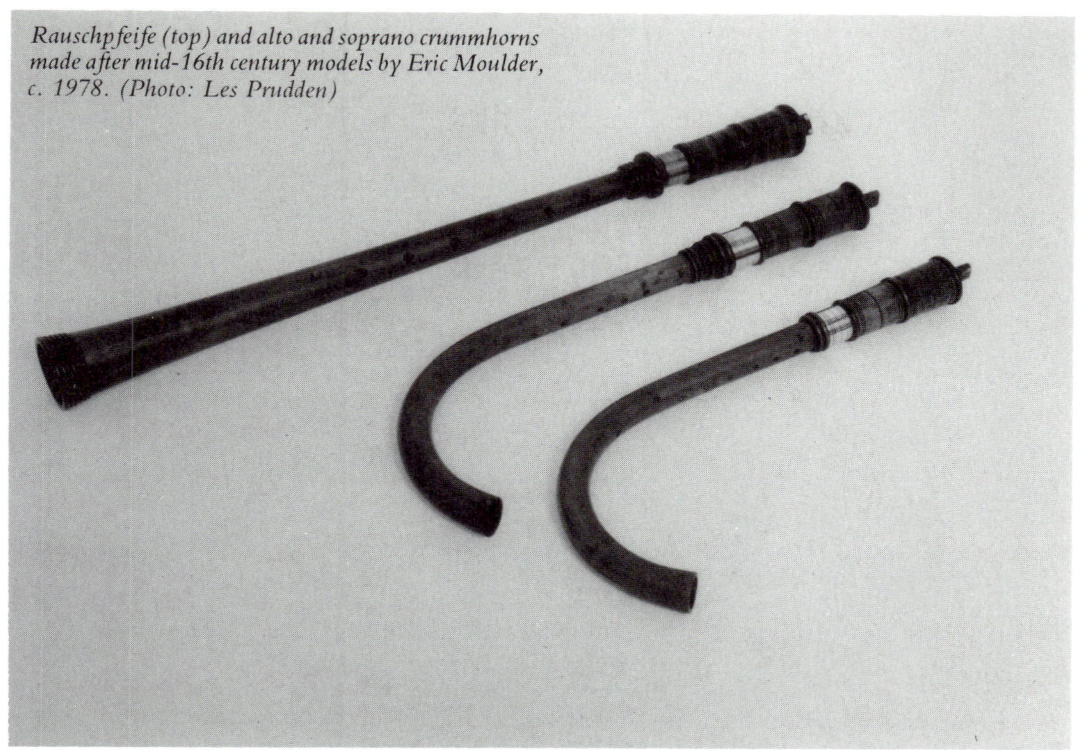

Rauschpfeife (top) and alto and soprano crummhorns made after mid-16th century models by Eric Moulder, c. 1978. (Photo: Les Prudden)

Berlioz, never one to neglect an interesting and spectacular effect, put one in his *Symphonie funèbre et triomphale* (1840).

Chorimori A bell rattle of ancient date from the Atacamá desert region of Chile.

Chromelodeon A harmonium invented by Harry Partch (see p 117) in Chicago in 1942 to produce his 43-tone scale.

Clarín A long, side-blown trumpet from the Atacamá desert region of Chile.

Clavicytherium is to harpsichord what upright grand is to piano, only higher. In a horizontal harpsichord (the usual type), the jacks which rise to pluck the strings fall back by gravity; in the clavicytherium they have to be helped back by springs. London's Royal College of Music possesses a clavicytherium dating from *c.*1480 (and therefore made within a decade or two of the instrument's invention) which is the oldest surviving keyboard instrument in the world. At 4ft 8in (142.5cm), with stand, its height is effectively greater and more imposing because it needs to be stood on a table to be played (that is, if it were in playing condition) since its keyboard otherwise is only a few inches off the floor.

Comb-and-paper (Mirliton) Mirlitons of great variety have existed throughout the last few thousand years. Today, the best-known example, and an ideal illustration of the principle, is the simple comb-and-paper. The voice is projected against a membrane, which resonates in sympathy, producing a rasping sound. The toy kazoo is another example, as are the Chinese flute, in which one hole is covered by a membrane, and the African mirliton, in which one end of a horn is covered by a type of tough spider-web.

With 100 Kazoos by David Bedford was written to be performed by the BBC Symphony Orchestra *and* the audience in London in 1972 but the conductor Pierre Boulez refused to include it in the programme. The instrument finds a more conducive place in jazz and popular music, but even this sphere of music might experience difficulty in accommodating the world's largest kazoo. It was reported by Barbara D. Stewart, 'Manager and Kazoo-keeper' of the Kazoophony, Rochester, New York, in July 1975. It weighs 43lb (19.5kg), measures 7ft (2.1m) high by 4ft 5in (1.3m) wide, and is played by four players simultaneously.

Cornu A Roman name for an instrument taken over from the Etruscans. It is made of brass, curved into a shape resembling the letter 'G', and a distinguishing feature is its wooden crossbar which is either grasped in one hand or supported on the shoulder. The bell of the instrument is sometimes fashioned into a reptilian or dragon-like mouth. Horace described its voice as 'a menacing murmur'.

Crembalum A mystery. The instrument was called for by Albrechtsberger in two concerti in the 1770s (Somfai Nos 8 and 10). Evidence points to an instrument comprising a wooden frame to which are attached up to 16 Jew's harps upon which the exponent might play a respectable melody (see Jew's harp, p 54).

Dactylomonocordo This is a single-stringed instrument to be played by one finger, invented by one Guida of Naples in about 1877.

Decachordum A '10-stringed instrument', according to references dating from the 14th century. It may equate with the 10-stringed psaltery — see dulcimer.

Didjeridoos were invented by mother Nature. Fallen branches hollowed out by termites lay around the primeval Australian landscape just waiting to be picked up by the first Aborigines, cleared of debris, cut to length if need be, and played. Various names survive in Northern Australia: *a:ra:wi, lhambilbilg, ganbag*, etc; but didjeridoo, in several spellings, thought up by white settlers, is a quaintly onomatopoeic name, more descriptive than the prosaic 'official' description, 'end-blown natural trumpet', which does nothing to convey the elemental throb produced by an expert a:ra:wi-ist. As a rhythmic one-note continuous drone it complements the sharp clicking of stick on stick or stick on didjeridoo at native song and dance festivals. The Australian composer George Dreyfuss (b.1928) wrote a Sextet for didjeridoo and wind in 1971.

Dulcimer, psaltery and zither A quick way of distinguishing between dulcimer and psaltery is to remember that the former is hammered and the latter plucked, but such generalizations never withstand examination, for some psalteries have been known to be hammered, while the not infrequent description 'hammered dulcimer' implies the existence of non-hammered (and therefore plucked) varieties. Furthermore, some dulcimer tutors recommend plucking with one hand and hammering with the other!

Both dulcimer and psaltery are antique instruments. A 12th-century ivory carving from Byzantium shows a trapezoidal instrument being struck with a stick but it is not certain whether strings or strips of wood are being struck — if the latter, the instrument would of course be a xylophone. There is, however, a soundhole, which indicates a stringed instrument but the artist can hardly be relied upon for, whatever the instrument is, it is standing almost vertically on its side and does not appear to be supported.

Unmistakeable references date from about 1440 and the word 'dulcimer' arose within about 50 years from the Latin *dulce melos* = 'sweet tune' or 'pleasant song'. The instrument has been known in most parts of the world, its design and name changing as it migrated: *yang-chin* (and related forms) in China and Japan, *psantin* or *santur* from Greece to India, *Hackbrett* in Germanic countries, and so on.

The idea of a box of strings struck with a hammer was then subjected to sophistication, mingled with harpsichord design, and evolved into the pianoforte (qv). The German composer and dulcimer player Pantaleon Hebenstreit (1669–1750) constructed a large and complicated dulcimer early in the 18th century and this had a century or so of currency as the *pantaleon* (see p 59). A local variety of dulcimer is the East European *cymbalom*. Zoltan Kodály incorporated one into his suite from the opera *Háry János* (1926), and the Byelorussian composer Valter Kaminsky has composed a concerto for cymbalom and folk-orchestra. The cymbalom is also used, often with incredible virtuosity, in Romanian folk bands.

The psaltery in early biblical references seems to be confused with a species of harp, an instrument with which its development was approximately contemporary. In its early forms the psaltery consisted of a shallow rectangular box across which about a dozen strings were stretched. The name comes from 'psalm': the instrument was frequently used to accompany psalm singing, and for a time its strings numbered 10, one for each commandment. Its outline varied greatly, from triangular, rectangular and pig-head shaped to elongated versions resembling a wing (see *Ala Bohemica*, above). Trapezoidal forms were rare. The strings were plucked with a plectrum or the fingertips, the instrument being stood or held vertically. As it developed, the instrument acquired more strings and a triangular shape and came to be laid flat. While the hammered varieties led ultimately to the development of the pianoforte, the plucked psaltery led, with the development of mechanical plucking agents

Seventeenth-century French dulcimer. (Prague University Library)

Philip Astle and Paul Williamson. Left: playing a tenor violin made by Nicholas Woodward in 1981 after an Amati of 1615; and a bass viol made by Norman Myall in 1979 after a late 16th-century model by Gasparo de Salò. In front, a typical Medieval large tabor, made by Paul Williamson in 1978. Above: playing a reproduction Medieval trumpet made by Edward Kirby in 1977, and nakers, made by Paul Williamson after Medieval models. (Photos: Les Prudden)

operated from a keyboard, to the harpsichord family. The psaltery has no real place in the orchestra today, but the Russian composer Barchunov has written a concerto for two psalteries with orchestra.

In simple terms the zither is a psaltery with frets. The word, which derives from Gk. *kithara* and Latin *cithara* (= harp), can denote any stringed instrument not covered by the general descriptions of harp, lute, lyre or viol. The huntsman's bow, therefore, becomes a zither as soon as it is twanged or bowed musically. Zithers were used occasionally in the serious music of the 19th century, notably by Johann

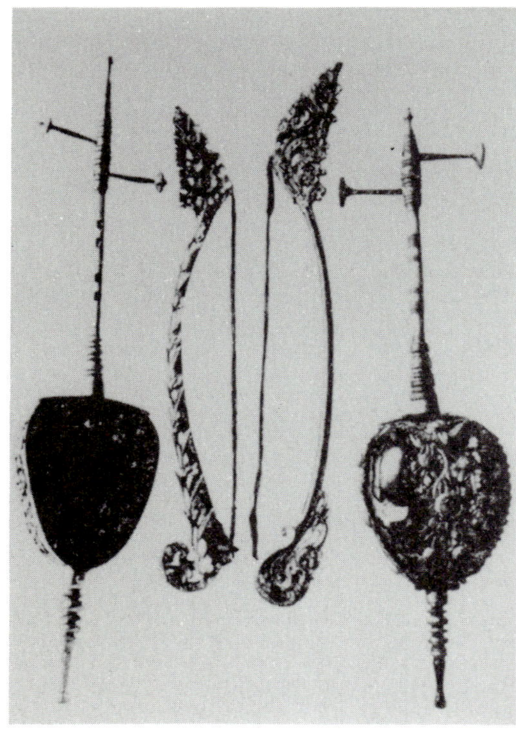

Strauss II, but it is as a café instrument that it achieved fame for its prominent part in the film music for Carol Reed's *The Third Man* (1949), from which the 'Harry Lime Theme', played by Anton Karas, became immensely popular. The American 'Appalachian dulcimer' is in fact a true zither.

Er-hu A Chinese violin or bowed lute with two strings and a snakeskin-covered soundbox. The bow hair is inserted between the strings.

Fidhla An Icelandic bowed zither of the 18th century and perhaps earlier, its body being a straight-sided elongated triangle, with the two (or sometimes three) strings running longitudinally and raised high off the body so that they may be stopped from below with the left hand. The *fidhla* may have given rise to the Norwegian *fidla* which in turn led to the Hardanger fiddle (see p 50).

Glass harmonica Also known as the 'euphon' and 'clavicylindre' the glass harmonica was the product of the imagination and sensitivity of the 18th century, but glass xylophones existed in the Far East from at least as early as the 11th century. Bascially, the principle stems from the idea of producing notes from glasses or tumblers which are tuned by being filled to different levels with water. 'Musical glasses' were performed by the Irishman Richard Pockrich in London in 1743 (but in 1759 he was killed in a fire which engulfed his glass-and-water instrument). In 1746 Gluck 'played a concerto on 26 drinking glasses tuned with spring water' at the Haymarket Theatre in London.

Benjamin Franklin, often given credit for inventing the 'glass armonica', merely adapted existing principles when he completed his instrument in 1763. The glasses, fitted one into the other, were half submerged and rotated by a treddle, their edges being activated by wetted fingertips.

Left: Japanese rebabs, with bows. (Photo: Les Prudden)

Much value was put on the ethereal sound thus produced. It was said to have magical soothing qualities, and the Swiss composer Franz Xaver Joseph Peter Schnyder von Wartensee wrote a descriptive piece entitled *Der durch Musik überwundene Wüterich* ('The Angry Man Calmed by Music') in about 1830, in which the volatile temper of the piano is gradually calmed by the soothing ministrations of the glass harmomica. Saint-Saëns included a 'harmonica' in the 'Aquarium' movement of his *Carnival of the Animals* (1886): probably the glass harmonica was the instrument he meant.

Gu-chin A Chinese fretless zither with silk strings overwound with metal. The *gu-jung* is similar, but with 12 or more strings and movable bridges.

Guitar Notwithstanding today's craze for building guitars in weird shapes, with strange projections, coloured lights, control knobs and trailing wires, the soundbox removed to give a skeletal effect because acoustic amplification has given way to overworked transistors, the traditional shape of the guitar remains recognizable. It is gracefully waisted, with one large soundhole, and the back is slightly bowed outwards. It is a shape found occasionally amongst lutes of the early Christian era, and the name bears a resemblance to Ancient Greek *kithara*. But the evidence for true guitars existing before the Renaissance is circumstantial.

The traditional shape of the guitar has remained recognizable for centuries. The amplification at this Crosby Stills and Nash concert may be a produce of 20th-century electrical wizardry but the instruments evolved in the early Christian era. (LFI)

■ *The largest and presumably also the loudest playable guitar in the world is one 10ft 1in (3.07m) tall, and in excess of 300lb (136kg) in weight, built by Sparkling Ragtime Productions of San Francisco, and the Guild of American Luthiers, Tacoma, Washington, USA in December 1980. The most expensive standard-sized guitar is the German chittara battente of Jacob Stadler, dated 1624, which was sold for £10 500 at Christie's, London on 12 June 1974.* ■

The earliest printed music for guitar was Mudarra's *Tres libros* of 1546, and it first appeared in a symphony in Boccherini's Symphony in C, Gér 523, arranged by the composer in about 1798 from his guitar quintet of 1771. Its earliest concerto appears to be Giuliani's, in A, Op 30, of 1808; earlier concertos (by, for example, Vivaldi) are arrangements of lute works. Of the many concerti written this century for the instrument by far the most famous is Rodrigo's *Concierto de Aranjuez* of 1939.

Gusle or gussly is the Yugoslav name for the violin, but it also denotes a folk fiddle made in one piece — neck and body — and played with a primitive bow. Folk singers tell long epic tales to the self-accompaniment of the gusle.

Gusli or gussly An instrument totally different from the above. The similarity of name doubtless arose because of the use in both instruments of strings (*gosl* in Slavonic). The gusli was common from about AD 1000 in Russia — Rimsky-Korsakov called for one in his opera *Sadko* (1896) — but has largely died out. It is a horizontal psaltery with strings numbering up to 36 which are plucked with the fingers. The earliest known gusli virtuoso was Vasiliy Fyodorovich Trutovsky (*c*.1740–1810), who not only entertained the Russian artistocracy but also collected folk songs and wrote music for his instrument.

Hardanger fiddle A Norwegian folk instrument named after the district in which it originated in the 16th century. The earliest surviving model, a six-string example made by Ole Johnsen Jaastad of Hardanger in 1651, is preserved in the Bergen museum. The instrument developed from early Norwegian fiddles such as the *gigja* and *fidla*, and from the viola d'amor. Its four strings cross a bridge which is less arched than that of a normal violin, making the production of multiple stopping an easy task for the players who make a speciality of highly embellished and harmonized variants to the basic dances for which the instrument is mainly used. Among these dances are the *halling, springar*, and *gangar*. Four or five sympathetic wire strings lie below the played strings. Norwegian composers have occasionally included the Hardanger fiddle in serious works: Nils Geirr Tveitt wrote two concerti for it (1956; 1965), and Eivind Groven composed *Fjelltonar* (1938) and *Margit Hjukse* (1964) in which the instrument is joined respectively by

Ugandan bow harp, a sophisticated development of the hunting bow. (Horniman Museum)

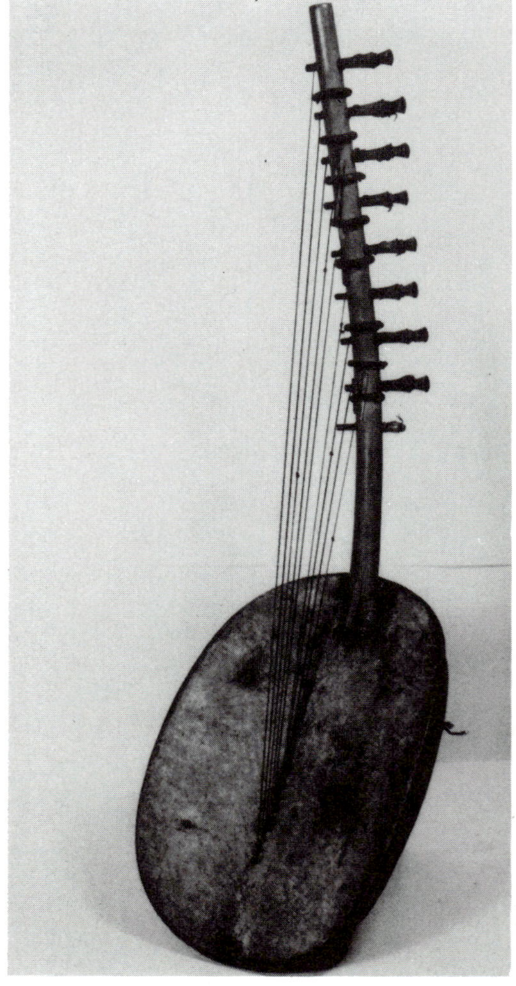

Hardanger fiddle made in 1651 by Ole Jonsen Jaastad (Historisk Museum, Bergen, Norway)

chamber orchestra and chorus. He also wrote two pieces in 1963 for two unaccompanied Hardanger fiddles.

Harp, in its simplest form, consists of a soundbox (resonator) and a curving or angled stem between which run a number of strings. It can be seen that the hunter's bow to which has been attached a resonator developed naturally into the harp; therefore the instrument is probably of prehistoric origin and was established in Egypt by at least the Fourth Dynasty (2723–2563 BC). Evidence from Sumerian culture suggests the existence of the *balang* (clearly an onomatopoeia), a boat-shaped harp from *c.*2800 BC.

The present word 'harp' may derive from the plucking action of the fingers (cf. Latin: *carpere* = pick, pluck; also 'harvest' and 'picking season'), but the Latin word for harp (also for lute and lyre) was *fides*, 'harpa' occurring first in France about AD 600 and therefore having little to do directly with Latin.

A Ruckers harpsichord dated 1628 with 18th-century decoration. This instrument sold for £68 200 at Sotheby's in December 1985. (Sotheby's)

The first harp concerto was written by Handel for incorporation in *Alexander's Feast* (1736); it was later published as an organ concerto, this having been the composer's alternative if no harp had been available. Gluck used a harp in *Orfeo ed Euridice* in 1762, and in the same year C.P.E. Bach composed a sonata for solo harp (W 139), but its début in a symphony did not occur until 1830, when Berlioz included two in his *Symphonie Fantastique*. Czerny once wrote a *Konzertstück* for 8 pianos and 12 harps; even the modern symphony orchestra customarily boasts only two.

The most aged instrumental player was a harpist. He was Denis A. Hempson, who achieved great fame in his native Ireland. He was born in 1695 and was blinded by smallpox three years later. He toured Ireland and Scotland playing Irish music exclusively and adhering tenaciously to the music and techniques of the past. For Hempson, Turlough Carolan, who died in 1738, was an avant-garde composer. Hempson died in 1807 at the age of 112.

Harpsichord An instrument akin in shape to a grand piano. The strings, however, are plucked by quills operated from a keyboard. Earliest reference to a 'clavicembalum' comes from Padua in 1397, an invention of one Hermann Poll, and the earliest depiction of such an instrument is a sculpture in a church in Minden, north-west Germany, which can be dated to 1425. A construction plan by Henricus Arnhault of Zwolle, dated 1435, shows five soundholes, a wing shape and 35 keys. The oldest harpsichord known to exist, and to which a date can be ascribed with certainty, was built by Hieronymus of Bologna in 1521 and is preserved in the Victoria and Albert Museum, London. The general design survives today, but with various embellishments such as swell devices, extra keyboards, etc.

The instrument's origin makes an interesting story. King David is seen playing an instrument in some early representations: it is plucked, has a sounding board behind the strings, and resembles a psaltery of the type brought to Europe by the Saracens and Moors in the early Middle Ages. The psaltery, branching off on its way to the dulcimer which led ultimately to the development of the pianoforte, eventually evolved into the harpsichord family, which reached its greatest popularity during the first half of the 18th century. Literally thousands of harpsichord sonatas appeared in print (Domenico Scarlatti alone wrote 555) but, perhaps due to its limited carrying power when in concert, it was slow to achieve solo status in a concerto. Circumstantial evidence suggests the background to the appearance of what may have been the first harpsichord concerti. Early in 1733 Johann Sebastian Bach's employer in Leipzig, Elector Friedrich August I of Saxony, died and a five-month mourning period began. During this period, of course, no music was heard in court, but in private Bach was testing the qualities of a newly-delivered harpsichord. It appears that he reworked several of his old concerti for the new instrument and invited his promising 19-year-old son Carl Philipp Emanuel to compose a concerto for the start of the new season in June. The keyboard versions of J.S.'s concerti are the only ones to survive in some cases, but C.P.E.'s concerto in A minor is lost in its original form, existing only in a revised version from 11 years later.

As part of the continuo, the harpsichord was included in the earliest symphonies, but the first part specifically designed for it in a symphony (although ironically it may have been played on a fortepiano) is a series of arpeggios introduced for performance by the composer towards the end of Haydn's Symphony No 98 in B flat (1792). During this century the harpsichord has recovered from its Victorian oblivion: Manuel de Falla (in 1926) and Frank Martin (in 1952) are amongst those who have provided concerti for the instrument.

Heckelphone Wagner, ever dissatisfied with the orchestra as he found it, approached the instrument-maker Wilhelm Heckel complaining of the hole in the woodwind department between oboe and bassoon. Wagner did not live to hear Heckel's response in 1904, but Richard Strauss snapped up the Heckelphone and used it prominently in his opera *Salome* the following year. It is a baritone oboe with a sonorous tone.

Hisser This comes in two models. The earlier were the *sibilatori* invented by Luigi Russolo in about 1913 but which no longer exist. They were members of a galaxy of formidable instruments with truculent names (exploders, howlers, roarers, etc) which formed the basis of the Futurists' musical experiments.

Perhaps inspired by this movement (but more likely not), Ernst Toch called for the sound of escaping steam in his Symphony No 3 (1955) and humorist Gerard Hoffnung rose to the occasion by 'inventing' a hisser. It consisted of a large cylinder of compressed air (with prominently displayed pressure gauges) and a rubber pipe to which was attached a valve. At points marked in the score, Margaret Cotton, the 'hissist' for the occasion, opened the valve to release a sound which suggested to Hoffnung 'all the venom and threat of a wild jungle creature spitting at its enemy'.

Horseshoes By suspending old horseshoes which he found in his uncle's village smithy, the opera composer John Davy (1763–1824) constructed an instrument upon which he could play simple tunes. This principle is also applied to the **stone star**, a horizontal instrument in the centre of which sits the player with striking stones in each hand. The stone star is still used in Africa.

Hurdy-gurdy This has existed in many forms since its introduction into Europe some time before the 9th century, and doubtless existed in varieties now lost during its previous period in the mysterious East. Basically, it consists of a body resembling a thickened violin, strings running the length of the body, a resined wheel underneath the strings at right-angles to them, a handle to turn the wheel, and a keyboard mechanism for stopping the strings. Of course, some of these features are expendable: the Swedish *Nyckelharpa* dispenses with the wheel and uses a bow instead while the German *Bauern Lyren* dispenses with the keyboard, and the *symphony*, or *symphonia*, dispenses with the shaped body and houses the workings in an oblong box. The hurdy-gurdy has the ability to play several notes at the same time, the continuously-turning wheel activating a drone or two while the player controls the melody with the keyboard. Well played, it can sound like a whole string band with rhythmic, almost percussive, effects. The sound, however, is unsubtle, and from a position of respectability during the Middle Ages it sank to the level of the street musician and the beggar. In the 18th century the tendency was for the instrument to improve its social standing since it had become associated with pastoral happenings, which were back in fashion among the aristocracy.

Leopold Mozart composed a concerto for bagpipes and hurdy-gurdy, written in such a way that one player, by changing instruments during pauses, could play both parts. The French composer Charles Baton was a virtuoso on the instrument, for which he also wrote chamber and concerted works, while Nicolas Chédeville arranged Vivaldi's *The Four Seasons* for hurdy-gurdy, violin, flute and continuo; and as recently as 1972 Sven-Eric Johanson wrote a Hurdy-gurdy Concerto.

One particularly odd hybrid was the **lyra-organizzata** an instrument played by street musicians in Naples (and elsewhere?) during the 1780s. In answer to a commission for six concerti (only five of which survive) from the King of Naples, Haydn wrote charming works for two lyrae-organizzata and small orchestra in 1786. No example of the instrument exists, but according to contemporary accounts it was a hurdy-gurdy to which was attached a set of pipes and a small bellows driven by the crank. Because of the necessity of turning the wheel, the player had only one hand available for operating the keyboard, so the strings and pipes presumably sounded in unison, which is why, in order to introduce some tonal variety, Haydn wrote for two.

Hydraulis Gk: *hydro* + *aulos* = water-pipe. The ancient East, so often blamed for the invention of weird instruments, is innocent of this one. Its appearance can be dated with certainty to 246 BC, and its inventor can be identified as an Alexandrian engineer called Ctesibius (300–250 BC), whose credits include the pneumatic catapult and the crossbow. His water organ (*pace* the Greek name) consisted of a water tank, cistern, air chest, bellows and pipes. Within the tank was a submerged bell containing part air, part water. Via a system of valves the bellows supplied air to the bell which in turn replenished the air chest. The interaction of weight and pressure ensured a steady supply of air to the pipes, its introduction controlled by keyboard-operated sliders. Ctesibius's invention was undoubtedly a wonder of the age, for three centuries later the Roman emperor Nero (the well-known 'fiddler') possessed one and marvelled at it. When threatened by imminent attack from the Gauls he called an urgent meeting of military staff — and spent several hours explaining and demonstrating his hydraulis.

A big advantage the water organ possessed over the bagpipes was that the cistern-and-bellows arrangement was capable of operating a far greater number of pipes than the bagpiper's lungs. Polyphonic music therefore theoretically became possible, though none survives from this period. Disadvantages were the water organ's expense — only the comfortably-off could afford to install one — and its weight, which meant that once installed it was somewhat less than portable.

Intonarumori Futurist music machines.

Jew's harp Familiarly a small flagon-shaped metal frame with a blade or tongue of metal fastened to the base. This blade is vibrated by the finger, and when the instrument is held against the player's mouth the resulting sound is amplified by the mouth cavity. There is no specific Jewish connection, nor has the version of the name 'jaw's harp' any foundation. A name 'jewjaw' or 'gewgaw', which survives in the north of England, may be onomatopoeic in origin and may also have given rise to the name 'jew's harp'.

Native versions of the instrument, sometimes with a wooden frame, have existed in most cultures of the world but, because of the disdain with which they and their players were usually regarded, few ancient examples have survived. Pictorial evidence exists that they were used in Egypt before Christian times. Suitable as a rhythmic accompaniment for dancing and singing, the Jew's harp has occasionally found its way into the recital room. Johann Heinrich Hörmann's *Parthia* in C for Jew's harp, two recorders, two muted violins, two pizzicato violins and continuo from about 1750 seems to be its first 'respectable' role. Two decades later much confusion was caused when Albrechtsberger's concerti for *trombula* or *crembalum* appeared. Recently the name *trombula* was taken for trumpet, but the nature of the part clearly precludes the trumpet of *c.*1770; apparently both names — *trombula* and *crembalum* — indicated types of multiple Jew's harp in which several instruments of different pitches were fastened to a wooden frame, thus making possible melodic playing in several keys. Albrechtsberger's works, for instance, are in D, E flat and F.

Jonkamentótzi A Peruvian cross flute made from a reed and lacking fingerholes. The 'melody' is made by sticking the finger in the lower end of the instrument and thus controlling the air-flow.

Jonkari Peruvian panpipes.

Kalumbu bow (and many other names in other places) is a primitive central African zither clearly derived from the hunting bow. To the bow is attached a gourd resonator and the string is plucked by the finger. Sophisticated models may have more than one string (and thus approach the harp in structure), and a widespread version is the small bow whirled on a cord round the player's head like the bull-roarer (qv).

Kamanga, kamancha, and many related works, refers to the spike fiddle, widespread in different forms from north-west Africa to the Black Sea and Persia. The 'spike' is the wooden rod that pierces the body to become the peg board at one end and the supporting foot at the other. Around this design may be bodies of round, oblong, square, pear or other shape, and the strings may number from one to six or more, played with a bow or plucked.

Kashmiri sarangi player. Formerly an instrument used by itinerant musicians, the sarangi is today well known in Indian 'classical' music.

Recorder, chitarrone (large lute) and violin. The violinist is reputed to be the young Handel. Eighteenth-century engraving.

Kazoo — see comb-and-paper.

Karnyx An Iron-Age Celtic trumpet up to 6ft (2m) long, the carved animal-horn bell held vertically above the warriors' heads as they went into battle.

Kemae A Peruvian rhythm instrument consisting simply of an empty turtle shell scraped with a stick.

Khong wong yai A Thai instrument comprising a circular rack of gongs.

Koto, specifically, refers to a Japanese zither some 6ft (2m) or more long which lies transversely in front of the player. It came to Japan from China during or before the 8th century and has developed into different varieties with different names, but the koto remains of prime importance in Japanese concert and domestic music-making. Each of its 13 strings has its own movable bridge by which tuning is carried out, and the strings are plucked with the fingers, sometimes wearing plectra.

Laka Chilean panpipes of the pre-Columbian era.

Lichiguayo A large Chilean notched flute of the pre-Columbian era.

Lituus A Roman war, or at least, processional, instrument made from metal (often bronze). It is a conical pipe terminating in an animal horn, the whole resembling the letter 'J' in shape. Possibly the Celtic *karnyx* (qv) derived from the lituus, and the lituus itself may be of Etruscan origin.

Lur Constructed of bronze in the shape of mammoth tusks, these early trumpets were widespread in northern Europe in the Bronze Age. They are relatives of the Roman lituus and the Irish karnyx, and examples have been found with remarkably sophisticated mouthpieces. They were mainly used in pairs in religious festivals.

Lyra organizzata — see hurdy-gurdy.

Maultrommel (Ger) = 'mouth-drum' = Jew's harp, qv.

Mirliton — see comb-and-paper.

Morin chur (or **khuur**) A Mongolian two-string fiddle played vertically like a cello by a squatting or kneeling figure. It has two horse-hair strings played with an arched horse-hair bow, and the animal motif is carried through by a carved horse-head at the top.

Nail violin The name refers to the method of discovery (rather than invention). Hanging his bow on a nail in a ceiling beam at his home in St Petersburg, the 18th-century German violinist Johann Wilde accidentally scraped the nail and was attracted by the resulting resonance. Subsequent experiment produced a semi-circular box of thick wood, the 'nails' or staples of which were driven in to different depths. The outermost bars of these staples are played with one or two violin bows. Some improvements have been made to the original instrument, such as the addition in 1780 of sympathetic strings, but no name of a composer rash enough to write a concerto for the nail violin has come to the authors' notice.

Nanga An East African arch harp made from a hollow block of wood open at the top but partly covered, as if by a part-opened lid, by a resonating board. Strings from the upper edge of the board run to curved sticks issuing from the other end of the block. The strings are plucked with the fingers.

Naseré An Argentinian wooden flute in the shape of a flattened globe.

Nihbash A Jordanian percussion instrument — actually a domestic pestle and mortar pressed into service to produce rhythmic sounds (rather than fine-ground coffee).

Nonengeige (Nun's fiddle) — see *tromba marina*.

Ocarina A word meaning 'little goose' in Italian. This wind instrument in the shape of an elongated egg is usually made of baked earth and provides a pure sound without overtones. Similar instruments were known in Upper Egypt 5000 years ago.

Oliphant — see *apunga*.

Ophicleide By about 1850 the ophicleide, a brass instrument, had replaced the serpent as the bass voice of the cornett family in French church music and in military bands elsewhere. It was patented in France in 1821 by Halary; the name comes from Gk: *ophis* = 'snake'; *kleides* = 'keys', therefore, a 'keyed serpent'. It was popular during the 19th century but gradually fell from use as its range became covered by the bass tuba. A wooden ophicleide, the serpentcleide, bastardizing the name as well as the instrument, was invented about 1850 by Thomas Macbean Glen of Edinburgh.

Organ The evolution of the organ, from a bundle of straws to the multi-ton masterpieces which grace our cathedrals, is far too involved to be given here, even in outline. The basic principles of its construction are given under hydraulis (qv), except that Ctesibius's water-pressure device has been replaced by manpower, steam and electricity at various times. Taken to its root in Ancient Greek, *uerg*, the word 'organ' denotes *any* device, not necessarily musical, which carries out work. Organology has come to mean the study of musical instruments in general, but it might just as correctly apply to the study of donkey engines or computers.

An organ comprises a keyboard, a windchest supplied with air from some mechanism, and a rank or ranks of sounding pipes. By the late 18th century it was being described as 'the king of instruments' (Mozart). Modern developments, which have introduced countless stops, several manuals and a whole range of effects from bells to steamship whistles, may have tarnished its regal status in some quarters, but when properly used on music written for it, it remains the noblest of instruments.

The first full-time organ-builder was Albert van Os, who worked in the Netherlands during the 12th century, and the earliest music to be written specifically for the organ dates from two centuries later. The peak of organ composition came with the music of J.S. Bach in the early 18th century. Apart from oratorio and other liturgical works, the organ is rarely heard in the orchestra today; when it is, as in Saint-Saëns's Third Symphony (1886), it makes an unforgettable impact.

In addition to several organ concerti, Handel is the only composer to have written one for two organs. The instrument is still featured occasionally, as for instance in the Concerto (1938) by Poulenc and in the three concerti (1947–8) by Siegfried Reda.

The organ has a large repertoire of solo music. The first composer to come to mind in this context is of course J.S. Bach, but he was preceded by important contributions by John Bull, Sweelinck, Frescobaldi, Buxtehude, Pachelbel and Bruhns. Until the late 18th century the literature for organ and for harpsichord overlapped to some extent: what sounded well on the one might sound equally well on the other. This applied even to some of the organ works of Haydn, Mozart and Beethoven, because, unlike those of Bach, the works were comparatively inconsequential and relatively unaffected by alteration of tonal colouring. But the organ pieces by 19th and 20th-century composers such as Mendelssohn, Brahms, Liszt, Franck, Reger, Widor, Nielsen and Messiaen are much more reliant on the effects produced by a good organist at a good organ, with variety of registration and weight of sound being of vital importance.

On a somewhat smaller scale were the mobile organs of the pre-Christian era which

The remains of a Roman organ supported by a perspex frame; this was discovered in Budapest at a site formerly called Aquincum and is probably the oldest surviving organ in the world. (Ilona Molnár)

developed into three main types by the 15th century: positive, usually played in a fixed position but movable on a cart and sometimes even played on the move; portative, a small organ with button-type keys that could be

■ *The loudest musical instrument ever made is an organ: the Auditorium Organ, Atlantic City, New Jersey. Built in 1930, the instrument has two consoles with a total of 12 manuals, 1477 stops, and 33 112 pipes ranging in length from $\frac{1}{16}$in (0.5cm) to 64ft (19.5m). Its 'flat-out' volume generated by blower motors of 365hp (370cv) once equalled that of 25 brass bands, but today the instrument is only partly functional. The ophicleide stop of the Grand Great in the Atlantic City Auditorium is the world's loudest organ stop. Operated by a pressure of 100in (254cm) of water, its pure trumpet tone is six times greater than the loudest of locomotive whistles. Just the thing to add that little extra to a Bach chorale.* ■

played by a marcher; and regal, a tiny reed organ that could be carried under one arm but was placed on the table for playing. One variety folded like a book when not in use, hence the name 'bible organ'.

Oud A five-string fretless Arab lute whose name is the (probably French-influenced) spelling of Arabian *al'ud* (= 'flexible stick'; cf. 'lute'). John Haywood and Salman Shukur have composed a Concerto for Oud and orchestra.

Panpipes or **Syrinx** Said to have been played by the god Pan to the water-nymph Syrinx, the simple panpipes are of extreme antiquity. They were known in Egypt by at least 330 BC. Each pipe produces only one note (in this respect the panpipes are in fact the simplest form of organ):

■ *The world's largest fully functional organ is the six manual 30 067 pipe Grand Court Organ installed in the Wanamaker Store, Philadelphia, Pennsylvannia, USA in 1911 and enlarged between then and 1930. It has a 64ft (19.5m) tone gravissima pipe. The world's largest church organ is that in Passau Cathedral, Germany. It was completed in 1928 by D.F. Steinmeyer & Co. It was built with 16 000 pipes and five manuals. The world's most powerful electronic organ is the 5000 watt Royal V. Rogers organ, designed by Virgil Fox with 465 speakers installed by Orient Shoji Co in Chuo-ku, Tokyo, Japan in June 1983. The chapel organ at West Point US Military Academy, NY has, since 1911, been expanded from 2406 to 18 200 pipes.*

The largest organ in Great Britain is that completed in Liverpool Anglican Cathedral on 18 October 1926, with two five-manual consoles of which only one is now in use, and 9704 speaking pipes (originally 10 936) ranging from tones ¾in to 32ft (1.9cm to 9.75m).

The longest interval between the known composition of a major composer, and its performance in the manner intended, is from 3 March 1791 until 9 October 1982 (over 191 years), in the case of Mozart's Organ Piece for a Clock, *a fugue fantasy in F minor (K 608), arranged by the organ builders Wm Hill & Son and Norman & Beard Ltd at Glyndebourne, East Sussex.* ■

Pi'pa, a Chinese lute with four silk strings, two of them double. (Photo: Les Prudden)

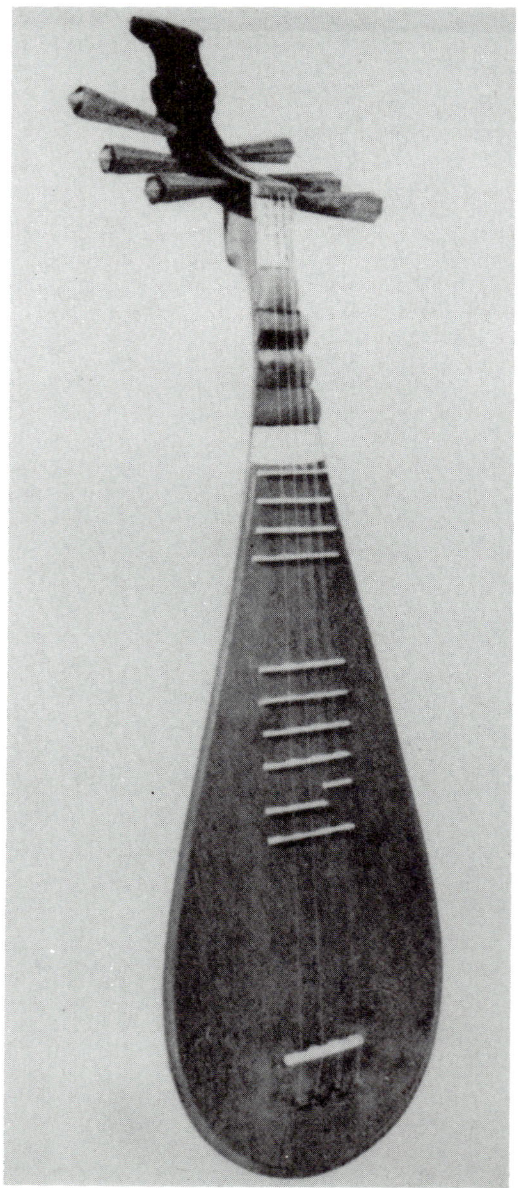

a collection of pipes is bound together in order of size, the lower ends being blocked. The instrument has played little part in concert music, being regarded mainly as a pastoral instrument, but the Romanian virtuoso Gheorghe Zamfir, who maintains that the panpipes are the oldest of all musical instruments, has recently composed concert works (a concerto and a rhapsody) for them. Romanian folk-orchestras still make extremely effective use of the panpipes, and there has recently been increasing interest in panpipes of the Andean regions through the exposure of such groups as Incantation, an English group which popularizes Andean music while respecting its traditions.

Pantaleon This oversized dulcimer (qv) took its name from the German composer Pantaleon Hebenstreit (1669–1750) who invented it by about 1697, calling it at first 'cimbal' (from whence, presumably, the modern Balkan dulcimer, *cymbalom*, takes its name) It was Louis XIV in 1705 who ordered that the instrument should carry the inventor's name (though whether as blame or honour has not been established). Hebenstreit was its sole virtuoso until his pupil Christian Siegmund Binder (1723–89) became well known as an exponent in about 1750. The largest stringed instrument ever constructed was a pantaleon. Made in 1767, it was 11ft (3.35m) long and possessed 276 strings — by comparison, Hebenstreit's own instrument had only 185.

P'ai-siao The original panpipes (see above) which originated in China. The pipes were set in line in a wooden frame.

■ *Whistles and flutes made from perforated phalange bones have been found at Upper Palaeolithic sites of the Aurignacian period (c.25 000–22 000 BC) e.g. at Istallóskö, Hungary and in Molodova, USSR. An Assyrian love song c.1800 BC to an Ugaritic god from a tablet of notation and lyric was reconstructed for an 11-string lyre at the University of California, Berkeley on 6 March 1974. Musical history is, however, able to be traced back to the 3rd millennium BC, when the yellow bell (*huang chung*) had a recognized standard musical tone in Chinese temple music.* ■

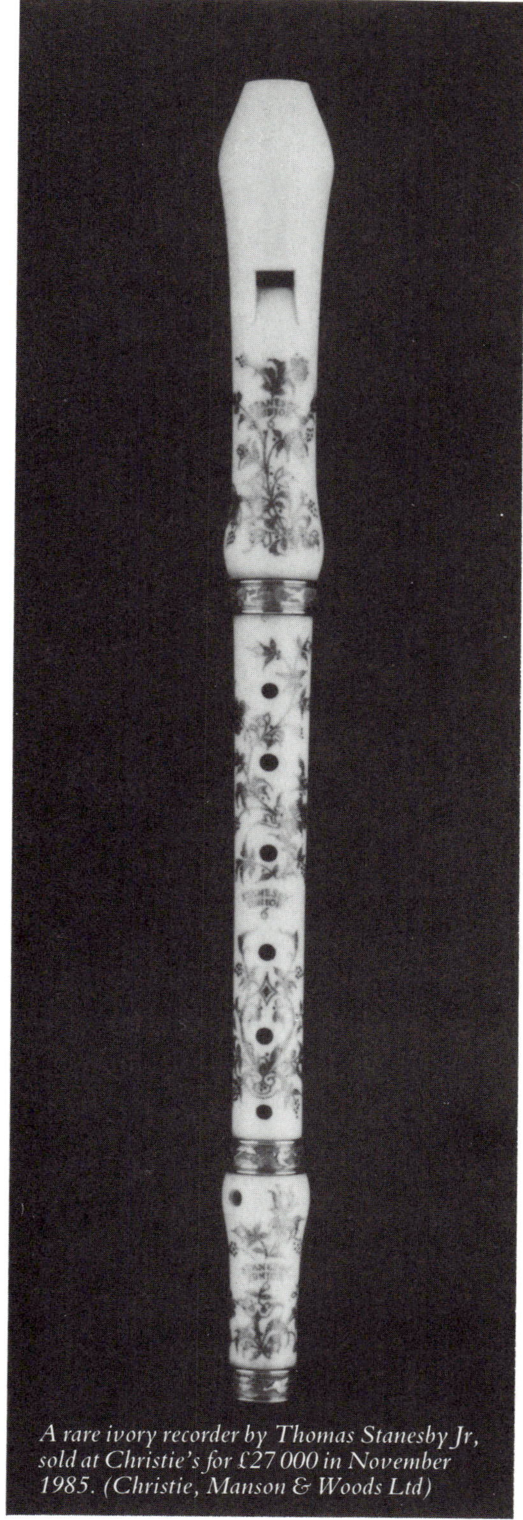

A rare ivory recorder by Thomas Stanesby Jr, sold at Christie's for £27 000 in November 1985. (Christie, Manson & Woods Ltd)

A Galaxy of Instruments

A Thames water party in the 18th century, with St Paul's cathedral in the background; Canaletto, detail. It was at such parties that Handel's Water Music *was first heard. (National Gallery, Prague)*

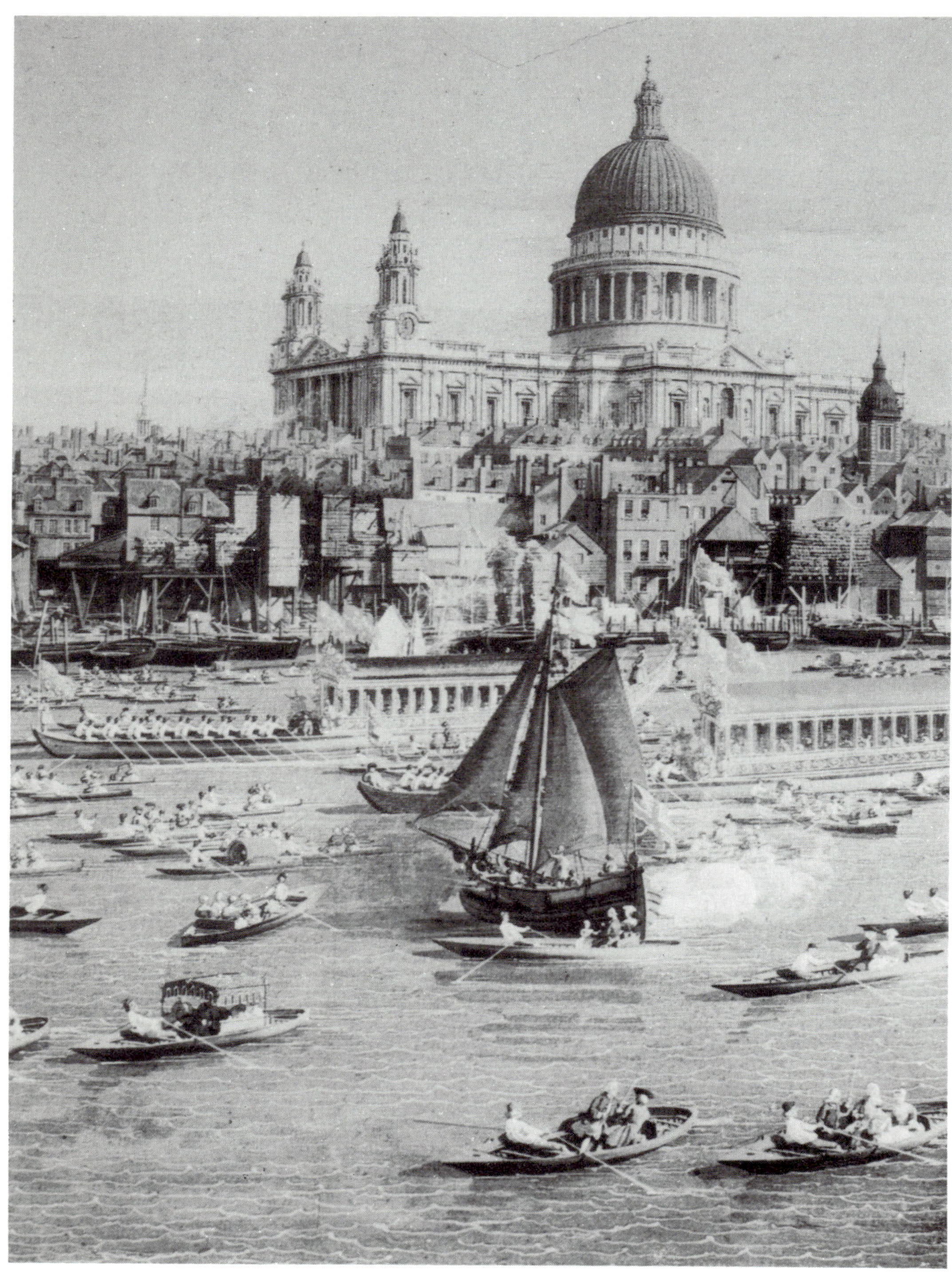

Pianoforte – see p 71

Pinkillo A small Chilean reed flute with a mouthpiece, derived from the European recorder. In Peru, *pinkillo* refers to a somewhat longer recorder-like flute.

Piom pirintzi A Peruvian bow held in the mouth and sounded by rubbing the string with a fibre from a palm leaf. A similar instrument, also from Peru, uses a second bow to play the first; thus, if a gourd or similar resonator were to be substituted for the mouth cavity, one would have a primitive violin.

Psaltery – see dulcimer.

Putu A natural horn of the Atacamá desert region, Chile.

Quena A very ancient flute, similar to the European recorder, end-blown and made of reed, bone, clay or metal; found in Bolivia.

Roekua A beeswax ocarina of Peru.

Sansa or **sanza** Thus named after the Congolese tribe among whom the instrument was first discovered, it is also known as kaffir piano, likembe, marimba, mbira, thumb piano, toum, zeze and many other names. It is extremely widespread throughout Africa and, through introductions by Africans, now also in the New World. Metal plates are fastened at one end to a sounding-board and the free ends are sprung down and released by the fingers and thumbs. George Crumb used a sansa in his *Night of the Four Moons* (1966).

Serpent A bass cornett of truly spectacular appearance and unreliability. Invented about 1590 by the French canon Edmé Guillaume, it was used primarily in church until about the middle of the 18th century, when it began to appear in military bands. Prior to that Handel has asked for it in the *Water Music* (1717) and *Musick for the Royal Fireworks* (1749) — a request today usually ignored — and later it was used, and sometimes criticized, by Mendelssohn, Berlioz, Rossini and Wagner. Its unpredictable tone production contributed to the serpent's demise in favour of low brass and woodwind instruments.

Made of two pieces of wood bound together, the serpent's tortuous shape was necessary in order to make the instrument manageable; a straighter model would have taken the fingerholes and, later, the keys, out of the player's reach. Never one to attract felicitous names, the serpent was the *Schlangenrohr* ('snake-tube') in Germany, and the 'black pudding' in the north of England.

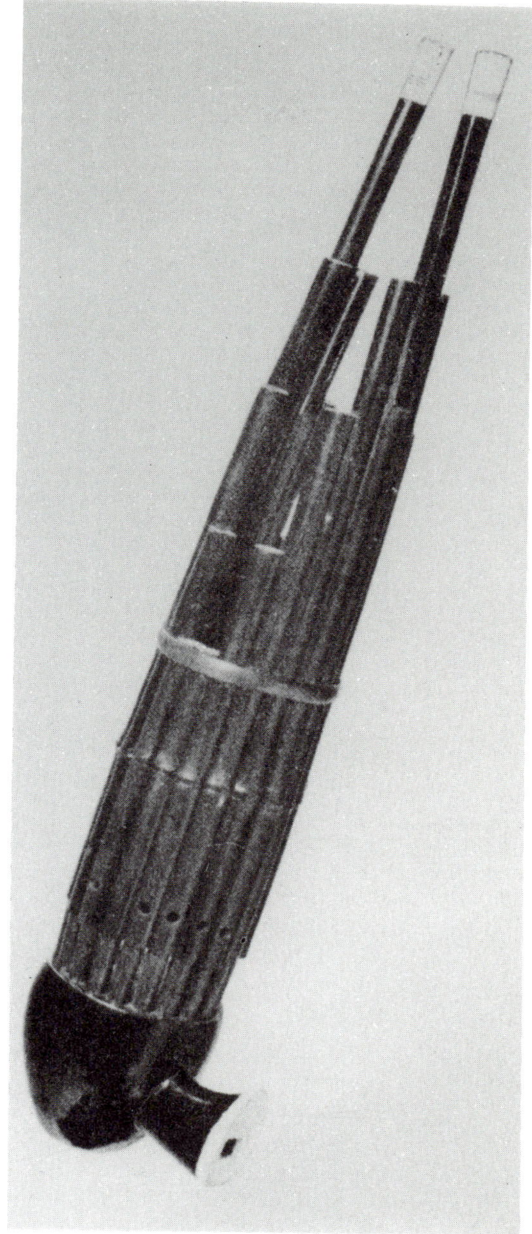

Sheng, a Chinese mouth-organ. (Photo: Les Prudden)

Sheng An ancient Chinese instrument at least 2500 years old, this has more title to the description 'mouth organ' than today's Western harmonica, for it actually resembles a miniature organ. The player fills an air-chest, now made of copper but originally a gourd, via a stubby mouthpiece, thus applying air to a bundle of 17 vertical bamboo pipes, one or more of which sounds continuously as a drone. In order to sound a pipe the player must cover the fingerhole.

Siku Peruvian reed panpipes.

Three-string lute (identified in some sources as Tan-chin*) from north-east China, formerly Manchuria. (Photo: Les Prudden)*

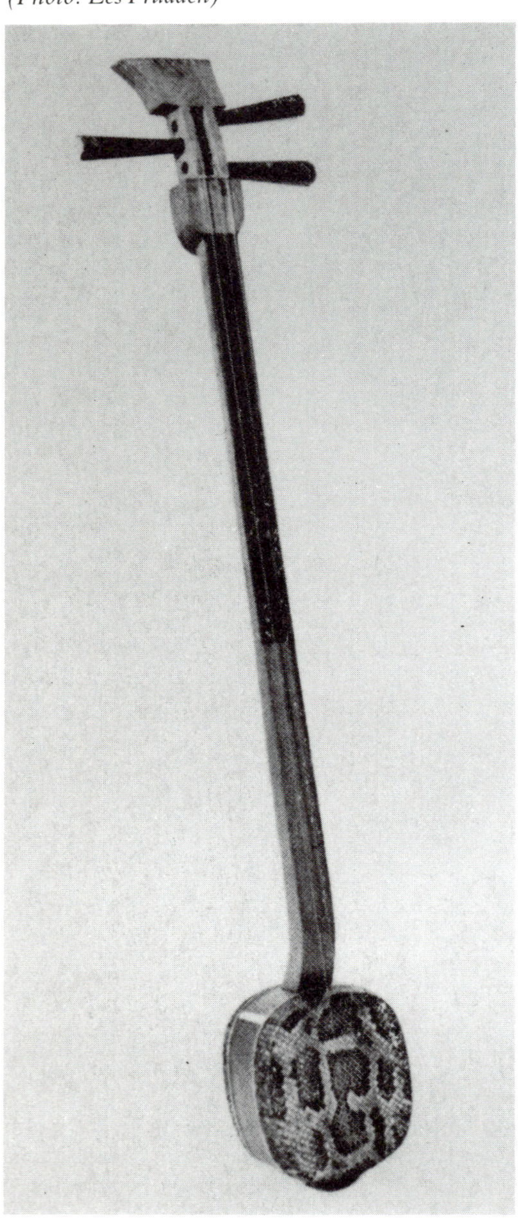

Stamping stick A simple and primitive rhythmic instrument, which evolved probably by accident. Some sticks which were used to beat drums were hollow and produced a definite independent resonance. With a shaped top these 'stamping sticks' were banged on a hard surface and became instruments in their own right.

Stone star — see horseshoes.

Tarka A Chilean wooden flute derived from the European recorder; similar to the Peruvian *pinkillo* and somewhat larger than the Chilean *anata* (qqv).

Tayuc An Indian horizontal bowed stringed instrument resembling a peacock in shape.

Thundersheet, in modern orchestras, is a large metal sheet up to 12ft (3.65m) high and 4ft (1.2m) wide which is suspended and beaten with soft-headed sticks to imitate thunder or other elemental effects. Other methods of obtaining such effects have included the rolling of large lead balls down a ramp. Richard Strauss is the first well-known composer to ask for thunder effects — in his *Alpine Symphony* (1915) — but doubtless such effects were required at times during the 19th century when more adventurous composers felt dissatisfied with instrumental imitations of the natural sounds so popular in Romantic music. John Cage was dissatisfied even with the thundersheet: he called for six of them in varying sizes in his *First Construction* (1962).

Tiama A Peruvian long flute with five fingerholes, made from bone, wood or reed.

Tijeras A Bolivian rhythm instrument for accompanying native dancing, this is merely a pair of scissors struck with a hard object.

Tiple A Columbian triple-strung zither.

Tontorentzi A Peruvian bow, larger than the *piom pirintzi* (above), played similarly but by women only.

Tromba marina Usually translated 'trumpet marine' to the continuing consternation of etymologists, this was a stringed instrument that apparently had nothing to do with the sea. It was a bowed monocord (i.e. with one string) which originated possibly in the Slav countries during the Middle Ages. The string runs virtually the whole length (up to 7ft 3in — 2.2m) of the body, which tapers from 7in to 2in (17.8cm to 5cm), often lacking shoulders, and roughly triangular in cross-section. At the lower end the string passes over a bridge which is partly free to vibrate against the table. The sound is so unbelievably harsh and unmusical that one is tempted to believe the instrument was used merely as a signalling device. Later makers attempted to improve the instrument's appearance, but its voice retained its piercing croak, despite which quite a large repertoire for the instrument grew up between 1660 and 1751, after which it died out.

In tackling the origin of the strange name writers have suggested that 'marina' might refer to the instrument's resemblance to a naval speaking trumpet, or to its common use in nunneries in place of brass instruments, 'marina' referring to the name of the Holy Mother (note a German name for the instrument: *Nonnengeige* = 'nun's fiddle'). The 'trumpet' component of the name is perhaps easier to account for. First, the voice is like the coarse blast of a natural trumpet; secondly, many models had flared bases looking like trumpet bells; thirdly, the earliest method of playing was to hold the thin end to the chest while the 'bell' end was held aloft at an angle — then the outline of player and instrument from a distance might be thought to have resembled that of a herald trumpeter.

Trutruka An inelegant Chilean and Argentinian trumpet consisting of a cane or similar vegetable stem some 6ft (2m) long with an animal horn fixed at right-angles to the end.

Ukulele = 'jumping flea' in Hawaiian. The instrument derives from the Iberian *machête de braça* which was introduced to Hawaii late in the last century. It is a small four-string guitar whose delights, as far as we have been able to ascertain, have so far been resisted by 'serious' composers.

Urusa Peruvian panpipes.

Vambi An arch-harp of the Bateke tribe of Central Africa. Its four strings run from a hollow wooden and animal-skin resonator to points on a gently curving stem; they are tuned by large pegs.

Viola pomposa Once thought to have been invented by J.S. Bach, this was never used by him. It is a five-string viola invented some time before 1725, used by Telemann, Graun and Lidarti, then allowed to slip back into history.

Yamstick An Australian Aboriginal instrument of the most basic kind: a simple stick for beating out the rhythm of the dance on trees, shields, the ground, or anything or anyone near at hand, simply to heighten the excitement at the wild ceremonial totemic dances known as 'corroborees'.

Zither — see dulcimer.

Drums

A drum is an instrument in which air inside a hollow vessel is made to vibrate when a membrane covering the vessel's opening is struck or otherwise activated. This simple general description covers an unimaginable multitude of different instruments which have existed since prehistoric times. The hollow vessel can be made of a variety of materials: gourd, tortoiseshell, wood, calabash, metal, bone, clay (e.g. china, earthenware, porcelain), plastic, glass, etc; it may be of almost any shape or size, and open at one end. The membrane may be of animal (or even human) skin, bark, cloth, plastic (used for all orchestral drums since about 1960) etc., (some cultures anoint the playing heads with a paste made of, for instance, an unappetizing mixture of boiled rice and iron filings). The striker might be the human hand, the foot, or a drum-stick of wood, bone, felt, leather, rubber, ivory, cloth, sponge, etc. or even reeds, birch twigs, wire brushes and bones.

Indian hour-glass drum. Sometimes erroneously called 'talking drum' due to its almost human ability to vary pitch infinitely and instantaneously; the true 'talking drum' is the log drum, often with only two different pitches. (Photo: Les Prudden)

A Galaxy of Instruments

The Roman Emperor Trajan (in the role of Ihy) holding a sistrum (primitive rattle) in his left hand.

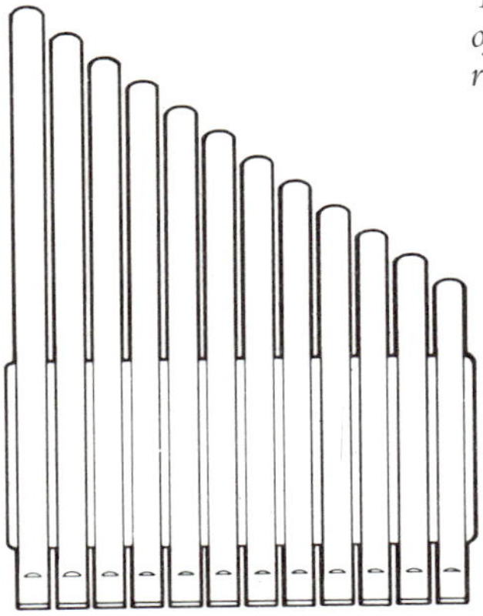

Panpipes

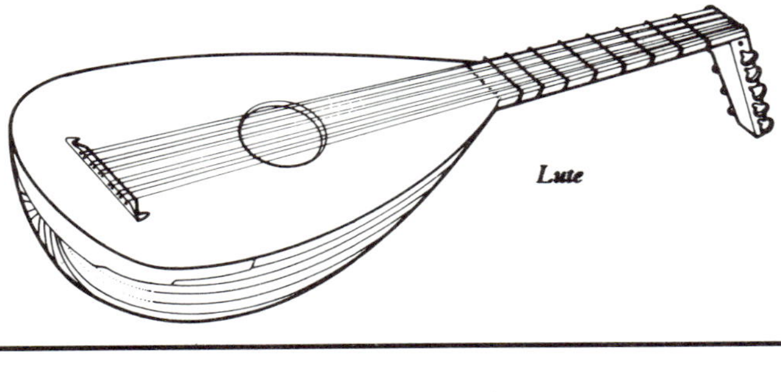

Lute

Guitar

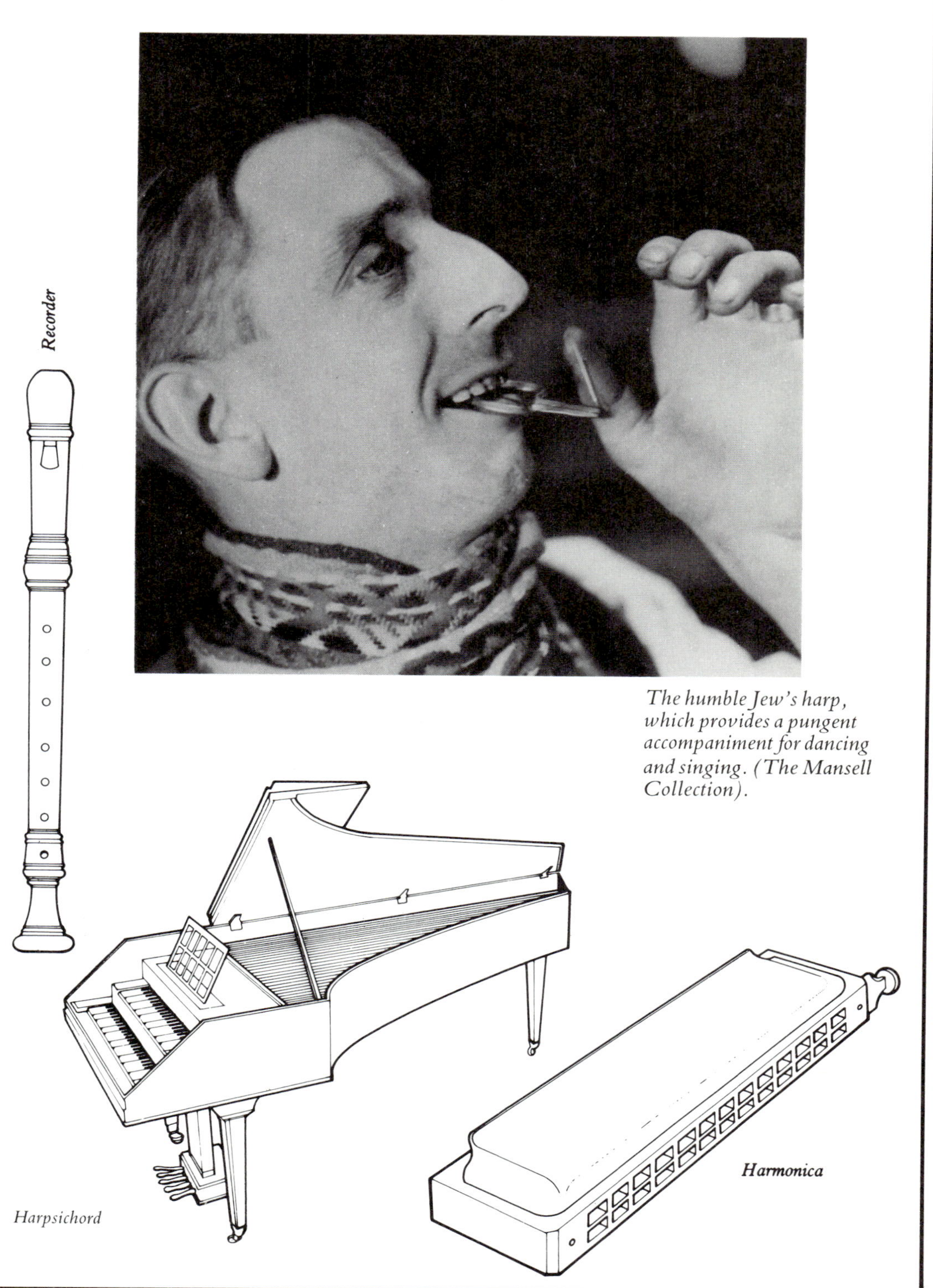

The humble Jew's harp, which provides a pungent accompaniment for dancing and singing. (The Mansell Collection).

Harpsichord

■ *The largest drum ever constructed was one 12ft (3.65m) in diameter weighing 600lb (272kg) for the Boston World Peace Jubilee of 1872.* ■

In the friction drum the membrane is pierced with a stick or cord which is manipulated with the fingers.

Sometimes a drum may have metal objects attached to it, or its body may contain sand, seeds, bones, pebbles, coins, bells, snares or metal springs to give added vibrations.

Older than the membrane drums are the slit drums of various types, the best-known example of which is the African message drum used for signalling across vast distances (up to 20 miles (32km) in exceptionally favourable conditions) of jungle terrain.

Composers of serious music have adopted the drum and progressively expanded its use until today's orchestral instruments have reached a high degree of sophistication. Yet their variety of tonal colour is seriously limited in comparison with ethnic drums, a limitation which is recognized by contemporary composers who call increasingly for exotic percussion in their scores.

Selected list of drums

Adapu Sumerian rectangular frame drum.

Alal Sumerian large frame drum.

Ānanda laharī Indian plucked drum. A cord passes through the membrane, is knotted below and held taut to be plucked by the fingers.

Atambor Persian two-headed drum.

Atumpan Ugandan message drums, used in pairs and beaten with curved sticks. See log drum.

Balag Sumerian generic word for 'drum'.

Bayan Bass of *tablā*, qv.

Baz Egyptian small kettledrum of the Middle Kingdom.

Bendir Arabian frame drum with snares under the head.

A group of instruments reconstructed expertly from natural materials. Top left: nakers with sticks. Top right: timbrel, a variety of tambourine designed to be played vertically. (Reconstructions by Paul Williamson). Front: Early Renaissance tenor rebec, reconstructed by Nicholas Woodward, c. 1979 (Photo: Les Prudden)

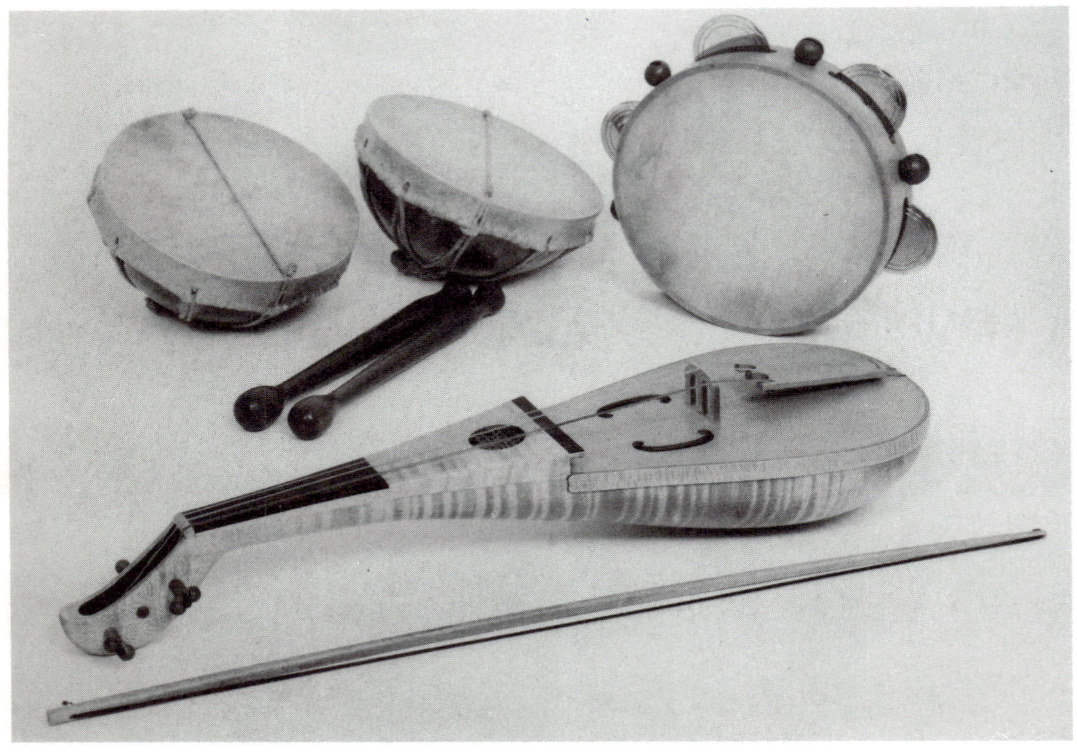

Berrigodea Singhalese two-headed drum played with the hand.

Bitin obonu = *kalengo*, qv.

Bombo South American two-headed goatskin frame drum up to 2ft (60cm) in diameter, but of different sizes and widespread throughout Chile, Argentina, Colombo, etc, and sometimes found in military bands. The heads *and* the frame may be struck with a beater or with the hand.

Bongos Small single-headed paired drums, sometimes physically joined by a stick, and played with the hands; much used in Latin American dance bands.

Boobams Chromatically-tuned small drums with resonators of various lengths to give different pitches. Of recent US origin.

Brummtopf Old German friction drum now called Reibtrommel ('rub-drum'). Similar to the lion's roar, qv.

Bukal 18th-century name for the stick friction drum.

Caccavella = *puttipu(ti)*, qv.

Caja South American two-headed frame drum of up to 18in (45.7cm) diameter and 6in (15cm) deep, often used by a piper to accompany himself.

Chakravādya Indian frame drum.

Chang-ku Chinese two-headed tunable drum, not unlike an empty cotton reel in shape. The cords form a 'W' pattern between the heads and are tensioned by metal rings.

Cuíca Latin American friction drum.

Culo-en-tierra Venezuelan drum of halved coconut shell and animal skin.

Da-daiko Japanese braced drum mounted on a special wooden structure and played with beaters. The two heads are each 4ft (1.2m) in diameter, and the body is 5ft (1.5m) deep.

Dahna Tibetan large kettledrum.

Da'ira Arabian frame drum.

Damarān Indian conical processional drums used in pairs and slung over the back of an ox. The player, astride the ox, plays with a straight stick in one hand, a curved stick in the other.

Dāmaru Indian clapper drum, similar to the Chinese *t'ao-ku* but made singly and minus the handle.

Damnya Tibetan small kettledrum.

Darabuka (and various other spellings) Turkish goblet drum made of wood and with one head, held under the arm and played with the hand. A similar name is given to Egyptian drums of various sizes and a Persian single-headed drum played horizontally and placed on a stand.

Dawul Turkish large two-headed barrel drum beaten on one head with a stick (knobbed or curved) and on the other with a light cane.

Dohl Indian barrel drum played with hands or stick; also used in Afghanistan and Tibet.

Dohlkee Indian; a small *dohl*.

Dof Moorish/Spanish frame drum with snares under the head.

Doira East European frame drum called for by Khachaturian in his ballet *Gayaneh* (1942).

Dōlak (or **dholak**) North Indian drum with two heads, also known in Pakistan. It is barrel-shaped, tunable with tension cords, and played with the hand or both stick and hand.

Donno Ghanaian two-headed hour-glass drum, played with a curved beater.

Doula Singhalese drum, similar to the *berrigodea* but played by the hand on one end, a stick on the other.

Indian dōlak, or barrel drum. (Photo: Les Prudden)

Douno = *kalenga*, qv.

Drum gong Chinese instrument from the 4th century BC, this is an all-bronze kettledrum comprising a cylinder with a thin bronze head at the top. Some examples are of considerable size. Both head and body are struck, the former with a heavy beater, the latter with a bamboo stick. The drum gong should not be confused with the gong drum, qv.

Duff (1) Arabic name for 'frame drum', usually square or angled.

Duff (2) Indian frame drum played with sticks.

Duffli Smaller version of *duff* (2).

Dundubhi A war kettledrum of ancient India, perhaps of Persian origin. Bronze bells are placed inside the instrument.

Embutu Ugandan kettledrum played with the hands.

Engalabi Ugandan cylindrical single-headed drum played with the hands.

Entenga African drum chime: 12 tuned drums played by four players with curved sticks.

Etwie 'Leopard drum' of Africa, its leopard-skin imitating the growl of the animal when a curved stick is rubbed across the drum.

Friction drum A small primitive drum whose skin is pierced by a stick or a cord which is then rubbed with resined fingers or twirled between the palms.

Fungu = *kalengo*, qv.

Ganggu Chinese large drum used for secular purposes.

Gem gem Ancient Egyptian drum, probably cylindrical.

Ghara Pakistani earthenware pot drum.

Ghirbāl Arabian large single-headed frame drum with snares under the head.

Gong drum A name sometimes given to the single-headed orchestral bass drum on account of its shape. Not to be confused with the drum gong, qv.

Gulu Ghanaian double-headed cylindrical drum.

Guntang Balinese slit drum.

Gyamadudu Ghanaian double-headed bass drum.

Hiuen-ku Very large Chinese drum of the Chou dynasty (1122 BC); as used in the Imperial palace it was associated with two much smaller two-headed drums of flowerpot shape.

Hour-glass drum = kalengo, qv.

Huehuetl Mexican vertical wood drum played with the hands and tensioned by ropes. Its name (= 'old, old') suggests extreme antiquity.

Huruk Indian hour-glass drum.

Idu-mān Tibetan kettledrums used in pairs.

Ingpongpo A primitive Bantu drum consisting of a dried animal skin either suspended from poles or held off the ground and hit with a stick.

Intambula A drum from Swaziland. The two components, a clay pot and a moistened, shaved, animal skin, are not joined together but are held tightly in place during the performance by the player, or by assistants, and hit with a stick.

Isigubu Zulu cylindrical drum with two heads, possibly derived from European military instruments. In some cases the heads are tuned by laces to give different pitches (unlike the European variety) and may be played with either hands or sticks.

Jackdaw Old English cord friction drum, probably named from the bird it imitates.

Kakko Japanese mounted drum with two heads braced by 'W' cords and a strap, used by the leader of the Bugaku (dance) orchestra. Possibly of Chinese origin.

Kalengo (hour-glass, or squeeze, drum) A double-headed hour-glass drum from Guinea and Nigeria, the tension on the heads being altered by leather thongs running between them, thus giving the impression of speech. Either one or the other head is played at a time, the non-played head being engaged in applying pressure. Similar drums occur in Japan (*tsuzumi*), India and elsewhere.

Kansar Indian framed metal disc struck with a stick (strictly a species of gong).

Kengang Balinese small drum.

Kero Small Chinese drum of the T'ang dynasty.

Khamak Indian string drum.

Khanjari Indian shallow single-headed drum.

Khol Indian conical clay drum.

Ko-daiko Japanese barrel-shaped two-headed drum with a diameter of 2ft 6in (76cm). In processions it is hung from a pole carried by two men, the player walking beside.

Kongtois Tibetan cylindrical drum.

Ko-tsuzumi Japanese tunable hand drum in

hour-glass shape, held over the right shoulder. The 'W' cords are tensioned by a central strap. This drum is much used in Noh plays.

Kultrun Widespread in Chile, Argentina and other South American countries, this is a kettledrum of hemispherical shape with pebbles within that can be agitated by shaking so that they strike the head. An external beater is also used.

Kurka Arabic kettledrum of the 12th century, of huge size.

Kūs Large Arabic kettledrum of the 10th century.

Lilis Sumerian bronze kettledrum with a bullskin head.

Lion's roar Modern cord friction drum, first used in Varèse's *Hyperprism* (1924) and other works.

Livika A hollow log-drum of Melanesia with cuts of varying depths on the surface to form teeth of different lengths. These teeth are rubbed with resined fingers. This drum has a unique combination of features: there is no membrane (unlike other friction drums), it is not hit, and it sounds several different notes. In principle it works similarly to the violin and the glass harmonica, i.e. by friction. Women are forbidden ever to see the *livika*; the male exponent is always hidden from view when playing.

Log drum (and **slit drum**) Prehistoric. In its simplest form it is a hollow tree trunk (standing or fallen) hit by a beater. By cutting a slit lengthwise in the trunk and modifying the thickness of the wood at each edge of the slit, resonance is increased and different tones are produced. Trunks of some 40ft (12m) have been used, but smaller ones are more wieldy. Some African tribes carve elaborate designs on the wood and form figures of animals from the logs. The slit may be made in the form of an 'H', giving greater possibilities for tonal variations. Stockhausen — in *Gruppen* (1957) — and Boulez — in *Rituel in Memoriam Maderna* (1974) — have asked for the log drum.

Ma-ch'un Tibetan hour-glass drum made from two human skulls joined at the crowns.

Mesi Sumerian small frame drum.

Message drum = log drum, qv.

Miya-daiko Large Japanese drum, made of zelkova wood with a cowhide head measuring up to 5ft 6in (170cm) and weighing *c.*570lb (*c.*400kg).

Moko Indonesian drum gong shaped like an hour-glass.

Monkey drum A clapper drum similar to the Indian *dāmaru*, sometimes played by the tame monkeys of travelling musicians.

Mpingtintoa Ghanaian single-headed gourd drum.

Mrdanga(m) South Indian two-headed drum, the body now made of wood but perhaps originally of clay. The heads are of slightly different sizes and the body of barrel-like shape but with straight sides, its widest part forming an obtuse angle. Tuning is carried out by sliding round wooden blocks in 'W' braces, and the drum is played with the hands.

Mujaguzo Ugandan royal drum of great size.

Murumbu A small version of the Transvaal *ngoma* (qv) and often used in conjunction with it.

Mu-yü Chinese slit drum which has entered the Western orchestra as the Chinese (or temple) block; see p 33.

Nāgarā Indian kettledrum, made of metal, sometimes of immense size; used for sacred and ceremonial occasions.

Nakers Small Medieval English kettledrums which originated in Arabia or some other Middle Eastern civilization as a small hand drum (Arabic: *naqqārah*). They arrived in Europe during the Crusades and by *c.*1300 were known in French as *nacaires*, and from then in Italian as *naccheroni*. They are usually used in pairs and struck with sticks, and have been associated with trumpets in England since at least the 14th century; Chaucer is amongst the writers who note this association. Nakers are the remote ancestors of modern timpani.

Naqqāra (nakara) Indian kettledrum with a single head, used in pairs and played with a stick. They are clearly related to the preceding and succeeding instruments.

Naqqarah Arabic large and small drum pair, hemispherical in form. (See Nakers)

Ngoma A Northern Transvaal drum with a single skin of cowhide fixed to the top of a wooden hemispherical body.

Ni-daiko Japanese braced drum with two heads, somewhat smaller than the *ko-daiko* but used in the same way.

Nihass Sudanese kettledrum some 3ft (1m) in diameter, usually played in pairs of different sizes.

Nin-an-da-gal-ki Sumerian drum of *c.*200 BC.

O-daiko Japanese 'Great Drum' measuring up to 6ft (2m) across the heads and weighing as much as 700lb (*c*.317kg); usually carried on a wooden wagon, and played by a drummer at each head with club-like sticks.

O-tsuzumi Japanese hour-glass shaped hand drum, supported on the left thigh and played with the fingers; used in Noh plays.

Pakhawaj Indian large wooden cylindrical drum.

Panchamukha vādyam Indian sacred drum of five faces, its very large bronze body incorporating five cylinders.

Pang-ku (1) Chinese single-headed drum, used in Chinese orchestras to give the rhythmic lead.

Pang-ku (2) = *t'ak*, qv; it is distinct from *pang-ku* (1).

Pash Mayan drum similar to the *huehuetl*, qv.

Piano-basque A keyboard instrument invented in 1841 by one Sormani in which two drumsticks operated from the keyboard play upon 13 small drums. This was an attempt to obtain a chromatic scale from drums without the necessity of retuning.

Pieng-ku Small Chinese drum with an internal metal spring which vibrates in sympathy.

Popo = *kalengo*, qv.

Puo-fu Chinese horizontal barrel drum with two heads played with beaters.

Puttipu(ti) Italian stick friction drum.

Qasa Arabic shallow drum of the 10th century. The name is possibly the origin of the French and Italian words for drum: *caisse* and *cassa*.

Rnga Large double-headed drum of Bhutan, played by a seated drummer who holds the drum aloft on a long pedestal and strikes it with a gracefully curved beater.

Rommel-pot = friction drum, qv.

Sahib-nahabat Indian 'master drum', a pair of kettledrums made of silver, with 5ft (1.5m) diameter heads and a weight of 450lb (204kg), mounted on an elephant for processional purposes. Each drum has its own player.

Sakara African (Yoruba) drum, small and shallow, with an earthenware body.

Sand-drum A membrane-less drum of New Guinea consisting of two holes dug in sand and joined by a tunnel. The player beats the sand between the holes. Often a pipe of earthenware of metal is inserted in the tunnel to prevent cave-ins and to increase resonance.

Squeeze drum = *kalengo*, qv.

Steel drum An invention of Trinidad, where oil drums are cut to resemble large side drums, their metal heads beaten and segmented to form tuned domes. An orchestral string section is emulated by the five different sizes, but these have unexpected names: ping-pong, double second, guitar, cello, and bass. Henze calls for steel drum in the film score *The Lost Honour of Katarina Blum* (1975), and in *Voices* for mezzo-soprano, tenor and instruments (1973).

String drum Extremely ancient form of drum in which the string of a hunter's bow is struck with a stick. This use may even antedate the plucked bow. String drums are widespread; they are sometimes embellished with jingles or bells and often placed on a resonator. Sometimes the wooden part of the bow is dispensed with altogether, the string being attached directly to a resonator (clay pot, gourd, etc) and tensioned by hand or some other means. When struck, these are string drums; when plucked they are closer to the lute. String drum is the name sometimes given to the friction drum operated by pulling a cord, e.g. lion's roar.

Sutri-nahabat Indian kettledrum pair mounted on a camel for processional use.

Tablā North Indian kettledrums used in pairs of different sizes and proportions and played with the hands. They date from at least as early as the 14th century. The paired drums are known, treble and bass, respectively as *tablā* and *bayan* or *bhaya*.

Tabl al-markab = *naqqāra*: Arabic kettledrum of the 10th century.

Tabor (1) Medieval drum with two heads, a snare sometimes running across the played head. Called in England the *taberett* and in Spain and Persia the *atambor*, in France the *taboret* and in Germany the *Timpanon*. Detail design changed with the name from region to region, but *tambourin* was used in both France and Germany, inviting confusion with a totally different instrument.

Tabor (2) Medieval European two-headed drum slung round the player's neck and struck with a stick. It was used in conjunction with a pipe that the same player operated with his other hand.

Tagna Tibetan frame drum of about 3ft (1m) diameter, struck with a heavy beater.

T'ak Small Chinese slit drum used by night-watchmen.

Talking drum = *kalengo*, qv (not the same as the message drum or log drum).

Tambattam Indian frame drum of large size.

Tamborine A small frame drum with jingles or bells fixed loosely in the frame. Of extreme antiquity and worldwide distribution.

Tambourin A typically French double-headed drum from the 15th century or earlier.

T'ang-ku Chinese barrel-shaped drum.

T'ao-ku Chinese clapper drum of the Shang dynasty (*c*.1766–*c*.1123 BC). A clapper drum consists of one or two small drums through the bodies of which passes a wooden handle. Attached to the drums themselves are beads or buttons on strings; these strike the heads as the instrument is twisted briskly.

Tapan Balkan two-headed drum tensioned by cords and struck with a wooden beater. Globokar calls for a tapan in *Étude for Folklora I* and *II* (both 1968).

Tapon tai Thai small barrel drum played with the hands.

Tās Persian hunting drum of AD *c*.600.

Teben Ancient Egyptian generic word for 'drum'.

Tef Turkish frame drum with jingles.

Teponaxtli Mexican slit drum of pre-Aztec origin with an 'H'-shaped slit.

Tomback = *zarb*, qv.

Tom tom Small double-headed drums, commonly played in jazz bands with side-drum sticks. John Cage called for 12 tom toms in *She in Asleep* (1943).

Toph (tupim) Biblical drum, probably indicating the frame hand drums of Egypt and Mesopotamia.

Tu-ku Chinese barrel-shaped large temple drum.

Tsuri-daiko Japanese drum hung from a frame and struck with short leather-headed sticks. Sometimes a second player uses sticks upon the body of the drum.

Tsuzumi Japanese hour-glass drum similar to the *kalengo*, qv.

Tungda Sikkimese kettledrum similar to the Indian *nāgāra*.

Tunkul Mayan name for *teponaxtli*, qv.

Tuntui A large Peruvian slit drum.

Tympanon Ancient Greek (up to the 4th century BC) bowl-shaped drum.

Uchiwa-daiko Small Japanese frame drum with handle.

Udakki Singhalese hour-glass drum.

Ushumgal-kalam-ma Sumerian drum, *c*.200 BC.

Uta-daiko Japanese braced drum with two heads placed on an angled stand and played with round sticks. This is the so-called 'song drum' of the Noh plays.

Water drum A clay or wooden drum found in Argentina. The water level in the shell can be adjusted to alter the pitch; for this purpose the head is detachable.

Wollogallu An Abyssinian membrane-less drum of the most primitive type: two cone-shaped holes of different size are dug in the ground and the openings are beaten with the flats of the hands.

Ying-ku Chinese barrel-shaped large temple drum of about 3ft (1m) in diameter.

Zambomba Spanish stick friction drum.

Zarb Middle-Eastern (Turkish, Iranian, etc.) goblet drum.

Zeir baghali Afghan goblet drum.

Zerbaghali Afghan drum played while held under the arm; probably merely an alternative spelling of *zeir baghali*.

The Pianoforte

When Bartolomeo Cristofori (1655–1731), keeper of instruments at the Florentine court of the Medici, began working in 1698 on his design for a harpsichord that would play both loud and soft, he was applying the principles of the dulcimer (a trapezoidal box of strings struck by hammers held in the hands) to the design of the harpsichord. By the nature of its tone production, in which strings are plucked mechanically but the force of plucking is the same regardless of finger pressure on the keys, the harpsichord had limited expressive powers. The dulcimer, however, is capable of wide dynamic gradations because of the intimate control possible with hand-held hammers.

By 1700 Cristofori had built his first model. He announced his perfected instrument in 1709 and examples exist from the 1720s. One, made in 1720 and heavily restored, is to be seen in the Metropolitan Museum in New York; another dated 1726 is preserved in the Kraus Museum, Florence. The latter still possesses the original leather hammer-heads.

■ *The highest price ever paid for a piano is $390 000 (then £177 273) at Sotheby Parke Bernet, New York City on 26 March 1980 for a Steinway grand of c.1888 sold by the Martin Beck Theatre and bought by a non-pianist.* ■

Those early pianos display most of the principles of the modern piano, although nearly three centuries of improvements have refined the instrument enormously. The name 'harpsichord with loud and soft' became usefully abbreviated to 'fortepiano' and 'pianoforte' ('loudsoft', 'softloud') early in the 18th century, and gradually the piano overtook the harpsichord in popularity. The first printed music for the piano was *Sonate da Cimbalo di piano e forte dello volgarmente di martelletti* (the reference to *martelletti* — 'little hammers' — leaves no doubt as to which instrument was intended) by Lodovico Giustini, printed in Florence in 1732. However, the instrument did not achieve any degree of popularity until a concert in London at the Covent Garden Theatre on 16 May 1767, when Charles Dibdin accompanied Miss Bickler in 'a favourite song' from Arne's oratorio *Judith* (1764) on the pianoforte: this is the earliest known appearance of the instrument in public. The first public piano solo was given in Dublin the following year by Henry Walsh, and a fortnight later in London — on 2 June 1768 — J.C. Bach performed on the instrument. This composer's *Sei Concerti per il Cembalo o Piano e Forte . . . Op VII*, dating from about 1776, are the first to admit the piano as a possible performer. However, in 1766 John Burton composed ten sonatas specifically for pianoforte, without the expected 'or harpsichord or organ' alternatives.

Pyramid piano, made by Sauer, Prague, in the early 19th century.

The upright 'parlour' piano is usually considered to be wholly typical of the Victorian age, but the first were made in Germany about 1770 by Christian Ernst Friederici at Gera. Attempts to sustain the tone of a struck piano string predates the invention of the instrument itself. The theory was put forward by Leonardo da Vinci in the 15th century that a 'mill' system would produce a sustained note from any stringed instrument; this is the device found in the hurdy-gurdy. In 1789, Schnell's 'Anemo-corde' vibrated the strings by a jet of air, and Hawkins produced an instrument employing rapidly repeating hammers in 1800.

As pianos improved and public concerts in large halls demanded ever greater volume from them, strings had to be thicker and tensions higher, so metal reinforcing members were introduced in the wooden frame from about 1800. Complete iron frames for the domestic 'square' pianos were first made by Babcock in the USA in 1825 and were introduced increasingly on all pianos, both in the New World and in Europe, during the next two decades. By about 1860 they were the norm, and with this improvement pianos reached a peak of popularity that continues in the concert hall and recital room even if radio and audio have supplanted them at home. The Russian music critic Vasily Petrovich Botkin (1812–69) was casting around for ideas for a pseudonym when he lighted upon the most commonly-heard object in the world of music — and he called himself Vasily Fortepianov.

32 hands and four feet

Music for two pianos and piano duet (two players at one piano) is common. Less so is music for two pianos/three players: Falla's *Nights in the Gardens of Spain* for piano and orchestra (1915) was arranged by the composer for piano soloist and piano duet, as was Glinka's *Divertimento brillante* on themes from Bellini's *La Sonnambula* (1832). A number of double piano duets exist (i.e. two pianos/four players), most of them arrangements of orchestral pieces (e.g. Grieg's *Peer Gynt* Suite, arr. Ruthardt), but Edmund Parlow (1855–1929) contributed an original *Tarantella* in 1904, and Edwin Schultz wrote a Serenade in F for this grouping. The amassing of three pianos, one player to each, is rarer still and is confined almost exclusively to arrangements; Mozart's Concerto for three pianos and orchestra, K 242 (1776), and Dallapiccola's *Musica per tre pianoforte* of 1935 survive to prove that it can be done.

Can piano multiplicity go further still? Apparently it can. Ivan Alexandrovich Vishnegradsky composed a Symphony 'Ainsi parlait Zarathoustra', Op 17, in 1930 for four pianos/four players, revising it six years later for the quarter-tone pianos he had invented. Milhaud requires four conventional pianos/four players for his *Paris*, Op 284, of 1948. This line of enquiry terminates (although avant-gardists may well extend it in future if they have not already done so) in Czerny's arrangement of Rossini's *Semiramide* Overture for octuple piano duet: eight pianos/sixteen pianists/32 hands/160 fingers, or nearly 600 keys on the pianos of Czerny's day. As one contemporary critic put it: 'There is nothing *semi* about this *ramide*'.

Four fingers and a thumb

More modestly, the literature for one-handed pianists is unexpectedly large and extends back to C.P.E. Bach's *Clavierstück für die rechte oder linke Hand allein* ('Keyboard piece for right or left hand alone') in A, W 117/1, of 1770. The purpose of Bach's exercise, and the artist for whom it was written, are not known. The genre received a boost through the activities of Paul Wittgenstein (see below), who wrote a *School for the Left Hand* in 1957. He lost an arm, but refused to abandon his career; however, he was by no means the first to show such resolve.

Géza Zichy (1849–1924) lost his right arm in 1863 at the age of 14. He wrote numerous works for piano left hand, including a Concerto in E flat and *Six Studies* (1878). By then, Frédéric Kalkbrenner (1785–1849) had contributed a left-hand Sonata, Carl Czerny had added to his mountainous stock of two-hand (and more!) piano works a set of *10 Grand Studies for the Improvement of the Left Hand*, Op 399, and *24 Easy Studies for the Left Hand*, Op 718; and Valentin Alkan (1813–88), whom we shall meet again, had offered a *Fantaisie* in A flat for the left hand in his *3 Études*, Op 76 (*c*.1838).

Hermann Wolfgang Waltershausen (1882–1954) also accidentally lost his right arm (along with his right leg) in 1892, which not surprisingly encouraged him to write left-hand piano works later, but his main concern was with writing operas. Meantime, two-handed composers also saw the need for left-hand piano works, among them Carl Reinecke (1824–1910), whose C minor Sonata, Op 179, dates from 1885. Alexander Scriabin (1872–1915) wrote *Two Pieces for Left Hand*, Op 9 (*Prelude* in C sharp minor and *Nocturne* in D flat) in 1894. Max Reger's *Four Studies* comes from about 1901, Béla Bartók's *Étude* in B flat appeared in his *Four Pieces* in 1903, and Saint-Saëns wrote *Six Études for Left Hand*, Op 135, in 1912.

Paul Wittgenstein (1887–1961) is the most famous of all one-armed pianists. This Austrian pianist faced a bleak future when he lost his right arm in battle in 1914. Repatriated from Siberia in 1916, he resumed playing despite his disability, but for him the half-hearted left-hand repertoire of the past was not good enough. He set about acquainting composers of his plight and of the expert use he could make of his left hand if only he could be freed from all those tedious exercises and studies, and he commissioned many works. Other composers simply wrote music for him without being asked. A full list may be impossible to compile, so successful was Wittgenstein in canvassing his case, but it will be seen from the list below that composers major and minor took up the left hand cause with enthusiasm, although, in Prokofiev's case, not wholly to his liking.

Works written for, or inspired by, Paul Wittgenstein and other one-handed pianists

* = commissioned by Paul Wittgenstein.

Bortkiewicz. Serge
Concert-Fantasy, Op 28 (1929); *Nocturno*

Bowen, York
Nocturne, from *Curiosity Suite*, Op 42 (1920)

Braun, Rudolf
Piano Concerto in A Minor (1927); *Serenade*; *Perpetuum mobile*

Bricht, Walter
Fantasy on themes from *Die Fledermaus* (*c*.1937)
Song without words; Album Leaf; *Perpetuum mobile* (1937)
Fantasy on themes from Gounod's *Faust* (1936)
Variations on a folk song, for piano, flute and cello (1942)

Bridge, Frank
Three Improvisations (1918)

Britten, Benjamin
**Diversions*, Op 21 (1940, revised 1954)

Gál, Hans
Piano Quartet in A, Op 13 (1915, revised for left hand *c.*1928)

Hindemith, Paul
*Concerto, Op 29 (1923)

Janáček, Leoš
Capriccio, 'Defiance', for piano and wind (1926)

Kastle, Leonard
*Concerto (1959)

Korngold, Erich
Suite for 2 violins, cello and piano left hand, Op 23 (1930)
Piano Quintet in E, Op 15 (1924)
Piano Concerto in C sharp, Op 17 (1923; premièred by Gary Graffman in November 1985)

Labor, Josef
Variations and Fugue on a theme of Czerny (1913)
Concert Piece in the form of variations (1916)
Concert Piece in B minor
Concert Piece in F minor (1936)
Trio in E minor for viola, clarinet and piano for left hand (1932)
Piano Quartet No 1 (1913)
Piano Quartet No 2 in C minor, Op 6 (1916)
Piano Quintet in E minor, Op 3 (1912)
Piano Quintet No 2 in D, Op 11 (1919)
Divertimento for piano left hand, flute, oboe, viola and cello in C minor
Sonata in E for piano and violin (1916)

Lipatti, Dinu
Sonatina (1942)

Prokofiev, Serge
*Piano Concerto No 4 in B flat, Op 53 (1931) (see below)

Ravel, Maurice
*Concerto for left hand (1930)

Schmidt, Franz
Quintet in B flat for piano left hand, clarinet, violin, viola, and cello (1932)
*Concertante Variations on a theme of Beethoven (1923)
Quintet in G for piano and strings (1926)
Quintet in A for piano and strings (1938)
Concerto in E flat (1934)
Toccata in D minor (1938)
Variations on a theme of Josef Labor for piano, clarinet, violin, viola and cello (1950)

Schütt, Eduard
Paraphrase for piano and orchestra (1929)

Strauss, Richard
**Parergon on Sinfonia Domestica* for piano and orchestra, Op 73 (1924)

Panathenäenzug: Symphonic studies in the form of a passacaglia, Op 74 (1927)

Tansman, Alexander
*Concert Piece (1943) (see below)

Walker, Ernest
Prelude for piano, Op 61 (1935)
Variations on an original theme for piano, clarinet, violin, viola and cello (1933)
Study for left hand (*c.*1938)

Wittgenstein's musical taste was conservative; he had grown up with the romantic school and firmly espoused all it had to offer. Therefore, when Prokofiev's Left Hand Concerto was presented to him in response to his commission, he found it 'aggressively modern' and refused to play it. Little wonder that Wittgenstein took the precaution of going to see Alexander Tansman, a relatively young composer, to ascertain that his style would be more congenial to him before commissioning the Concert Piece.

When Leopold Godowsky (1870–1938), the famous pianist, became partially paralysed in 1930 he provided himself with many left hand pieces, amongst them arrangements of 19 Chopin *Études*, a Suite in D, a Fugue on BACH, and an *Intermezzo* and *Étude macabre*. Less permanent, fortunately, was Harriet Cohen's injury to her right hand in 1949, but Arnold Bax nonetheless provided her with a *Concertante* for left hand and orchestra.

Alkan's *Fantaisie* for left hand, mentioned earlier, is the first movement of his *Trois grandes études*, Op 76, of *c.*1838. Its second movement is an introduction, variations and finale for the right hand, and the two hands are united in the third movement, *Étude à mouvement semblable et perpetuel*. *Souvenir* by Gustave Samazeuilh (1877–1967) is for right hand only, and York Bowen's *Curiosity Suite*, Op 42, of 1920, includes a *nocturne* for the left hand and a *caprice* for the right. When Cyril Smith suffered a stroke in 1956 and lost the use of his left arm it seemed that his duet partnership with his wife Phyllis Sellick would be at an end. However, the following year the pair were playing music for three hands. In 1968 Sir Arthur Bliss, with Clifford Phillips's assistance, arranged his Concerto for two pianos for the Sellick-Smith three-hand team, and in 1969 Gordon Jacob composed his Concerto for three hands at one or two pianos for them, as did Malcolm Arnold his *Concerto for Phyllis and Cyril*, Op 104.

On the whole, it seems that the right hand is more at risk in pianists. What to do if both arms are lost? In such a tragedy it seems the only thing left is to equip oneself with a similarly afflicted friend and a pedal piano or organ and play Alkan's *Bombardo-Carillon* for two armless pianists (*c.*1872), for four feet.

In an article 'Pidgin, the Language of Friendship' in *Readers' Digest* (July 1976), Olaf Ruhen tells how the concept of a piano is conveyed in New Guinea by the use of a colourful and surprisingly accurate extended description in the English-derived Pidgin language of the area:

'Bokis bilong musik I-gat tit olsem pukpuk, sapos y paitim hat, I-krai aut' (= a box of music with teeth like a crocodile's, suppose you fight it hard, it cries out).

Fighting a piano hard to make it cry out seems an ungrateful, brutal, way of treating this noble instrument, but serious abuse began within a century of its invention. In *The Battle of Marengo* (1802) by the Frenchman Bernard Vignerie (1761–1819) the player is instructed (at points marked in the score by a cross-and-circle) to represent cannon-shots by stretching both hands flat over the lowest three octaves of the keyboard and banging down to sound every note simultaneously. Many modern composers have directed that the strings should be played without the keyboard's interference (first, perhaps, in 1923, in Henry Cowell's *Aeolian Harp*), using such objects as finger-nails, nail files, combs, spoons, carpenter's hammers, brushes, etc., and by 'preparing' the piano in various ways in order to modify the tone. Mauricio Kagel, in *Transition II* (1959), requires two pianists to play entirely upon the inside of the instrument with drumsticks and other weapons, and in *Und so weiter . . .* (1975) Luc Ferrari, in addition to amplifying the tones electronically and mixing them with

Square piano with sustaining pedal, by Buntebart & Sievers, London, 1786. (Gemeentemuseum, The Hague)

■ *The longest continuous non-repetitious piano piece ever published has been 'The Well-Tuned Piano' by LaMonte Young first presented by the Dia Art Foundation at the Concert Hall, Harrison St, New York City on 28 February 1980. The piece lasted 4 hr 12 min 10 sec.* ■

quadraphonic tape sounds, instructs that billiard balls and other objects should be placed on the strings and soundboard; and the soprano in David Bedford's *Music for Albion Moonlight* (1965) screams the word 'Hell' into the piano's interior to make the strings resonate, while milk bottles are applied direct to the strings in the same composer's *Come in Here Child* (1968).

Erik Satie was probably the first to interfere with the piano's innards. In the first performance of the Quadrille in *Le Piège de Méduse* in 1914, apparently on impulse, he inserted paper between the strings of the instrument, an unheard-of liberty then, but amongst avant-garde composers these excesses are so common that they have moved out of the category of 'unusual use'. John Cage has written a full-scale concerto for 'prepared' (i.e. tampered-with) piano, and to prove that other keyboard instruments are not immune from such attack, Hermann Rechberger includes ten prepared glockenspiels in his children's piece *Mobile 4* (1977).

But unusual use does not always result in abuse; consideration for the instrument can go too far. LaMonte Young, for instance, wrote his *Piano Piece for David Tudor No 1* in 1960, the instructions for the performance of which are as follows:

'Bring a bale of hay and a bucket of water onto the stage for the piano to eat and drink. The performer may then feed the piano or leave it to eat by itself. If the former, the piece is over after the piano has been fed. If the latter, it is over after the piano eats or decides not to.'

Electric Instruments

For thousands of years instruments were quite content to be sounded by finger-, fist-, leg-, or lung-power, sometimes assisted by tools such as the bow or the drumstick. Amplifying devices were entirely 'natural' — resonating boards and boxes, flared horns and the like. With the 19th century's increasing use of electricity it was inevitable that this new force should enter the world of music. It did so first, not to everyone's liking, soon after the century turned.

Thomas Edison floated an idea for an 'air relay' system of amplifying sound in 1876 but it was not truly launched until Sir Charles Parsons patented the compressed-air **Auxetophone** in 1903. At a demonstration in London in October 1906 two vast helical horns resembling Sousaphones faced a Promenade concert audience in the Queen's Hall and were hooked up to various instruments. Each proceeded to emit 'sound-waves identical in quality and intonation but richer in tone and larger in volume than those produced by the instrument itself unaided by the Auxetophone', according to Parsons. The new invention should have sent a shiver of excitement through the musical world; instead, it merely succeeded in sending the audience to the back of the hall with their hands clasped over their ears. Furthermore, misgivings amongst the orchestra were crystallized by Sir Henry Wood's supremely ill-considered and untimely pronouncement that the Auxetophone 'will be able to reinforce five stringed instruments . . . sufficiently to combat the complete woodwind and brass of the Wagnerian orchestra.' Visions of mass unemployment among the hapless string players quickly brought an end to the Auxetophone for concert use.

During the 1930s electricity was used — directly, and without the loud hiss of the Auxetophone's escaping air — for electric pianos (e.g. the 'neo-Bechstein') and for guitars, the latter indispensable today in pop music; a related species was known during the 1940s as the Hawaiian guitar. These and Parsons's invention amplified the sounds of conventional instruments (or modifications thereof) through loudspeakers. They are a group apart from the next to use or abuse electricity in the name of music: instruments whose sound production relies entirely upon electricity when played by a human agent.

Once again the year 1906 marks the beginning of the rot. In that year Thaddeus Cahill, a Canadian scientist, demonstrated his **Telharmonium** in New York. No-one has survived to tell of its onslaught on the senses, and by World War I the instrument was 'lost', which must be put down to sheer carelessness, since it weighed 200 tons/tonnes.

After the war, in 1920, the Russian inventor Lev Sergeyevich Termin (b. 1896) demonstrated in

Petrograd an extraordinarily clever instrument which he called the **Etherophone**. It consisted of a box with an antenna like a whip aerial. The player at no time touches the instrument during play. Pitch depends on the remoteness or proximity of his right hand to the aerial; amplitude was at first controlled by his left hand's position relative to a second, loop-like, antenna. In the improved model (1928) the left hand controls a cut-out device to separate successive notes while a foot-operated pedal controls volume. The strange waving and weaving of the player's hands has perhaps more appeal than the disembodied sound of moulded oscillators — recent demonstrations on TV have been visually mystifying but musically anonymous — but the Soviet composer Andrei Filippovich Pashchenko was sufficiently impressed in 1924 temporarily to abandon choral and opera composing to become the first to write for what was by then known as the **thérémin** or thereminovox (made by an inventor who by this time was known as Leo Thérémin).

Joseph Schillinger was next: in 1929 he included a thérémin in his *First Airphonic Suite*. Apparently there was not to be a second.

Ken Gray's Man in Static-Mind in Transit *for sound sculptures and installations, as seen in Manchester early in 1986. (*Classical Music*)*

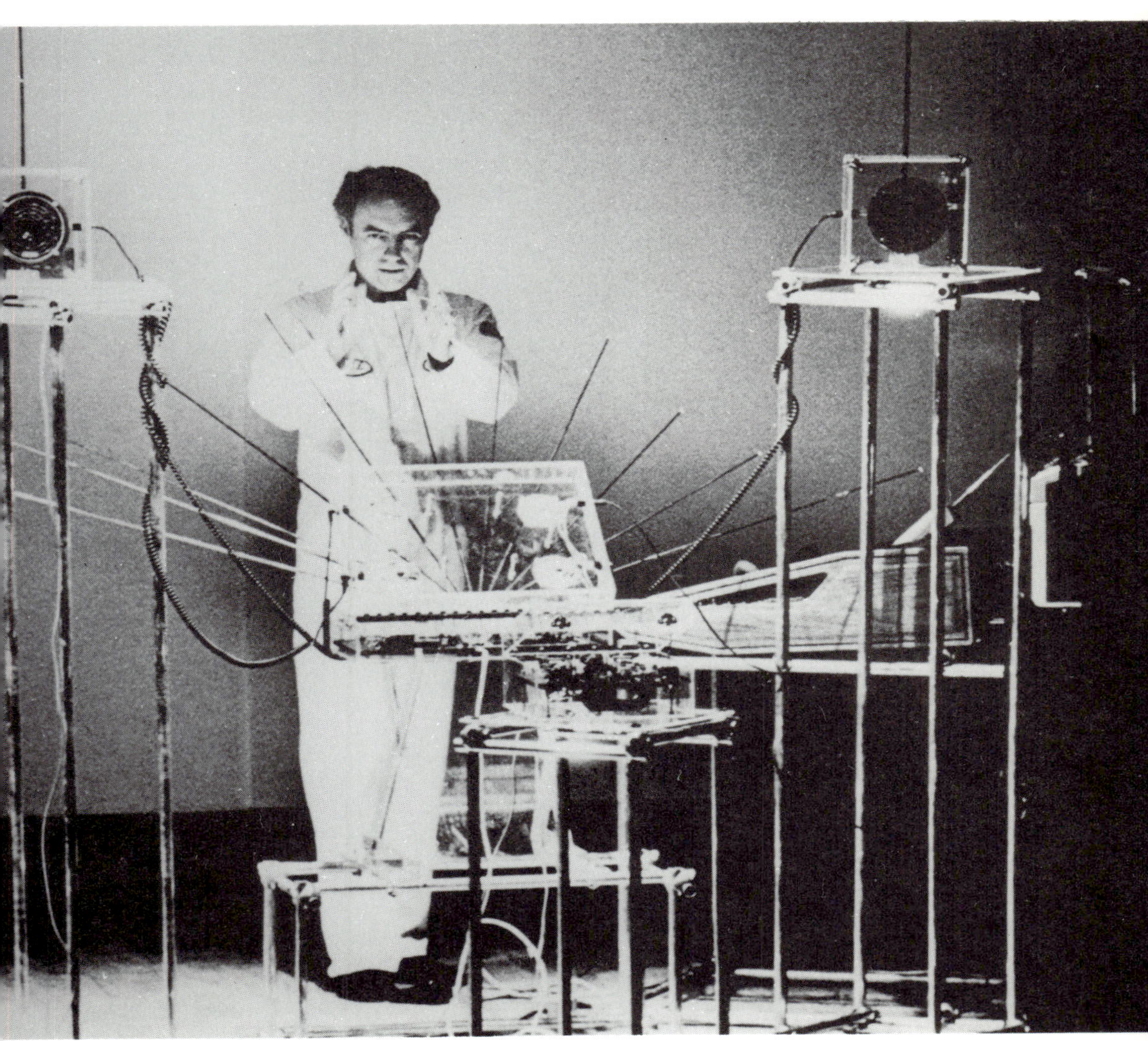

In 1923 came Jörg Mager's **Spherophone** in Germany, a species of electronic organ that, with sophisticated additions, became the **Partiturophone** before becoming history. But the Frenchman Maurice Martenot scored a real hit when on 20 April 1928 his **ondes musicale** was premièred in the first performance of Levidis's *Poéme Symphonique*. Like Thérémin's instrument, the ondes musicale quickly changed its name to honour its inventor, and the **ondes Martenot** has appeared in scores by Boulez, Honegger, Ibert, Jolivet, Koechlin, Milhaud, Schmitt, Varèse and others. Messiaen, in *Fêtes des belles eaux* (1937) requires six of the beasts. A keyboard controls the frequency of a variable oscillator in the bowls of the ondes, the amplified signal issuing from a loudspeaker. Alternatively, a sliding ribbon operated by a finger ring activates the oscillator for glissando effects. Part-writing is not possible, for the instrument is capable of producing only one note at a time. Bach, at least, was safe for a time.

Tortured oscillators protesting through a loudspeaker also feature in Friedrich Adolf Trautwein's invention in Berlin in 1930. Not for Trautwein the false modesty of a fancy name for his instrument: he came right out with it and called it the **Trautonium**. A wire and a metal rail are connected to an oscillator. The performer presses wire to rail at certain marked points to select the notes, the pressure controlling the amplitude; timbre is modified by push buttons. Composers as notable as Richard Strauss and Hindemith (and as obscure and unwise as Genzmer, Höffer and Weismann) have written for the instrument, while one Sala modified it to become the Mixtur-Trautonium.

Three years later, Oskar Vieling in Berlin also made an oscillator-based instrument, the **Electrochord** (he spared us 'Vielophone'), but the year 1933 is remembered for a rather more lasting device. Laurens Hammond (1895–1973) in the USA invented an 'organ' in which rotating wheels in a magnetic field induce currents which are amplified and modified electronically. The **Hammond Organ** continues to enjoy popularity in the light music field because its clever design enables an extremely wide variety of sounds to be produced on a relatively compact console instrument.

Since World War II electronics have increased so hugely in sophistication that their invasion of the musical scene has transformed our listening, and our playing. The Yamaha **Clavinola**, a recent development of the electric piano, can sound like a piano or like most other instruments; the keyboard even lights up to assist students to find the right notes. The Clavinola will record what you play automatically, and if you use headphones the speaker is muted so that the neighbours stay sweet.

Electro-acoustic music and synthesizer music have merged into one (see below), but a quick glance at the beginnings of synthesizer music is necessary to complete our survey of electric instruments.

Synthesizers grew out of the machinery developed by electronic composers; this in turn grew out of a marriage between some of the electric instrument ideas noted above and the 'tape-recorder-school' of *musique concrète* composers. In 1954 Robert Moog began manufacturing thérémins in New York and 11 years later made his first synthesizer. However, as early as 1960, Drs J.R. Pierce and M.V. Mathews at the Bell Telephone Laboratories were constructing digital programmes to feed into an IBM 7090 computer and obtaining music via a digital-to-analog transducer. A recording called *Music from Mathematics* was issued in 1962 (indisputably the very first digital recording) by the American Decca Record Company. It contains compositions by the two doctors and others and includes *Bicycle Built for Two* 'sung' by the computer.

However, it was **Moog**'s synthesizer of 1965, and the 1969 CBS disc *Switched-on Bach* (arrangements by Walter Carlos that showed the Moog was capable of doing what Martenot could not) which really caught the imagination. The modern Moog (correctly pronounced to rhyme with 'vogue') is an electronic jungle of keyboards, amplifiers, oscillators, filters, mixers, reverberators, etc., all geared to make sounds that Sir Henry Wood's fiddlers could never have imagined, let alone produced. Synthesizer music is now widely heard and is particularly popular with producers of TV commercials, selectors of TV and radio signature tunes, and for dramatic sound effects. Doubtless the first concerto for synthesizer and orchestra is imminent, though the depth and width of the synthesizer's capabilities would make the orchestra superfluous.

The genesis of electro-acoustic music

As already stated, an integral part of the modern synthesizer's development was the evolution of electro-acoustic music, and in particular that part of it known as electronic music. Apart from specially designed instruments such as the springboard and shozyg invented by the British composer Hugh Davies (b. 1943), today's electronic music is generated by computers, sometimes minicomputers, employing transistors and integrated circuits. An example is the **Fairlight Computer Synthesizer** used by the BBC's Radiophonic Workshop in London as part of the equipment used to produce artificial music for radio and TV programmes. The department was set up in 1958. Similar studios exist in many countries, either as independent bodies or attached to universities (Utrecht, Toronto, etc.), broadcasting stations (Milan, Warsaw, etc.) or electronics companies (such as Siemens in Munich, Philips in Eindhoven).

Composers in these studios not infrequently call in 'live' musicians to sing or play a part complementary to computer-generated sounds or to provide sounds which, once on tape, may be modified electronically. A link is therefore forged with pure electronic music and the older *musique concrète*, a concept which came to prominence in the 1950s when a group of Parisian experimental composers headed by Pierre Schaeffer formed the Groupe de Recherche de Musique Concrète in 1951, this in turn emerging from the Club d'Essai founded in 1948.

Musique concrète became a force in experimental music only when the tape recorder became available. Before that the 'concrete' sounds with which the composers worked were taken from 78rpm records which were tampered with in some way: one or two grooves would be repeated over and over to provide a rhythmic ostinato base against which other records might be similarly manipulated, or played backwards, or have their sounds fragmented or mutilated according to the whims of the operator who wielded the pick-up head (or soundbox). Much 'concrete' music was invented in this way, but the system was hit-and-miss: every performance would be subject to variations, the successful realization of planned effects would often be a matter of luck, and there was no way of preserving what was composed for future listening and study.

The tape recorder changed all that. With its aid not only was it possible to record the experiments, but recordings could now be made of the components of music wrested from those long-suffering 78rpm discs, and these could be manipulated further by electronic means. Control was vastly improved with the ability to splice tape and to judge more accurately the speed variations and other mutations to which the sounds on tape might be subjected. The **Phonogène**, invented by Pierre Henry in 1950, used revolving tape 'record' and 'replay' heads which enabled the composer to alter the speed at which a sound source is recorded and reproduced. In addition, the range of sound sources was no longer restricted to what might be drawn from disc surfaces: sounds of birds and animals, traffic, railways, aircraft, overheard speech, musical instruments, the clatter and chatter of public places, random radio noises — all could be taped for use. It was only a short step then to the noises being specially generated for recording: metal objects dropped onto a hard surface, twanged rubber bands, water dripping on to a resonating object — a thousand different sounds could be produced from every-day household, office or studio paraphernalia, then recorded and altered in a thousand different ways. The electronic nature of *musique concrète* was further established as these sounds were amplified, filtered, exaggerated, echoed, muted and otherwise transformed to become fuel for the *musique concrète* composer's inventive fire.

All this was prophesied more than 300 years earlier by Francis Bacon. In *The New Atlantis* (1624) he describes the workings and products of an Atlantean electro-acoustic studio, plus the micro-tones used by composers such as Alois Hába (1893–1973), echo-plates, stereo, landlines and speaker-cables, and even, apparently, hearing aids! It is an astonishing vision that repays close study:

Wee have also Sound-houses, wher wee practise and demonstrate all Sounds, and their Generation. Wee have Harmonies which you have not, of Quarter-Sounds, and lesser Slides of Sounds. Diverse Instruments of Musick likewise to you unknowne, some sweeter than any you have; Together with Bells and Rings that are dainty and sweet. Wee represent Small Sounds as Great and Deepe; Likewise Great Sounds, Extenuate and Sharp; Wee make diverse Tremblings and Warblings of Sounds, which in their Originall are Entire. Wee represent and imitate all Articulate Sounds and Letters, and the Voices and Notes of Beasts and Birds. Wee have certaine Helps, which sett to the Eare doe further the Hearing greatly. Wee have also diverse Strange and Artificiall Eccho's, Reflecting the Voice many times, and as it were Tossing it: and some that give back the Voice Lowder than it come, some Shriller, and some Deeper; Yea some rendring the Voice, Differing in the Letters or Articulate Sound, from that they receyve, Wee have also meanes to convey Sounds in Trunks and Pipes, in strange Lines and Distances.

Cheironomy: the indicating of melodic movement by hand gestures. Right: Iti, the earliest-known female composer; left: Hekenu, the earliest identifiable musician. Fifth Egyptian dynasty (c. 2450 BC). (Photo: Cairo Museum)

III

Notes on Composers

First came the singer, then the instrumentalist, then the composer. Once man discovered that he might make others listen in admiration or awe when he lifted his voice in a semi-musical howl, and that others might join him in the howl or accompany him on instruments, the composer became necessary. There are two reasons for this: the purely practical one that it is necessary to control people if their combined noises are not to become a diabolical row, and the creative one that if one or more of those people hit upon a succession of notes or some idea that could be considered pleasant it would be handy to commit them to some kind of written record for future use.

Many 'compositions' have been improvized by an expert story-teller, and as the stories were handed from generation to generation they came to be associated with certain tunes that were memorized and handed down as inseparable from the stories. But man is an inventive animal. Perhaps a son had a keener ear or a sharper imagination than his father (or simply wanted to change things for the fun of it) and altered the melody; in this way old tunes die out and new versions grow. It is only natural that some fathers would wish to preserve the tunes taught to them by *their* fathers, so they sought some means to write them down in a series of mnemonics, thus making them available to future generations regardless of what their sons might do. The Egyptians of the Fourth Dynasty (2723–2563 BC) used cheironomy — a system of hand and arm movements, still not fully understood, that indicated to other performers the direction in which the 'composer' wished the melody to go. Cheironomy was also used elsewhere in pre-Christian times but became obsolete as notational systems developed.

In early days each 'composer' would have invented his own system of notation, probably a hasty and ill thought-out affair of signs that was intelligible to others only if laboriously explained. Clearly a universal and completely unambiguous system was needed. Perhaps it still is.

The practical reason for notation concerns the control of forces. If discipline were introduced at those early concerts it might have been possible to produce a listenable result. Singers would agree as to which notes to sing simultaneously and which combinations to avoid as unpleasant, and there would be timed entries for singers or players against a played or implied rhythmic background. This called for a sophisticated system of writing down sounds that was intelligible to all participants: the forerunner of the modern score. It evolved slowly and has today reached a stage approaching, but not attaining, perfection — for scores still contain ambiguous directions open to more than one interpretation.

The oldest surviving musical notation dates from at least 1800 BC. It is a heptatonic scale which was deciphered from a clay tablet by Dr Duchesne Guillemin in 1966–7. The tablet was discovered at Nippur Sumer, now in Iraq.

The beginnings of the present notation system were created about the year 1020 by the Italian monk Guido d'Arezzo (*c.*990–1050). He saw the need for a method by which to teach his singing pupils to sing unfamiliar songs on sight, and the

Balinese dancers accompanied by percussion (left), as pictured in 1889 (Illustrated London News)

system he invented has the genius of simplicity. His singers knew a great many hymns by heart, so, by taking various prominent syllables from a well-known hymn, the relative pitches of which were firmly implanted in the minds of his pupils, he devised a scale based on the vocal sounds 'ut-re-mi-fa-sol-la-(te-ut)'. The notes in parentheses were added later to complete the scale. Today the syllable 'doh' sometimes replaces 'ut'. The text of the hymn d'Arezzo chose runs:

UTqueant laxis REsonare fibris MIra gestorum FAmuli tuorum, SOLve polluti LAbii reatum, Sancte Johannes.

D'Arezzo's next step was to establish a bass line in red ink to indicate the note 'fa' (F), another above it in yellow for 'ut' (C), and between them a scratched line made with a needle for 'la' (A). Using the lines, and all the spaces below, between and above them, he was able to indicate positions for all the notes of the range E to D. Later another line was added, clefs were invented to establish registers, and the other conventions were introduced to lead, by the mid-17th century, to the musical notation we know now.

Contrasts in notation. Top: Part of Tchaikovsky's manuscript of the ballet Swan Lake. *Bottom: Gregorian, a short extract from an Ash Wednesday tract.*

Notes on Composers

The American composer Earle Brown (b. 1926), dissatisfied with conventional notation, rejected it and constructed his own 'open-form' system during the 1950s. In his *December 1952* (the title is the date of composition), Brown introduced a graphic notation of black rectangles positioned on the page to represent a space through which the performer must pass. Such indeterminacy (for no two performers will reach an identical interpretation) circumvents the need for accuracy which centuries of endeavour have sought to enshrine in conventional notation.

The earliest composers may have found ways of writing down what they had composed, but rarely did they think to add their names to it unless, of course, they were a part of a select set who habitually signed things: nobility and royalty. Later, composers associated with or employed by royalty began to append their names to works written for court, but which might also be heard outside, but then only as 'Giovanni at the court of Luigi IV' or some such. It became usual for composers to identify themselves only during the 16th century.

But how far back must we go to learn the name of the earliest composer? Obviously, Stone Age men did not leave records of their names, although it is evident that music existed for them and its performance must have been 'controlled' to some extent. Those individuals were the world's first composers. We must come forward in time to Sumeria and Ancient Egypt before we find evidence of music-making on a large scale. Musical instruments dating from about 5000 years ago have been preserved, particularly in the dry atmosphere of Egyptian graves, but actual names of performers, who must have composed the music they played, are not known until perhaps the Fourth Dynasty (2723–2563 BC). Hemre was a female musician, the earliest named musician in history, who led the court music, in which capacity she probably also 'composed' the works performed. During the same Dynasty, Mery, who sang and played the drum, was the earliest known male musician. A singer and leader of vocal music, Iti, another lady, became famous during the Fifth Dynasty (2563–2423 BC): she may certainly be classed as a composer. She is also notable as the first musician whose portrait has survived.

Nero (AD 37–68), Roman emperor from 54 to 68, is probably the first notable composer of the Christian era who can be identified with certainty. He composed long, often tragic, narrative poems which he sang in 'a thin, husky voice' to his own accompaniment on a lute or *kithara*, a kind of lyre made of wood. Nero gave serious attention to his musical education and refused to appear before an audience until he, at least, was satisfied with his proficiency. He first sang publicly in Rome in the year 59 and toured Greece in 66. He knew nothing of the 'fiddle', but he may well have sung to his own accompaniment during the week-long fire which destroyed much of Rome in 64. Given his consuming passion for music, and his powerlessness to do anything to quench the blaze that was not already being done by better-qualified fire fighters, it would be difficult to imagine his acting otherwise.

Nero's musical memorial as the emperor who 'fiddled while Rome burned' nonetheless endures, but he himself erected a larger, if less permanent, monument. A vast palace, the Golden House, built on the site later occupied by the Colosseum, and a bronze statue of himself in excess of 100ft (30m) high, form the grandest memorial ever built to commemorate a composer.

ROYAL MUSIC

Royalty has often attracted music, and vice versa. The pomp and ceremony of a state occasion would be incalculably reduced if music were excluded. Music enhances the image man tries to create for himself: what makes a royal wedding more memorable, the words of the oath or the splendour of music resounding in a cathedral? At the opposite extreme, natives may paint their faces and carry weapons to intimidate their enemies, but their belligerent intentions are enormously accentuated by the beating of drums and the blowing of trumpets. Music heightens the occasion, and when the occasion is regal it calls for regal music to enhance it further.

That most pagentry-conscious of all nations, Great Britain, is the only country to appoint a national Master of the Monarch's Musick, the archaic spelling revealing the antiquity of the post.

Today, the appointment is made by the ruling monarch in consultation with advisers, and the duties are nominal. The composer thus chosen may provide music for the most important state occasions but there is no binding obligation to do so, and the Master of the Monarch's Musick carries out the honour without the drudgery which attended the post in its earlier history. Once, these duties ranged from obtaining and copying parts for performance, rehearsing and conducting, to being responsible for the behaviour of the court musicians both inside and outside the concert room.

James I perhaps employed a specific court composer, but the post was not officially recognized until 13 June 1626, when Charles I made provision for the position as part of the royal household. He awarded the title on 11 July 1626, when Nicholas Lanier was appointed the first Master of the King's Musick. Lanier served Charles I until the latter's execution in 1649, and was reinstated to the post by Charles II after the Restoration.

Of the 19 Masters to date, only three (Nos 2, 6, and 12) have retired from the post. In all other cases they were serving at the time of death.

EQUAL OPPORTUNITIES

Composers must compose. Neither illness, deprivation, plague, nor even politics, will stop them. But where do women stand in this assertion of the social and physical barriers to creativity?

A woman's place was in the home and this was

MASTERS OF THE MONARCH'S MUSICK

Composer	*born*	*appointed*	*died*	*served*
1. Nicholas Lanier	1588	1626	1666	James I; Charles I; Charles II
2. Louis Grabu	*c.*1638?	1666	1694?	Charles II (ret: 1674)
3. Nicholas Staggins	?	1674	1700	Charles II; James II
4. John Eccles	*c.*1668	1700	1735	Anne; George I; George II
5. Maurice Greene	1696	1735	1755	George II
6. William Boyce*	1711	1757	1779	George II; George III
7. John Stanley	1712	1772	1786	George III
8. Sir William Parsons	1746	1786	1817	George III
9. William Shield	1748	1817	1829	George III; George IV
10. Christian Kramer	*c.*1788	1829	1834	George IV; William IV
11. François Cramer	1772	1834	1848	William IV; Victoria
12. George Frederick Anderson	*c.*1801	1848	1876	Victoria (ret: 1870)
13. Sir William George Cusins	1833	1870	1893	Victoria
14. Sir Walter Parratt	1841	1893	1924	Victoria; Edward VII; George V
15. Sir Edward Elgar	1857	1924	1934	George V
16. Sir Henry Walford Davies	1869	1934	1941	George V; Edward VIII; George VI
17. Sir Arnold Bax	1883	1941	1953	George VI; Elizabeth II
18. Sir Arthur Bliss	1891	1953	1975	Elizabeth II
19. Malcolm Williamson	1931	1975		Elizabeth II

*Boyce took over duties unofficially in 1755 on the death of Greene; he retired on account of deafness in 1772.

Grazyna Bacewicz (1909–69), Polish composer. (Interpress Publishers, Warsaw)

so for thousands of years — but not at the desk writing music. The honour of receiving the muse's inspiration was deemed to lie wholly with the male half of the population.

In 1981 Aaron Cohen published the results of eight years of information-gathering in his monumental *International Encyclopedia of Women Composers* (Bowker, New York and London) that shows just how mistaken is this attitude. It lists over 4000 women together with their biographies and works. Since then his further research has revealed 2000 more women who have dared to invade this area of man's territory; one wonders just what will be Mr Cohen's final total for his second edition!

A fascinating breakdown he sent recently to the authors, and quoted here by kind permission, shows that, of the women composers whose existence he has been able to verify, up to the beginning of the 13th century there had been 104, the 13th to 17th (five centuries) produced 163, and the 18th alone 182. Then came a really spectacular increase: 19th century — 1093; 20th century — 3919. Together with 612 composers for whom not even the century of their activity is known, the total (so far) is 6073 female composers.

A geographical breakdown shows that Egypt and Greece started well, with 11 and 10 respectively up to the 4th century AD, but these countries produced only about ten more each since then. Arabia could boast of 34 by the 9th century but only 37 in total, after which France had 42 up to the 15th century (and 386 since) and Italy took the lead in the 16th to 19th centuries with 161 (and a total to date of 303). During the 18th century France (48) and the United Kingdom (45) were the front-runners; in the 19th these were still well represented (133 and 197 respectively) but Germany (180) and America (165) had taken second and third places. The clear leader this century has been that land of opportunity, America, with no less than 1695 so far. America's nearest rivals are the UK (302), France (201), the USSR (180), Germany (167, including the DDR), and Canada (130).

Women were composing before the 5th century AD in Byzantium and Sumeria, as well as in the areas now called Arabia, China, Hawaii, Hungary, India, Persia (Iran), Israel and Italy, and the feminine art had spread by the start of the 19th century to Austria, Belgium, Britain, Chile, Denmark, Eire, Japan, Mexico, Monaco, the Netherlands, Norway, Poland, Portugal, Spain, Sweden and Switzerland, as well as those countries mentioned above. On the other hand, Arabia has not produced a single female composer since the 11th century and Persia not one since the 4th.

Composers in the Stars

Do astrological influences affect the musical quality, nature or character of composers, linking them together in some occult fashion? In an attempt to find an answer, sixty of the greatest composers have been listed under their respective birthsigns. Although inconclusive, the list is interesting in that it assembles composers into groups that the believer may examine for similarities (note the amazing fecundity of some of the composers born under Pisces and Aquarius, for example) while the cynic will point gleefully to the dissimilarities (e.g. under Taurus).

Aquarius (21 January — 19 February)
27 January 1756 **Mozart**
29 January 1862 **Delius**
31 January 1797 **Schubert**
3 February 1809 **Mendelssohn**
9 February 1885 **Berg**
15 February 1571 **Praetorius**
17 February 1653 **Corelli**

Pisces (20 February — 20 March)
23 February 1685 **Handel**
29 February 1792 **Rossini**
1 March 1810 **Chopin**
2 March 1824 **Smetana**
4 March 1678 **Vivaldi**
8 March 1714 **C.P.E. Bach**
13 March 1681 **Telemann**
13 March 1860 **Wolf**

Aries (21 March — 20 April)
21 March 1685 **J.S. Bach**
21 March 1839 **Mussorgsky**
25 March 1881 **Bartók**
31 March 1732 **Haydn**
1 April 1873 **Rachmaninoff**

Taurus (21 April — 21 May)
23 April 1891 **Prokofiev**
2 May 1660 **A. Scarlatti**
2 May 1813 **Wagner**
7 May 1833 **Brahms**
7 May 1840 **Tchaikovsky**
7 May 1875 **Ravel**

Gemini (22 May — 21 June)
1 June 1804 **Glinka**
2 June 1857 **Elgar**
6 June 1865 **Nielsen**
8 June 1810 **Schumann**
11 June 1864 **R. Strauss**
15 June 1843 **Grieg**
17 June 1882 **Stravinsky**

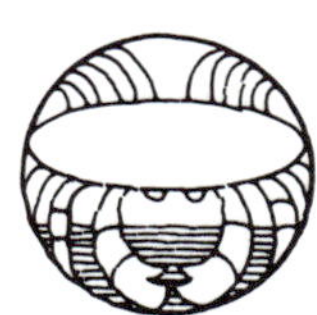

Cancer (22 June — 23 July)
2 July 1714 **Gluck**
7 July 1860 **Mahler**

Leo (24 July — 23 August)
22 August 1862 **Debussy**

Virgo (24 August — 23 September)
4 September 1824 **Bruckner**
8 September 1841 **Dvořák**
13 September 1874 **Schoenberg**
?23 September 1683 **Rameau**

Libra (24 September — 23 October)
25 September 1906 **Shostakovich**
9 October 1835 **Saint-Saëns**

Igor Stravinsky (Photograph of Hurrah, 1951). (Royal College of Music)

Edvard Grieg. (National Museum, Stockholm)

10 October 1813 **Verdi**
12 October 1872 **Vaughan Williams**
17 October 1844 **Rimsky-Korsakov**
22 October 1685 **D. Scarlatti**
22 October 1811 **Liszt**

Scorpio (24 October — 22 November)
25 October 1825 **J. Strauss**
10 November 1668 **F. Couperin**
16 November 1897 **Hindemith**
18 November 1786 **Weber**
22 November 1913 **Britten**

Sagittarius (23 November — 21 December)
29 November 1632 **Lully**
3 December 1883 **Webern**
8 December 1865 **Sibelius**
8 December 1890 **Martinů**
11 December 1803 **Berlioz**
15/16 December 1770 **Beethoven**
17 December *c.*1525 **Palestrina**

Capricorn (22 December — 20 January)
22 December 1858 **Puccini**

Franz Liszt. (Mary Evans Picture Library)

Ninety Not-out

Verdi wrote *Otello* during his 74th year and *Falstaff* six years later; Vaughan Williams continued to compose until shortly before his death at the age of 86; Stravinsky, too, remained remarkably active until the last of his 89 years. Here is a list of composers who achieved the magical figure of 90.

90 years old

Adam, Johann Ludwig (or Jean-Louis) (1758–1848), Alsatian pianist and composer.

Alcock, John (1715–1806), Doctor of Music (Oxon), organist in London, Plymouth, Reading and Lichfield; composition pupil of John Stanley. As a novelist he wrote under the pseudonym 'Piper' (= organist).

Carrillo-Trujillo, Julián Antonio (1875–1965), Mexican conductor and composer who experimented with microtones. He wrote works subtitled 'Debussy' and 'Beethoven' (string quartets), and 'Paganini' (violin sonata).

Esplá, Oscar (1886–1976), prolific Spanish composer of music in the post-impressionist style.

Gui, Vittorio (1885–1975), Italian composer and conductor.

Harris, Sir William Henry (1883–1973), English organist and composer, mainly for his instrument and for chorus.

Hüe, Georges Adolph (1858–1948), French opera composer.

Huygens, Sir Constantijn (1596–1687), Dutch musician, politician, poet, diplomatist, gymnast, artist and playwright.

Spengel, Heinrich Ritter von (*c.*1775–1865), German composer.

91 years old

Foerster, Joseph Bohuslav (1859–1951), Czech nationalist composer of many types of music.

Grechaninov, Alexander Tikhonovich (1864–1956), Russian composer of songs, piano music and the once-popular 'Credo' from his Liturgy No 2 (1908).

Heger, Robert (1886–1978), German conductor, and composer of five operas, etc.

Huss, Henry Holden (1862–1953), American composer and teacher; he was a descendant of the Czech national hero Jan Huss.

Jiránek, Alois (1858–1960), Czech pupil of Fibich.

Malipiero, Gian Francesco (1882–1973), one of the most prominent modern Italian composers, he was also a writer and musical editor concerned chiefly with ancient Italian music.

Rieger, Gottfried (1764–1855), Moravian composer of sacred music.

Ropartz (1864–1955), whose name is given as

Joseph Guy-Ropartz and as Guy Marie Ropartz. He was a French pupil of Massenet.

Scott, Cyril (1879–1970), English symphonist, pianist, poet and writer.

Siret, Nicholas (1663–1754), French composer and keyboard player.

Tritto, Giacomo (1733–1824), Neapolitan opera composer.

92 years old

Boulanger, Nadia (1887–1979), French composer and renowned and influential teacher. Kendal's biography of her is titled *The Tender Tyrant*.

Friml, Rudolf (1879–1972), Czech, naturalized American, composer of light operettas, for example *Rose Marie* (1924) and *The Vagabond King* (1925).

Marin, Marie-Martin Marcel de, Vicomte (1769–1861+), French composer, violinist and harpist, at least 92 at death.

Seeger, Charles Louis (1886–1979), American conductor and composer. He and his wife Ruth Crawford brought into the world three children who have made their marks in folk music: Pete, Peggy and Michael.

Sibelius, Jan Julian Christian (1865–1957), one of the greatest of 20th-century symphonists and the greatest composer yet to emerge from Finland.

Strong, George Templeton (1856–1948), American composer; friend of Liszt.

Zavertal, Ladislao Joseph Philip Paul (1849–1942), British conductor and composer of Czech descent who worked in Italy and the British Isles.

93 years old

Bertini, Giuseppe (1759–1852), Italian musician, writer on music, and, apparently, composer of much sacred music.

Widor, Charles-Marie-Jean-Albert (1844–1937), Parisian writer, organist and composer of the popular *Toccata* from the Organ Symphony No 5. He was also active in opera, orchestral and chamber music, and as a song writer.

94 years old

Hartmann, Johann Peter Emilius (1805–1900), Danish composer whose music has a strong nationalist bias.

Mouton, Charles (1626–?) French lutenist, said to have been still living in 1720.

Perti, Giacomo Antonio (1661–1756), Bolognese opera and sacred music composer.

Preyer, Gottfried (1807–1901), Austrian church composer and organist.

Stolz, Robert Elisabeth (1880–1975), Austrian, a pupil of Humperdinck and the composer of operettas, film music, etc.

95 years old

Caffi, Francesco (1778–1874), Venetian musicologist, composer amd writer.

Charpentier, Gustave (1860–1956), French composer chiefly of dramatic works.

Ganz, Rudolf (1877–1972), Swiss conductor, pianist and composer.

Gossec, François-Joseph (1734–1829), Belgian composer of operas and about 100 symphonies, one of which is now thought to be by another nonagenarian: Witzthumb (see below).

Ruggles, Carl (1876–1971), American painter and composer of deeply thought and uncompromising music.

96 years old

Araújo, João Gomes de (1846–1942), Brazilian composer.

Brian, Havergal (1876–1972), English composer of 32 symphonies and much other music, including operas.

Casals, Pablo (1876–1973), the world-famous Spanish expatriate cellist who was also a skilful composer.

Mascitti, Michele (or Michel, etc.) (*c.*1664–1760), Neapolitan violinist and composer chiefly for his own instrument.

Witzthumb, Ignace (1720–1816), symphonist (see Gossec, above) of Austrian origin who settled in Brussels.

97 years old

Floyd, Alfred Ernest (1877–1974), English organist, conductor, composer and broadcaster who spent most of his life in Australia.

98 years old

Berger, Francesco (1834–1933), English song-writer, piano composer and teacher in London. Hon. secretary of the Royal Philharmonic Society.

99 years old

Rein(c)ken, Jan Adam (1623–1722), Dutch or German organist and composer. It is said that the great Bach walked many miles to hear his improvizations in Hamburg.

Weinert, Antoni (1751–1850), Czech/Polish *opera-buffa* composer.

101 years old

Busser, Paul-Henri (1872–1973), French organ pupil of Franck and Widor; composer primarily of dramatic works.

Cervetto, Giacobbe Basevi (*c.*1681–1783), Italian composer and cellist who worked in London from 1738. At his death he was reported to have been *at least* 101.

104 years old

Lang, Margaret Ruthven (1867–1972), American pupil of, among others, Chadwick and MacDowell, began composing aged 12. Works include over 100 songs, choral and other vocal music, piano and chamber works, orchestral music.

17 000 years old?

Le Comte de Saint-Germain, according to confused reports, was born about 1660 and is still alive. Other incredible claims include his own 18th-century report that he had discovered a potion that would prolong life indefinitely, as it had already prolonged his own for 2000 years. He also claimed to be able to make gold and diamonds, that he could speak virtually all the European languages, and that he is the finest violinist and composer who ever lived. The authors have not heard him play but we have examined his 13 sonatas in the British Library (published by Walsh, 1750, and by Johnson, 1758). They are average works for their period, and Dr Burney pronounced some of his songs 'insipid'.

A sober estimate of his dates is *c.*1710–*c.*1780 (*Encyclopaedia Britannica*), while *New Grove* commits itself only to a death date: 27 February 1784. Both fail to take account of his reported conversation with Rameau in Venice in 1710 and a Paris appearance in 1789. In addition to being an alchemist, scientist, composer and violinist, he was a singer in those days and travelled widely through Europe and the Middle East, from London (where he met Horace Walpole in 1743) to Persia, from Tunisia to St Petersburg.

What is the answer to this riddle? Are we dealing with two Saint-Germains, father and son, both gifted in deception and proficient in music and the sciences? Various reports from widely separated centres (there is one from India dated 1756), and the claim of the discovery of the elixir of life, would lend credence to the longevity story in those superstitious days, and the discrepancy in age could be masked by clever itineraries.

The numerous reports lessened as the 18th century wore on, and a final isolated one in 1821 seems to have been the end of the matter – until the 1970s. On 28 January 1972 a Richard Chamfrey appeared on French television claiming to be the genuine Comte de Saint Germain. The audience witnessed him 'change lead into gold', a trick which has apparently enabled him to give up the strenuous activity of music. Chamfrey's claims are now somewhat more ambitious: he now commutes between Earth and Mars, and his age is 17 000 years.

WHICH TCHAIKOVSKY? – BROTHERS AND STRANGERS

Music librarians will tell you of the 'brother nightmare' and the 'father-and-son syndrome'. In earlier centuries, when sons were obliged to follow their fathers' trades if at all possible, and when simply to be a musician implied that you should also compose, families produced several composers, many of whom, with total disregard for the ulcers of 20th-century cataloguers, signed their family names only, omitting their given names. Some of the twisted threads that result will never be untangled.

But what about those obscure figures bearing names identical to those of more familiar composers? A relationship may be suspected but does not invariably exist. Our list of like-named composers has been compiled with a view to identifying each individual with a few descriptive details and noting his relationship, if any, to others. Musicians other than composers have been included only where necessary, and particularly obscure composers are ignored unless their names and/or dates and work locations are sufficiently close to those of their namesakes to cause confusion.

ARNOLD

Carl (1794–1877), German; son of Johann Gottfried.

Georg (?–1676), Austrian; worked in Germany; also organist.

Gustav (1831–1900), Swiss; also organist and conductor.

György (1781–1848), Hungarian; also organist.

Johann Gottfried (1773–1806), German; also cellist; father of Carl.

Malcolm Henry (b. 1921), English; composed approachable, skilful music.

Samuel (1740–1802), English; mainly operas.

Yury Karlovich (1811–98), Russian; also writer.

Apart from J.G. and Carl, all the above apparently are unrelated.

Above: Malcolm Arnold — not one of a crowd. (Faber Music Ltd. Photo: John Carewe) Below: Bach's greatest son, Carl Philipp Emanuel. Engraving by A. Stöttrup. (Royal College of Music)

BACH

The largest family tree in music belongs to the Bachs. Some 76 musicians are known, no less than 53 of whom possessed the given name Johann — four of them were Johann Christians, eight were Johann Christophs! A complete list is out of the question in a book of this size, but the best-known and most important members are given, plus some minor figures with identical forenames (included for reference only). The nicknames attached to J.S. Bach's four composing sons refer to the musical centres in which they mainly worked.

Carl Philipp Emanuel (1714–88), 'Berlin' or 'Hamburg' Bach; second musical son of Johann Sebastian.

Johann Bernhard (1676–1749), distant cousin of Johann Sebastian.

Johann Christian (I) (1717–38), son of Johann Nicolaus.

Johann Christian (II) (1735–82), 'Milan' or 'London' Bach; sixth musical son of Johann Sebastian.

Johann Christian (III) (1743–1814), nephew of Johann Ludwig.

Johann Christoph (I) (1642–1703), brother of Johann Michael (I); father of Johann Nicolaus.

Johann Christoph (II) (1671–1721), brother of Johann Sebastian.

Johann Christoph (III) (1702–56), son of Johann Christoph (II).

Johann Christoph Friedrich (1732–95), 'Bückeburg' Bach; fifth musical son of Johann Sebastian.

Johann Ernst (1722–77), son of Johann Bernhard.

Johann Ludwig (1677–1731), uncle of Johann Christian (III).

Johann Michael (I) (1648–94), brother of Johann Christoph (I).

Johann Michael (II) (1745–1820), no relation to the J.S. Bach line.

Johann Nicolaus (1669–1753), distant cousin of Johann Sebastian.

Johann Sebastian (1685–1750), father of six musicians, including C.P.E., J.C. (II), J.C.F. and W.F.

Wilhelm Friedemann (1710–84), 'Halle' Bach; first musical son of Johann Sebastian.

Wilhelm Friedrich Ernst (1759–1845), son of Johann Christoph Friedrich.

BENDA

The Bohemian Benda family had moved to Potsdam by 1742 to work for King Frederick the Great. Germanic versions of their names were then used, but references to the Bohemian forms are still seen (including Johann Georg, originally Jan Jiří, but the Germanic form is retained here to avoid confusion with his father).

Bernardine Juliane (1752–83), daughter of František; wrote keyboard sonatas and songs; married the composer J.F. Reichardt.

František (Franz) (1709–86), son of Jan Jiří; half brother of V.I. Brixi, qv; wrote almost entirely instrumental music.

Friedrich Ludwig (1752–92), son of Georg Anton; wrote several operas, other vocal and orchestral music.

Friedrich Wilhelm Heinrich (1745–1814), son of František; wrote three operas; otherwise mainly instrumental music.

Georg Anton (1722–95), son of Jan Jiří; wrote many operas, symphonies, etc., often emotionally highly charged.

Jan Jiří (Johann Georg) (1686–1757), father of František, G.A., J.G., and Joseph.

Johann Friedrich Ernst (1749–85), son of Joseph; wrote just one set of variations for the harpsichord.

Johann Georg (1713–52), son of Jan Jiří; small output of violin and flute music.

Joseph (1724–1804), son of Jan Jiří; wrote a small quantity of violin music.

Karl Hermann Heinrich (1748–1836), son of František; wrote only one violin sonata.

Maria Carolina (1742–1820), daughter of František; wrote songs; married the composer E.W. Wolf.

BERG

There is no known family connection between any of these composers.

Alban (1885–1935), Austrian; a disciple of Schoenberg.

Carl Natanael (1879–1957), Swedish late romantic composer of five operas and five symphonies.

George (*fl.c.*1770), English, perhaps of German origin; wrote a small amount of keyboard and vocal music.

Gunnar Johnsen (b. 1909), Danish; like Alban Berg, an exponent of atonalism.

Josef (1927–71), Czech; prolific *avant-gardist* and experimenter.

BERWALD

German family who settled in Sweden.

Christian August (1798–1869), brother of Franz; wrote a handful of instrumental pieces.

Christian Friedrich Georg (1740–1825), violinist, the first Berwald to settle in Stockholm (in 1772), father of C.A. and F.A.

Franz Adolf (1796–1868), brother of C.A; an intensely original composer, Franz was virtually unknown outside Sweden until after World War II.

Johann Fredrik (1787–1861), nephew of C.F.G.

BONONCINI

Italian family.

Antonio Maria (1677–1726), son of G.M. (I); also cellist; wrote many operas.

Giovanni (1670–1747), son of G.M. (I); prolific writer of operas, cantatas, etc.

Giovanni Maria (I) (1642–78), father of the other three; composed 13 sets of published works.

Giovanni Maria (II) (1678–1753), son of G.M.

(I); wrote some vocal works; also a multi-instrumentalist.

BOURNONVILLE

French family.

Jean de (*c.*1585–1632), father of V; wrote sacred music.

Valentin de (*c.*1610–63+), son of J; also wrote sacred music, all lost.

BRANDTS BUYS

Dutch family.

Cornelis (1757–1831), not a composer himself, he instead founded a dynasty of them.

Cornelius Alexander (1812–90), son of Cornelis; father of M.A. (I), L.F., and H.F.B. Wrote some songs.

Hans Sebastiaan (1905–59), son of M.A.(II); composer, teacher, conductor, keyboardist, author of film music, etc.

Henri Francois Robert (1850–1905), son of C.A; wrote an opera; also conductor.

Jan Willem Frans (1868–1939), son of M.A.(I); wrote eight operas, instrumental and orchestral works.

Ludwig Felix (1847–1917), son of C.A; wrote vocal music; also organist and conductor.

Marius Adrianus (I) (1840–1911), son of C.A; father of J.W.F. and M.A.(II); composer, organist and arranger.

Marius Adrianus (II) (1874–1944), son of M.A.(I); wrote a handful of vocal works.

BRIXI

Czech family of three (probably distantly) related branches.

František Xaver (1732–71), son of Šimon; wrote sacred and instrumental music, including five organ concerti; also organist.

Jan Josef (?1712–62), father of V.N; one mass survives.

Jeroným – see Václav Norbert.

Šimon (1693–1735), father of F.X; wrote mainly church music; also organist.

Václav Norbert (1738–1803), son of J.J; wrote church works; also organist; signed himself by his priestly name Jeroným.

Viktorin Ignác (1716–1803), half-brother of František Benda, qv; wrote church music.

BRUNETTI

Two distinct Italian families.

Antonio (I) (*c.*1735/45–86), son of G.G; not a composer; the violinist for whom Mozart wrote several works.

Antonio (II) (?1767–1845+), ?son of Giuseppe; wrote many operas and much church music.

Giovan Gualberto (1706–87), father of Antonio (I) and Giuseppe; wrote a substantial number of operas and sacred works.

Giuseppe (*c.*1734/45–80), son of G.G; wrote two operas.

The following have no connection with the above, or with each other.

Domenico (*c.*1580–1646), composer and organist.

Gaetano (1744–98), worked in Spain mainly as a composer of chamber music and over 30 symphonies; also violinist.

Giovanni (active 1613–31), wrote vocal music.

CALEGARI

Italian family.

Antonio (1757–1828), brother of Giuseppe; prolific writer of operas and sacred music.

Giuseppe (*c.*1750–1812), brother of Antonio; wrote vocal music; also cellist and impresario.

Luigi Antonio (*c.*1780–1849), ?son of Giuseppe; nephew of Antonio; wrote 10 operas and some instrumental works.

No known connection with the above:

Francesco Antonio (1656–1742), worked in Venice and Padua; wrote much sacred music.

Isobella Leonarda (1620–1700), nun; wrote mainly vocal music, but also some instrumental.

Maria Cattarina (1644–?62), nun; wrote some vocal pieces, all lost; also singer and organist.

CANNABICH

German family.

Carl Konrad (1771–1806), son of J.C.I.B; prolific composer, but less so than his father.

Johann Christian Innocenz Bonaventura (1731–98), son of M.F., father of C.K; prominent in the 'Mannheim School'; wrote many ballets, symphonies, chamber works, etc.

Martin Friedrich (?1675–1759), father of J.C.I.B; flautist and composer for his instrument.

CARDON

French family.

Jean-Baptiste (1760–1803), son of J.-G; also harpist.

Jean-Guillain (also Jean-Baptiste) (1732–88), father of J.-B. and L.S; wrote small instrumental music, and vocal works; also violinist.

Louis Stanislas (?–1797), son of J.-G; ?composer; violinist.

No connection with the above:

CARDONNE, Jean-Baptiste (also Philibert) (1730–92), wrote operas, ballets and some instrumental works.

CASADESUS

French family of Catalan origin.

Francis Louis (1870–1954), son of Luis; pupil of César Franck; wrote operas and some orchestral works; also collaborated with H.G. and M.R.M. in faking works by 'C.P.E. Bach', 'J.C. Bach', 'Mozart' and 'Handel'.

Gaby (Gabrielle) (b. 1901), wife of R.M; pianist; not a composer.

Henri Gustave (1879–1947), son of Luis; wrote operettas; also violist.

Jean-Claude (b. 1935), grandson of H.G; wrote stage and film music.

Jean Michel (1927–72), son of R.M. and Gaby; died in a road accident; pianist, not a composer.

Luis (1850–1919), father of F.L., H.G., M.L.L., M.R.M., and R.-G; printer and amateur musician.

Marcel Louis Lucien (1882–1914), son of Luis; killed in World War I; cellist; not a composer.

Marius Robert Max (1892–1981), son of Luis; wrote instrumental music; also a violinist.

Robert-Guillaume (1878–1940), son of Luis; wrote songs and operettas; also actor.

Robert Marcel (1899–1972), nephew of F.L; husband of Gaby; wrote instrumental works mainly for piano, also six symphonies; famous as a pianist.

CLEMENTI

Three separate composers of similar name.

Aldo (b. 1925), Italian composer mainly of orchestral music.

Johann Georg (*c.*1710–94), correctly Clement or Clemens. German composer of masses and other sacred music.

Muzio (1752–1832), Italian/English founder (with Longman) then figurehead of the famous London instrument makers and publishers. Prolific composer chiefly for the piano.

ENGELMANN

German father and son.

Georg (I) (*c.*1575–1632), wrote mainly vocal music; also writer and organist.

Georg (II) (1601/5–63), son of above; wrote part songs; also organist.

ERKEL

Hungarian family.

Elek (1843–93), son of F; wrote operettas, etc; also conductor and drummer.

Ferenc (1810–93), father of E., G., L., and S; wrote many works in all forms; also conductor and pianist.

Gyula (1842–1909), son of F, similar career to that of his father, but with a smaller output.

László (1844–96), son of F; piano teacher of the young Bartók; not a composer.

Sándor (1846–1900), son of F; composed little, but collaborated with his father on operas; also conductor and timpanist.

FABER

German composers; no link is known between them.

Benedikt (1573–1634), wrote mainly sacred music.

Gregor (*c.*1520–54), theorist.

Heinrich (*c.*1500–52), theorist; also possibly a singer.

Johann Christoph (early 18th century), wrote cryptographic music in which, for instance, notes stood for numbers or letters.

Nicolaus (*fl.c.*1516), Tyrolean composer, sometimes given as Nikolaus Georg Fabri.

Stephen (*c.*1580–1632), composer and organist.

FABRI

A widespread name, sometimes confused with FABER. Only two of these figures are related.

Annibile Pio ('Balino') (1697–1760), Italian; there is a small collection of unpublished music; also tenor.

Martinus (*fl.c.*1400), ?Flemish, wrote secular vocal music.

Stefano (I) (?–1609), Italian; father of Stefano (II); wrote two vocal pieces.

Stefano (II) (*c.*1606–58), son of Stefano (I); wrote sacred vocal pieces.

Thomas (*fl.c.*1400–12), French/Flemish; wrote sacred vocal music.

FRANCK

There is no known connection between any of these figures.

César-Auguste-Jean-Guillaume-Hubert (1822–90), famous Belgian/French composer.

Eduard (1817–93), German; wrote some piano pieces; also pianist and teacher.

Johann Wolfgang (1644–*c.*1710), German composer of operas, cantatas and other vocal pieces.

Melchior (*c.*1579–1639), German; wrote much vocal and some instrumental music.

Michael (1609–77), German composer of sacred songs; also poet.

GRAF

German family.

Christian Ernst (Graaf) (1723–1804), son of J; wrote mainly symphonies and other instrumental works; also violinist. He added the second 'a' to his name when he went to work in The Hague in 1762.

Friedrich Hartmann (1727–95), son of J; wrote chiefly chamber music but also some orchestral and choral; also flautist. He worked for a time with his brother in The Hague but apparently did not modify the spelling of his name.

Johann (Graf(f)) (1684–1750), father of both the above; wrote some string works; also violinist.

GRÄFE, Johann Friedrich (1711–87), German composer of one opera, songs etc; also poet. No connection with the above family.

HAYDN

Austrian brothers.

Franz Joseph (1732–1809), worked in Esterházy; extremely prolific.

Johann Michael (1737–1806), worked in Salzburg with Mozart and Mozart's father; also prolific, but the proportion of sacred music is higher than with F.J.

(Joseph HAYDA was a composer and organist in Vienna in the late 18th century, but his precise dates are not known. He was an admirer of the music of both Haydn brothers, and a church work by Hayda was so similar in style to Joseph Haydn's work as to be published mistakenly as by Haydn as recently as 1959.)

HALFFTER

Spanish family of German origin.

Cristobal (b. 1930), nephew of E. and R; wrote much orchestral music; recent works employ electronics.

Ernesto (b. 1905), brother of R; wrote ballets, orchestral, vocal, instrumental and film music.

Rodolfo (b. 1900), brother of E; similar output to E., but one opera and no film music.

IVES

Charles Edward (1874–1954), American composer of highly original experimental music.

Simon (I) (1600–62), English; ?father of Simon (II); much instrumental and some vocal music.

Simon (II) (*c.*1626–before 62), English; ?son of Simon (I); wrote a handful of pieces for lyre-viol.

KLEINKNECHT

German family.

Jakob Friedrich (1722–94), brother of J.W; wrote much instrumental music; also flautist.

Johann Wolfgang (1715–86), brother of J.F; wrote some instrumental and orchestral music; also violinist.

(J.F. and J.W.'s father had another son, Johann Stephan (1731–91), and J.F. had a son, Christian Ludwig (1765–94), but neither was a composer.)

LOEILLET

Flemish family; no connection with the French Lully family.

Jean-Baptiste (I), 'John of London', sometimes called 'Lully' (1680–1730), brother of Jacques; cousin of J.-B. (II); wrote harpsichord, flute and recorder music, etc.

Jean-Baptiste (II), 'de Gant' (i.e. Ghent) (1688–

c.1720), cousin of Jacques and J.-B. (I); wrote mostly recorder music.

Jacques (Jacob) (1685–1748), brother of J.B.(I); cousin of J.-B (II); wrote flute and oboe music.

(Pieter Loeillet (1651–1735) was J.-B.(II)'s father and J.-B.(I) and Jacques's uncle; and Etienne Joseph (1715–97) was Pieter's second son. Pierre (1674–1743) was the eldest brother of J.-B. (I) and Jacques. All were instrumentalists, not composers.)

LULLY

French family.

Jean-Baptiste (I) (1632–87), father of all the others; wrote many operas and other stage works.

Jean-Baptiste (II) (1665–1743), son of J.-B. (I); wrote a small number of occasional works.

Jean-Louis (1667–88), son of J.-B. (I); collaborated with Louis in some works.

Louis (1664–1734), son of J.-B. (I); wrote stage works.

MOZART

Austrian father, son and grandson.

Franz Xaver (later known as Wolfgang Amadeus) (1791–1844), son of W.A; wrote much piano music; also vocal pieces, etc; also pianist.

Johann Georg Leopold (1719–87), father of W.A; wrote much church and other music, including at least 65 symphonies; also violinist and theorist.

Wolfgang Amadeus (christened Johannes Chrysostomus Wolfgangus Theophilus) (1756–91), son of J.G; father of F.X.

NAUMANN

German family.

Emil (1827–88), grandson of J.G; wrote vocal and some instrumental pieces.

Johann Gottlieb (1741–1801), grandfather of E., and K.E; wrote mainly vocal works, but also 12 pieces for the glass harmonica; it is said that the constant playing of this instrument caused a disorder of his nervous system. Also conductor.

Karl Ernst (1832–1910), grandson of J.G; wrote chamber and instrumental works, also sacred pieces; also conductor.

Siegfried (b. 1919), Swedish composer of advanced music; no known connection with the German family.

NEUSIDLER

German family.

Conrad (1541–1604+), son of Hans; wrote a few lute pieces; also lutenist.

Hans (*c*.1508/9–63), father of C. and M; wrote much lute music; also lutenist and lute-maker.

Melchior (1531–90), son of Hans; wrote much lute music; also lutenist.

NIELSEN

No known connection between any of the following:

Carl August (1865–1931), the greatest Danish composer.

Carl Henrik Ludolf (1876–1939), Danish composer of ballets, operas, symphonies, etc.

Hans (*c*.1580–1626+), Danish madrigalist and lutenist.

Ludwig (b. 1906), Norwegian; wrote much sacred and organ music; also conductor and organist.

Riccardo (b. 1908), Italian atonalist.

Tage (b. 1929), Danish *avant-gardist*; wrote instrumental music and some songs.

PERGAMENT

Moses (1893–1977), Finnish/Swedish; wrote works of most types, often concentrating on Jewish subjects.

Ruvim (1906–65), Russian composer of operas, choral works, etc., some with Karelian folk-music links.

PEZ

Johann Christoph (1664–1716), German chiefly vocal composer; also singer and lutenist.

PEZEL

Johann Christoph (1639–94), German composer of much municipal tower music; also brass player.

PEZOLD

Christian (1677–1733), German keyboard composer; also organist.

SÆVERUD

Harald Sigurd Johan (b. 1897), Norwegian,

father of Ketil; prolific composer of orchestral music.

Ketil (b. 1939), son of Harald; instrumental works; also organist; violist. Changed his name to HVOSLEF in 1980.

SCHMIDT/ SCHMITT/SMITH

In the 18th century, as now, these names give a dire problem of identification. Many alternative forenames are given and variants of the family name abound, but the following can be identified with reasonable certainty.

SCHMID, Balthasar (1705–49), German; father of J.M. Schmidt; wrote mainly keyboard music; also printer.

SCHMID, Ferdinand (*c.*1694–1756), Austrian; wrote sacred works.

SCHMID, Johann Michael (*c.*1720–92), German; wrote mainly church works.

SCHMIDT, Johann Christoph (I) (1664–1728), German vocal composer.

SCHMIDT, Johann Christoph (II) = J.C. Smith.

SCHMIDT, Johann Michael (1741–93), German composer; son of B. Schmid.

SCHMIDT, Johann Philipp Samuel (1779–1853), German opera and song composer; also pianist.

SCHMIEDT, Siegfried (*c.*1756–99), German vocal and keyboard composer; worked with the publishers Breitkopf und Härtel in Leipzig.

SMITH, John Christopher (originally Johann Christoph Schmidt) (1712–95), German composer and Handel's amanuensis; wrote some instrumental and vocal music.

SMITH, John Stafford (1750–1836), English composer of vocal music.

SCHMITT, Joseph (1734–91), German; wrote many orchestral and other works; worked in the Netherlands as a music publisher.

SMITH, Robert Archibald (1780–1829), Scottish writer of vocal music; also instrumentalist.

SMITH, Theodore (*c.*1740–*c.*1810), ?German, active in London; much instrumental and some vocal music. (Perhaps equates with Theodor Schmidt, active in Paris *c.*1765).

SCHUBERT

Austrian family.

Ferdinand Lukas (1794–1859), brother of F.P; wrote vocal music.

Franz Peter (1797–1828), brother of above; wrote an incredible quantity of music of all kinds.

SCHUBERT

Dresden family.

Franz (1808–78), son of F.A; wrote violin music; also violinist.

Franz Anton (1768–1827), father of Franz; wrote chiefly sacred music; also double bass player.

SCHUBERT

Miscellaneous.

Johann Friedrich (1770–1811), German composer of one opera, a concerto, etc; also violinist.

Joseph (1757–1837), German composer of four operas and instrumental works; also instrumentalist.

Louis (1828–84), German composer of operettas, etc; also violinist.

Manfred (b. 1937), German atonalist.

SCHUMANN

German composers; only two are related.

Clara Josephine (1819–96), née Wieck; wife of R.A; wrote a piano concerto and many other piano works and songs; famous as a pianist.

Frederic Theodor (*fl.* 1760–80); wrote chamber music and songs; also guitarist.

Georg Alfred (1866–1952), orchestral, chamber and choral music composer; also instrumentalist and conductor.

Robert Alexander (1810–56), husband of Clara; wrote piano music, Lieder, orchestral and chamber music; also pianist.

STAMITZ

Bohemian family, originally Stamic.

Anton Thadäus Johann Nepomuk (1750–?1809), son of J.V.A., became prominent in Paris after moving from Mannheim in 1770; composed chiefly chamber works and concerti; also violinist, violist.

Carl Philip (1745–1801), son of J.V.A., important in the 'second generation' Mannheim School; prolific writer of symphonies, concerti, chamber works (his two operas are lost); also

The Strauss Brothers, a woodcut caricature. Left to right: Josef, Johann and Eduard. (Österreichische Nationalbibliothek)

violinist, violist.

Jan Václav Antonín (Johann Wenzel Anton) (1717–57), father of Anton and Carl; co-founder (with Holzbauer and Richter) of the so-called Mannheim School; important early symphonist; wrote also sacred music; also violinist.

František (late 18th century), Czech cornist who wrote for his instrument; no apparent connection with the above family.

STRAUS

Oscar (1870–1954), Austrian; wrote operettas, film music, etc; also conductor.

STRAUSS

Austrian family.

Eduard (1835–1916), son of J.B.(I); father of J.M.E; wrote chiefly waltzes and polkas.

Johann Baptist (I) (1804–49), father of J.B.(II), Josef and Eduard; wrote waltzes, etc; also violinist.

Johann Baptist (II) (1825–99), son of J.B.(I); 'The Waltz King'; however, he wrote much else: stage works, other dances, marches, concert pieces; also violinist.

Johann Maria Eduard (1866–1939), son of Eduard; wrote operetta; also conductor. His son Eduard Leopold Maria (1910–69) conducted but did not compose.

Josef (or Joseph) (1827–70), son of J. B. (I); wrote dance music.

Little or no connection with the above family:

Christoph (*c.*1575/80–1631), Austrian choral composer and organist.

Franz Joseph (1822–1905), German; father of R.G; wrote orchestral works; also cornist.

Isaac (1806–88), French; his waltzes and other dances were sometimes published as being by 'Strauss', without the first name; also violinist.

Richard Georg (1864–1949), German; son of F.J; wrote operas, orchestral music, etc.

TAGLIETTI

Giulio (*c.*1660–1718), Italian; ?brother of Luigi; wrote concerti grossi, sonatas; also violinist.

Luigi (1668–1715), Italian; ?brother of Giulio; wrote concerti grossi, sonatas; also tromba marina player.

TCHAIKOVSKY

The following are unconnected:

André (1935–82), Polish pianist and composer.

Boris Alexandrovich (b. 1925) (name often spelled Chaykovsky), Russian; wrote chiefly orchestral and chamber music; also pianist.

Pyotr Ilyich (1840–93), Russian. Possibly the most popular composer of all time.

WAGNER

German family.

Siegfried Helferich Richard (1869–1930), son of W.R; father of Wieland Adolf Gottfried (1917–66) and Wolfgang Manfred Martin (b. 1919), both of whom were producers at Bayreuth.

Wilhelm Richard (1813–83), German; father of S.H.R; wrote music dramas, operas, etc.

No known connection with the above family:

Georg Gottfried (1698–1756), German composer of sacred and instrumental music; also violinist.

Gotthard (1678–1738), German composer of sacred music.

Joseph Franz (1856–1908), Austrian; wrote marches (including *Under the Double Eagle*), dances; also bandmaster.

Karl Jacob (1772–1822), German; wrote orchestral works, operas, etc; also oboist.

WEBER

German family.

Carl Maria Friedrich Ernst (1786–1826), son of F.A; wrote *Der Freischütz, Oberon* and other operas, much other music; also conductor and pianist.

Franz Anton (1734–1812), father of C.M., F.E.K., and F.S.J; wrote Lieder; also string player.

Franz Edmund Kaspar Johann Nepomuk Joseph Maria (1766–1828), son of F.A; wrote two operas, orchestral and instrumental music.

Fridolin Stephan Johann Nepomuk Andreas Maria (1761–1833), son of F.A; wrote minor works; also violinist.

No known connection with the above:

Alain (b. 1930), French; pupil of Messiaen.

Bedřich Diviš (1766–1842), Bohemian; wrote vocal and instrumental pieces.

Ben (b. 1916), American atonalist.

Bernhard Anselm (1764–1821), German; wrote stage music; also pianist and conductor.

Bernhard Christian (1712–58), German organist and composer for his instrument.

Georg (*c.*1610–53), German; wrote chiefly sacred music; also singer.

Gustav (1845–87), Swiss; small output of choral and instrumental pieces; also organist, conductor and writer.

Jacob Gottfried (1779–1839), German; wrote church works and some instrumental pieces.

Joseph Miroslav (1854–1906), Czech; wrote stage works, a violin concerto, etc; also violinist.

Ludwig (1891–1947), German, wrote instrumental and stage music.

PEN NAMES AND PET NAMES

There are many reasons why a composer should come to be known by a name other than his own. For practical reasons he might choose to make his name more understandable to his new countrymen when he emigrates; alternatively, if he is English, he might be ashamed that his name betrays his origin in a country often considered to be 'without music', so he will choose a foreign name — Italian is favourite.

Composers who are performers, or vice versa, may wish to assume a different identity for each activity, and some composers who are authors publish their books under an assumed name. Others simply shorten or otherwise modify their real names. Those 18th-century Italians who entered the Arcadian Academy were given florid Arcadian names, a procedure far more common than our selective list indicates.

Most picturesque and helpful are the nicknames. They might refer to a composer's place of origin, a physical characteristic, or his assumed place in music. One wonders whether the name given to il Divino Boemo was sincere flattery or an expedient device.

What follows is merely a small sample of composers' false names. Some nicknames have been omitted deliberately because, in the authors' view, they should now be forgotten — preferably, they should never have been dreamed up in the first place.

Adams, Stephen, pseudonym of the composer of *The Holy City*, Michael Maybrick.

Arcimelo, Arcadian name of Arcangelo Corelli.

Arma, Paul, pseudonym of the Hungarian-born French pianist and composer Imre Weisshaus, a pupil of Bartók.

Belgian Orpheus, The, admiring nickname of Roland de Lassus (Orlando di Lasso), born in the Flemish town of Mons in 1532.

Ben Haim, Paul, adopted name of Paul Frankenberger (b. 1897), when he fled from Germany to Tel Aviv in 1933.

Berlijn, Anton, adopted name of Aron Wolf (1817–70), Dutch composer.

Berlin Bach, The, nickname of C.P.E. Bach, who worked there; he also worked in Hamburg, with a similar result.

Berlin, Irving. When Israel Baline, Russian-born song writer, composed the song *Marie from Sunny Italy* in 1907, a New York publisher misprinted his name as 'Berlin'. The change of forename followed.

Bounce, Benjamin, a pseudonym adopted by Henry Carey, 18th-century English composer, for his burlesque opera *Chrononhotouthologos* in London in 1734. For a set of cantatas he chose the name of Sigr. Carini.

Botelero, Enrique, pseudo-Italian name used by the 17th-century English composer Henry Butler.

Buranello, Il, nickname of Baldassare Galuppi, who was born on the Venetian island or Burano.

Caesar, William, pseudonym of William Smegergill, 17th-century English composer, adopted perhaps in honour of the dean of Ely cathedral where he sang as a boy.

Capilupi, Gemignano, the assumed name of the early 17th-century Italian composer G. Lovetti.

Carini — see Bounce.

Caro Sassone, Il, name given by admiring Italians to the German Johann Adolf Hasse.

Clemens non Papa. Confused stories surround this nickname, given to Jacob Clement, the Flemish composer, in 1545. It was said that its use prevented confusion with a Flemish poet, Clemens Papa, but that poet apparently was called Jacobus Papa. Just as likely is its adoption as a denial of a paternity suit.

Copland, Aaron, is the correct name of the American composer of *Rodeo, Billy the Kid* and other favourites, but his father, who emigrated from Poland to New York in the 1870s, changed his name from Kaplan.

Coprario or Coperario, Giovanni, name adopted by the London composer John Cooper (or Cowper), possibly after a visit to Italy.

Divino Boemo, Il, (the divine Bohemian), nickname of Josef Mysliveček, Bohemian composer also known as Josef Venatorino — anything, it seems, to relieve his Italian and Austrian colleagues from wrestling with his real name.

Duke, Vernon, adopted name of Vladimir Alexandrovich Dukelsky, American composer of Russian birth who fled from the Revolution.

Dvorsky, Michael, composing pseudonym of Josef Hofmann, the Polish-born American pianist.

English Bach, The, nickname (to distinguish him from other members of the dynasty) of Johann Christian Bach. Also called the London Bach and, because of his early sojourn there, the Milan(ese) Bach.

Father of Swedish Music, The, not wholly accurate nickname of Johan Helmich Roman.

Foss, Lukas, adopted name of Lukas Fuch, German-born composer and pianist who emigrated to America in 1937 and took American nationality.

Fürstenberger, von, pseudonym (together with 'Zeuner') of the Italian pianist Luigi Gordigiani, who composed under these names.

German, Sir Edward. Edward German Jones, in order to avoid confusion with Edward Jones, another student, became known as Jones Edward German, later dropping the first name.

Gore, Gerald Wilfring, one of eight pseudonyms (this one strictly anagramatic) of the American composer Wallingford Riegger, adopted when writing commercial arrangements.

Halévy, J.F.F.E. The family name was changed from Levy in 1807 when the composer was eight years old.

Notes on Composers

Hammer, F.X., translated name of the German or Bohemian 18th-century composer Franz (František) Xaver Marteau.

Hardelot, Guy d', adopted name of Helen Rhodes, French composer. She took 'Hardelot' from her birthplace and added it to her maiden name.

Hervé, pseudonym of French composer and singer Florimond Ronger.

Hopkins, Antony, adopted name of Antony Reynolds, English composer, broadcaster and author.

Hunchback of Arras, The, nickname given during his lifetime to Adam de la Hale. He did indeed come from Arras (in about 1250), but the origin of the rest of his name is a mystery: his back was straight.

Imareta, Tirso, anagramatic pseudonym of the Spanish author, poet and composer Tomás Iriarte, whose surviving music is limited to ten short orchestral works. He is perhaps the only composer to have been born (in 1750) in the Canary Islands.

Ireland, Francis, pseudonym, when a composer, of the Irish 18th-century writer of catches and glees. When a violinist he used his own name: Francis Hutcheson.

Joncières, Victorin de, pseudonym of Félix Ludger Rossignol, 19th-century French critic and composer.

Kéler-Béla (full given names: Béla Albrecht Pál), original and ethnically correct form (with family name first) of the Hungarian composer/conductor also called Adalbert Paul von Keler.

Klenovsky, Paul, pseudonym adopted by the English conductor Sir Henry Joseph Wood when orchestrating Bach's Toccata and Fugue in D minor.

Lara, Adelina de, romantic pseudonym of Lottie Tilbury, English pupil of Clara Schumann.

Linhauna, Jaakko Armas, Finnish composer who changed his name in 1935 from J.A. Lindemann.

Linko, Ernst Frederik, Finnish composer who changed his name in 1906 from E.F. Lindroth.

Linnala, Eino Mauro Aleksanteri, assumed name of Eino Borgmann, 20th-century Finnish composer.

London Bach — see English Bach.

Longstrides, nickname of Johannes Bedyngham (and variants), 15th-century English sacred music composer, presumably of ample gait.

Lourdault, a nickname given to Jean Braconnier, 16th-century French composer. The name was no disparagement (it means 'clod') but merely refers to a song he was wont to sing.

Mathis, G.S., pseudonym of the Hungarian-born British composer Mátyás Seiber which he used when writing for accordion.

Meyerbeer, Giacomo, assumed name of Jakob Liebmann Meyer Beer, famous German opera composer.

Milan Bach — see English Bach.

Music's Prophet, an appropriate name given to Claudio Monteverdi, from whom sprang opera and other vital forms.

Napoleon of Music, The, a name given to the composer whose music conquered Europe: Rossini.

Nipredi, anagramatic form of T. Pedrini, ?Italian composer at the Chinese emperor's court in the 18th century.

Novello, Ivor, assumed name of David Ivor Davies, Welsh composer of the song known as *Keep the Home Fires Burning* (real title: *Till the Boys Come Home*) and many successful stage musicals. Novello was his mother's maiden name.

O'Byrne, Dermot, pseudonym assumed by the Celtophile English composer Sir Arnold Bax for his novels published in Dublin.

Old Nosey, nickname given to the centenarian Italian composer Giacobbe Basevi Cervetto during his London days, i.e. the last 45 years of his life, to 1783.

Ostern, Claudianus, Arcadian name of the 18th-century Moravian composer Edmund Pascha ('Ostern' and 'Pascha' both mean 'Easter').

Pinto, George Frederick, pseudonym of G.F. Sanders, English piano prodigy and composer who died at the age of 20. He took his mother's maiden name.

Prince of Music, The, the name engraved upon the lid of the coffin of Palestrina.

Red Priest, The, nickname of the red-haired Vivaldi, an ordained priest who never said mass.

Regnal, Frédéric, backwards form of Frédéric

d'Erlanger's family name, a naturalized English composer of German/American parentage.

Riadis, Emilios, simplified name of the Greek composer Eleftheriadis Khu.

Rudhyar, Dane, Hindu name adopted by the French composer and astrologer Daniel Chennevière when he took American citizenship in 1926.

St Gilles, pseudonym used by Jean Baptiste Andreas André, 19th-century pianist and composer, son of the famous publisher J.A. André.

Senez, Camille de, pseudonym adopted by the Hungarian composer Gabriel von Wayditch, writer of 14 operas.

Sharm, anagramatic form of the surname of John Marsh, English 18th-century composer.

Signor Crescendo, an affectionate nickname for one of the foremost exponents of the orchestral 'steamroller', Rossini. However, the crescendo was used at least a century before Rossini employed it.

Siklós, Albert, changed his name from Schönwald in 1910.

Sommer, Hans, pseudonym of the German composer Hans Friedrich August Zincken who also used a near-backward form of his name: Neckniz.

Strauss of Italy, a name dreamed up by envious Italians for Respighi.

Strinfalico, Eterio, name adopted by Alessandro Marcello upon entry to the Arcadian Academy.

Stuart, Leslie, assumed name of Thomas Augustine Barrett, English musical comedy writer. His best known show was *Floradora* (1899), and his most widely-sung song *Soldiers of the Queen* (1895).

Suppé, Franz von, simplified name of Francesco Ezechiele Ermenegildo Cavaliere Suppé Demelli, composer of many light operas.

Sweetest Swan, The, nickname of Luca Marenzio, Italian madrigalist of the late 16th century. This name and another, 'The Divine Composer', were applied to Marenzio apparently on the strength of his earlier works. The later ones were less agreeable because more exploratory in manner.

Thorn, or Thorne, Edgar, pseudonym used for his early publications by Edward MacDowell, American composer who died insane in 1908.

Venatorini, J. — see Divino Boemo, Il.

Vincent, Heinrich Joseph, pseudonym of H.J. Wunzenhörlein, 19th-century Viennese opera composer.

Warlock, Peter, pseudonym of the English composer Philip Arnold Heseltine, who committed suicide in 1930.

Wundermann, Der. If Saint-Germain's claims are true (see p 90), he was indeed a wonderful man. Perhaps, like so much else, the name came out of Saint-Germain's imagination.

Wynne, David, prolific Welsh composer who uses the simplified form of his name David Wynne Thomas.

Zeuner — see Fürstenberger.

Multiple pseudonyms seem to be a 19th-century phenomenon amongst musicians. The English composer Charles Arthur Rawlings (1857–1919) used at least 62, his brother Alfred William Rawlings (1860–1924) used at least 28, and the American gospel hymn composer Philip Paul Bliss (1838–76) hid his light, it is said, under about 60, but since he was the compiler (with Ira David Sankey) of a volume of hymns by various composers there may be confusion between what he composed and what he compiled.

Sunday Composers

When the desire to compose first hits him, no composer knows whether he possesses that divine flair that will take him to the top of the profession. Yet without it, no matter how strong the inner compulsion to compose, he will starve. Little wonder that most take up a stand-by profession to fall back on if their composing lets them down. In many cases this stand-by takes over, leaving composing as a spare-time occupation.

What follows is only a selection from the list of countless hopefuls for whom composing was an absorbing hobby — and a paying one only in a minority of cases. Priests and cantors are omitted because the dispensing of music was in most cases an integral part of their duties.

Belcher, Supply (1752–1836), American innkeeper who wrote an opera titled *The Harmony of Maine*, produced in Boston in 1794.

Berners, Lord (Gerald Hugh Tyrwhitt-Wilson) (1883–1950), composer of the ballet *The Triumph of Neptune* (1926) and many parodic and ironic works (e.g. *Du bist wie eine Blume*, a song dedicated to a pig), was also diplomat, painter, novelist and illustrator.

Notes on Composers

Billings, William (1746–1800), one of the earliest American composers; a song-writer and lyricist noted for his fugal hymn tunes, he was by trade a tanner.

Bittner, Julius (1874–1939), Austrian pupil of conductor Bruno Walter, and opera composer; a lawyer by profession.

Borodin, Alexander Porphyrevich (1833–97), world-renowned composer of *Prince Igor* (1890) and other works, was in fact an amateur musician, his time being absorbed largely by research into chemistry for a Russian university.

Bowles, Paul Frederick (b. 1910), American composer, linguist, and author of novels and short stories.

Brühl, Hans Mortiz, Count Brühl of Martinskirche, was the Saxon ambassador to London from 1764 and interested himself in the musical events of the capital. He was friendly with Clementi and Schroeter, knew Abel and J.C. Bach and doubtless met Mozart and Haydn on their respective visits to London. Brühl was also an astronomer. He involved himself in improvements to the piano and composed sonatas for it, with and without violin.

Burghersh, Lord John Fane (1784–1859), 11th Earl of Westmorland. He had a distinguished political and military career as Member of Parliament (1806–16), army officer, serving in the Napoleonic wars and rising to the rank of general, British envoy in Florence (1814–30), Berlin (1841–51), and at the Viennese Imperial Court (1851–5). He founded the Royal Academy of Music, London, in 1822, served as its president from then until his death, and was created earl in 1841. His compositions, reported to be of little worth, include seven operas, three symphonies, a mass and other sacred music.

Butler, Samuel (1835–1902), the famous English author, so admired the music of Handel that he was encouraged to compose in the same style. Butler's cantatas *Narcissus* (1886) and *Ulysses* (1902) faithfully copy the style of a composer who died three-quarters of a century before he was born!

Caffi, Francesco, born 1778, became a magistrate in Venice and a judge in Milan, retiring in 1850. As a hobby he wrote vocal works and an oboe concerto as well as several scholarly books on the history of Venetian music.

Cage, John (b. 1912), American experimental composer, has so many other activities that he might be described as an all-rounder: commercial artist, critic, teacher, poet, writer, lecturer, etc.

Musician and astronomer Sir William Herschel, with his plan of Uranus and its satellites. (Mary Evans Picture Library)

Campian, Thomas (1567–1620), English song-writer, also poet, lawyer and physician.

Cui, César Antonovich (1835–1918), a general in the Russian army; also a critic and writer on music.

Dahl, Ingolf (1912–70), German-born American composer, writer and teacher. His non-composing musical activities were so time-consuming that his actual musical output is quite small.

Dibdin, Charles (1745–1814), English composer of numerous operas; also theatrical manager, publisher, author, actor and singer.

Herschel, Wilhelm Friedrich (1738–1822), the famous German astronomer who discovered the Martian polar caps and the planet Uranus (which he called 'Georgium Sidus'), and who postulated the theory that some so-called 'variable' stars are in fact double stars (a theory since proved correct). It was also a talented composer and organist.

Hoffmann, Ernst Theodor Wilhelm (1776–1822), the German writer immortalized in Offenbach's opera *The Tales of Hoffmann* (1881), was a theatrical manager, lawyer, artist and municipal officer. He revered Mozart, adopting the name Amadeus to replace Wilhelm, and he composed instrumental music, several stage works, a symphony, etc.

Ireland, Francis (real name: F. Hutcheson) (1721–80), Irish doctor and glee composer.

Ives, Charles (1874–1953), American experimental composer who was also a successful businessman until ill health in his late 40s dictated a less strenuous career.

Kryzhanovsky, Ivan Ivanovich (1867–1924), Russian army doctor and composer.

Lichtenthal, Peter (1780–1853), Austrian doctor and amateur composer. In 1826 he published a four-volume dictionary of music in Milan.

Moore, Patrick (b. 1923), English broadcaster and amateur astronomer, composer of two operas.

Morgan, Justin (1747–98), American full-time horse breeder, also teacher, innkeeper and composer.

Mussorgsky, Modest Petrovich (1839–81), Russian composer of *Boris Godunov* (final version 1873) and *Pictures from an Exhibition* (1874), was an army officer and later a civil servant.

Netherclift, Joseph (1792–1863), owned a London printing establishment and was one of the 19th century's most noted calligraphic experts. In his spare time he composed madrigals and sacred music.

Rimsky-Korsakov, Nikolay Andreyevich (1844–1908), Russian naval officer before turning to music full time.

Rousseau, Jean-Jacques (1712–78), the Swiss author, philosopher, religious and political thinker, was an active composer in France. His best-known work is the one-act 'Intermède' *Le devin de village* (1752).

Roussel, Albert Charles Paul Marie (1869–1937), was undecided when young whether to go for a career in music or in the navy. At first the sea won: he became a cadet at 18 in 1887 and was later commissioned, but he left the navy in 1894, intending to give his life to composing. Despite a doubtful health record, he joined the French army in 1915 as an artillery officer. After the war he became a leading composer and music educationalist until his death.

Teplov, Grigorii Nikolayevich (1719–89), the composer of the first Russian 'art songs'; also a prominent politician.

Xenakis, Iannis (b. 1922), Romanian-born Greek composer, assistant during the 1950s to Le Corbusier, the architect.

IV

Composers of Note

THE NOTABLE AND THE NOTORIOUS

Ultimately it is their music that counts more than their personal oddities, but nonetheless the appearance, strange habits and eccentricities of composers, just as of other personalities, are of abiding interest to the curious. Some stories concerning composers' appearances are not necessarily true. **Handel** became exceptionally obese in later life — this we know from contemporary accounts, from portraits and from the statue in Westminster Abbey, London; but the story that **Domenico Scarlatti** became so fat that he could not play cross-hands passages on the harpsichord (thus explaining why his late sonatas contain no such passages) is mere rumour and is not supported by any evidence. **Beethoven** and **Haydn** were reputed to be ugly — one cannot place much reliance upon portraits, whose painters have been known to flatter their subjects — and Stravinsky is reported to have described the well-built and morose **Rachmaninoff** as 'a six-foot scowl', which seems to receive photographic support. Death-masks of composers do not reveal their appearance in life, for face muscles sag under the weight of clay and the 'windows of the soul', the eyes, are closed.

Chopin's death mask cast in bronze. (Museum of the Frédéric Chopin Society, Warsaw)

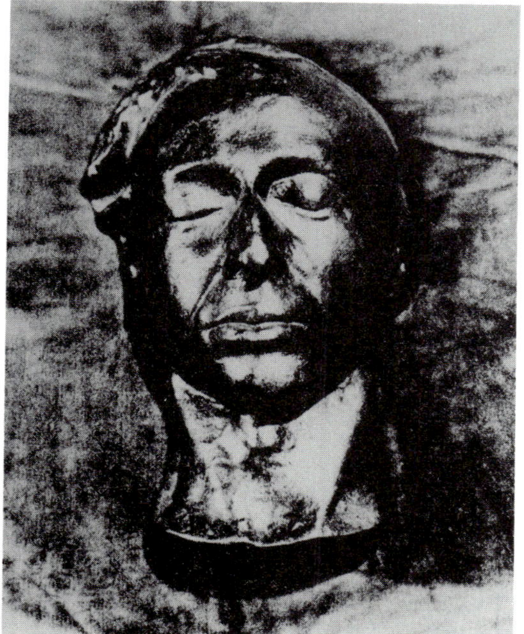

Wagner as seen by Spy. (BBC Hulton Picture Library)

Sergei Rachmaninoff in 1924. (BBC Hulton Picture Library)

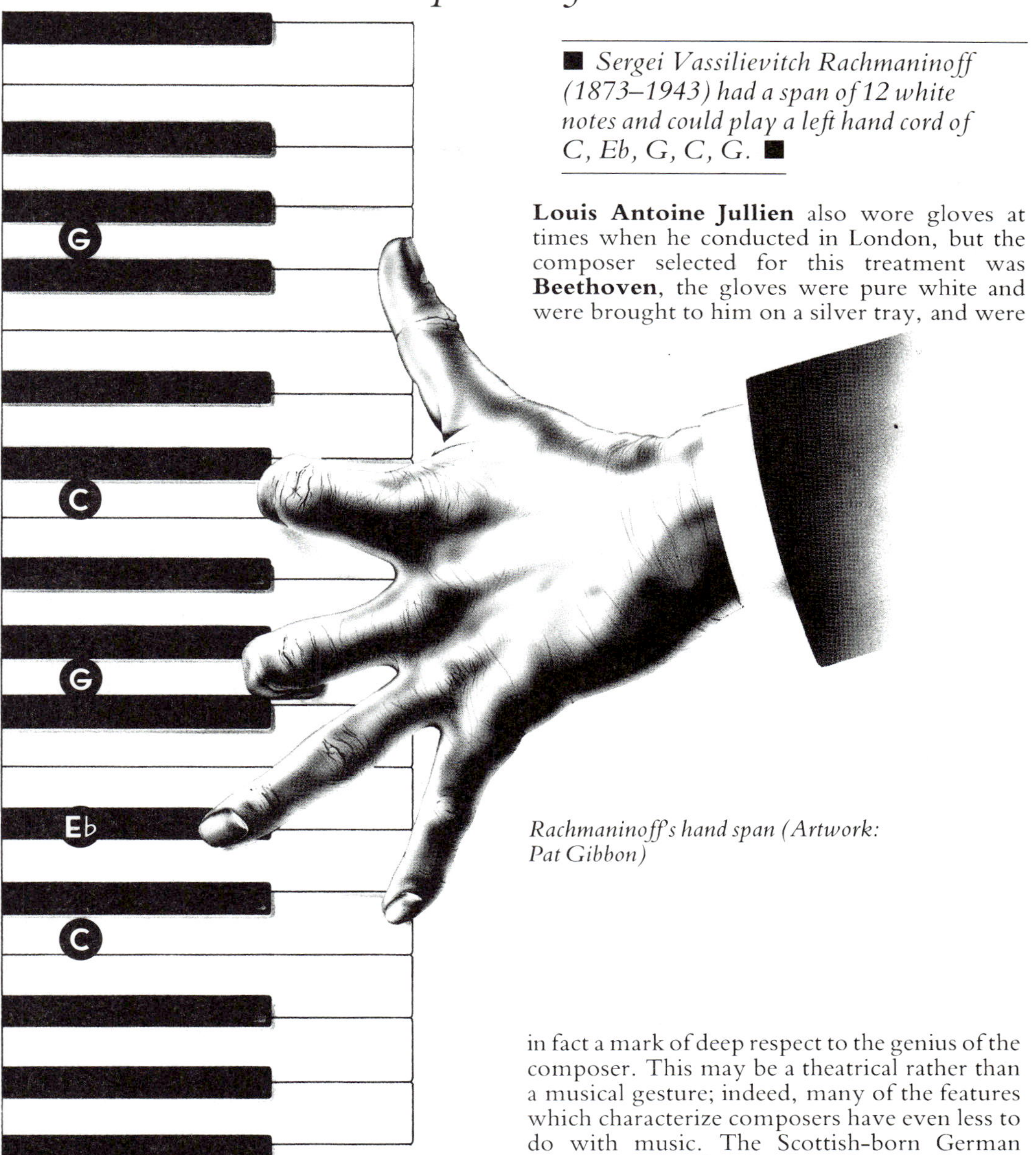

■ *Sergei Vassilievitch Rachmaninoff (1873–1943) had a span of 12 white notes and could play a left hand cord of C, Eb, G, C, G.* ■

Rachmaninoff's hand span (Artwork: Pat Gibbon)

Reports of personal encounters tell us all we need to know about character: that **Wagner** was so conceited and arrogant that he refused to conduct the music of Mendelssohn unless he was wearing gloves, the reason being that Mendelssohn was a Jew. At the end of the performance Wagner would remove the gloves and throw them to the floor, to be swept up by the cleaners. It was partly due to this anti-Semitic attitude that the Third Reich 'adopted' Wagner's music and the Wagnerian ideal, at the same time banning the performance of Mendelssohn's, and all Jews', music.

Louis Antoine Jullien also wore gloves at times when he conducted in London, but the composer selected for this treatment was **Beethoven**, the gloves were pure white and were brought to him on a silver tray, and were in fact a mark of deep respect to the genius of the composer. This may be a theatrical rather than a musical gesture; indeed, many of the features which characterize composers have even less to do with music. The Scottish-born German composer of Italian descent, **Eugene Frances Charles d'Albert** (1864–1932) is perhaps remembered less for his opera *Tiefland*, one of 20 stage works, than for the fact that he married six times; and the modern American **Walter Carlos** may well suffer the ignominy of being forgotten for his sterling work on Moog synthesizers but remembered only for changing sex (she is now called Wendy). Then **Thomas Brewer** (1611–*c*.70), English composer employed to play the viol and compose songs, catches and dances for Sir Nicholas Lestrange's household, is not remembered for his contribution to English music but for the fact

From left to right:

Ralph Vaughan Williams. (Royal College of Music)

Ludwig van Beethoven. (Royal College of Music)

Johann Strauss, Jr. (Mary Evans Picture Library)

Thomas Linley, Jr, painted by Thomas Gainsborough. His promising composing career was terminated by a boating accident in Lincolnshire at the age of 22. (Dulwich College, London)

that he paid too much attention to the profession reflected in his surname, for, according to his employer, he possessed 'a very Rich and Rubicund Nose' on account of his 'Pronenesse to good Fellowshippe'.

Mention of names brings us again to the white-gloved Mr Jullien mentioned above. When his father, a violinist at the Philharmonic Society at Sisteron, France, announced the arrival of a son on 23 April 1812, each of the 36 members of the Society insisted upon standing as godfather. Jullien may be remembered as an important figure in the popularizing of promenade

concerts in London, but who can forget his forenames? Who, indeed, can remember them?

Louis Georges Maurice Adolphe Roch Albert Abel Antonio Alexandre Noé Jean Lucien Daniel Eugène Joseph-le-Brun Joseph Barême Thomas Thomas Thomas-Thomas Pierre-Arbon Pierre-Maurel Barthélemi Artus Alphonse Bertrand Dieudonné Emanuel Josué Vincent Luc Michel Jules-de-la-plane Jules-Bazin Julio César Jullien.

Other composers are noteworthy through no fault of their own. The American **Roy Harris**, whose Third Symphony is amongst the finest of 20th-century works, could have boasted (but probably did not) that he had as many broken bones as a stuntman. In 1913, when only 15, he was carried off the football field with a broken left arm, a broken finger on his right hand and a broken nose; in 1930 he fractured his spine; and as a grand finale he was involved in a car accident in 1953 that left him with a right knee broken into 20 pieces. He died (peacefully at home in bed) at the age of 81.

It falls to some composers never to fulfil their potential or even to reach full maturity. The tragic drowning of **Thomas Linley Jr** at

Grimesthorpe, Lincolnshire, in 1778 at the age of 22 perhaps robbed English music of a great talent. Sadder still was the fate of the Finnish composer **Heikki Theodor Suolahti** who wrote an *Agnus Dei*, a violin concerto and a *Sinfonia Piccola* but was not able to complete a piano concerto, an opera, a ballet and some tone poems when he died in 1936 at the age of only 16. The surviving compositions were described in *Grove V* as 'amazingly mature works of romantic style'.

Schubert and **Mozart** both lived long enough to establish themselves as amongst the greatest of all geniuses. By the age of four Mozart was composing; some of his music from this period has survived, unlike the early works of **Saint-Saëns** which were said to have been written when he was three. Mozart was only 35 when he died; Schubert was younger still (31), yet wrote over 1000 works in 18 years and five months (May 1810, when he was 13, to October 1828) and therefore must be considered to be the fastest composer of all.

Hugo Wolf, one of the world's greatest song writers. (Mary Evans Picture Library)

Hugo Wolf sometimes wrote three songs in a day, **Telemann** and **Vivaldi** could scribble masterpieces faster than copyists could prepare the music for printing or performance, and there are other examples of rapid composition (Hindemith's 15-minute *Meditation* for viola and strings was completed in just over five hours on 20 January 1936 in memory of King George V who had died that day), but none equals Schubert's sustained pace.

Vivaldi's incredible output of 238 violin concerti, 45 operas, over 100 chamber works, etc., etc., is often cited as the work of an abnormally prolific composer, but easily exceeding Vivaldi's total is the output of Georg Philipp Telemann. Bach and Handel were immensely prolific, but Telemann's volume is said to exceed their *combined* totals. A recent listing gives the following:

100 concerti
135 orchestral suites
*c.*400 chamber works
*c.*200 instrumental solos
*c.*130 songs
*c.*100 secular vocal pieces
*c.*30 operas
*c.*150 passions, oratorios, masses, etc.
*c.*1270 cantatas, etc.

Telemann also found time to write about music and to edit volumes of other composers' music for publication.

Telemann's total is large enough, but his range is also wide. He composed in the French, German and Italian styles, he introduced elements of folk music from Poland and other east European ethnic groups into the concert room, and he wrote for virtually every instrument known to 18th-century society. By contrast, **Chopin** and **Leopold Godowski** (1870–1938), both expatriate Poles (they lived respectively in France and America), limited themselves basically to one instrument. Each and every one of their compositions includes the piano. Both wrote songs and some pieces for piano with another instrument, and *Les Sylphides* is one of several purely orchestral pieces based on Chopin's piano music by arrangers; but neither composer ever forsook the instrument.

Finally, let us look at the music itself. Two 18th-century Italian composers represent dynamic extremes. **The Abbé Giovanni Pietro Maria Crispi** (1737–97) is credited with writing the noisiest symphonies of the era. Of his 18 symphonies, 16 are in D major, a key which encourages the use of drums and trumpets and elicits the most brilliant tone from the violins.

■ *Among composers of the classical period the most prolific was Wolfgang Amadeus Mozart (1756–91) of Austria, who wrote c. 1000 operas, operettas, symphonies, violin sonatas, divertimenti, serenades, motets, concerti for piano and many other instruments, string quartets, other chamber music, masses and litanies of which only 70 were published before he died aged 35. His opera* La Clemenza di Tito *(1791) was written in 18 days and three symphonic masterpieces,* Symphony No. 39 in E flat major, Symphony in G minor *and the* Jupiter Symphony in C, *were reputedly written in the space of 42 days in 1788. His overture* Don Giovanni *was written in full score at one sitting in Prague in 1787 and finished on the day of its opening performance.* ■

George Philipp Telemann.

An attractive study drawn by Mazas from a bust reputed to be of Luigi Boccherini. (Photo: Louis Picquot: Notice sur la Vie et Catalogue raisonné des oeuvres de Luigi Boccherini, *Paris, 1851)*

Sir Charles Burney described Crispi's music as 'too furious and noisy for any room or, indeed, for any other place'.

On the other hand, **Luigi Boccherini** was anxious to lull his listeners with the most charming and ingratiating music he could devise. If he had access to an Italian thesaurus he might have raided it constantly for synonyms of 'sweetly' or 'gracefully'. Examination of his some 600 works, amounting to about 1400 movements, reveals the following directions to the players: *affettuoso* ('affectionately'), *grazioso* ('gracefully'), *con grazia* ('with grace'), *amoroso* ('lovingly'), *soave*, *soave assai*, etc. ('sweetly', 'caressingly'), *dolce*, *dolcissimo* ('sweetly', 'gently'). These directions are found 284 times, but their antonyms *appassionato* ('passionately'), *con brio* ('with fire') and *con forza* ('with force') occur only 15 times.

IT'S A FAKE!

No two composers, then, can ever be the same. This does not prevent them from trying at times to be someone else.

Henri Casadesus, the French composer, in collaboration with two of his brothers, wrote music in pale imitation of 18th-century composers. Works said to be by Johann Christian Bach, Carl Philipp Emanuel Bach and others are still current. Unlike Kreisler (below), the brothers never admitted their forgeries.

Fritz Kreisler (1875–1962), the world-renowned Austrian violinist and composer, frequently played items said to be by ancient composers: Vivaldi, Pugnani, Dittersdorf, for example. In 1935 he announced to the world that these items (which were thenceforth titled '. . . in the style of . . .') were of his own composition.

Ferdinando Pellegrini (*c.*1715–*c.*66), was an Italian composer who so admired the music of his compatriots **Galuppi** and **Rutini** that he took their works to London, copied them out, and had them published as his own amidst a set of harpsichord sonatas in 1765 (Op 2). His admiration extended to **Platti**, whose Fantasia he purloined for inclusion in his swansong, Op 10, just before his death. Doubt has been cast upon other of his works, too, since the musical styles of adjacent sets of sonatas seem too suspiciously dissimilar to be the work of one composer.

Charles Zulehner (1770–1830), a German composer who worked in Mainz (where many of his compositions are still preserved in the Schott Archiv) passed off his music as by Mozart. Is there a clue here to the identity of the true composer of 'Mozart's' A minor Symphony, K 16a, discovered in Odense, Denmark, in 1982, a work which experts have so much trouble in accepting as genuine? The earliest knowledge we have of this supposedly 'early' work of Mozart's comes from 1793, two years after his death. By then, Zulehner was 23.

DIFFERENT DRUM

If a man does not keep pace with his companions, perhaps it is because he hears a different drummer. Let him step to the music he hears, however measured or far away.

Thoreau — *Walden* (1854)

In history's cavalcade of composers we find a number who march to the beat of a different drum. For them, existing tenets are inadequate. In seeking to change them they often endure ridicule, and ridicule can be a fearsome weapon. It has destroyed minds; but, with its escort indifference, it can induce even greater excesses. What follows will illustrate the power of the original mind; also, what circumstances can do to folk.

John Barnett

John Barnett began his career unremarkably as a singer who wished to widen the appeal of opera in England by presenting it so that it might be understood — in English. He ended it as a quarrelsome individual who considered that in matters musical he was the only one in step.

Born in Bedford in 1802 of German/Hungarian parents, young John made his first stage appearance in *The Shipwreck* at the London Lyceum at the age of 11. His father had already discarded the family name of Beer for something more English. John soon began composing songs, piano works and stage music, and, when S.J. Arnold, who had given him his first singing opportunity, transformed the Lyceum into the English Opera House in 1834, Barnett revived the obsolescent English opera style with his *The Mountain Sylph*, an immediate and enduring success.

Perhaps that success helped to turn Barnett's head. In an ugly episode he accused his old mentor Arnold of duplicity, took his next operas to Drury Lane, and in 1838 launched his own English Opera House at St James's Theatre. Its rapid failure pushed Barnett further into a mood of suspicion and paranoia. In a series of letters to newspapers he accused many prominent English musicians of trying to defeat the cause of English music, and after another disastrous attempt to form his own company, this time at the Prince's Theatre, he gave up and moved with his wife to Cheltenham as a singing teacher.

His letters to the press, however, continued. His views became ever more contentious (Sir Henry Bishop, he wrote, composed some music worthy of Mozart), his language ever sharper. In 1845 he finally abandoned opera and spent the next 45 years until his death in relative obscurity, writing songs, teaching, and blaming the musical establishment for any artistic crime to which he could lay his pen. It may be significant that one of his rare excursions into concert music was in a symphony called *The Hypocondriac*; certainly, he was one of the first to investigate the efficacy of homeopathic medicines.

John Cage

There are those who aver that reading about John Cage's music is a thousand times more entertaining than listening to it. This is not altogether just — perhaps 500 times would be fairer. One critic referred to Cage's contribution to a disc of experimental music by several composers as 'the least successful in a collection of absolute disasters', and the previous editions of the present book have made easy fun of some of Cage's creations.

John Cage, born in 1912, describes himself as a hunter or an inventor; he was in fact the son of an inventor and many of his experimental extravagances may be attributable to his having inherited an inquiring inventor's mind which just happened to apply itself to music. But his experiments are so uncompromisingly radical that he has frequently aroused in his audiences hostility and the desire to escape, and he has relied for his living on other careers (see p 103) — and on the identification of mushrooms. The

John Cage in 1966. (BBC Hulton Picture Library)

cumulative effect of his music-making, however, has proved immensely important, and in recent decades he has become the centre of attention for younger experimentalists and a cult figure with audiences.

Arnold Schoenberg was amongst his teachers, and Cage for a time in the 1930s composed in his own version of the 12-tone discipline, but he left this behind, his interest in music for dancing leading him towards works for percussion alone. By 1938 he had invented the prepared piano, in which erasers, metal bolts, screws and nuts and other objects are slid between the strings at carefully determined points to alter the character of the sound, and by 1940 (in *Second Construction*) he was specifying 'glissando' for gong, a seemingly impossible direction which is satisfied only by lowering the ringing gong into a bowl of water. In 1942 he composed *The Wonderful Widow of Eighteen Springs* for voice and piano, in which the pianist 'plays' upon various parts of the instrument's anatomy while keeping the lid closed.

To Cage, the true essence of sound was becoming apparent. He saw beauty and value in any and every sound, and the random juxtaposition of sounds became a consuming passion, their source a matter often of chance or indifference. In *Imaginary Landscape I* (1939) he became the first electro-acoustic composer by including recorded sine waves together with cymbal and muted piano, and shortly afterwards he extended his inventory of electronic instruments to include oscillators and buzzers, sine wave disc recordings on variable-speed turntables, and contact microphones to amplify normally inaudible sounds. From the early 1950s he employed tape extensively, but live electronics were introduced in 1951 in *Imaginary Landscape IV* for 24 'players' at 12 radios. Twelve of the operators play with the volume controls while the others twiddle the station selector knobs. Station frequencies, volume and other variables are decided by the fall of tossed coins. A more recent experiment, *Inlets 2* of 1983, employs four operators each with a cassette player and six tapes of Irish folk drumming.

This largely random art was suggested to Cage by his study of Eastern philosophy, particularly I Ching, the Chinese 'classic of changes', a divination text concerning the figures of divided and undivided lines called the eight trigrams and 64 hexagrams. The 43-minute piano piece *Music of Changes* (1951) resulted, its content determined by interchangeable charts and the flip of coins.

By 1952 he was ready to launch onto the world his most notorious composition, *4′ 33″*. For four minutes and 33 seconds any number of performers at any type of instruments stay silently upon the stage. The 'composition' which results is made up of involuntary noises produced by the performers and the audience, and by any sounds which drift in from outside. This work represents the ultimate in chance, for no two 'performances' can ever be the same. When the composer performed *4′ 33″ (No 2)* (also called *0′ 0″*) ten years later he used contact microphones to pick up his actions as he peeled and sliced vegetables, liquidized them in an electric blender, then drank the concoction.

There is, for Cage, absolute freedom to do virtually anything and call it music, whether it be pouring water into buckets, playing two or more of his compositions simultaneously, playing one note on a cello without variation for 15 minutes, waving or making faces at the audience, or organizing an 'environmental extravaganza' of rock groups, dance, electronic music, movies, singing and other simultaneous musical activities (as in *Musicircus*, 1967). Yet, despite the apparent randomness (some say anarchy) of his music, he and his associates sometimes spend many months preparing a piece, the components of which are then jumbled together to create the true indeterminacy Cage seeks. He feels that it is not the composer's place to bring order out of the chaos which is life, but rather to drift with that chaos and appreciate it for what it is.

Charles Dibdin

Charles Dibdin was born in Southampton in 1745, one of at least 14 children of the parish clerk. Young Charles showed himself to be good at everything, but not good enough to get into Winchester college, despite his later claims. He was particularly good at words and music: by the time he was 20 he had taught himself music, had published a collection of songs and cantatas, had written a pastoral (a kind of rural operetta), had it accepted for performance at Covent Garden, and had sung the lead there. He was also married. At Covent Garden he secured character parts in other operas, and his operatic career and personal future seemed assured. The management at Covent Garden encouraged him to contribute to operas (some of his contributions were somewhat experimental and unlikely to endear him to other artists, such as when the leading lady in *Love in the City* had to sing while fighting) rather than write complete operas. For a time this worked quite well.

But Dibdin was hearing a different drum.

Abruptly he left Covent Garden for Drury Lane, an appointment which gave him more artistic freedom both at the theatre and outside it, for the young man's name was by now well known. But by his 30th birthday he seems to have shot his bolt. Audiences began to drift away and his marriage collapsed when he ran off with, first, a dancer, then a singer, apparently intent on repopulating London with young Dibdins.

He lost his Drury Lane position in 1775 and was unable to find another. By the following summer his creditors were after him, so he moved to France with his second mistress (the singer) until the hunt was over. He might have stayed there had the political climate not been so antipathetic towards foreigners; on his return to London he repaid all his debts, presumably from money made in France, and found a job back at Covent Garden, now under new management — a management which had no experience of Dibdin's sharp tongue, quarrelsome ways, and, by now, sadly diminished abilities.

Dibdin stormed out during a row over a libretto and found himself on the street with neither food nor job. By sheer luck he became involved in a new theatre and a new enterprise, a kind of children's circus featuring short operas, ballets and riding displays, but he bungled this enterprise, too, putting the theatre and himself into debt. This time he landed in prison.

Upon his release his forgiving associates re-employed him, but for Dibdin nothing was right. He misread their intentions and in a fury of paranoia he resolved to leave all his commitments to their fate and emigrate to India. He got as far as Torbay in the west of England. Seasickness was no more to his liking than anything else.

If nothing in existence would suit him, Dibdin had to invent something which would. He came up with what he called 'Table Entertainments', a succession of songs interspersed with stories and jokes. To his surprise these entertainments, assisted by Dibdin's gift for imitating accents and dialects, became a popular London attraction, and after a few years he was able to build his own tiny theatre, open a publishing house and start a magazine. He wrote copiously: novels, articles, textbooks, and an autobiography, and he painted with skill. But for all his energy and new-found ability, he was unable to adjust to commercial and artistic life, his bad temper contributing to his downfall. When he died aged 69 in London he had scarcely a friend or a penny.

Percy Grainger

Percy Grainger, the composer of such jolly trifles as *Handel in the Strand* and *Molly on the Shore*, was one of the most original and audacious free-thinkers in the history of music.

Born in Melbourne, Australia, in 1882, just three weeks after Stravinsky, he moved to London in 1901 and established his reputation as a pianist by touring widely in England and abroad. In 1905 he began collecting English and other nations' folksongs (using an Edison Bell cylinder phonograph for the purpose), but moved to America in 1914, and took American citizenship in 1918. He died at White Plains, New York, in February 1961, aged 78.

Although his folksong setting deservedly remain popular, the real nature of Grainger is to be found in his more serious works, many of which anticipate by many years the experiments of 'modernist' composers. Because of their severe demands upon musicians and resources they are rarely performed; another reason may be that they are likely to remain 'ahead of their time' for many years to come.

In *The Warriors* (1916) he called for two, or preferably three, conductors; he anticipated the modern school of indeterminacy (i.e. leaving to chance the sounds his audiences actually heard) by giving the xylophone a part but advising the player 'The actual notes do not matter; anything of this sort will do equally well'. His percussion forces are unusually large for the period: glockenspiel, celesta, three pianos, marimbas (both wooden and steel), tubular bells, staff bells and timpani in addition to the xylophone.

Hill Song No 1 (1902) was not given in its original form until 1969 (at Northwestern University, Evanston, Illinois): it calls for a large wind section including euphonium, with strings, percussion and harmonium, and it contains bars of distinctly odd meters, e.g. 13/8, 10/8, 5/8, 7/8, 1/4, 5/16. In *Love Verses from 'The Song of Solomon'* (1900), a vocal and instrumental piece, one passage of 28 bars changes time signature 20 times (including the possibly unique measure of 2¼/4), while *Sea Song* (1907) takes this freedom still further: its opening 13 bars, in an explosion of metrical chaos, call for 1/4, 7/32, 3/32, 5/64, 5/16, 3/8, 7/64, 3/32, 5/64, 9/32, 3/8, 7/64, 5/16, consecutively, and *fast!*

The reason for this apparently perverse and meaningless jumble lies in Grainger's folk music studies. He found that untrained and unsophisticated country people sing with a free-flowing, natural rhythm as dictated by the rise and fall of the words, and the only way to relay

Australia Post first day cover commemorating Percy Grainger's centenary in 1982.

to trained musicians and thence to his audience this unaffected flow was by adopting constantly shifting meters.

The indeterminacy noted above was taken to its extreme in *Random Round* (1914). Its six sections may be repeated *ad lib* by the wordless voices and instruments, and anyone can join in or not at any time. A person standing before the artists holds up cards at random to indicate which section is to be heard next, the conductor giving one bar's warning of change by some audible means (hand clap, whistle, stamp, etc). He also decides when he has heard enough permutations by bringing *Random Round* to an end with an exciting free-for-all. Grainger made a 'set version' for three soloists and nine instruments in 1943.

Perhaps Grainger's most radical ideas were embodied in his concept of *Free-Music*, 'a scaleless, pulseless music' which he considered performable only by mechanical means. The 'scaleless' aspect originated in Grainger's fascination at the age of 10 (1892) with the properties of air and water. If natural elements were not subject to instantaneous changes of level, pressure, displacement, etc., why should music be doomed to progress, as do melodies played on the piano, by a series of jerky steps? His analogy was to a painter being deprived of the use of curving lines. This idea could not be realized until the invention of electrical instruments such as the Thérémin (see p 77), with its infinitely graded scale, and of his own complicated Free-Music Machines (made with the assistance of Burnett Cross) after World War II.

The 'pulseless' aspect has already been noted: his fluid time signatures, and his refusal to give some pieces barlines at all, partly realized his ideal of a music unfettered by regular downbeats. Apparently some of his metrical experiments were conceived as early as 1899.

Grainger's other ideas were distinctly modern — striking the piano keyboard with the fist in *Country Gardens* of 1918, and playing the instrument 'directly' with soft mallets on the strings in *Tribute to Foster** of 1914; or breezily attractive and unconventional — the audience sings along in *Tribute to Foster* while the ladies of the chorus play with moistened fingertips upon drinking glasses 'tuned' with water, and the original 1901 version of *Marching Song of Democracy* called for voices and whistlers. Grainger's 'elastic scoring' echoed the 18th century's freedom of instrumentation, in which sonatas and concerti were often made available for several different instrumental possibilities to attract more sales, making many of his works performable by a wide variety of vocal and/or instrumental groups.

*'Foster' is Stephen Foster (1826–64), author of *Old Folks at Home*, *Oh! Susanna*, *Camptown Races* and other songs.

Wind instruments attracted Grainger, especially those with 'fierce' tones like the *zampogna* and Oriental oboe (e.g. the Indian *Shanai*). He once wrote that his favourite sonority was that of the bagpipes, and some of his scores call for bass oboe and sarrusophone. But, as Thomas C. Slattery has written in *The Percy Grainger Companion*, 'almost any general statement made about his (Grainger's) music can be refuted by citing abundant examples of decidedly the opposite', and indeed Grainger did not neglect to explore the more exotic possibilities of brass, strings and percussion.

By nature he was insistently non-conformist. When young he refused to give a recital without having his toy suit of armour on stage with him, and as he matured he made no secret of his opinion that Beethoven was a frivolous and shallow composer. In his writings he loved to use the awkward suffix ('keeping-on-ness', 'aristocraticness', 'unfoldment'), feeling no doubt that the English language needed help to handle his subtle shades of meaning. His scores, similarly, reveal a lack of faith in conventional Italian and English terms: he used the following, *inter alia*, whose meanings are not unfailingly self-explanatory: 'band-boss' (conductor), 'dished up' (arranged), 'don't soften' and 'keep it up' (*tenuto*), 'harped' (*arpeggiando*), 'linger slightly' (*poco rubato*), 'louden lots' (*crescendo molto*), 'quicken lots bit by bit' (*molto accelerando, poco a poco*), 'room-music' (chamber music), 'tone-tool' (instrument), 'tone-work' (composition), and 'woggle' (*tremolo*).

Grainger's wedding, on 9 August 1928 to the Swedish beauty Ella Viola Ström, did not take place in a conventional location: he chose the Hollywood Bowl, before thousands of witnesses, at the end of a concert at which he conducted the première of his bridal tribute *To a Nordic Princess*, the wedding present to his bride as touching as the occasion was spectacular.

Harry Partch

'One's beginning is a decent and honourable mistake, and long before life has run its course one is obliged to contemplate — both dazed and undazed — the endless reaches of one's innocence.'

The last word of Harry Partch's credo might equally well read 'ignorance', for his musical experiments are a feverish and determined attempt to widen his audience's awareness and acceptance of sound, of exotic cultures, and of the unexpected. To these ends he built his own instruments, sometimes based on, for example, percussion found in Polynesia, but at other times founded on new (or very ancient) principles, and he uses a scale of 43 notes to the octave. Like Percy Grainger (above), he was disturbed by the arbitrary selection of a handful of given frequencies in the scale; in addition, he returned to just intonation.

Disenchanted with conventional music, Harry Partch went to extremes to invent his own. Like author George Orwell, who went in search of experiences amongst the lowest levels of society in England, Partch sought his music 'riding the rails' for eight years, associating with hobos and learning about the rougher fibres of American life. To quote Wilfred Mellers (*Music in a New Found Land*), 'His (Partch's) works, like Aristophanes and Japanese Kabuki, use monophonic chant, dance, mime, slapstick and juggling for social-religious ends. It is not his fault that the religion he celebrates is that of the outsider, the bum'.

Amongst Partch's influences were the Balinese gamelan, Aboriginal American Indian music and chant, Japanese theatre, and Tin-Pan Alley. He seemed interested in decrying and satirizing the sophisticated trappings of modern society.

Harry Partch with his bell-tree and cone gongs.

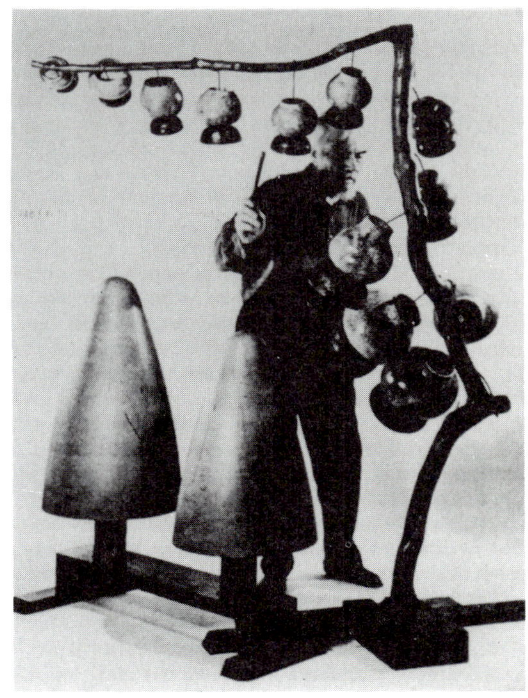

Together, these factors gave him a powerful motive for inventing his own distinct music, and with it his theoretical structures and his own instruments.

What Partch's music sounds like may be guessed to a certain extent from his interests and from the names and materials of his invented instruments. He has 'adapted' the viola and guitar (*cf.* John Cage's 'prepared' piano) by lengthening their fingerboards, and these instruments together with his 'chromelodeon', a specially tuned reed organ, are capable of producing the microtones demanded by his 43-tone scale. The 'boo' is a marimba made of bamboo, the 'cloud chamber bowls' are glass, the cone gongs (resembling tall toadstools a yard or more high) are metal, and for his 'diamond marimba' and 'gourd tree' Partch utilized wood and gourds respectively. The sonorous ringing quality of these percussion instruments is set against the sharper sounds of 'waving drums', 'belly drums' and other small percussion, often adapted from native instruments.

Recordings give some idea of Partch's music but its full value may be understood only visually. The gourd tree, with different-sized gourds hanging apparently randomly from a crooked branch rising awkwardly from the stage, and the cloud chamber bowls suspended chaotically from a frame, themselves have considerable visual impact, which is increased by the players' athletic antics as they move to reach their targets with their strikers. But his musical pieces designed for staging offer splendid opportunities to imaginative designers.

In his *US Highball* (1943), for instance, a tramp called Mac intones railroad station names, graffiti, and random thoughts about his life and the alternative life promoted by line-side advertisements, while Partch's eerie instruments give an evocative background of saloon tunes, hill-billy songs and the popular hits of the day.

More adventurous is *Water! Water!* (1961), in which the stage is occupied to the right by a deserted nature scene with distant mountains, and to the left by an imaginary American city, Santa Mystiana, peopled by a radio baseball commentator, a disc-jockey, an alderman and a mayoress. Man's control over nature is represented by a vast dam which at present is dangerously low due to prolonged drought. Partch shows his interest in magic by turning subsequent events on the intervention of a black jazz band with occult powers to appeal to the Water Witch for rain. At length the appeal is only too successful: the Second Flood bursts the dam, ruins the baseball game, and brings civilization to an end. The sueing of the jazz leader and the Water Witch for $1m each in compensation is merely a part of this surrealist 'tragic farce' in which values have no perspective, and in which at one point the diverse characters sing 'We really love each other in 43 whines to the octave'.

Pietro Raimondi

There is little doubt that if Pietro Raimondi had been born a century earlier he would have rivalled Bach, in technical wizardry if not in invention and inspiration. Unfortunately, Raimondi appeared in 1786 (in Rome), a time when the skills of counterpoint and fugue were considered old hat, and he grew up in a climate of Romanticism in which such classical forms were deemed as dry as a museum.

His early counterpoint training under the unimaginative and conservative Giacomo Tritto must have influenced Raimondi so deeply that he determined to practise scholarly composition at every opportunity. Indeed, it became a way of life for him. Although primarily a stage composer (with more than 50 operas and 22 ballets to his credit), he also gravitated towards sacred vocal music for the chance it gave him to practise his learned style. Raimondi, in mid-19th century Romanticism, heard a different drum; one that he believed would lead music back to the contrapuntal styles of a century earlier. Fugues and double canons of ever-increasing complexity brought him fame of a sort. When Rossini was asked to write a mass for Naples in 1820 he sought Raimondi's help, for Rossini was at that time overworked. The mass was duly completed and performed, and the critic and composer Carl von Miltitz wrote, 'I cannot say whether Rossini or Raimondi wrote the *Sanctus* and *Agnus [Dei]* but I can say that they are worth little. There is a kind of weeping fugue which ran through all 12 notes of the scale'. As well as looking to the past, then, Raimondi was already presaging the 20th century.

Soon he was writing multiple fugues, a line of development which led him to the simultaneous performance of as many as six four-part fugues in different keys. But still Raimondi's crossword-puzzle mind was not content. Next came a fugue for 16 four-part choirs — 64 lines of independently weaving music, followed in 1836 by two masses, each for eight-part choir with orchestra, which could be performed separately or simultaneously. This, however, was still child's play.

Three oratorios, *Putifar, Giuseppe* and *Giacobbe*, appeared in 1848, each complete in itself. The three works, despite their minute-by-minute differences of tempo, rhythm, mood, etc., had of course been designed for simultaneous performance. It was four years before anyone took the plunge; then, on 7 August 1852 in Rome, the three oratorios were performed consecutively, then brought together in simultaneous performance by a choir of 250 and a combined orchestra numbering 150. The three conductors were under the overall direction of Raimondi, and the complete concert had lasted for six hours by the time the end came. Raimondi met the 'colossal' ovation by falling in a dead faint.

There was, however, yet one more mountain for Raimondi to climb. The serious opera *Adelasia* and the comic opera *I quattro rustici* were planned for simultaneous performance on a divided stage, the two totally different plots and moods to be interlinked like a gigantic sonic jigsaw. It was not to be. The composer's death in 1853 intervened, and a pupil's completion of the project has never been mounted. The ultimate in visual and aural counterpoint has yet to be presented.

Gioacchino Rossini

Gioacchino Rossini was outwardly a normal operatic composer of the first half of the 19th century. He wrote 39 operas, two large choral works and about 200 smaller items. Apart from the scintillating quality of many of his operatic overtures, some of which have become highly prized concert pieces, there is nothing remarkable about his musical style. But look closer at his life and character, however, and one perceives elements of high farce.

He attained 76 years but only 20 birthdays, for he was unfortunate enough to be born on leap-day 1792. For much of his life he was troubled by irrational superstitions which turned on him at last by terminating that life on Friday the 13th (November 1868). Baptized Gioacchino Antonio, he could never remember the spelling of his first name, habitually omitting one of the 'c's. In his early life he was taught harpsichord by a priest named Prinetti who had acquired the peculiar knack of being able to sleep standing up.

Rossini suffered chronically with a 'social disease', due, said a doctor, to 'the abuse of Venus when very young'. This occasioned serious concern that his brilliant career might be terminated early: his obituary appeared in Naples and Paris in 1818, somewhat to the composer's surprise, and rumours of his death were again heard in 1834.

Food was Rossini's third favourite pastime and success brought him masses of it so that before middle-age he was 'broad'. Wagner said 'Rossini is stuffed not with music but with mortadella'. Many of the anecdotes surrounding the composer have food as a basis. Eating cheese, he is supposed to have said, makes good oratorio composers; *Di tanti palpiti* from *Tancredi* is called the 'rice aria' because he wrote it in the time taken to boil rice (one is reminded of the name 'the egg-timer' given to the Overture to *The Marriage of Figaro* by Rossini's hero Mozart, which plays for precisely four minutes); and it was reported that Rossini would see a visiting Russian princess only on condition that she brought a gift of asparagus.

More reliable is the story of Rossini's escapade while shopping with a friend in Paris. They entered a pasta shop and the composer requested Neapolitan macaroni but was offered something else. He knew the difference. 'No!' said Rossini, 'if all you have is Genoese macaroni we shall leave'. Rossini's friend, lingering behind, told the shop-keeper that he had just offended the great composer Rossini. 'Rossini?' answered the shop-keeper. 'Never heard of him; but if he knows tunes like he knows macaroni he must write beautiful music'. The composer, when told of this exchange, exclaimed that no-one had ever complimented him more highly.

In 1814 he ordered a marzipan ship, mast broken, sails torn, foundering in a sea of cream. On the ship's side was the name *Ciro*, the title of his recently failed opera. Much later, at a time of abysmal physical ebb in 1853, Rossini displayed the old wit in abundance in a letter thanking an admirer for sending some sausage and ravioli from Modena. Treating the food as music, Rossini wrote, 'I found your collected works totally complete, and am impressed by the internal expertise and finesse of your renowned compositions . . .', and much more in the same vein. The letter was received in a frenzy of delight by the Modenese: he read it repeatedly to friends, framed it, circled it with candles, and was overcome for days with excitement and had to be 'protected' in an asylum 'for a rest'. Upon release he immediately despatched further comestibles to Rossini but was this time bitterly disappointed with the acknowledgement, which informed him that Rossini was too ill to eat.

When he was 37 Rossini retired from opera composing and wrote little music of any sort for many years. He had made a fantastic fortune, partly during his seven months in London in 1824 (during which he taught rich young ladies to sing, charging £100 per lesson 'to compensate me for suffering the tortures of their creaky voices.')

The composer built his Villa Rossini by the Bois de Boulogne on a site chosen because its shape resembled that of a grand piano, and he had flower beds dug in the shape of musical instruments. A gilt lyre on the gate told visitors that Rossini was at home. The villa was demolished by a subsequent owner, perhaps in an attempt to recover the hoard of medals, jewels and coins rumoured to have been buried in its foundations.

In old age, Rossini went as bald as a melon and wore a wig. When it was cold he wore two; in freezing weather, three!

In 1857, after 28 years of virtual silence, Rossini began composing again. This coincided with a marked health improvement. These *Sins of my Old Age* as he called them comprised over 150 small pieces; he dedicated those for piano 'to pianists of the fourth class, to which I have the honour to belong'. There was also a *Stabat Mater* and the *Petite Messe Solonelle*, the latter, according to commentators, being not little (it plays for 80 minutes or more in the 1863 version for four soloists, eight-part chorus, two pianos and harmonium; and the vocal/orchestral version of 1866/7, though slightly shorter, runs to about 500 pages), hardly a mass in the accepted sense, and certainly not uniformly solemn. Its autograph score includes a punning letter to God: '. . . Is it sacred music (*musique sacrée*) or abominable music (*sacrée musique*) I have written?' He called the Mass 'the last sin of my old age'. Characteristically, a number of musical 'sins' followed it.

Rossini's music is famous for its wit and vivacity. Some comically agile double-bass solos occur in the sonatas for strings written when he was 12, and the Overture to *Il Signor Bruschino* (1812) is notable for the direction that second violins should tap their candle reflectors with their bows during pauses in the music. Not all the farcical aspects of his music were Rossini-made, however. The stage machinery required for *Mosè in Egitto* (1818), where two halves of the Red Sea, their edges towering over the cast, were pushed aside by all-too-visible stagehands, reduced the audience, at a dramatic moment, to tears of mirth. The farcical irony of a commentator's complaint in 1852 that Rossini's *The Siege of Corinth* (1826) was too noisy — with bass drum, other percussion, trombones, cornets, ophicleide, organ, bells and military bands — becomes apparent when one learns the critic's name: Hector Berlioz. Earlier, Weber, a composer totally opposed to the Rossinian ethos, fled half-way through *La Cenerentola* because he feared he was beginning to like it.

Rossini — a charming man, as ready with a quip as with a generous remark, a man who encouraged the impression that he was lazy yet wrote *The Barber of Seville*, fully orchestrated, in 13 days — left a final contradiction. Along with music designed wholly to delight, he bequeathed the saddest of epigrams: 'Glory is no compensation for the trials of living.'

Erik Satie

Not the least of Erik Satie's oddities was the string of contradictions which characterized his life. He detested music school yet returned to it in middle-age; he was a radical socialist (joining the Communist Party in 1920) yet mingled with, and enjoyed the patronage of, the upper classes; amongst the least 'influenced' of composers, he wrote advanced and intensely personal music, yet borrowed freely from composers of the past; he jealously guarded his solitary privacy yet joined a number of clubs and institutions; and he respected his art so religiously that he thought of little else, yet advocated an early form of Muzak.

He was, he said, 'born very young into a world very old' in 1866. 'Erik' was an affectation; he was christened 'Eric'. During his seven years at the Paris Conservatoire he was lazy and a truant — his composition teacher thought he should concentrate on the piano, while his piano teacher advised him to compose. Invalided out of the army in 1887 with self-induced bronchitis (he stood outside, part-naked, in mid-winter), he developed an interest in mysticism, Gregorian chant and Gothic art, befriended Debussy (whom he later renounced), embraced the Rosicrucian faith, then founded his own religious order, a severe and vengeful organization called the Metropolitan Art Church of Jesus the Conductor. It had but one member: Erik Satie.

In 1898 he moved to a shabby Parisian suburb, called himself Saint Erik of Arcueil, and supported himself as a café pianist and provider of stage music, those stages, disappointingly, being in music halls. His compositions for piano, including the now famous *Gymnopédies* of 1888, attracted little attention. At the age of

Erik Satie, as seen by the whimsical pen of an unknown artist. (Mary Evans Picture Library)

39 he entered the Schola Cantorum and graduated in 1908, his patchy musical education at last repaired.

A certain fame came at last in 1911 via Ravel's interest, but Satie's real success was with *Parade* (1917), a ballet written in collaboration with Cocteau and with Picasso's designs, in which the scoring includes siren, typewriter, lottery wheel and pistol shot. The scandal surrounding *Parade* brought Satie to court: to a hostile critic he sent a postcard saying: 'You are an arse; moreover an unmusical arse'. Satie was sentenced to prison and a heavy fine, but won on appeal.

He became a kind of figurehead for the group of composers called *Les Six* without ever becoming the seventh (it was largely due to Satie's moods that the group disintegrated in the early 1920s), and in 1920 he organized a programme of 'furnishing music' (*cf.* today's 'wallpaper music', marketed by Muzak) consisting of well-known pieces against which the audience was implored to talk, smoke, move about . . .

Satie's final work marked also his final appearance. At the end of the ballet/movie *Relâche* he acknowledged the audience's reaction (which was not applause) by driving round the stage in a small Citroën car. He died of drink, aged 59, in 1925.

Satie's love of umbrellas is legendary — it is said that 200 were found in his apartment after his death. So, too, were six unworn identical grey velvet suits, the remainder of the dozen he is reported to have purchased with a small legacy when young. He did not wash, finding pumice stone more effective — and cheaper — than soap. He called the sun 'a bore' and 'a bully', preferring inclement weather (hence, no doubt, the umbrellas), and he had a quirky visual sense, writing letters in a kind of imitation medieval script, drawing fantastic sketches of impossible machines and buildings, and writing his scores in coloured inks.

His musical imagination was similarly weird. Titles of his works include *Flabby Preludes (for a dog)*, *Penultimate Thoughts*, *Disagreeable glimpses*, *Memories of an amnesiac*, and *Sketches and exasperations of a big wooden twit*. Artists faced with Satie's musical directions might need to pause for thought before playing, for instance, 'like a nightingale with toothache'. *Vexations* must be played 840 times, very slowly, with the minimum of variety (an 'impossible' joke that has in fact been carried through more than once by adventurous pianists.)

Satie's programmes are equally crazy. There is an anticipation of *Goon Show* surrealism in his *Sonate bureaucratique* of 1917 when the civil servant 'hums an old Peruvian tune picked up from a deaf-mute in Brittany'. The third of his *Trois Valses distinguées du précieux dégoûté* (1914) describes how the dandy admires his own slim legs: 'he is proud of them; not for *them* inferior dances . . . he would like to carry them under his arm but they slither about sadly and become haughty. He hugs them and ties them round his neck, and will not imprison them in gaiters.'

Sorabji

He is a composer and pianist who hates people, especially musicians, critics and all those connected with concert-giving. For him, audiences are an intolerable intrusion, and to those investigators with a genuine interest in his background he deliberately gives false information, regarding such inquiries as 'stupid and impertinent'. As if further to bewilder the curious he changed his first names from Leon Dudley to the almost unpronounceable Kaikhosru Shapurji. As a final defiant insult he threatens legal action on anyone who has the temerity to attempt to play his compositions in public — that is, if the ferocious difficulties of the music for both performer and listener were not already sufficient deterrent.

Does he deserve an entry in a book of this kind, or indeed in any book? Or should he expect the world to turn its back on him?

L.D. (or K.S.) Sorabji must have *something*, for he has soundly abused the musical scene for years, yet the world still attempts to beat a path to the door to his house in Dorset, England, which has the sinister name of 'The Eye'. Most path-beaters are repulsed, but pianist Yonty Solomon, by some magic formula unknown to the rest of us, managed in 1976 to obtain permission to perform (and perhaps ultimately to record) Sorabji's music, thus partially lifting a ban which had lasted since 1932 (according to most reports, or since 1940 according to *New Grove*). Since then Michael Habermann apparently has also received permission and has recorded two discs of Sorabji's piano works.

If Sorabji's smoke-screen concerning biographical details has been pierced with accuracy, we may give his birth date as 14 August 1892 and his birthplace as Chingford, London. His mother was a Spanish Sicilian, his father a Parsi. Largely self-taught, Sorabji became a brilliant pianist, a music critic with a mordant turn of phrase, and a composer whose works impressed a small group of connoisseurs, before he abandoned public musical activities.

During his long career he has produced music of the most phenomenal complexity and scale. Most notorious is his *Opus clavicembalisticum*, completed in 1930, a 12-movement piano work written on three or four staves throughout and occupying 250 pages of music playing for nearly three hours. But some later works are longer still, the piano writing occasionally extending to as many as seven staves. The composer once suggested that the reason for the performance ban was that adequate performances were not attainable in the foreseeable future; today, computer programmers may well realize his impossible demands electronically. We shall then learn whether the charisma surrounding Sorabji's music is justified.

Daniel Steibelt

Daniel Steibelt, virtuoso pianist and composer, was born in Berlin in 1765. His career began promisingly but ended amid disgrace, for his irresponsible attitude made him many enemies.

His early promise as pianist and composer was already threatened with oblivion when he deserted from the Prussian army at the age of 19, lying low for several years to avoid the inevitable penalty. He was not pardoned until 1799, by which time he had travelled widely in Europe, had published several compositions, made a name as a showy virtuoso, and defrauded a Parisian publisher, which required an abrupt move to London. There, he passed off other composers' music as his own, sometimes thinly arranged, and married an English girl who was also a pianist.

This skill was of little use to Steibelt, but her other skill, as a virtuoso tambourine player, offered new possibilities. He took her to Prague where he bought 'nearly a whole cartload' (Tomášek) of tambourines, then gave a series of recitals of his own piano works to which he had added brilliant tambourine parts. This started a craze amongst the ladies there, all of whom wished to show off their arms and hands to admiring tambourine buffs. For 24 ducats these gullible ladies could obtain a tambourine and a 12-lesson course on how to play it.

With full pockets, the couple then visited Vienna, where Steibelt rashly entered into a piano-playing contest at the house of Count Fries. It was unfortunate that his opponent happened to be a 30-year-old pianist called Beethoven. The result was predictable, and once it had been passed round the musical capital of Europe there was only one course open to Steibelt: to leave quietly. In Paris he dismayed audiences with his own rewritten version of Haydn's *The Creation* and eventually had to flee from creditors, his growing reputation as a charlatan having adversely affected his income.

Eventually he found sanctuary in St Petersburg, where he was put in charge of the French opera, and he died there in 1823 after a long illness.

In Prague, the composer Tomášek heard Steibelt pass off a piano quartet as his own work but considered it so vastly superior to Steibelt's other music that he suspected fraud, a suspicion confirmed both by Steibelt's refusal to let outsiders see the music parts (he rehearsed it in a locked room), and by the lack of any work of this description in the long list of his authentic works. For Steibelt, however, authenticity was a relative thing, for he frequently reshaped old music (sometimes his own) for publication as 'new', and added unnecessary extra parts to piano sonatas in order to sell them to unsuspecting violinists and other players. As a performer his style was showy, often vulgar, and displayed poor left-hand technique, 'banging away awkwardly', as Tomášek put it.

Steibelt's arrogance was notorious. Even the trouncing he received in Vienna at Beethoven's hands did nothing to lessen it, and he is reported to have kept his audiences waiting, sometimes for an hour, before arriving with feigned breathlessness but without apology. He discarded his native tongue and habitually spoke French.

Steibelt composed music for the stage, concert hall and recital room, but a complete list is not possible because of his multiple publication of works in the same or slightly different form.

Herbert Taylor

This section has been called 'Different Drum' and it brings to attention some of the composers who have travelled their own roads at their own paces despite persistent opposition, hostility, and in many cases posterity's almost total neglect. The section would be incompete without reference to a contemporary composer who has examined palindromic experiments of the past and found them lacking, and who feels that there is a real future for works that last forever. He is Herbert F. Taylor of London, who, in a letter to the authors dated 14 March 1981, puts forward his own compositions as having uniquely superlative qualities. He says:

> '. . . some of my works play *for ever, infinitum*, and one piece not only plays for *evermore*, the two violins play upside down, *and backwards* way, for *evermore*, and the piano part plays *backwards and forwards only*, for evermore, is this a record?'

V

Music Sung

With some exceptions, sacred music *is* vocal music. To dispose of the exceptions first, these are instrumental, and occasionally orchestral, compositions designed to be performed before, during, or after a sacred service or mass. Giovanni Gabrieli and Adriano Banchieri wrote works in the 16th and early 17th centuries for such use (some may have been played softly during the reading of the epistle), and the baroque *sonata da chiesa* included movements which could be used as appropriate. Mozart's 'Epistle Sonatas' were played singly half-way though the Catholic mass, immediately before the epistle. Even these exceptions, then, were used in conjunction with voices in places of worship.

When primitive man first raised his voice in something approaching song it was undoubtedly in praise of some deity who, being invisible, must be distant and therefore needed to be hollered at. A Mesopotamian bas-relief of the 7th century BC, preserved in the British Museum, London, shows a choir of six women and nine children with instrumentalists nearby. One woman, presumably the leader, is squeezing her larynx in order to obtain a pinched and piercing tone that would carry over long distances. Such singing may still be heard in the Middle and Far East.

HRONOLOGY OF ACRED MUSIC

ompilation of any chronology is hampered by e lack of early written records, but the llowing is an attempt to indicate the probable quence of events.

th century BC The earliest surviving hymn xt is a two-line fragment by Eumelius, a poet Corinth.

ncient Greece The hymn fulfilled various unctions, rarely if ever religious, and was often companied by dancing.

138 BC First Delphic Hymn to Apollo. The xt on this incomplete stone slab is glossed ith clear musical indications (Greek letters presenting notes: M = C; I = D; Y = A flat, nd so on, in Reinach's transcription of 1893) nd it is the earliest known example of written usic as hymn accompaniment. (See p 126).

th century AD Plainsong. Ambrosian chant ased on four scales codified by Bishop mbrose of Milan. *c.*333–397.

th century Proclus defined the hymn as a (religious) composition 'sung by a stationary chorus to a *kithara* accompaniment'. 'Stationary' in this instance may mean simply 'not dancing'.

By no means all hymns were set to music; indeed, music has often been banned by church leaders, and the recital of hymn texts without music, and certainly without dancing, persisted for centuries.

6th century Gregorian chant, with four scales added to Ambrosian chant reputedly by Pope Gregory 'The Great' (ruled 590–604). However, the cross-fertilization with contemporary Old Latin chant results in confusion as to priority. Chants were sung in unison.

9th century The beginnings of polyphony. Organum: addition of another part a fourth below.

10th century Liturgical drama.

Mid-12th century Conductus, a sacred song to Latin text which arose in southern France and spread north and east. It was sung as the bible or other text was 'conducted' (i.e. carried) to the lectern. The rise of polyphony called for a stricter control of rhythm.

Music Sung

■ *There are more than 950 000 Christian hymns in existence. The music and parts of the text of a hymn in the* Oxyrhynchus Papyri *from the 2nd century are the earliest known Christian hymnody. The earliest exactly datable hymn is the* Heyr Himna Smióur (Hear the maker of heaven) *from 1208 by the Icelandic bard and chieftain Kolbeinn Tumason (1173–1208)* ■

13th century Introduction of the Motet; Canon; 10-part polyphony.

14th century Anthems.

15th century Passions.

16th century Introduction of Antiphonal polyphony; homophony; sacred (i.e. vocal) concerti and symphonies.

1550 The first services set to music by John Merbecke (*c.*1505/10–*c.*85) for use in parish churches.

17th century Oratorio: that is, voices with instrumental backing in church.

18th century 'Symphonic' masses (e.g. by Haydn, Mozart); National anthems.

19th century Spread and consolidation of sacred forms outside sacred venues.

First Delphic Hymn to Apollo: stone fragment showing musical indications; c.138 BC.

20th century Further interest in and development of 'symphonic' choral music for concert use (e.g. Stravinsky's *Symphony of Psalms*; Janáček's *Mša Glagolskaya* (*Glagolitic Mass*)).

Mass

High Mass

The High Mass (or *Missa Solemnis*) is a large-scale choral work, often with orchestra since the 17th century, divided into a number of sections. Vocal soloists usually take a prominent part in the presentation of the words, which are always the same. The sections of the Latin text of the Ordinary are as follows:

Kyrie eleison Lord have mercy on us
(Ancient Greek response, from pagan origins)

Christe eleison Christ have mercy on us
(Gregorian addition in the 6th century)

Gloria in excelsis Deo Glory to God on high
(Latinized from the Greek, *c.*600)

Credo in unum Deum I believe in one God
(Officially incorporated in 1014)

Sanctus Dominus Deus Saboath Holy Lord God of Hosts
(Jewish, from *c.*1000)

Benedictus qui venit in nomine Domini Blessed is he that cometh in the name of the Lord
(Subsection of the *Sanctus*)

Agnus Dei Lamb of God (John i.29)
(Added late in the 7th century)

Settings of the mass are numerous. Palestrina (1525/6–94) wrote 104, F.X. Brixi (1732–71) about 100, and the line extends through Bach, Haydn, Mozart, Beethoven, and on to Bruckner. Then, in 1903, the exuberant symphonic treatment often given to the text was abruptly terminated by a Papal Bull issued by Pope Pius X. This instructed that the words should take a higher priority than the music. Thenceforth, composers diversified by producing masses with secular texts (e.g. Delius's *A Mass of Life*, 1905) or in languages other than Latin (Janáček's *Mša Glagolskaya*, 1926, a setting of a 9th-century Slavonic text). More recent examples have sought to integrate into the mass forms popular music, as in Geoffrey Beaumont's *Twentieth Century Folk Mass* (1956), which uses various then-contemporary dance rhythms behind easily remembered tunes, and English words, and John Dankworth's *Folk Mass* (1970). The *Missa Luba* and *Missa Criolla* bring ethnic (respectively Black African and Creole) idioms to the mass.

Durham cathedral as the choir enters to take its place. (Mary Evans Picture Library)

Missa Brevis

The Missa Brevis (= 'Short Mass') compresses all the text of the mass into the space of half an hour or less, which is useful during wintertime in an unheated church.

Requiem

The Requiem, or *Missa pro Defunctis* (= 'Mass for the Dead') is a composition of mourning, once again set always to the same words. The sections of the text, which is a modified version of the High Mass, are as follows:

Requiem aeternam dona eis Eternal rest given unto them

Music Sung

Palestrina receiving benediction from Pope Julius III in return for his mass. (Mary Evans Picture Library)

Kyrie eleison Lord have mercy on us

Christe eleison Christ have mercy on us

Dies irae Day of Wrath

Tuba mirum Wondrous trumpet

Rex tremendae majestatis King of majesty tremendous

Recordare, Jesu pie Think, kind Jesus

Confutatis maledictus When the wicked are confounded

Lacrimose dies illa Day of mourning

Domine Jesu Christe Lord Jesus Christ

Hostias et preces tibi, Domine We offer Thee, Lord

Sanctus Holy

Benedictus qui venit in nomine Domini Blessed is he that cometh in the name of the Lord

Agnus Dei Lamb of God

Robert and Clara Schumann. (Mansell Collection)

Such musical gatherings were common amongst the wealthy in France and elsewhere in the 18th century. (Mary Evans Picture Library)

Le Concert.
A Madame la Comtesse de Sain Brisson

Right: The console of the world's largest organ — the great John Wanamaker organ in the Grant Court, Philadelphia.

Below: With 451 stops, 964 controls and weighing nearly 2½ tons its installation in the Grant Court was completed in 1911, following its manufacture in successive stages.

Benjamin Britten. (National Portrait Gallery)

Below: Giuseppe Verdi, who wrote Falstaff, *one of his greatest operas, at the age of nearly 80. (Mary Evans Picture Library)*

Below: Rossini as a young man, before alopecia and cold weather induced him to wear a wig . . . or two . . . or three. *See p. 120* *(Mary Evans Picture Library*

Egyptian harper with a primitive 10-string harp, pictured on the Tomb of the Kings, Thebes. (Mary Evans Picture Library)

'Three little maids from school' The Mikado *is one of the most popular products of the most successful composer/librettist partnership in music: Gilbert and Sullivan. (Mary Evans Picture Library)*

Dec 19 1937

BEECHAM SUNDAY CONCERTS

ROYAL OPERA HOUSE COVENT GARDEN

Chinese instruments — list to right: er-hu (bowed lute), sheng (mouth organ), san-hsien (3-stringed lute), pi'pa (4-stringed lute). (Mary Evans Picture Library)

George Frideric Handel, composer of the oratorio Beyond the Veil *which does not appear in any work-list of his music.* *See p. 226* *(Mary Evans Picture Library)*

Benjamin Britten, composer of the powerfully pacifist War Requiem *which uses Wilfred Owen's anti-war poems. (Decca Record Co. Ltd)*

Ockeghem's *Requiem* of possibly as early as 1470 is the oldest extant example; prominent subsequently are those by Michael Haydn (1771), Mozart (1791), whose setting was completed by Franz Xaver Süssmayr, his pupil; and more recently by others: Berlioz (Paris, 1837); Bruckner (1849, revised 1854 and 1894); Verdi (St Mark's, Milan, 1874); Fauré (1887); Brahms's *German Requiem*, first heard in Bremen Cathedral in 1868; and Benjamin Britten (*War Requiem*, 1962), in which Wilfred Owen's war poems are interspersed amidst the requiem text. Neither of these last two is a true Requiem since the Britten is based on English war poems, and the Brahms is based on German words from the bible; they should more correctly be called oratorios.

ORATORIO

Established in Rome in *c.*1600 as a semi-dramatic treatment of a sacred subject performed in the oratory, but not called 'oratorio' until 1640, this form has received attention from many distinguished composers, most notably Bach and Handel. The first oratorio was Emilio de Cavalieri's *La Rappresentazione dell' anima e del corpo* ('The Representation of Soul and Body'), given in the oratory of the Church of Santa Maria in Vallicella, Rome, in 1600.

The spread of oratorio after its appearance in Italy came about in the following way:

First German oratorio *Historia der Auferstehung Jesu Christi* (1623) by Heinrich Schütz. This work, however, is an adaptation of the *Resurrection* of about 1573 by Antonius Scandellus (or Antonio Scandello).

First French oratorio *Le Reniement de St Pierre* by Marc-Antoine Charpentier, composed about 1600.

First oratorio heard in England Handel's *Esther*, of 1720. The original title of the work was *Haman and Mordecai*.

First oratorio written in Russia Giuseppe Sarti's *Oratorio for Catherine the Great*, of about 1800.

First oratorio heard in America Samuel Felsted's *Jonah*, which had reached New York by 1775. However, the **first oratorio to have been composed by an American** was *Hora Novissima* of 1893 by Horatio Parker.

Oratorio was, however, not restricted to Europe and North America: *Oratoria ao Menino Deos para a Noite de Natal* was composed by the Brazilian Ignacio Parreiras Neves in 1789.

In its earliest days oratorio was often accompanied by stage action, and even during the 19th century the more dramatic oratorios were sometimes presented as stage dramas. Perhaps the safest way to tell oratorio apart from opera is to decide whether a performance of a given work will be less effective *without* stage presentation. If so, the work is an opera. The definition is nevertheless vague, and it is because of this that it is impossible to state the identity of the most prolific composer of oratorios. If sacred works alone are considered, Handel's total is 18, and there are a dozen or so secular choral works. Antonio Draghi's total is 13 oratorios and 29 *sepolcri*, which were in effect staged oratorios. (See also Motets, below.)

The best known of all oratorios is *Messiah* by George Frideric Handel. *Messiah* is known and loved the world over by musicians and, inexplicably, by those with neither religious nor musical interest in the work and who would admit to listening to no other example of serious music. The reason for this may be the vast exposure given to the work, hardly a year passing without it being given at Christmas-time, and also often again at Easter, in most of the English-speaking musical centres of the world. This tradition took a few years to become established: the early history of *Messiah* performances may be seen in the adjacent chart.

A performance in London's Westminster Abbey on 26 May 1784, held to commemorate the 25th anniversary of Handel's burial there, was planned on a mammoth scale: 95 violins, 26 violas, 21 cellos, 15 double basses, 26 oboes, 26 bassoons, 6 flutes, 12 trumpets, 4 sets of kettle drums and, to enrich the lower line, a double bassoon, and specially-made 'double base (*sic*) kettle drums'. The chorus numbered 257 voices in addition to the soloists, and Joah Bates directed the performance from a harpsichord specially designed with levers connecting it to the organ, 19ft (5.8m) away. The Royal Choral Society, established in London in 1873, celebrated its 230th performance of *Messiah* on Good Friday, 9 April 1982, so the tradition which lived through the Handel Festivals at the Crystal Palace annually from 1859 to 1926 (frequently with a choir of 4000) continues to the present day.

An unusual secular oratorio appeared in 1935. Its title is *Wagadu Destroyed* by Vladimir Vogel, and it is scored for solo voices and chorus (sometimes using *Sprechgesang*, 'speech-singing') and just five saxophones. See also Raimondi's multiple oratorios on pp 118–9.

Early Messiah Performances

Below we follow the early history of *Messiah* performances, showing the slow start it had in London, and the first performances it received in the provinces. At first, in London, *Messiah* met resistance because it appeared unseemly that a sacred work with this title should be given in a common play-house. It was not for some years, and then only by building a reputation for giving performances for charity, that Handel and his promoters were emboldened to mount *Messiah* invariably under its proper name.

Dublin 13 April 1742, first performance in The Music Hall, Fishamble Street (a number of performances followed in Dublin, usually for charity).

London 23 March 1743, in the Covent Garden Theatre, as 'New Sacred Oratorio'.

London February 1744, given by the Academy of Ancient Music as 'Messiah, A Sacred Oratorio'.

London 9 April 1745, at the King's Theatre, Haymarket, as 'The Sacred Oratorio'.

London 11 April 1745, at the King's Theatre, as 'A Sacred Oratorio'.

London 23 March 1749, at Covent Garden Theatre.

Oxford April 1749, organised by William Hayes in the Radcliffe Camera.

London 1 and 15 May 1750 at the Foundling Hospital Chapel (and every year thereafter until 1759).

Salisbury 4 October 1750, directed by John Stephens.

Bath May 1755, in Wiltshire's Rooms, organised by Giuseppe Passerini.

Bristol January 1756, in the New Musick Room.

Gloucester 1757, in Booth Hall, conducted by William Hayes.

Worcester 1758, in College Hall.

Hereford 1759, in the Cathedral, conducted by Richard Clack.

Passion

Although akin to oratorio, the passion's purpose specifically is to enact the Passion of Jesus Christ during Holy Week. Its roots lie in the old miracle and passion plays and in the semi-dramatic presentation of the Passion story in church, in which the words of Christ (only) were chanted.

The earliest musical passions date from 10th-century England and were performed at mass on Holy days. At these the music was monophonic but from about 1450 the choral sections were polyphonic, the solos plainsong. Latin settings were supplemented by the vernacular for greater accessibility by Johann Walther during the 1520s. In direct contrast to the sombre message of the passion comes the *Te Deum*, which is a Latin chant of praise to God on some glorious occasion, such as a military victory or the consecration of a bishop. The *Te Deum* orginated at least as early as the 4th century AD; some of its roots may go back a further two centuries. It is not a frequently chosen genre today, but Sir William Walton's *Te Deum* of 1953 written for the coronation of Queen Eliabeth II is a superb modern example.

Secular Music

The secular song is as old as man. Its descendants are diverse and are not always clearly differentiated from sacred song.

■ *The oldest known song is the* shaduf *chant, which has been sung since time immemorial by irrigation workers on the man-powered pivoted-rod bucket raisers of the Nile water mills (or* saqiyas*) in Egypt. The oldest known harmonized music performed today is the English song* Sumer is icumen in *which dates from c.1240.* ■

Chronologically, the introduction of the various *genre* was as follows:

*c.***1200** Motet. This grew out of the sacred conductus and, for a time, continued to have liturgical connections, the word 'motet' being a diminutive of the Old French *mot* (= 'given word', *cf.* 'motto') or scriptural saying. Generally unaccompanied and with up to 10 independent parts, the motet was immensely popular up to about 1700. A comprehensive list of prolific composers of motets serves little point here. Numerically, Lassus (with 526) would head the list, with Palestrina (382), A. Grandi (212), Josquin (*c.*180) and Campra (161) following, but Grandi's and some other composers' motets are short and slight works which bear no relation in size, complexity or scope to Lalande's 72 *Grandes motets*. Furthermore, the whole issue is confused by terminology. Although Pérotin composed the first motets about 1200, he did not necessarily call them by that name; and Charpentier's 48 'dramatic motets' are really oratorios and should not be added to his 157 other works called motets.

*c.***1350** Madrigal, first described in Northern Italy in *c.*1425. The origin of the word is unclear and in any case disputed. The first madrigal-style works were written perhaps by Majister Piero (?–*c.*1352); they are two-voiced settings of secular verses.

*c.***1400** *Lied*. The German 'polyphonic *lied*' (i.e. two vocal/instrumental parts) was written about or before 1400 by a composer known only as the Monk of Salzburg; but what is commonly understood today by *Lied* is the German art song for one voice with instrumental accompaniment. This arose in Berlin in 1752 with the publication of C.S. Krause's (1719–70) *Lieder*, included with which were certain ground rules as to what the *Lied* should be: simple folklike songs which reflect the meaning of the texts and may be sung without accompaniment if need be. Probably the most prolific of all *Lieder* writers is Schubert, with a total of *c*.600.

1620 Cantata, a work to be sung, just as a sonata is a work to be played. It began modestly in Italy with *Cantade et arie* (before 1620) by Alessandro Grandi. It was a popular form set for voices, almost always with instruments, and it culminated in Bach's prodigious total of over 200. However, he was far from being the most prolific cantata composer. That honour goes to Telemann with his total of about 1270.

OPERA

An Opera *is a Poetical Tale, or fiction, represented by Vocal and Instrumental Musick, adorn'd with Scenes, Machines and Dancing. The suppos'd Persons of this Musical* Drama, *are generally Supernatural, as Gods and Goddesses, and Heroes, which at least are descended from them, and in due time are to be adopted into their number.*
John Dryden

Dryden's 17th-century view of opera goes on in its snobbish way grudgingly to admit 'meaner persons' such as shepherds only if they are essential to the action, but the common person was strictly excluded for most of the time. Opera's subjects were later to include all manners and classes of people, and we may assume that the earliest ancestors of opera were also a little less class conscious.

Claudio Monteverdi, whose Orfeo *was probably the first opera to place musical considerations above ludicrous stage effects. (Mary Evans Picture Library)*

These are the known facts concerning the components which led to the establishment of opera and its spread.

400 BC Greek tragedy of this period seems to have included singing as part of the drama. For instance, Euripides's play *Orestes* was performed with accompanying music, some of which may have been sung.

c.**1283 AD** Adam de la Hale (*c*.1240–88), a French *trouvère* known as the 'Hunchback of Arras', wrote *Le Jeu de Robin et de Marion*, which was performed in Naples at about this time. It is a kind of proto-opera in which a story is told in music.

1472 Angelo Poliziano's play *Orfeo* was produced in Mantua. Edward J. Dent suggests that its structure indicates that many of the poems were sung.

16th century The Italian composer Vincenzo Galilei, father of the astronomer Galileo Galilei, produced songs and lute solos which may have assisted in the development of opera as a distinct art form. During the century, the setting of sacred texts and miracle plays to music gradually took three separate ways. These resulted in the following concepts which, despite elements from each which could be found in the others, had crystallized by about 1600 into:

Masque — a usually mythological play with poetry, music, dancing and other stage presentations, in which the actors wore masks.

Oratorio — a presentation of a liturgical story with music. (See above)

Opera — the Italian word for 'work' (compare *opus*: the Italian word for opera is *Melodramma* = 'melody' + 'drama').

Another contributory stream was the *Commedia harmonica* productions of Orazio Vecchi around 1590. These comprised a series of madrigals arranged to form a dramatic continuity, but they were for chamber use and do not appear to have been produced on stage with 'props'.

1597 The earliest true opera: *Dafne* by Jacopo Peri. Although the music is lost, the libretto by Rinuccini survives together with some of the directions for the production. A big, terrifying serpent is required which is controlled by a man

An example of the elaborate stage settings common in the 17th and 18th centuries. This was for an intermède. *(Motley Books Ltd)*

on all-fours within. The creature is made to sway and undulate, to flap its wings and to breathe fire.

1600 The earliest surviving opera: *Eurydice* by Peri and Giulio Caccini. Later that year Caccini reset the same Eurydice story without assistance from any other composer. These works were performed at the house of Giovanni Bardi, Count of Vernio, in Florence.

1607 The earliest opera which is still occasionally performed is Monteverdi's *Orfeo*.

1627 The first German opera was *Daphne* by Heinrich Schütz. It was produced at Torgau but has since entirely disappeared.

1629 The first Spanish opera (or 'pastoral eclogue') was *La Selva Sin Amor* ('The Forest Without Love'), sung in honour of King Philip IV. The composer's name and his music are lost, but it is known that the text of this one-act piece was by Lope de Vega. It was a predecessor of the *Zarzuela*, but this name did not come into use until *El Golfo de las Sirenas* (music anonymous, text by Calderón de la Barca), which was given at the Palace of La Zarzuela on 17 January 1657. Calderón's is the earliest surviving *Zarzuela*.

1629 The first Yugoslav opera was *Atalante* by Junije Palmotić.

1637 The first public opera house at which an admittance fee was charged was the San Cassiano Theatre in Venice. The first performance there was of *Andromeda* by Manelli, with a libretto by Ferrari.

1656 The first English opera, and the first ever heard in England was *The First Dayes Entertainment at Rutland House by Declamation and Musick: After the Manner of the Ancients* with a libretto by Sir William Davenant, who later became poet laureate. It was a series of speeches between which vocal and instrumental music was performed. The music is lost, as is the composer's name.

1671 The earliest surviving French opera is *Pomone* by Robert Cambert. In 1659 Cambert had written *La Pastorale* which is lost, and *Ariane* which, however, was not performed until 1674, and then only in London (see below). *Ariane* also is lost.

Music Sung

1674 At a performance of Locke's *Tempest* at Dorset Gardens Theatre, London, the orchestra was for the first time brought down from its high platform above the stage and placed below and in front of the stage, where we would normally expect to find it now. In the same year came the first foreign opera to be heard in England: *Ariane* by Louis Grabu, with a libretto by Cambert. It was in fact given in an English translation, and was performed on the occasion of the wedding of the Duke of York and Mary of Modena.

c.**1675** The beginnings of a breakaway form — pantomime — are to be found in the stage parodies of Thomas Duffett, whose operatic caricatures probably contained the origins of the conventions of the 'Principal Boy' being taken by a young actress, and the 'Dame' by a male comedian.

1682 The first Italian opera to be performed outside Italy was Francesca Caccini's *La liberazione di Ruggiero dall'isola d'Alcina* of 1625, which was given in Warsaw in 1682.

1688 The first opera written in the Netherlands was Servaas de Konink's *De vrijadje van Cloris en Roosje*.

1692 The first opera to be based on a Shakespeare story was Purcell's *The Fairy Queen* adapted from *A Midsummer Night's Dream* and given at the Dorset Gardens Theatre, London, in April.

1701 The first opera produced in the New World was *La purpura de la rosa*, given in Lima, Peru. The composer was the Spanish-born Tomás de Torrejón y Velasco who became a court official to Pedro Fernández de Castro y Andrade and moved with him to Peru in 1667.

1704 The first opera to be heard in Prague was Sartori's *La Rete di Vulcano*.

1710 The first opera in England to be performed entirely in Italian was *Almahide*, a pastiche by a group of composers led by Giovanni Bononcini. It was Italian opera in London which prompted Dr Johnson's famous description of opera as 'an exotick and irrational entertainment'.

1711 The first opera by a Mexican was *La Parténope* by Manuel Zumaya, given on 1 May at the Viceregal Palace, Mexico City.

1731 The first opera performed in Russia was Giovanni Alberto Ristori's *Calandro* of 1726.

1732 Covent Garden Theatre, London, was opened. It was modelled on the famous King's Theatre in the Haymarket, site of most of Handel's premières. Fire destroyed Covent Garden in 1808 but it was rebuilt.

1733 The first opera by a Portuguese composer was *La Pazienza di Socrate* (written in Italian) by Francisco António de Almeida. The same year Antonio José da Silva wrote the first Portuguese language opera: *Vida do grande D. Quixotte de la Mancha*.

1733 The first *opera buffa* was said to be Pergolesi's *La Serva Padrona*, designed to be performed between the acts of his *opera seria Il Prigioneri Superbo*.

1735 The first opera heard in America was *Flora, or Hob in the Well* (a popular English ballad opera, composer unknown), produced at Charles Town — later Charleston — South Carolina.

1737 The first opera composed in Russia was Francesco Araia's *Il finto Nino*.

1743 The birth of *Singspiel*, a German form of the English ballad opera, took place in Berlin with a translation of Coffey's *The Devil to Pay*. The style became more popular in 1764 when J.A. Hiller set the same story for performance at Leipzig. Hiller became known as 'the father of *Singspiel*'.

1751 The first opera performed in Scotland was Lampe's *The Dragon of Wantley*, given in Edinburgh.

1755 The first Russian language opera was *Cephal i Prokris* by Araia, libretto by Sumarokov, produced in St Petersburg on 10 March. The first opera composed by a Russian (but in Italian) was *Demofonte* (*c*.1770) by Berezowski; this was also the first opera by a Russian to be performed abroad: in Bologna and Livorno in 1773. The first Russian language opera by a Russian appears to have been *Miller, Wizard, Cheat and Marriage-broker* (1779) by Sokolovsky.

1756 The first Danish opera was *Gram og Signe* by Sarti and Kleen, libretto by Bredal.

1767 The first ballad opera composed in America was *The Disappointment: or the Force of Credulity* (composer unknown), which included the song 'Yankee Doodle', also known as 'The Lexington March', adopted as America's unofficial anthem in 1782.

1778 The first Polish opera was *Nedza Uszczésliwiona* ('Misery Contented') by Maciej Kamieńsky.

1786 The first opera to be performed in Turkey was by Heidenstam (name of opera unknown) given at Pera on 22 February.

Music Sung

1788 The first opera to be written by a Canadian was *Colas et Colinette* by Joseph Quesnel.

*c.***1790** The first Hungarian opera was *Pikko Hertzeg és Jutka Perzsi* by József Chudy.

1794 The first American opera was *Tammanny* by James Hewitt. The first American opera on a native subject was G.F. Bristow's *Rip van Winkle* (1855).

1809 The first Brazilian opera was *Le due gemelle* by José Maurício Nunez Garcia.

1824 The first Norwegian opera was *Fjeldeventyret* by Waldemar Thrane.

1837 The first opera performed in Greece was Rossini's *The Barber of Seville* (1816).

1843 The first opera written in Australia was Isaac Nathan's *Merry Freaks in troublous Times*, on the life and times of Charles II, not performed complete and not published until 1851. Nathan, an ancestor of Sir Charles Mackerras, was described in C.H. Bertie's books as 'Australia's first composer'. The first opera to be staged in Australia was Rossini's *La Cenerentola* (1817), in Sydney on 14 February 1844.

1845 The first grand opera by a native American was *Leonora* by William Henry Fry.

1846 The first opera written in Chile was *La Telesofra* by Aquinas Pied, a native of Bavaria.

1848 The first Romanian opera was *The Witch Hîrca* by Alexandru Adolf Flechtenmacher.

1866 The first true Czech opera was *The Bartered Bride* by Smetana, one of his eight operas.

1866 The first musical comedy was *The Black Crook*, words by Charles Barras, the music assembled from popular tunes of the day by Giuseppe Operti, which opened on Broadway, New York and ran for 474 performances in that production. It remained popular for a further quarter of a century in New York and the provinces.

1867 The first Greek opera was *O ypopsifios vouleftis* ('The Parliamentary Candidate') by Spyridon Xyndas.

Royal Opera House, Covent Garden, London, completed in 1809. It replaced the original theatre which was burnt down in 1808, and itself suffered the same fate in 1856. The present theatre, built in 1858, stands on the same site. (Mary Evans Picture Library)

Queen Victoria watching Cavalleria Rusticana *at Windsor Castle, surrounded by members of her family. (The Mansell Collection)*

1874 The first musical comedy with original music was *Evangeline*, an 'American Extravaganza' by Edward E. Rice.

1883 The Metropolitan Opera House, New York, opened with the first American production of Gounod's *Faust*.

1897 The first Argentinian composer to write operas with South American settings was Arturo Berutti, whose *Pampa* dates from this year.

1898 The first Finnish language opera was *Pohjan neito* ('The Maid of Bothnia') by Frans Oskar Merikanto, with a libretto by Antti Rytkönen (produced at Viborg, 18 June 1908).

1904 The first New Zealand opera was *Tapu*, composed by the Australian Alfred Hill but based on a Maori theme.

1909 The first Bulgarian opera, strictly, was *Detsa i ptichki* ('Children and Birds'), a children's opera by Panayot Pipkov, but the first opera for adults was *Borislav* (1911) by Georgi Athanassov.

1912 The first Western-type Japanese opera was *The Depraved Heavenly Maiden*, written in Germany by Kosaku Yamada; its Oriental première was in Tokyo in 1929.

1914 The first Argentinian nationalist opera in Spanish was *Tucamán* by Felipe Boero.

1934 The first Turkish opera was Ahmet Adnan Saygun's *Özsoy*.

How Many Operas?

Frankly, no-one can say. In his *Annals of Opera 1597–1940* Alfred Loewenberg lists some 3500, while in their research into 18th-century music the authors have examined some 1500 from that period alone which are not listed by Loewenberg. It has been estimated that some 25 000 operatic libretti were written before 1800, and some of these were set to music more than once — a few many times. It is not possible always to be accurate as to the number of operas written by a given composer. Albinoni, for instance, claimed to have written over 200 operas, never spending more than a week on any one, but only about 57 are known to us. Often two or more composers shared the writing of an opera, and sometimes it is difficult to draw a distinction between, say, opera and oratorio or cantata. The totals in our chart, then, are somewhat provisional but in any case it may help to put them in perspective if we remember that, of operas, musical plays, serenatas, etc., Rossini wrote 39, Verdi 28, Mozart 22 and Puccini 10. This does not imply criticism of Mozart in favour of Müller, or of Puccini in favour of Piccinni. Quantity does not necessarily equate with quality.

OPERATIC LEAGUE TABLE

*c.*250 Müller, Wenzel (1767–1835): Singspiele, operas, pantomimes, etc.
209 Casimiro, Joaquin, Júnior (1808–62): operas, musical plays, etc.
*c.*200 Caballero, M.F. (1835–1906): zarzuelas
122 Draghi, Antonio (1634–1700): operas
122 Piccinni, Nicolò (1728–1800): operas
119 Bishop, Henry Rowley (1786–1855): operas, masques, melodramas, musical plays, etc.
105 Galuppi, Baldassare (1706–85): operas (including five doubtful)
101 Offenbach, Jacques (1819–80): operas, operettas, plus four vaudevilles
97 Scarlatti, Alessandro (1660–1725): operas, including 28 serenatas
91+ Guglielmi, Pietro Alessandro (1728–1804): operas, plus contributions to six pastiches, and many doubtful operas
91 Paisiello, Giovanni (1740–1816): operas
86(?) Cimarosa, Domenico (1749–1810): operas, including a small number doubtful
81 Keiser, Reinhard (1674–1739): operas, Singspiele, etc.
74+ Hasse, Johann Adolf (1699–1783): operas, including 11 intermezzi
60+ Caruso, Luigi (1754–1822): operas

Who Wrote the Stories?

One component of an opera which is sometimes overlooked, often disregarded, and frequently libelled, but without which there would be no opera, is the libretto. The great majority of libretti are completed before the composer sets to work on the music. No matter how much it may seem that the reverse is true, it is rarely possible to set the words of a drama to music which already exists.

But do the words make sense, and, furthermore, is there any logic to the combination of score, libretto and stage production? Francesco Algarotti (1712–64), a famous Italian writer on opera, described late baroque opera as 'a languid, disconnected, unlifelike, monstrous and grotesque composition'; and Lord Chesterfield remarked 'Opera is a magic scene contrived to please the eye and the ear at the expense of the understanding'.

■ *The longest operatic encore, listed in the* Concise Oxford Dictionary of Opera, *was of the entire opera: Cimarosa's* Il Matrimonio Segreto *at its première in 1792. This was at the command of the Austro-Hungarian Emperor Leopold II (1790–92).*

It was reported on 5 July 1983 that Placido Domingo received 83 curtain calls and was applauded for 1 hour 30 minutes after singing the lead in Puccini's La Bohème *at the State Opera House in Vienna, Austria.* ■

The word 'libretto' ('little book') comes from the time, near the beginning of operatic history, when the story and the music were bound separately. The earliest operatic singers were primarily actors who learnt their vocal parts by ear: to have the music *and* the words bound together would have made the book unnecessarily cumbersome.

Many famous writers have provided stories upon which operas have been based, while other writers have made a speciality of the operatic libretto. The casual attitude towards plot and narrative is typified by an incident which took place in Dublin in 1868 during a performance of Weber's *Oberon*. The popular German soprano Therese Tietjens (1831–87) was applauded for a quarter of an hour after singing 'Ocean, thou mighty monster', and thus the progress of the story was seriously disrupted. Rather than attempt to pick up the thread, the audience demanded that Tietjens sing 'The last rose of summer'; but the orchestra did not have the musical parts for the song to hand, so Oberon and five demons dragged a piano onto the stage, a pianist was found, and the soprano sang her song, to adoring applause. Weber's masterpiece was then allowed to continue.

From early on in the history of opera, libretto writing was an art distinct from the musical side of opera production. The librettist built up for himself a reputation for producing stories mainly in poetic form — the more musical the words, the more successful the opera was likely to be. Unfortunately, the result of putting poetry and music first was that the story had to go last: nowhere are there such ludicrous, involved, fatuous stories as those in opera libretti.

Henry Rowley Bishop, the most prolific English stage composer. (Mary Evans Picture Library)

Some composers have tried to avoid the complications inherent in the task of setting another's words to music by producing their own libretti. Wagner is the best-known example: not once did he trust the story of another man, and he thereby evaded the deep philosophical questing for 'the right story' which Beethoven suffered.

The world's first librettist was Ottavio Rinuccini (1562–1621). He provided the stories for the first operas: *Dafne* (1597) and *Euridice* (1600), both with music by Peri. The most successful was undoubtedly Pietro Antonio Domenico Bonaventura Trepassi (1698–1782), the Italian poet who is better known by the name given to him by his adoptive father Vincento Gravina: Metastasio. The texts he wrote, over 70 in number, were so popular during his lifetime that a list of his stories and the composers who set them would take on the appearance of a history of 18th-century opera. His most popular libretti were:

Didone Abbandonata (1724)
Siroe (rè di Persia) (1726)
Catone in Utica (1727)
Ezio (1728)
Alessandro nell'Indie (1729)
Semiramide riconosciuta (1729)
Artaserse (1730)
Adriano in Siria (1731)
Demetrio (1732)
Démophon (1733)
Olimpiade (1733)
Il Clemenza di Tito (1734)

Metastasio, the world's most successful librettist. Engraving by T.E. Mansfield, after the portrait by J.N. Steiner. (Országos Széchényi Könyvtár, Budapest)

After 26 stories which met with less acclaim came *Il Rè Pastore* (1751) and a further series of less successful libretti, culminating with his last, *Lucio Silla*, set by Mozart in 1772 and J.C. Bach two years later.

Other prominent librettists are:

Barbier, Jules (1822–1901), worked with Carré on *Les Noces de Jeanette* (Masse, 1853); *Faust* (Gounod, 1859); *Philemon et Baucis* (Gounod, 1860); *Mignon* (Thomas, 1866); *Roméo et Juliette* (Gounod, 1867); *Hamlet* (Thomas, 1868), *Tales of Hoffmann* (Offenbach, 1881).

Calzabigi (or Calsabigi), Raniero da (1714–95) was friendly with Gluck, with whom he worked to bring about various operatic reforms. He provided Gluck with a number of libretti including *Orfeo ed Euridice* (1762), *Alceste* (1767), and *Paride ed Elena* (1770). He also wrote libretti for other composers (e.g. *La critica teatrale* by Gassmann, 1769).

Cammarano, Salvatore (1801–52), author and theatre manager. His stories include: *Lucia di Lammermoor* (Donizetti, 1835); *Don Pasquale* (Donizetti, 1843); *Il Trovatore* (Verdi, 1853).

Carré, Michel (1819–72) — see Barbier.

Forzano, Gioachino (or Giovacchino) (1883–1958), provided the libretto for two-thirds of Puccini's *Il Trittico* (1819), i.e. *Suor Angelica*, and *Gianni Schicchi*. The story for the first part of the triptych, *Il Tabarro*, was written by Giuseppe Adami.

Ghislanzoni, Antonio (1824–93). His most famous story is *Aïda* (Verdi, 1870).

Gilbert, William Schwenk (1836–1911), the only librettist to be billed consistently above the composer. His career with **Sir Arthur Sullivan** (1842–1900) began with *Thespis* (1871) and continued with the following successes: *Trial by Jury* (1875), *The Sorcerer* (1877), *H.M.S. Pinafore* (1878), *The Pirates of Penzance* (1879) and *Patience* (1881). In 1881 the specially built Savoy Theatre opened, the players there being known as 'The Savoyards'. The series continued with *Iolanthe* (1882), *Princess Ida* (1884), *The Mikado* (1885), *Ruddigore* (1887), *The Yeomen of the Guard* (1888), *The Gondoliers* (1889), *Utopia Limited* (1893) and *The Grand Duke* (1896).

Their partnership lasted a surprisingly long time in view of its tempestuous nature. Gilbert was pompous and arrogant. 'I know nothing about music', he boasted one day to Sullivan. 'I merely know that there is composition and decomposition. That is what your song is — rot!' Sullivan was mild-mannered and forgiving. The partnership eventually collapsed over the most trivial of matters: the choice of a carpet for the Savoy Theatre.

Goldoni, Carlo (1707–93). Known as the 'Father of Opera Buffa', Goldoni wrote 78 libretti, often using his pastoral name (Polisseno Feglio) or humorous anagrams (sometimes inexact) of his own name: Aldimiro Clog; Loran Glodici; Calindo Grolo; Sogol Cardoni. Galuppi was the best customer for Goldoni's libretti, setting about 20 stories, but as will be seen from the selection which follows, he was by no means the only composer to show an interest in these charming comedies: *La Generosità Politica* (Marchi, 1736); *Il Negligente* (Ciampi, 1749; Paisiello, 1765); *La Contessina* (Maccari, 1743; Gassmann, 1770); *Il Mondo della Luna* (Galuppi, 1750; Haydn, 1777; Paisiello, 1783); *Arcifanfano* (Galuppi, 1750; Dittersdorf, 1777); *La Buona Figliuola* (Duni, 1757; Piccinni, 1760); *La Pescatrice* (Paisiello, 1766; Piccinni, 1766; Haydn, 1770); *Lo Speziale* (Pallavicini, Act I, and Fischietti, Acts II and III, 1759; Haydn, 1768); *Il Ciarlatano* (Scolari, 1759).

Halévy, Ludovic (1834–1908), nephew of the composer Fromenthal Halévy. His collaboration with Henri Meilhac produced several Offenbach operettas, including *La Belle Hélène* (1864), *Barbe-Bleue* (1866), *La Vie Parisienne* (1866), and *La Périchole* (1868), and Bizet's opera *Carmen* (1875), and in association with H. Crémieux, Offenbach's *Orphée aux Enfers* (1858).

Illica, Luigi (1857–1919), best known for his partnership with Giuseppe Giacosa for Puccini's *La Bohème* (1896), *Tosca* (1900), and *Madame Butterfly* (1904). Illica was also responsible for many other less successful libretti: *Cristoforo Colombo* (Franchetti, 1892); *Andrea Chenier* (Giordano, 1896); *Iris* (Mascagni, 1898); *Germania* (Franchetti, 1902); *Siberia* (Giordano, 1903); *Tess* (Erlanger, 1909); *Isobeau* (Mascagni, 1911).

Piave, Francesco Maria (1810–76) wrote the libretti for Verdi's operas *Ernani* (1844), *Macbeth* (1847), *Rigoletto* (1851), and *La Traviata* (1853). He also collaborated with Boïto for Verdi's *Simon Boccanegra* (1857) but this was revised by Boïto in 1881.

Planché, James Robinson (1796–1880), best known for his *Oberon* (Weber, 1826).

Ponte, Lorenzo da (1749–1838), born Emanuele Conegliano, he worked as a writer in Dresden and Vienna until 1791, when he moved to London and opened a publishing house. From 1805 to his death he lived in Columbia, USA, and became an American citizen. As Mozart's best-known librettist, he produced *Le Nozze di Figaro* (1786), *Don Giovanni* (1787), *Cosí fan Tutte* (1790), as well as books for Bianchi (*Antigona*, 1796; *Merope*, 1797), Martín y Soler (*Una cosa Rara*, 1786; *L'Arbore di Diana*, 1787; *La Scola de'maritati*, 1795), and Salieri (*Il Ricco d'un Giorno*, 1784; *Axur, Ré d'Ormus*, 1788).

Romani, Felice (1788–1865), the author of some 80 libretti, ten of which were set by Donizetti and sixteen by Mercadante. Bellini also chose a number of stories: *Il Pirata* (1827); *Zaira* (1829); *La Straniera* (1829); *I Capuletti e i Montecchi* (1830); *Norma* (1831); *La Sonnambula* (1833) and *Beatrice di Tenda* (1833). Romani's stories were also set by Carlo Conti, Carlo Coccia, Mayr, and Verdi (*Un Giorno di Regno*, 1840).

Schikaneder, Emanuel (1751–1812) is best known for *Die Zauberflöte* (Mozart, 1791); he produced altogether over 50 libretti.

Scribe, Augustin Eugène (1791–1861), the so-called 'creator' of grand opera. He wrote the following stories set to music by Auber: *La Muette de Portici* (also called *Masaniello*, 1828); *Fra Diavolo* (1830); *Le Dieu et la Bayadère* (1830); *Le Philtre* (1831); *Gustav III* (1833); *Le Domino Noir* (1837); *Le Lac des Fées* (1839); *Crown Diamonds* (1841), and *L'Enfant Prodigue* (1850), among others. He achieved considerable success with Boieldieu — *La Dame Blanche* (1825); with Halévy — *La Juive* (1835); *Guido et Ginevre* (1838); *Le Juif Errant* (1852); and with Meyerbeer — *Robert le Diable* (1831); *Les Huguenots* (1836); *Le Prophète* (1849); *L'Etoile du Nord* (1854), and *L'Africaine* (1865).

Zeno, Apostolo (1668–1750) wrote a number of stories which were set to music by various Venetian composers. Among these libretti were *Faramondo* (1699); *Temistocle* (1700); *Antioco* (1705); *Lucio Papiro* (1719); *Ormisda* (1721); *Alessandro in Sidone* (1721), and *Ornospade* (1727).

Among the most popular stories to be selected for operatic treatment are:

Alceste, a tragedy written in 432 BC by Euripides (*c.*485–407 BC), which has been set under its own name and under *Admetus*, *Getreute Alceste*, etc., notably by Handel (1727 and 1750) and Gluck (1767).

Armida, based on a poem by Torquato Tasso (1544–95) called *Gerusalemme liberata* and completed in 1575; it also has been set numerous times under different names as well as its own, for example by Handel (1711), Vivaldi (1718) and Haydn (1784).

Orpheus, the legendary son of Apollo and the Muse Calliope, was written up by Ovid, Aristophanes, Boëthius and others and has been

Don Quixote *by Cervantes has inspired nearly a hundred musical works. (Popperfoto)*

treated operatically as *Orpheus*, *Orfeo*, *Favola d'Orfeo*, *Morte d'Orfeo*, *Orfeo ed Euridice* and other variations, first by Peri (1600), then notably by Gluck (1762), J.C. Bach (1770), Offenbach (1858) and others well into the present century.

Don Quixote, Cervantes' famous tale, according to a list sent to the authors recently by Aaron Cohen, the South African musicologist and researcher, has received the following attention:

Operas	43
Operettas	7
Zarzuelas	3
Ballets	14
Music Dramas	1
Incidental music	5
Cantata	1
Orchestral works	14
Miscellaneous	7
Total	95

Semiramide, a legend dating from 1593, set to music by F.P. Sacrati in 1648, made for the stage as *Semiramide riconosciuta* in 1729 and treated by Voltaire as *Semiramis* in 1748. The story was set for the musical stage by L. Vinci (1729), Paisiello (1772), Meyerbeer (1819), and Rossini (1823), among many others.

The most popular figure in English opera of the 18th century was Harlequin, who appeared in countless roles and guises, and was often introduced gratuitously in a kind of balletic aside known as the 'Harlequinade'.

What *is* Opera?

No two operas are the same, yet the stereotype persists in people's minds: a heroine, a hero, perhaps another couple to provide a sub-plot, a 'baddie', sometimes a chorus, always an orchestra, and stage settings offering the final word in escapist surrealism or impossible grandeur. The story proceeds fitfully, its course being interrupted for various set pieces: arias, ensembles, choruses. Duration? A couple of hours or so, plus an interval or two.

Stockhausen does not agree with this last rule. For him, an opera should take a week to perform; at least, that is his estimate for his *Licht* (Light), which he began composing in the 1970s

Title page of Monteverdi's Orfeo. *(Archiv für Kunst und Geschichte)*

L' ORFEO
FAVOLA IN MVSICA
DA CLAVDIO MONTEVERDI
RAPPRESENTATA IN MANTOVA
Anno 1607 & nouamente data in luce
AL SERENISSIMO SIGNOR
D. FRANCESCO GONZAGA
Prencipe di Mantoua, & di Monferato, &c
In Venetia Appresso Ricciardo Amadino
M D C IX.

and hopes to complete within 20 years. *Licht* will be, in fact, a cycle of operas, as is Wagner's *Der Ring des Nibelungen*, parts of which may be performed independently. Not so Robert Wilson's seven-act *The Life and Times of Joseph Stalin*, which played for over 13 hours when performed on 14–15 December 1973 at the Brooklyn Academy of Music. Gabriel von Wayditch's *The Heretics* (1958) and Rosenberg's *Joseph and his Brethren* (1948) are mere bagatelles in comparison at only eight hours each.

Steven Oliver's three 'instant operas' for children, *Old Haunts*, *Paid Off* and *Time Flies* (1976) detain their listeners for a mere nine or ten minutes each; shorter still is Milhaud's *The Deliverance of Theseus* (1928) at seven minutes 27 seconds. If time-saving is a consideration, Pietro Raimondi (see p 00) is here to help: his serious and comic operas may be performed either separately or simultaneously.

Today's operas sometimes convey a pointed social or political message, but the use of opera as a weapon is by no means new. Samuel Arnold's *The Genius of Nonsense*, Op 27 (1780), subtitled *An Original, Whimsical, Operatical, Pantomimical, Farcical, Electrical, Naval and Military Extravaganza* makes fun of the 'Temple of Health' run by a Dr Graham, who claimed to cure patients of sterility with an electric 'Celestial Bed'. The doctor was furious, but he never carried out his threatened libel action. However, an injunction was issued against the performance of Hindemith's *Neues vom Tage* (1929) on behalf of the Breslau gas-heating company, for in the opera the heroine takes a bath heated by electricity, singing the while of its benefits against the drawbacks of gas: 'No horrid smell, no danger of explosion'.

A tub of hot water on stage is the least of the stage manager's worries. Giordano's *Fedora* (1898) requires bicycles, Křenek's *Jonny Spielt Auf* (1927) calls for a car, and Herold's *Zampa* and Meyerbeer's *Robert le Diable* (both 1831) each requires a church organ. Verdi's *Aïda* (1871) has been staged, in particularly grand productions, with a procession of elephants.

The Opera that Never Was
For many years the 'first Polish Opera' was given as *La fama reale* (1633) by Piotr Elert (*c.*1600–53). The supposition was based on a text of this title having been printed by Elert, who was publisher as well as composer. Then it transpired that the text was that of a speech by Paolo Piazza, given for the succession to the throne in 1632 of King Władysław IV; it has nothing whatever to do with music or any stage production.

■ *The longest of commonly performed operas is* Die Meistersinger von Nürnberg *by Wilhelm Richard Wagner (1813–83) of Germany. A normal uncut performance of this opera as performed by the Sadler's Wells company between 24 August and 19 September 1968 entailed 5 hours 15 minutes of music.* ■

Operas About Composers
Below is a small group of works for which inspiration was drawn from the lives of earlier composers. The opera by Paul Graener takes a fact and exaggerates it; this, and a novel on the same subject by A.E. Brachvogel, has given posterity the completely wrong impression of Friedemann, the much-slandered son of J.S. Bach. Likewise, the opera by Rimsky-Korsakov takes a thread of suspicion and turns it into a drama which might easily be believed by the gullible.

Die Abreise, oder Flauto solo (1905), by D'Albert, about the flute-playing composer King Frederick the Great.

Adam de la Hale (1880), by Ernst Frank.

Chopin (1901), by Giacomo Orefice.

The Damask Rose (1929), by George Clutsam. This is about Chopin, with music based on that of Chopin.

Friedemann Bach (1931), by Paul Graener.

Lavotta szerelme ('Lavotta's Love'). János de Izsépfalva et Kevelháza Lavotta (1764–1820) was a Hungarian composer whose exploits inspired operas of that name by Hubay and Barna, and another piece, *Lavotta elsö szerelme* ('Lavotta's first Love'), once attributed to Lavotta but actually by József Kossovits.

Lilac Time (1922), about Franz Schubert, and using his music. This is an English version by Clutsam of the operetta *Das Dreimädelhaus* (1915) by Heinrich Berté.

Lully et Quinault, about a composer and his principle librettist, by Isouard (1812) and Berens (1859).

Mozart and Salieri (1898), by Rimsky-Korsakov.

Paganini (1925), by Franz Léhar.

Palestrina (1917), by Hans Erich Pfitzner.

Pergolesi (1868), by Paolo Serrao.

Rossini à Paris, ou le grand dîner (1823), by Mazères.

Rossini in Neapel (1936), by Bernard Paumgartner.

Franz Schubert (1864), by Franz von Suppé.

Alessandro Stradella, by Friedrich von Flotow (1844) and by Abraham Louis Niedermeyer (1846).

Taverner (1970), by Peter Maxwell Davies.

Trillo del Diavolo (1899), by Falchi, based on a supposed incident in the life of Tartini.

Ochsenmenuette (1823), by Seyfried, based on a supposed incident in the life of Joseph Haydn.

Wolfgang A. Mozart (1971), by Wilhelm Breuker.

Eduard Lassen wrote a *Beethoven* Overture, not as an operatic prelude but as an independent concert piece.

Robert Russell Bennett in 1925 wrote an opera about a famous opera singer: *Maria Malibran*.

ARTISTS, ARTISTS

The human voice is by far the most flexible musical instrument, capable of extremes of amplitude: a vocalized sound — as opposed to a whisper — can be barely audible to another person in the same room, while under freak conditions a voice has been heard at a distance of 10½ miles (16.9 km) across still water at night. Concerning extremes of pitch, composers have been more modest in their requirements than human ability allows. The highest written notes are by Mozart in the Concert Aria *Popoli de Tessacaglia*, KE 300B (K 316) of 1778–9, and by Massenet in the opera *Esclarmonde* in 1889: both G'''; and the lowest, again by Mozart in *Il Seraglio*, K 384 of 1782 in which Osmin descends to D,. But Mozart is reported to have heard **Lucrezia Aguiari** ascend to C''' in an improvized cadenza, and **Mr J. D. Sumner** of Nashville, Tennessee, in his recording *Blessed Assurance*, reaches C,,,. (See chart below.)

Miss Aguari's high C, however, was not as high as it seems. Since her day concert pitch has risen by approximately a semitone, so her C''' would probably sound to us as B'''. This high B is attained by **Cleo Laine** in 'Being Alive' by Stephen Sondheim in the recording *Cleo's Greatest Show Hits*.

Left: Antonio Salieri, the composer who didn't *murder Mozart. (Archiv für Kunst und Geschichte)*

Right: Janós Lavotta, Hungarian violinist and composer (1764–1820) whose dissolute life, which inspired three operas, ended in an alcoholic stupor at the age of 56. (Photo from a contemporary portrait)

Highest and lowest written vocal notes

Massenet and Mozart

Mozart

Highest and lowest attained vocal notes

Aguiari

Sumner

Rivalry between singers, especially prima donnas, has always been fierce, but today it is less publicly visible than hitherto. **Domenica Casarini** (*fl.* 1743–58 in Italy) was imprisoned for putting out a death contract on a rival, while extraordinary riots were witnessed around the King's Theatre in London in February 1727 as factions centred upon the Countess of Burlington, Sir Robert Walpole and others, fought to determine which was the greater soprano, **Francesca Cuzzoni** or **Faustina Bordoni**. Later that year, during a performance of Bononcini's *Astianatte*, these two sopranos were brought together by an impresario who should have known better. Inevitably, the opera was impeded and finally terminated as the two wildcats fought on stage, egged on, as if at a boxing match, by opera-lovers in the audience.

Two years later in Naples the two leading ladies in Caballone's opera *Ammore vò speranza,* **Rosa Albertini** and **Francesca Grieco**, came to blows on stage. Apparent rivalry over a man fuelled the flames of professional jealousy, and Francesca retired hurt. Soon afterwards Rosa was assassinated by a partisan youth named Giulio Lerro — he escaped with a fine imposed by a pro-Francesca court.

The battling prima donnas: Bottom: Faustina Bordoni. Top: Francesca Cuzzoni. (Mary Evans Picture Library)

Right: Cleo Laine who hit high B in Stephen Sondheim's 'Being Alive' *recorded for posterity on the* Cleo's Greatest Show Hits *album. (EMI Records Ltd)*

■ *The youngest opera singer in the world has been Jeanette Gloria La Bianca, born in Buffalo, New York on 12 May 1934, who sang Rosina in* The Barber of Seville *at the Teatro dell'Opera, Rome, on 8 May 1950 aged 15 years 361 days, having appeared as Gilda in* Rigoletto *at Velletri 45 days earlier. Ginetta La Bianca was taught by Lucia Carlino and managed by Angelo Carlino.* ■

It is not only the ladies who displayed tantrums. Gaetano Majorano, known as **Caffarelli** (1710–83), for whom Handel wrote the famous 'Largo' *Ombra mai fu* in *Xerxes*, behaved like a spoilt prima donna, was vain, arrogant, insubordinate, and enjoyed twitting his colleagues. Fighting occurred frequently and Caffarelli once ended up in jail. During one performance of an opera in 1747 the action required a dart to be thrown. It bounced off its target and by sheer bad luck caught Caffarelli, drawing blood. In a blind rage, and deaf to abject apologies, the wounded singer fell upon his unintentional assailant and had to be restrained by the rest of the cast. The audience roared its delight.

A similar incident, but inverted, occurred when a librettist, exasperated by Caffarelli's habitual truancy, challenged him to a duel. Neither was hurt in the duel, but a stray bullet wounded (some reports say killed) a bystander. On yet another occasion Caffarelli hid in a cistern to escape the wrath of an unreasonably jealous husband — unreasonable because Caffarelli was a castrato.

But despite his reputation, Caffarelli is reported to have donated large portions of his fortune to charity.

In efforts to appease singers' oversize egos, composers have sometimes written especially accommodating parts: the Prologue to Leoncavallo's *I Pagliacci* was specially composed for **Victor Maurel**. Rossini was perhaps the most diplomatic where singers were concerned, though he learnt the art slowly. He described his contralto pupil **Marietta Alboni** as 'an elephant', adding hastily when he realised that she might have heard: '. . . with a nightingale inside'. For another lady whose only good note was B flat, Rossini wrote an aria in *Ciro in Babilonia* (1814) in which that is the only note given to the singer. Two years later, in *Le nozze di Teti e di Peleo*, the bass **Matteo Porto** was booked to sing the river god but was concerned that the venerable part would reflect his advancing age. Rossini was quick to reassure him: the river god, he said, was aged between 30 and 35. Porto was pacified.

A mathematician in 1883 computed that when **Adelina Patti** sung *Semiramide* in Rossini's opera in Washington, DC, she earned $42\frac{5}{8}$ cents per note; Rossini received $7\frac{1}{10}$ cents less per note for composing the whole opera, much to Patti's satisfaction.

Not all creators are willing to indulge their artists. Mozart's librettist Da Ponte said of the Austrian soprano **Dorothea Bussani** that 'she was popular for her clowning and exaggerations among cooks, grooms, servants, lackeys and wigmakers'; and of her husband, who sang bass, Da Ponte remarked that he knew something about every profession except that of gentlemen. Instrumentalists, too, need to be brought down at times. The well-known story of Handel waiting patiently while his violinist travelled in a leisurely manner through key after key, finally arriving at the tonic only to be greeted by Handel's loud sarcasm, 'Welcome home, **Mr Dubourg**', is matched by the experience of another violinist, **Felice de Giardini**. During a Jommelli opera, 'I gave loose to my fingers and fancy; for which I was rewarded by the composer with a violent slap in the face.'

The skill of some singers has brought unexpected results. **John Braham**, the English tenor (1774–1856) sang so well at a private royal function that King George IV spoke of knighting him there and then, even as Napoleon had knighted **Girolamo Crescentini** (1762–1846) for his voice. **Carlo Broschi**, famous throughout Europe as the castrato **Farinelli** (1705–82), is said to have cured King Philip V of Spain's melancholia by singing the same four songs every night for nearly ten years, an experience that might have induced melancholia in many others, but the King duly knighted Farinelli — though whether for the size of his repertoire or for the domestic politics

Enrico Caruso, often described as the greatest tenor who ever lived. (EMI Records Ltd)

the singer involved himself in has not been determined.

Jean Buck, who sang the Governess in Britten's *The Turn of the Screw* at Sadler's Wells, has the distinction of causing a flare in the gas lighting whenever she hit G sharp. Two centuries earlier a fashionable hair-adornment in Madrid in the 1770s owed its name, *caramba*, to the nickname applied to **Maria Antonía Vallejo Fernández**, who had made a hit with a song in which the advances of a pompous pip-squeak (sung by Miguel Garrido) are scornfully rejected with the exclamation *Caramba!* (roughly, 'Great heavens!' or 'Blow me down!'). This word was sung with such tremendous spirit that it became Fernández's popular nickname, and thence that of the coloured bow she wore in her hair.

Who was the greatest singer of them all? Was it the legendary **Adelina Patti**, who never needed to attend rehearsals? Or **Caruso**, a natural-born singer whose only instruction when young had been sitting in on other singers' lessons for a year? Or the only operatic artist to sell over a million copies of a record: **Mario Lanza's** *Be My Love*? Or **Count John McCormack**, whose repertoire extended from popular Irish ballads to grand opera and who, at various times, owned Stradivarius and Guarnerius violins as well as 12 Rolls Royces? Or the little-known **Bernardine Hammaekers** who, at the Paris Opéra in the 1860s, sang a one-minute trill in *Caro Nome* from Verdi's *Rigoletto*? And who can deny the sheer pluck of **Giovanni Martinelli**, who stood in for an ailing tenor early in 1967 at the age of 81?

The 'Swedish Nightingale', Jenny Lind, one of the finest 19th-century sopranos, who set an artistic example other attempted to follow. (BBC Hulton Picture Library)

There is no 'greatest'. There is, however, a well-documented 'worst'. **Florence Foster Jenkins** (1868–1944) sang with such exquisite disregard for pitch, rhythm, phrasing and tempo that she developed a unique following among cognoscenti. Her *Flower Song* from Bizet's *Carmen* was notable for the large basket of roses she carried; as the aria ended and the audience showed their appreciation of a truly unforgettable experience she took the roars as a sign of approval and cast the roses one by one into the auditorium. With all the flowers gone and the uproar continuing, she cast the basket too. She refused to prosecute a taxi driver when she was injured in a motor accident because she claimed that the crash had made her F higher still. Some writers suggest that she never suspected the applause she received was wholly ironic; that she was convinced that she was the 20th century's answer to Jenny Lind, 'the Swedish Nightingale'. But a chance remark made towards the end of her life betrays the fact that she knew she had a good gimmick: 'People may say I *can't* sing but no-one can ever say I *didn't* sing'.

VI
What's the Key?

Ever since the late 16th century Western music has relied upon a system of tonality based upon complicated principles which are explained in musical textbooks and need not concern us here. The force behind these principles, however, is easily recognized by the Western listener: if a melody makes logical sense and does not introduce incongruous sequences of notes in its horizontal progress across the page, it is following tonal principles, whereas if it moves away from these principles it begins to sound 'Oriental' or in some other way 'foreign'. A good example of this is 'Peter's Theme' in Prokofiev's *Peter and the Wolf*, which begins in C major but abruptly alights upon a 'foreign' note (in this case E flat) which sounds all the more alien for entering upon a strong beat and then recurring twice more on strong beats. Similarly, if a vertical chord makes a satisfying sound, and a succession of chords progresses 'easily', tonal principles are being observed, but if foreign elements are introduced discords result.

For most of this century there have been composers who have sought to abolish this system by taking the introduction of foreign elements to its ultimate conclusion. Schoenberg, although not the first, was the most prominent figure in the move towards 'atonality' ('without tonality'). He and his followers argued that the tonal system was worn out. He saw no need to limit a piece only to the notes c d e f g a b (c) (i.e. the C major scale, employing seven different notes) when the other five notes (i.e. the black keys on the piano: c sharp/d flat, d sharp/e flat, f sharp/g flat, g sharp/a flat, and a sharp/b flat) are every bit as valuable and make up, with the other seven, a whole-tone, or twelve-tone, scale. Hence the term 'dodecaphonic' = Gk: 'of twelve sounds'. Schoenberg introduced strict compositional methods for ensuring complete tonal integration in which no note or group of notes should receive any kind of priority over any other, so each should be sounded as often as the others in a strict series. Hence 'serialism'.

Two composers interested in moving away from established tonal principles: Debussy (standing) and Stravinsky. (BBC Hulton Picture Library/The Bettmann Archive)

Most composers, though, still rely on tonal rules, and even though notes 'foreign' to a scale may be used freely, they do not threaten the comfortable tonal foundation of a piece except in some dramatic or colouristic context. Writers of TV jingles and pop songs do not use serialism (unless their intention is to be deliberately outlandish); nor do marketers of Muzak. They have learnt the strength of tonal recognition of the human brain; and because this recognition is largely unconscious it follows that tonality must be based on a natural, or instinctively acquired, acoustic law.

Strict adherence to all aspects of this law was demanded of 18th-century composers, and a great deal of dull, workaday music was written. But skilful composers used the law of tonality imaginatively, clearing the way for the greatest imaginative genius of the tonal era: Beethoven.

'Tonality' and 'key' mean the same thing but in English usage one more easily speaks of a work as being 'in a key' (rather than a 'centred upon a tonality'). Apart from the feeling of variety imparted by a concert of several pieces in different keys (a feeling only subconsciously recognized by most listeners), the choice of key in the 17th and 18th centuries was dictated largely by the instrumental resources available. Trumpets could play only in C and D; woodwind sounded best in 'soft' keys (i.e. with flats in the key signature), strings 'rang' more tellingly in 'sharp' keys (e.g. D major, A major), and so on. Later, with improvements in instrumental design, composers were less limited and were enabled to concentrate more on the musical effects created by certain keys. And so began the convention that 'sharp' keys made confident music, 'flat' keys comfortable music, major keys were optimistic, minor keys pessimistic. In some cases this formula is justified but in others it is not; its successes and failures may be judged by reference to the Key Chart, pp 154–162.

Another analogy, which gained popularity for a time but is now largely discredited, concerns the claimed relationship between sound and colour*. Early experimenters were led to believe that because there are seven different notes in an octave and seven colours in the rainbow (red, orange, yellow, green, blue, indigo, violet) there must be some connection. Intermediate keynotes such as F sharp or B flat would, of course, equate with intermediate colours: turquoise, perhaps, or yellowish-green. Many musicians have drawn up concordance lists; we give some of their necessarily subjective relationships in our Key Chart.

The futility of such relationships was demonstrated conclusively in London as long ago as 1886, when proponents of the key-equals-colour movement were invited to witness an experiment. A pianist played a piece of music in G major, which has one sharp and should therefore be considered a 'bright' key, evoking 'bright' colours. Supporters of this concept then agreed that the performance did indeed produce 'optimistic' and 'positive' colours, although the actual colours suggested ranged from pink to leaf green, via vermilion.

The same piece of music was then played again, this time in A flat, the key's four flats producing in the listeners a subdued, sad feeling which evoked dark colours, from maroon to bottle green. The self-congratulatory atmosphere amongst the key-equals-colour brigade was abruptly terminated when it was revealed that between the two pieces the pianist had thrown a lever which brought into play an automatic transposing device on the piano: the second performance had sounded precisely the same as the first, and the key-equals-colour experts had been misled by watching the pianist's fingers playing in A flat while the piano actually sounded G major.

One might try other experiments. The composer and writer E.T.A. Hoffmann described one of his heroes, Johann Kreisler, as 'a little man whose coat was the colour of C sharp minor with an E major collar'. If outline drawings of a little man in a coat were to be sent to musicians, and those musicians could be persuaded to colour in the picture according to Hoffmann's description, how many pictures would coincide?

Why should not the seven basic keynotes equate with the Seven Wonders of the Ancient World, the Seven Deadly Sins, the seven (*sic*) rings of Saturn, or the seven days of the week? Does B flat minor really sound best at 2.45 on a Sunday morning?

One wonders whether the ordinary listener is expected to pay too much attention to the key of a piece of music. Is it really necessary in concert programmes or on record sleeves solemnly to print the key (and the opus number) each time, say, Beethoven's Symphony No 7 is offered to the public? More ludicrous still is the oft-heard radio announcer's formula: 'the orchestra will now play Beethoven's Symphony No 7 in A major' — as if they had an alternative. Much better, surely, to scrap all reference to key (and to opus number) and quote instead the date of composition. The group of syllables 'Beethoven's Symphony No 7' can mean only one piece of music in this world. Key and opus number are of academic interest only, but if the date of composition were to be added (1812) it

*At a concert in Paris in 1891 the audience was treated to simultaneous onslaughts on ear, eye *and* nose, and an 'experimental perfume concert' was staged in New York the following year.

What's The Key?

Composer and author E. T. A. Hoffmann. (Mary Evans Picture Library)

would throw the work into a rather interesting historical context.

In some cases, of course, the key may be necessary to a work's identification, as in Mozart's piano concerti where the generic number is wrong and the Köchel number may not be readily remembered, but the convention of quoting the key for *every* such work is now so firmly rooted that we cannot ignore it.

Let us, then, take it a step further. The list of works arranged by key in the Key Chart includes many for which the key is rarely, if ever, given. It remains, rightly, of concern only to the performers. By listing them with other works of like key the reader may notice some hitherto unsuspected affiliation or affinity. But first a word of caution. A musical work rarely holds tenaciously to one key: it is therefore ludicrous to suggest that Liszt's *Les Preludes* is 'in C major', but no more so than to say that Schubert's 'Trout' Quintet is 'in A major', for both works spend considerable periods in other keys. The 'Trout' variations are in D and are based on a song in D flat!

Famous Works by Key

This list gives the key 'signature' (i.e. the clue given to the performer at the head of a piece to direct him to sharpen or flatten the right notes for the key), and the related key in the opposite mode. Works are identified in the simplest possible way consistent with clarity.

Although the subject of key in relation to colour has been alluded to, and we have seen that there is no scientific basis for an analogy, certain musicians have given their opinions about such relationships. Rimsky-Korsakov and Scriabin both compiled lists, and the French mathematician Louis-Bertrand Castel (1688–1757) constructed an ocular harpsichord which interested, for one, Telemann. This instrument displayed strips of colour according to the pitches being sounded. The impressions of these three, together with those of some other authorities, are noted against the keys concerned simply for the reader's interest. Their opinions (identified by their initials: C, R-K, and S) are as interesting for their discrepancies as for their agreements.

Alexander Scriabin in 1914. (Novosti Press Agency)

Other authorities have imparted specific characteristics to certain keys; these also are given. Mattheson's impressions were listed in his *Das neu eröffnete Orchester* (Hamburg, 1713), where he revealed his strong affection for some keys and extreme distaste for others.

C major

An 'open' key, i.e. no sharps or flats in the signature. Relative minor: A minor

C: blue
R-K: white
S: red

Mattheson described C major as rough, bold, suitable for joyful occasions but also, in the right hands, for tenderness
Bach: Orchestral Suite No 1
Balakirev: Symphony No 1
Bartók: String Quartet No 4
Beethoven: Overtures: *Consecration of the House; Prometheus; Leonora* Nos 1, 2 and 3; Piano Concerto No 1; String Quartet Op 59/3, 'Razumovsky'; Symphony No 1; Triple Concerto
Berlioz: Overtures: *Corsair; King Lear; Symphonie Fantastique*
Berwald: *Symphonie Singulière*
Bizet: Symphony No 1; Symphony No 2, 'Roma'
Gluck: Overture: *Orfeo*
Haydn: Cello Concerto No 1; 'Drum' Mass; String Quartet Op 76/3, 'Emperor' (but the 'Emperor's Hymn' movement is in G major); Symphony No 48, 'Maria Theresia'; Symphony No 82, 'Bear'
Kodály: Cello solo Sonata, Op 8
Liszt: *Les Preludes*
Mendelssohn: Wedding March
Mozart: 'Coronation' Mass; Overtures: *Clemenza di Tito; Cosí fan tutte; Impressario;* Piano Concerti K 467; K 503; String Quartets K 465; K 499; String Quintet K 515; Symphonies Nos 28, 34, and 41, 'Jupiter'
Prokofiev: Piano Concerto No 3; Symphony No 4
Ravel: *Boléro*
Rimsky-Korsakov: Symphony No 3
Rossini: Overture: *La Scala di Seta*
Schubert: Overture: *Rosamunde*; String Quintet; Symphonies Nos 6 and 9, 'Great'; Wanderer Fantasy
Schumann: Symphony No 2
Shostakovich: Symphony No 2, 'October'; Symphony No 7, 'Leningrad'
Tchaikovsky: Serenade for Strings
Vaughan Williams: A Sea Symphony; *Sinfonia Antartica*
Wagner: Overture: *The Mastersingers*
Weber: Overture: *Die Freischütz*

C minor

Three flats: b, e, a. Relative major: E flat.

Often chosen for its dark and dramatic quality. Mattheson regarded the key as sweet, sad, and useful for depicting sleep, Quantz as suitable for music of audacity, rage and despair. Mozart, Beethoven and Schubert chose C minor for some of their most poignantly elegiac or crushingly violent works. It is the key, also, of the so-called *Suicide Song* (see p 224).
Beethoven: Overture: *Coriolan*; Piano Concerto No 3; Piano Sonatas: 'Pathètique'; Op 111; String Quartet Op 18/4; Symphony No 5
Brahms: Overture: 'Academic Festival'; Piano Quartet Op 60; String Quartet Op 51/1

Johannes Brahms, drawn by Professor W. von Beckerath. (Popperfoto)

Bruckner: Symphonies Nos 1, 2 and 8
Dvořák: Symphony No 1, 'Bells of Zlonice'
Glazunov: Symphony No 6
Gluck: Overture: *Iphigenia in Aulis*
Grieg: Symphony
Haydn: Keyboard Sonata No 33
Mahler: Symphony No 2, 'Resurrection'
Mendelssohn: Overture: *Ruy Blas*; Symphony No 1, Op 11
Mozart: Mass K 427; Piano Concerto K 491; String Quintet K 406
Myaskovsky: Symphony No 27
Prokofiev: Symphony No 3, 'Flaming Angel'
Rachmaninoff: Piano Concerto No 2
Saint-Saëns: Piano Concerto No 4; Symphony No 3, 'Organ'
Schubert: Quartet movement D 803; Symphony No 4, 'Tragic'
Shostakovich: Piano Concerto No 1; String Quartet No 8; Symphonies Nos 4 and 8
Tchaikovsky: Symphony No 2, 'Little Russian'
Vivaldi: Concerto for strings, 'Al Santo Sepolcro'
Weber: Concertino for clarinet

C sharp minor

Four sharps: f, c, g, d. Relative major: E

Beethoven: Piano Sonata, 'Moonlight'; String Quartet Op 131
Haydn: Keyboard Sonata No 49
Mahler: Symphony No 5
Prokofiev: Symphony No 7
Shostakovich: Violin Concerto No 2

D flat major

Five flats: b, e, a, d, g. Relative minor: B flat minor

R-K: dusky, warm
S: violet
Khachaturian: Piano Concerto
Prokofiev: Piano Concerto No 1
Rimsky-Korsakov: Harmonica Romance

D major

Two sharps: f, c. Relative minor: B minor

C: green
R-K: yellow, sunny
S: yellow, brilliant

Beethoven in C minor mood. Impression by Eichstadt. (The Mansell Collection)

A martial, military key suitable for festive occasions where instrumental brilliance is required. Mattheson saw D major as forthright, arrogant, warlike and animated.
C.P.E. Bach: Magnificat
J.S. Bach: Brandenburg Concerto No 5; Magnificat BWV 247; Orchestral Suites Nos 3, and 4

What's The Key?

Bartók: String Quartet No 6
Beethoven: Piano Trio Op 70/1, 'Ghost'; String Quartet Op 18/3; Symphony No 2; Violin Concerto
Berwald: *Symphonia Capricieuse*
Boieldieu: Overture: *Caliph of Bagdad*
Brahms: Symphony No 2; Violin Concerto
Cherubini: Symphony
Cimarosa: Overture: *Secret Marriage*
Dvořák: Symphony No 6, Op 60
Elgar: Pomp and Circumstance March No 1: 'Land of Hope and Glory'
Glazunov: Symphony No 3
Glinka: Overture: *Ruslan and Ludmilla*
Handel: Musick for the Royal Fireworks; Water Music (the section with trumpets)
Haydn: Cello Concerto No 2; Harpsichord Concerto Hob XVIII:11; Horn Concerto Hob VII:d3; Symphonies Nos 73, 'Hunt'; 93; 96; 101, 'Clock'; 104, 'London'
Mahler: Symphony No 1
Mendelssohn: Overture: *Calm Sea and Prosperous Voyage*; Overture: 'Fingal's Cave' (partly in B minor)
Mozart: 'Haffner' Serenade; Horn Concerto No 1 K 412; Overtures: *Don Giovanni;*

Idomeneo; Marriage of Figaro; Piano Concerto K 537, 'Coronation'; 'Post-Horn' Serenade; String Quartet K 575; String Quintet K 593; Symphonies Nos 31, 'Paris'; 35, 'Haffner'; 38, 'Prague'; Violin Concerto K 218
Pachelbel: Canon and Gigue
Prokofiev: Symphony No 1, 'Classical'; Violin Concerto No 1
Rodrigo: *Concierto de Aranjuez*
Rossini: Overture: *Semiramide*
Rubbra: Symphony No 2
Saint-Saëns: Piano Concerto No 1
Schubert: Symphonies Nos 1 and 3
Shostakovich: Symphony No 5
Sibelius: Symphony No 2
Tchaikovsky: Symphony No 3, 'Polish'; Violin Concerto
Wagner: Overture: *Rienzi*
Weber: Overture: *Oberon*

D minor

One flat: Relative major: F
A brooding and passionate key, sometimes chosen for its semi-religious feeling. It has the advantage that trumpets and drums may be used to give emphasis at cardinal points. Mattheson found it devotional, tranquil, but at the same time noble.
Arriaga: String Quartet No 1; Symphony
Bach: Harpsichord Concerto No 1; 2-violin Concerto; Toccata and Fugue, BWV 565
Balakirev: Symphony No 2
Beethoven: Piano Sonata Op 31/2, 'Tempest'; Symphony No 9, 'Choral'
Brahms: Piano Concerto No 1; Overture: *Tragic*
Brian: Symphonies Nos 1, 'Gothic'; 6, 'Tragica'
Britten: Young Person's Guide to the Orchestra (the closing Fugue is in D major)
Bruckner: Symphonies Nos 3 and 9
Dvořák: Serenade for Wind Instruments; Symphonies Nos 4, Op 13; 7, Op 70
Haydn: 'Nelson' Mass; String Quartet Op 76/2, 'Fifths'; Symphonies Nos 26, 'Lamentatione'; 80
Mahler: Symphony No 3
Marcello, A: Oboe Concerto
Mendelssohn: Symphony No 5, 'Reformation'; Violin Concerto No 1
Mozart: Piano Concerto K 466; Requiem Mass
Mussorgsky (arr. Rimsky-Korsakov): *Night on the Bare Mountain* (ends in D major)
Prokofiev: Symphony No 2
Rachmaninoff: Piano Concerto No 3; Symphony No 1; 'Youth' Symphony (1891)
Schubert: String Quartet, 'Death and the Maiden'
Schumann: Symphony No 4
Shostakovich: Symphony No 12, 'The Year 1917'
Sibelius: String Quartet; Violin Concerto; Symphony No 6
Strauss, R: Burlesque for piano and orchestra
Vaughan Williams: Symphony No 8; Violin Concerto
Vivaldi: Concerto Grosso Op 3/11
Wagner: Overture: *The Flying Dutchman*

E flat major

Three flats: b, e, a. Relative minor: C minor

R-K: dark, gloomy, bluish grey

S: steel colour, with a metallic lustre

This is Beethoven's 'heroic' key, but few other composers have seen it in this light. Usually it is adopted for music of mellow beauty and grace. For Mattheson, however, E flat represented pathos, earnestness and sorrow, and is absolutely devoid of sensuality.
Arriaga: String Quartet No 3
Beethoven: Piano Sonata, 'Les Adieux'; Piano Concerto No 5, 'Emperor'; Septet; String Quartets Op 74, 'Harp'; Op 127; Symphony No 3, 'Eroica'
Borodin: Symphony No 1
Brahms: Clarinet Sonata Op 120/2; Horn Trio Op 40
Bruckner: Symphony No 4, 'Romantic'
Dvořák: Symphony No 3, Op 10
Elgar: Overture: *In the South;* 'Nimrod' (from *Enigma* Variations); Symphony No 2
Glazunov: Saxophone Concerto; Symphonies Nos 4 and 8
Gounod: *Petite Symphonie* for Wind
Haydn: Keyboard Sonata No 62; Symphonies Nos 22, 'Philosopher'; 55, 'Schoolmaster'; 99; 103, 'Drum Roll'; Trumpet Concerto
Liszt: Piano Concerto No 1
Mendelssohn: Octet for Strings
Mozart: Divertimento for string trio K 563; Horn Concerti Nos 2–4; Horn Quintet K 407; Overture: *The Magic Flute*; Piano Concerto K 482; Piano Quartet K 493; Piano and Wind Quintet K 452; Sinfonia Concertante K 364; String Quartet K 428; String Quintet K 614; Symphony No 39
Paganini: Violin Concerto No 1 (usually played in D)

Prokofiev: Symphony No 6
Saint-Saëns: Piano Concerto No 3
Schubert: Piano Trio D 929
Schumann: Overture: *Manfred*; Piano Quintet; Symphony No 3, 'Rhenish'
Shostakovich: Cello Concerto No 1; Symphonies Nos 3, 'May Day'; 9
Sibelius: Symphony No 3
Strauss, R: Horn Concerti Nos 1 and 2
Tchaikovsky: Overture: *1812*
Vivaldi: Violin Concerto Op 8/5, 'Storm at Sea'
Weber: Clarinet Concerto No 2; Overture: *Euryanthe*

E major

Four sharps: f, c, g, d. Relative minor: C sharp minor

C: Yellow

R-K: blue, sapphire, sparkling

S: bluish white

For most composers this is a friendly, confident key, but for Mattheson it evoked fatal sadness and despair; pain akin to death.
Bach: Violin Concerto No 2
Beethoven: Overture: *Fidelio*
Bruckner: Symphony No 7
Dvořák: Serenade for strings
Goldmark: Rustic Wedding Symphony
Handel: Harpsichord Suite No 5, 'Harmonious Blacksmith'
Mendelssohn: Overture and Nocturne: *A Midsummer Night's Dream*
Raff: Symphony No 5, 'Lenore'
Rossini: Overtures: *The Barber of Seville; William Tell* (also partly in E minor)
Scarlatti, D: Harpsichord Sonata Kk 380, 'Cortège'
Smetana: Festival Symphony
Spohr: Octet Op 32
Sullivan: Symphony, 'Irish'
Vivaldi: Violin Concerto Op 8/1, 'Spring'
Wagner: *Siegfried Idyll;* Overture: *Tannhäuser*
Weber: Overture: *Jubel*

E minor

One sharp: f. Relative major: G

An ambiguous key, with a certain exotic grandeur, brilliance and self-confidence, but with a dark and thoughtful side. Quantz linked this key with C minor as suitable for music of audacity, rage and despair; Mattheson heard it as thoughtful, profound and sad: fast music in E minor will never be happy.
Beethoven: String Quartet Op 59/2
Brahms: Symphony No 4
Chopin: Piano Concerto No 1
Dvořák: 'Dumky' Trio; Symphony No 9, 'From the New World'
Hanson: Symphony No 1, 'Nordic'
Haydn: Symphony No 44, 'Mourning'
Khachaturian: Symphony No 1
Mendelssohn: Violin Concerto No 2
Rachmaninoff: Symphony No 2
Rimsky-Korsakov: Symphony No 1
Rossini: Overture: *William Tell* (storm music)
Shostakovich: Piano Trio No 2; Symphony No 10
Sibelius: Symphony No 1
Smetana: *Vltava* Tone Poem
Tchaikovsky: Symphony No 5
Vaughan Williams: Symphonies Nos 6 and 9
Verdi: String Quartet
Weber: Horn Concertino

F major

One flat: b. Relative minor: D minor

C: aurore ('dawn')

R-K: green

S: red

The traditional 'pastoral' key, and the key of hunting horns (as is D major). For Mattheson it expressed beautiful sentiments, generosity, love and other virtuous feelings; it is like a proud, handsome and wholly good person.
Bach: Brandenburg Concerti Nos 1 and 2; *Italian* Concerto for harpsichord solo
Beethoven: Overture: *Egmont*; Romance No 2 for violin and orchestra; String Quartets Op 18/1, Op 59/1, Op 135; Symphonies No 6, 'Pastoral'; No 8; Violin Sonata 'Spring'
Berlioz: Overture: *Les francs juges*
Brahms: Symphony No 3
Dvořák: String Quartet, 'American'; Symphony No 5, Op 76
Glazunov: Symphony No 7
Handel: Water Music (the section with horns); Organ Concerti Op 4/4; 'The Cuckoo and the Nightingale'
Hofstetter: String Quartet 'Op 3/5' (attrib: Haydn)

Mozart: Oboe Quartet; String Quartet K 590
Nicolai: Overture: *The Merry Wives of Windsor*
Raff: Symphony No 3, 'Im Walde'
Saint-Saëns: Piano Concerto No 5, 'Egyptian'
Schubert: Octet
Shostakovich: Piano Concerto No 2
Spohr: Nonet
Vivaldi: Violin Concerto Op 8/3, 'Autumn'
Weber: Bassoon Concerto; Overture: *Ruler of the Spirits*

F minor

Four flats: b, e, a, d. Relative major: A flat

One of the darkest of the commonly-used keys, this has drawn from some composers their bitterest music. Mattheson regarded it as tranquil, tender, but then went on to add that it has a depth and power close to anxiety and despair: black melancholy, provoking horror in the listener.
Beethoven: Overture: *Egmont*; Piano Sonata, 'Appassionata'; String Quartet Op 95
Brahms: Clarinet Sonata Op120/1
Chopin: Piano Concerto No 2
Dukas: *The Sorcerer's Apprentice*
Haydn: Symphony No 44, 'La Passione'
Shostakovich: Symphony No 1
Tchaikovsky: Symphony No 4
Vaughan Williams: Tuba Concerto; Symphony No 4
Vivaldi: Violin Concerto Op 8/4, 'Winter'
Weber: Clarinet Concerto No 1

F sharp minor

Three sharps: f, c, g. Relative major: A

For Mattheson, 'here is the sadness of love, unrestrained and outlandish'.
Haydn: Symphony No 45, 'Farewell'
Mahler: Symphony No 10 (incomplete)
Myaskovsky: Symphony No 21
Rachmaninoff: Piano Concerto No 1

G major

One sharp: f. Relative minor: E minor

C: red

R-K: brownish gold, bright

S: orange-rose

An optimistic key, not often used for deep music. For Mattheson it was rhetorical — an all-purpose key, at once earnest and gay.
Bach: Brandenburg Concerti Nos 3 and 4
Beethoven: Romance No 1 for violin and orchestra; Piano Concerto No 4; String Quartet Op 18/2
Berlioz: *Harold in Italy* Symphony; Overture: *Beatrice and Benedict*
Dvořák: Symphony No 8, Op 88
Elgar: Pomp and Circumstance March No 4, 'All Men Must be Free'
Grieg: *Holberg* Suite (also in G minor)
Handel: Water Music (the sections without brass)
Haydn: Symphonies Nos 92, 'Oxford'; 94, 'Surprise'; 100, 'Military'
Mahler: Symphony No 4
Mozart: *Eine Kleine Nachtmusik*; Piano Concerto K 453; Symphony No 32, 'Overture in the Italian Style'; Violin Concerto K 216
Prokofiev: Piano Concerto No 5
Ravel: Piano Concerto
Tchaikovsky: Piano Concerto No 2
Vaugham Williams: A London Symphony (No 2)

G minor

Two flats: b, e. Relative major: B flat

Mozart's 'tragic' key, this has been used also by other composers to express deep emotion. But for Mattheson it was perhaps the most beautiful key, combining earnestness, sweetness, liveliness, grace and tenderness.
'Albinoni': Adagio for strings and organ (actually by Giazotto)
Berwald: *Symphonie Serieuse*
Brahms: Piano Quartet No 1
Bruch: Violin Concerto
Bruckner: Overture
Corelli: Concerto Grosso Op 6/8, 'Christmas'
Dvořák: Piano Concerto
Elgar: *Introduction* (in G minor) *and Allegro* (in G); *Enigma* Variations (in G minor and G; 'Nimrod' is in E flat)
Handel: Concerto Grosso Op 6/6
Haydn: *Salve Regina*; String Quartet Op 74/3, 'Horseman'; Symphonies Nos 39; 83, 'Hen'
Mendelssohn: Scherzo: *A Midsummer Night's Dream*

Moeran: Symphony
Mozart: Piano Quartet K 478; String Quintet K 516; Symphonies Nos 25 and 40
Nielsen: Symphony No 1
Prokofiev: Piano Concerto No 2; Violin Concerto No 2
Rachmaninoff: Piano Concerto No 4
Roussel: Symphony No 3
Saint-Saëns: 'Africa', for piano and orchestra; *Danse Macabre*; Piano Concerto No 2
Shostakovich: Symphony No 11, 'The Year 1905'
Tchaikovsky: Symphony No 1, 'Winter Daydreams'
Vaughan Williams: String Quartet
Vivaldi: Violin Concerto Op 8/2, 'Summer'
Walton: Symphony No 2

A flat major

Four flats: b, e, a, d. Relative minor: F minor

R-K: greyish violet

S: purple violet

Elgar: Symphony No 1
Haydn: Keyboard Sonata No 31
Saint-Saëns: 'Wedding Cake' Caprice
Sibelius: *Finlandia* Tone Poem

A major

Three sharps: f, c, g. Relative minor: F sharp minor

C: violet

R-K: rosy, clear

S: green

The brilliance associated with the Beethoven and Mendelssohn symphonies listed below is due partly to the fierce and raw tone of horns pitched in A. The key has also attracted composers for the solo clarinet. Mattheson described it as affecting and brilliant, suited to sad feelings and to violin music.
Arriaga: String Quartet No 2
Beethoven: String Quartet Op 18/5; Symphony No 7; Violin Sonata, 'Kreutzer'
Berlioz: Overture: *Roman Carnival*
Brahms: Piano Quartet Op 26
Bruckner: Symphony No 6
Dvořák: Overture: *Carnival*
Liszt: Piano Concerto No 2
Mendelssohn: Symphony No 4, 'Italian'
Mozart: Clarinet Concerto; Clarinet Quintet; Piano Concerto K 488; String Quartet K 464; Symphony No 29; Violin Concerto K 219, 'Turkish'
Roussel: Symphony No 4
Schubert: Piano Quintet, 'Trout'
Scriabin: Piano Sonata No 8
Shostakovich: Symphony No 15; Violin Concerto No 1

A minor

'Open, i.e. no sharps or flats. Relative major: C

Music of strength and seriousness, with a misty, undefined sadness. For Mattheson, it was somnolent, in a plaintive, refined way, and suitable for keyboard music.
Bach: Violin Concerto No 1
Bartók: String Quartets Nos 1 and 2
Beethoven: String Quartet Op 132
Borodin: Symphony No 3
Brahms: Clarinet Trio; Double Concerto for violin and cello; String Quartet Op 51/2
Dvořák: Violin Concerto
Grieg: Piano Concerto
Mahler: Symphony No 6
Mendelssohn: Intermezzo: *A Midsummer Night's Dream*; Symphony No 3, 'Scots'
Rachmaninoff: Symphony No 3
Schubert: String Quartet D 804
Schumann: Piano Concerto
Sibelius: Symphony No 4
Spohr: Violin Concerto No 8, 'Singing Scene'
Walton: String Quartet
Weber: Overtures: *Abu Hassan; Preciosa*

B flat major

Two flats: b, e. Relative minor: G minor

A happy self-confident key, to which older composers often turn as a vehicle for their most mature thoughts. It is odd that neither Castel nor Rimsky-Korsakov gave any colour judgement for this commonly-used key, but Scriabin saw it as steely, with a metallic lustre, and Mattheson described it as magnificent but also delicate.
Bach: Brandenburg Concerto No 6
Bartók: String Quartet No 5
Beethoven: Piano Concerto No 2; Piano

Sonata, 'Hammerklavier'; Piano Trio, 'Archduke'; String Quartets Op 18/6; Op 130; Symphony No 4
Brahms: Piano Concerto No 2; String Quartet Op 67; Variations on *St Antoni Chorale*
Bruckner: Symphony No 5
Chausson: Symphony
Glazunov: Symphony No 5
Haydn: Masses: 'Creation'; 'Harmoniemesse'; 'Heiligmesse'; 'Theresienmesse'; Overture: *Armida*; Sinfonia Concertante; String Quartet Op 103 (unfinished); Symphonies Nos 85, 'La Reine de France'; 98; 102, 'Miracle'
Hindemith: Symphony for Concert Band
Mendelssohn: Symphony No 2, 'Hymn of Praise'
Mozart: Bassoon Concerto; Piano Concerto K 595; String Quartets, K 458, 'Hunt'; K 589; String Quintet K 174; Symphony No 33
Prokofiev: Piano Concerto for the left hand; Symphony No 5
Rubbra: Symphony No 5
Schubert: Piano Trio No 1; Symphonies Nos 2 and 5
Schumann: Symphony No 1, 'Spring'
Tchaikovsky: *Marche Slave* (partly in B flat minor)
Vivaldi: Violin Concerto Op 8/10, 'Hunt'

B flat minor

Five flats: b, e, a, d, g. Relative major: D flat

An emotion-filled and sometimes angry key.
Chopin: Piano Sonata No 2
Shostakovich: Symphony No 13, 'Babi Yar'
Tchaikovsky: *Marche Slave* (partly in B flat); Piano Concerto No 1
Walton: Symphony No 1

B major

Five sharps: f, c, g, d, a. Relative minor: G sharp minor

C: purple

R-K: sombre, dark blue, shot with steel

S: bluish white

Few major works have been centred on B major, perhaps because most composers agree with Mattheson that it is aggressive, hard, ill-mannered and desperate.
Brahms: Piano Trio No 1
Haydn: Symphony No 46

B minor

Two sharps: f, c. Relative major: D

Tchaikovsky's 'black despair' key, and used also for music of religious strength and forceful tragic drama. Bach's use of it in the B minor Mass enables him to brighten to the key's relative major for the introduction of trumpets and drums. On one occasion Beethoven described the key as 'black'; Mattheson saw it as moody, glum and bizarre.
Bach: Mass, BWV 232; Suite No 2 for flute and strings
Borodin: Symphony No 2
Brahms: Clarinet Quintet
Chopin: Piano Sonata No 3
Dvořák: Cello Concerto
Handel: Concerto Grosso Op 6/12
Liszt: Piano Sonata
Mahler: Symphony No 7
Mendelssohn: Overture: 'Fingal's Cave' (partly in D)
Moeran: Cello Concerto
Nielsen: Symphony No 2, 'The Four Temperaments'
Schubert: Symphony No 8, 'Unfinished'
Shostakovich: Piano Sonata No 2; Symphony No 6
Tchaikovsky: Symphony No 6, 'Pathètique'
Vivaldi: Symphony, 'Al Santo Sepolcro'
Wagner: *Ride of the Valkyries*

VII
Music Played

'There are three kinds of music: first, the music of the universe; second, human music; third, instrumental music.'

These words were written in the year AD 515 by the Roman philosopher Anicus Manlius Severinus Boëthius under the heading 'De Institutione Musica'. By 'music of the universe', presumably he meant the mysterious harmony of space and/or natural phenomena, but there is no doubt that by 'human music' he meant music which is sung. Last, and by implication least important, comes 'instrumental music'.

Since Boëthius's time instruments have become infinitely more reliable (if not more diverse) and a repertoire has grown up which is at least equal in quantity to that of vocal music. We have attempted to indicate this quantity: unfortunately, research is not complete as to which composer wrote the most symphonies and, as so often, variable nomenclature clouds the issue in many areas. We have also drawn attention to some of the more unusual works that have appeared, and created chronological lists where most useful.

THE SYMPHONY

The first symphony, by which we mean a work for instruments in several movements composed for concert performance (other types of symphony — or *sinfonia* — are disregarded for the moment) was composed before 1700. It cannot be pinpointed in time precisely; neither can the first symphonist. But it would be pleasant to think that a certain Symphony in C (Giegling 33) by Giuseppe Torelli (1658–1709) qualified for the honour, for it is a grand and impressive three-movement piece for four trumpets, four oboes, two bassoons, timpani and a large string orchestra, dating from well before 1700. Its brilliant fanfares, written to resound across the aisles of the San Petronio Cathedral in Bologna either before a mass or during intervals, seem to announce the arrival of an important new member of the musical dynasty and say 'watch this space'.

Alessandro Stradella (1644–82) introduced his operas and other stage works with a *sinfonia* for instruments alone. *Il Barcheggio* (1681) is an extended piece in four movements (fast-slow-fast-moderate), but since it is scored for a solo trumpet and strings it is an ancestor of the solo concerto, rather than of the symphony. His *sinfonie* and sonatas for two violins and continuo, for which no dates are known, are multi-movement works foreshadowing the concerto grosso of Corelli.

Much thought has been given to who might have written the first four-movement symphony; that is, a normal three-movement (fast-slow-fast) work with a minuet inserted in second or third place. G.M. Monn (1717–50) is usually credited with the invention, for his four-movements-with-minuet Symphony in D is dated 24 May 1740. There is, however, at least one earlier candidate: Alberto Gallo's string symphony in C, published in 1724, has the movement sequence fast-minuet-slow-fast. An even earlier work, broadcast about 1952 by the BBC as a Symphony in D minor by Gioseffo Placuzzi and given the date 1692, is in fast-slow-minuet-fast form, but it turns out to be a *Suonata* from his Op 1 of 1667 and is a chamber work for lute, two violins and continuo.

The First Symphonies by Country
In compiling the chart of regional firsts we have had to consider the fact that the symphony developed fully a century after the opera. Therefore most countries, as they witnessed their musical culture changing from 16th-century conventions (i.e. that 'serious' music consisted of sacred vocal pieces sometimes with instruments, while 'folk' music was largely

spontaneous and so might use voices or instruments and was rarely written down), founded an operatic tradition much earlier than a concert tradition. The instumental piece preceding the performance of an opera (the Italian *sinfonia*) was a forerunner of the concert symphony; when orchestral pieces came to be required for concert performance these *sinfonie* were frequently detached from their operas and used separately. It is not always possible to recognize which concert symphonies originated in this way because many of them lost their operatic identities during the move. Furthermore, Mozart among others composed *sinfonias* which could be used for both operatic or concert performance, with or without alteration.

No two regions took the same path of symphonic development, so our chart attempts the impossible in trying to identify the appearance of the first *concert* symphony. There is often no means of knowing which work fulfils the requirements, i.e. that it should have been written in the country concerned specifically for concert use. Some very early three-movement *sinfonias* (see, for example, England) would not make viable concert symphonies but they have to be mentioned as examples of the form we are dealing with. In other cases (e.g. Russia) the earliest symphonies can be identified, but they may have had operatic use, and furthermore they were almost certainly antedated by operatic *sinfonias* which *could* have had concert use.

Not all the earliest symphonies of a country were composed by native musicians. Often (e.g. Russia again) there was a firmly established tradition of imported foreign composers holding important posts long before native musicians began to produce their own music.

First Symphonies by Country

1 Italy **before 1700** see Torelli in text, p 163.

2 Netherlands **1698** 12 *Symphoniae introductioniae* (1698) by Hendrik Anders (1657–1720?), possibly performable separately but doubtless intended to be operatic *sinfonie*.

3 England **1703** Overtures by William Croft (1678–1727): *The Twinn Rivalls* (1703), and John Barrett (*c.*1676–1719): *Tunbridge Wells* (1703) are short three-movement pieces which *may* have been performed separately in concert; William Boyce's Symphony in B flat for *Peleus and Thetis* (*c.*1734) almost certainly was.

4 Austria **1709** J.J. Fux's Sinfonia in C to the opera *Gli Ossegni della Notte* (1709) is a slow-fast-slow overture; G.M. Monn probably composed the first purely concert symphonies by 1740.

5 Sweden **?1730** A suite-type Symphony in E by J.H. Roman (1694–1758) may date from as early as 1730; several of his true symphonies date from 1737 or just after.

6 Germany *c.***1735–41** J.V.A. Stamic's Symphony in G, Wolf G10, of *c.*1735–41 is the first to be written on German soil; first German symphonist: C.P.E. Bach, Symphony in G, W 173 (1741).

7 France *c.***1735–45** A Symphony in F for strings, *c.*1735–45 may be by M.-A. d'Ambreville or by the Italian Antonio Brioschi, (dates for both unknown). First undoubtedly French symphonies (albeit on a foreign plan): the six 'in Italian Style' for two violins and bass, Op 6, published 1740, by Louis-Gabriel Guillemain (1705–70).

8 Portugal *c.***1740** Carlos de Seixas (1704–42), noted harpsichord composer: wrote a Symphony in B flat (*c.*1740) which owes much to Vivaldi's style; intended for concert rather than operatic use.

9 Poland *c.***1740** Symphony in D (*c.*1740) by Jacek Szczurowski (*c.*1721–73).

10 Norway *c.***1750** Symphony in D by Johan Daniel Berlin (1714–87), probably *c.*1750.

11 Hungary *c.***1760** Two Austrians, F.J. Haydn and Anton Zimmermann (*c.*1741–81) worked in Hungary, wrote symphonies there from early 1760s.

12 Russia **1767** First symphony composed on Russian soil probably by the Italian Baldassare Galuppi, *c.*1767. First by a (presumably) Russian composer was an anonymous Symphony in C, *c.*1790, discovered in Jaroslav in 1971.

13 Yugoslavia **before 1770** Luka Sorkočević (1734–89) had written seven symphonies by 1770.

14 Denmark **by 1770** Symphonies by Johann Ernst Hartmann (1726–93), published 1770.

15 Spain *c.***1790** Pablo de Moral (*c.*1747–*c.*1805?): Symphony in C, *c.*1790.

16 Brazil **1790** José Mauricio Numes Garcia (1767–1830), *Sinfonia funèbre*, 1790.

17 America *c.***1835** Anthony Philip Heinrich (1781–1861), American composer of Bohemian origin, wrote a *Gran sinfonia eroica* in *c.*1835. First American-born symphonist: George Bristow (1825–98), Symphony in E flat, Op 10, 1848.

18 Finland **1847** Axel Gabriel Ingelius (1822–68): Symphony No 1, 1847.

19 Greece **before 1872** Nicolaos Mantzaros (1795–1872) wrote 24 overtures ('sinfonie') which are undated; probably stage-related. First concert symphony: No 1 in G, 'Greek' (1929) by Petros Petrides (1892–1979).

20 Mexico **1883** Ricardo Castro Herrera (1864–1907): Symphony No 1, 1883.

21 Australia **1896–1900** Alfred Francis Hill (1870–1960): Symphony No 1, 'Maori' by 1900.

22 Romania **1905** George Enescu (1881–1955): Symphony No 1 in E flat (1905). He also wrote a number or earlier symphonies while a student in Paris.

23 Japan **1912** Kosaku Yamada (1886–1965): Symphony 'The Shout of Victory and Peace', 1912.

24 Bulgaria **1912** Nikolao Athanassov (1886–1969): Symphony No 1, 1912.

25 China *c.***1940–45** Hsien Hsing-Hai (1905–45) wrote two symphonies, *c.*1940–45.

26 Turkey **1946** Ulvi Cemal Erkin (1906–72): Symphony No 1, 1946.

27 New Zealand **1948** Douglas Lilburn (b. 1915): Symphony No 1, 1948; A.F. Hill's 'Maori' Symphony (see 21 Australia) was begun in New Zealand and is based on an Aboriginal subject.

Symphonies of Note

Some cynics blame prolific composers for writing symphonies indistinguishable one from another, and in previous centuries the works of Haydn and Mendelssohn have been imitated by those wishing to share their success; but in the main the man who writes a symphony is anxious that it should be as different as possible from previous examples. He might set about securing this difference in one or more of several ways.

His best bet is to write a symphony of such surpassing quality that it will stand as an immortal monument to his genius. Unfortunately, this is not given to many. So composers are forced to turn to other devices to make their music memorable.

■ *The longest of all commonly performed symphonies is the orchestral symphony No 3 in D minor by Gustav Mahler (1860–1911) of Austria. This work, composed in 1896, requires a contralto, a women's and boys' choir in addition to a full orchestra. A full performance requires 1 hr 40 min, of which the first movement alone takes between 30 and 36 min. The Symphony No 2 (the* Gothic, *or No 1), composed in 1919–27 by Havergal Brian (1876–1972) was played by over 800 performers (4 brass bands) in the Victoria Hall, Hanley, Staffordshire on 21 May 1978 (conductor Trevor Stokes). A recent broadcast required 1 hr 45½ min. (See also p.203). Brian wrote an even vaster work based on Shelley's 'Prometheus Unbound' lasting 4 hr 11 min but the full score has been missing since 1961. The symphony* Victory at Sea *written by Richard Rodgers and arranged by Robert Russell Bennett for NBC TV in 1952 lasted for 13 hr.* ■

One might begin with a playful effect. At the start of Derek Bourgeois's Symphony No 4 of 1979 all the players insert their fingers in their mouths and 'pop' them out to imitate a cork being pulled from a bottle. Thus begins the 'Wine Symphony'. Or one might resort to extreme shock tactics, as in Ives's Symphony No 2 of 1902. Most of its considerable length (five movements) sticks closely to a mid-Romantic musical language, described by one commentator as 'Brahmsian', building to a grand climax topped with a piercing and excruciatingly indecisive chord.

Although all the best symphonies seem to be in four movements, there is no law about it. We have just met Ives's five-movement work, with its honourable predecessors by Haydn (Nos 7 and 45), Beethoven ('Pastoral'), Berlioz (*Symphonie Fantastique*) and Schumann ('Rhenish'), and Haydn once experimented with six movements (No 60), as did Mahler (No 3). Bourgeois's 'Wine Symphony' is in nine, representing nine wine-growing areas, and Messiaen's monumental *Turangalîla-symphonie* (1949) is in ten. The Japanese composer Yasushi

Akutagawa's 'Erolla' Symphony of 1958 is in 20 movements. The composer is not concerned as to which order they are performed. Probably the greatest number of separate sections is the 24 of Alan Hovhaness's 'St Vartan' Symphony of 1950.

Louis Spohr in 1838. Portrait by Roux. (Spohr Society, Kassel)

'St Vartan' runs for just less than an hour, a wholly reasonable call on our attention when compared with the world's longest symphony, Norman Rutherlyn's 18-movement 'A Legend in Music of the Life and Times of Sir Winston Churchill'. The composer's estimate of 'approximately 2½ hours' is yet to be confirmed by a performance. By contrast, Darius Milhaud's six symphonies for small orchestra (1917–23) each takes four minutes or less to play.

Symphonies of 'normal' length and 'normal' movement-count may yet display odd contents. František Krystof Neubaur's Symphony in D, 'La Bataille' (1789) falls short of introducing actual musket shot and cannon fire (failings to be rectified later by Beethoven's 'Battle' Symphony and Reicha's Grand Symphony of *c.*1815 — see p. 168), but in its description of the victorious battle of Prince Friedrich Josias of Saxe-Coburg-Saalfeld on 22 September 1789, when a mighty Turkish army was defeated on the Rymnik River, it faithfully depicts reveille. the general addressing his troops (a pompous bassoon solo), battle and victory, return to camp, and the victory celebration ball. Even more colourful is Pavel Vraničky's *Quodlibet Symphony* (1798). It begins with the arrival of the orchestra one by one (the order *and* method — walking, running — specified by the composer), who then commence to build up the first movement. The middle two movements consist of a collection of arrangements of popular folk and concert items of the day by Weigl, Paisiello, Salieri, Meyer, Haibl and Mozart, including a complete performance of the *Magic Flute* Overture. The *Quodlibet Symphony* then closes with a movement based on a folk-tune also used by Leopold Mozart, in which the orchestra gradually disperses. This final trick recalls Haydn's tactful joke in the finale of his *Farewell* Symphony of 1772 (See p. 187).

In his Symphony No 6 (1839), Spohr gives us a history lesson — or attempts to. Its movements are written respectively in the style of 'the Bach-Handel Period 1720', 'the Haydn-Mozart Period 1780', 'the Beethoven Period 1810', and 'the most recent period 1840'. Schumann rather cruelly deflated the project by saying that it all sounds like the Spohr Period 1839.

Right: Schwertsik's Symphony (see p.168) echoes the 'penny dreadfuls' so popular early in the century. (Mary Evans Picture Library)

No. 1.] Nos. 2, 3 and 4 are Presented, Gratis, with this No. [Price 1d.
VARNEY
THE
VAMPIRE.
OR THE
FEAST OF BLOOD
A ROMANCE OF EXCITING INTEREST.
BY THE AUTHOR OF
"GRACE RIVERS; OR, THE MERCHANT'S DAUGHTER."
LONDON: E. LLOYD, SALISBURY-SQUARE, AND ALL BOOKSELLERS.

Neubaur's battle scene mentioned above brings to mind the purely musical battles in Nielsen's 4th and 5th symphonies, in which musical elements fight for supremacy. The strain put upon Soviet composers by the conflict between political pressure and artistic conviction must have produced severe internal stress, much of it resolved before the results were published. But two odd examples give clues to what really happened. 'Soviet Realism' was the prescription that symphonies had to be understandable and optimistic. A composer might wish to close in a restrained mood if it gave a convincing artistic conclusion to his work, but this was not permitted. Prokofiev hit upon the most extraordinary solution: for his 7th symphony (1952) he provided alternative endings, one pensive, the other positive. The conductor may 'plug in' whichever ending better suited his audience.

A less well-known but even more curious history surrounds Shostakovich's Symphony No 4. It was actually in rehearsal when the Soviet authorities launched a vicious attack upon the composer's opera *Lady Macbeth of Mtsensk* in 1936. He withdrew his symphony and nothing more was heard of it until 1961. When it re-emerged it was realized that Shostakovich, either soon after its withdrawal or at some more recent time, had made the work commit suicide! Towards the end of the last movement the timpani turn on their own symphony and ruthlessly batter it into a kind of coma. The work ends in a painful, lingering death.

Even more grotesque, but with tongue firmly in cheek, is Kurt Schwertsik's (b. 1935) 'Transylvanian Symphony' for strings (1968), titled *Drakulas Haus– und Hofmusik*. Its four movements depict the times of day when Dracula is most active: *Taglied* (he practises his violin); *Nachtstück* (he conducts bats and werewolves); *Morgengrauen* (he delights in making variations on his grave song); *Abendrot* (a drinking song lends him wings).

Many composers have augmented or reduced the normal symphony orchestra. Messiaen, for instance, introduced an *ondes martenot* into the *Turangalîla-symphonie*, Mozart's father concocted a hunting symphony with four horns, shotgun and strings, and the Polynesian composer Dai-Keong Lee wrote a 'Symphony with a Tahitian Happening'. What happens? A grass-skirted dancer appears!

Should all symphonies employ strings? The first to answer this question negatively was Georg Glantz, *Kapellmeister* in Pressburg (now Bratislava) in 1763–75. He wrote a symphony for Turkish instruments in 1774: woodwind, brass, Turkish percussion (cymbals, triangle and bass drum) but no strings. Gossec's 'Military' symphony of 1794 is for wind alone, and Gounod (*Petite Symphonie* in E flat, 1885), Hindemith (Symphony for Concert Band in B flat, 1951) and John McCabe (Symphony for 10 Wind Instruments, 1964) are amongst those who have followed. Alan Hovhaness's Symphony No 17 'for metal orchestra' is scored for six flutes, three trombones and five percussionists. Henry Kling (1842–1918) dispenses altogether with orchestral instruments in his 'Kitchen Symphony' for piano, funnel trumpet, wine glass, bottle, saucepan, fire irons, milk jug and tin covers.

Others have retained the strings but thrown out the violins and everything else: Leopold Mozart's *Sinfonia burlesca* in G makes do with two violas, two cellos and bass, while Albert Siklós (1878–1942), a Hungarian who changed his name from Schönwald in 1910, felt even this to be too bright for his Symphony No 3, *Aethérique*, of 1899. He reduced the scoring to just 12 double basses.

Some composers, however, are not troubled by self-restraint. The most extreme example is mentioned on p 203, but ambitious symphonic plans go back at least as far as 1815, when Anton Reicha, a French/Bohemian composer, wrote a four-movement Symphony in D, the full title of which is *Musique pour célébrer des grandes hommes qui se sont illustres du service de la nation française*. This work was designed to be performed in the open air, the audience to be placed at a position 50 paces from the orchestras, behind which, at a distance of a further 100 paces, were the drums. Two orchestras were to take part, these being separated by at least 30 paces, and also included in the scoring were parts for cannon and infantry march-past.

One orchestra, then, was not enough for Reicha, but here again he had been beaten to the idea. The Dutchman Charles-Joseph van Helmont (1715–90) wrote a symphony for two orchestras in 1754 (perhaps transferring Vivaldi's two-orchestra concerto technique, which was known in Holland, to the symphony); three by J.C. Bach were published in London in *c*.1781, perhaps spurring on John Marsh (writing under the name Sharm) to produce his own charmingly-titled 'Conversation Symphony' five years later; and the idea had spread to Portugal by 1793, when Antonio Leal Moreira (1758–1819) wrote his Symphony in D for double orchestra. Louis

Spohr's Symphony No 7 in C, *Irdisches und Göttliches im Menschenleben* (1841) is also for double orchestra, but Elliott Carter's 'Symphony of Three Orchestras' (1976) goes further still. Orchestra I is on the left, its brass, timpani and strings balancing the woodwind, horns, untuned percussion and strings of Orchestra III on the right. Between lies Orchestra II, a concertante group of three clarinets, piano, percussion and strings. There are 12 short interlocked movements, four for each orchestra.

Finally, a brief glance at symphonies that need no orchestra at all — at least not in the accepted sense. George Antheil's Jazz Symphony of 1923 is a one-movement piece for jazz instruments which represents the highly syncopated spirit of the time. The Soviet composer Bogdan Iakovlevich Trotsyuk (b. 1931), however, invoked the 'cool' moody modern jazz of the 1950s in his three-movement Jazz Symphony, with jazz-type instruments being abetted by a handful of somewhat self-conscious 'normal' instruments.

Overtures and Beginners

Types of Overture

1 The single-movement, symphonic, sonata-form Opera Overture in which the development section is either abbreviated or omitted altogether. Mozart's *Marriage of Figaro* is a good example; there are others by Beethoven, Mendelssohn, Weber and Wagner.

2 As above, followed by a slow movement and a quick finale. The 18th century abounds with examples by virtually every operatic composer. Mozart provides perfect examples of this Italian Overture form in his so-called 'Symphonies' Nos 23 and 24 (K 181 and 182). The first was Alessandro Scarlatti's introduction to *Olympiade* (1697), and the first by an Englishman was William Boyce's overture to *Pelleas and Thetis* (1738). In many cases the finale is a greatly shortened version of the first movement: Mozart's Symphony No 32 in G, K 319, illustrates this form precisely. A mongrel type is found in the same composer's *Magic Flute* overture: a slow introduction leads to a rapid main movement, then a 'slow movement' (just three groups of developing chords), a development of the rapid material and a full recapitulation. The whole is capped by a short coda.

Types 1 and 2 were (are still in some countries) called *sinfonia*.

3 The so-called French *Ouverture* (note spelling), introduced by Lully about 1660, consists of a declamatory slow introduction in strongly dotted rhythm, followed by a fast movement usually of a fugal character. In some cases French-style dances follow,. This style travelled to Germany early in the 18th century and was taken up with enthusiasm by Telemann, Fasch, Hartwig, and many others.

4 The Concert Overture. In form this may be similar to 1, often with a slow introduction, but it is not associated with a stage work and is often descriptive in character. Mendelssohn's *Fingal's Cave* is the archetypal example: Brahms's two overtures also fall into this category.

Overtures of Note

The first overture in which the mood of the music was meant to prepare the audience for the drama to follow in the opera was that written by Gluck for *Alceste* in 1767. It is an overture of type 1 but is unusual in maintaining a slow tempo throughout. The composer explained: 'I feel that the overture should acquaint the audience with the mood of the opera'.

We noticed above the 'plug-in' alternative final bars of Prokofiev's Symphony No 7. Rameau found himself in a similar position two centuries earlier when the daringly atmospheric start of his overture to the 'heroic ballet' *Zaïs* (1748), with its solo muffled drum, was considered too advanced for the Paris audience and had to be replaced with a new opening. Thereafter, either opening might be 'plugged in' to the main part of the overture.

The first overture designed to be played *after* the rise of the curtain on the first act of the opera is Grétry's *Le Jugement de Midas* of 1778; and the only overture to include a part for solo voice is that to the opera *Uthal* (1806) by Méhul, at the climax of which a soprano utters two declamatory notes. The unconventional scoring calls for full orchestra but minus trumpets and violins.

Symphonic and Tone Poem

This is a large-scale orchestral work of descriptive character, the limits of which shade off into three other forms: concerto (Richard Strauss's *Don Quixote* with cello solo; Berlioz's *Harold in Italy*, a 'symphony' for viola solo); symphony (Berlioz's *Symphonie Fantastique*; Debussy's *La Mer*); and overture (Beethoven's *Egmont* and *Coriolan*, and Dvořák's *Hussites*). The symphonic poem is a direct descendant of the mood-setting overtures of Gluck, Cherubini, Méhul, Weber and Mendelssohn.

The earliest symphonic poem was César Franck's *Ce qu'on entend sur la montagne*, after Victor Hugo, completed about 1846, while the first British symphonic poem was *The Passing of Beatrice* (1892) by William Wallace.

SUITE, DIVERTIMENTO, SERENADE, ETC.

Of these, the suite is the oldest, being a string of dance movements which gradually evolved into a cogent and contrasting order, often including bourrée, courante, sarabande, minuet, gigue, etc., but with endless variations in their sequence. J.S. Bach's four orchestral suites are of overture type 3 and are still called *Ouvertüren* in Germany. Later in the 18th century, out of the suite and the lighter type of symphony grew the divertimento, serenade, cassation, etc., bright and entertaining pieces of many movements, liberally sprinkled with minuets (the one dance form which survived from the old suite and was later to develop into the symphonic scherzo) and usually ending with an extended rondo. The biggest of these compositions were called serenades; they often contained concerto elements in one or more movements. Mozart's Serenade in D, K 203, is a good example: an eight-movement work in which is buried a three-movement violin concerto. The Divertimento in D, K 251, has six movements in which the solo oboe is given a concertante part.

CONCERTO

The many different types of concerto were described in the second edition of this book, to which the reader is invited to refer. Those descriptions are replaced here with a short history of the concerto in its many forms and many locations.

Barely any modern instrument has escaped the attention of concerto writers. Woodwind, from piccolo (Bucchi) to double bassoon (Badings); brass, from high trumpet (Blacher) to bass tuba (Vaughan Williams); strings, from *violino piccolo* (Bach) to double bass (Dragonetti); and percussion of most types (Milhaud, Salzedo). All these, either independently or in groups, have been honoured with solo status — even the lowly Jew's harp has featured in two concerti by Albrechtsberger. On the other hand, the authors are not aware of a banjo concerto but it would be dangerous to deny that one exists.

Leaving aside the vocal use of the word 'concerto', known since 1519 as an ensemble of singers, and the 1565 meaning of a mixed group of singers and instrumentalists, the history and spread of the concerto may be seen in the adjacent chart. The composer of by far the most concerti is Antonio Vivaldi, whose grand total of 488 includes no less than 238 for violin. The largest corpus of concerti for the same instrument is the 312 for flute by Johann Joseph Quantz (1697–1773), who wrote them while in the service of the flute-playing King Frederick the Great. It is said that the king played them in strict rotation, so many per night, and when he had exhausted the stock he started again at the beginning.

The History of the Concerto

1607 First 'concertos', so called, were written in Carinthia (a part of southern Austria abutting Italy) by the Italian Giulio Radino, who died prior to their publication in Venice in 1607. The title *Concerti per sonore et cantare* (concerti for instruments and voices) might lead one to believe that they were works combining these forces; actually, there are canzonas for voices and other works for instruments — but there is no trace of the later concerto style.

1627 First Polish concerti were *Canzoni e concerti* by Adam Jarzębski (?–1649?), but again the instrumental works are not of true concerto type, being 'fantasias' based on compositions of others.

1675 Alessandro Stradella experimented with orchestral forces in his serenatas and cantatas, hitting upon a soloist-versus-main group in his serenata *Qual prodigio è ch'io miri*. He later extended the idea to introductory sinfonias and an independent sonata for two violins, lute and strings, in which the 'concertino' group plays against a 'concerto grosso' (main group). It is

Sanssouci Palace, Potsdam, residence of the flute fanatic King Frederick the Great. (*The Mansell Collection*)

perverse of musical history to introduce the first true concerti as serenatas, sinfonias and sonatas!

1682 Georg Muffat reported hearing Corelli's concerti grossi, although they were not published until 1714. They follow Stradella's format by setting a string trio (two violins and a cello) against a larger string group.

*c.***1690** First solo concerto was written by Giuseppe Torelli for the trumpeter at Bologna, Giovanni Pellegrino Brandi.

1698 First German concerti published: Muffat's *Florilegium* shows the clear influence of Corelli. The first concerti to include solo violin were published in Torelli's *Concerti musicale*, Op 6.

1701 First cello concerti published. Amongst the ten concerti of Giuseppe Maria Jaccini published in Bologna, six contain parts for solo cello.

1727 Boismortier was the first French composer to adopt the Italian name 'concerto' (in his Op 15). Two years later he composed the first French solo concerto, for cello or viol or bassoon, Op 26.

1733 First keyboard concerti. During a period of mourning at the Leipzig court where he worked, Bach took delivery of a new harpsichord. So impressed was he with its capabilities that he refurbished several of his old concerti for various instruments and turned them into harpsichord concerti. He also invited his 19-year-old son Carl Philipp Emanuel to compose for the instrument. J.S. Bach's modified works were the first harpsichord concerti, but C.P.E. Bach's A minor Concerto was the first original work in the genre. In about 1721 J.S. Bach had written the *Brandenburg Concerto* No 5 which has a prominent harpsichord solo (together with flute and violin); this may be antedated by Vivaldi's Concerto in C, RV 555, which employs two harpsichords along with nine other soloists and string orchestra.

*c.***1735** First Portuguese concerto: a harpsichord concerto in A by Carlos de Seixas (1704–42).

*c.***1750** First Norwegian concerto: harpsichord concerto by Johan Daniel Berlin (1714–87).

*c.***1776** First piano concerti. J.C. Bach's set of concerti Op 7, published about this time, were the first to specify *Piano e Forte* (pianoforte), although the alternative of harpsichord was prudently given.

1787 First Russian concerto: a piano concerto by Dmitry Stepanovich Bortnyansky (1751–1827).

*c.***1808** First Finnish concerto: a violin concerto by Erik Eriksson Tulindberg (1761–1814).

1834 First American concerto: for kent bugle by Anthony Philip Heinrich (1781–1861).

1902 First Mexican concerto was a cello concerto by Ricardo Castro Herrera (1864–1907), but Gustavo Emilio Campa (1863–1934) wrote a *Mélodie* for violin and orchestra in 1890.

1915 First Australian concerto: a trumpet concerto by Alfred Francis Hill (1870–1960).

?1929 First Greek concerto may have been a concerto grosso for wind and timpani by Petros Petrides (1892–1979).

1932 First Turkish concerto: a piano concertino by Ulvi Cemal Erkin (1906–72).

*c.***1965** First Chinese concerto was the 'Yellow River' Concerto for piano and orchestra, arranged by the Central Philharmonic Society of Peking from the 'Yellow River' Cantata by Hsien Hsing-hai (1905–45).

Concerti of Note

Vivaldi seems to have created the largest group of soloists in a concerto; or, in fact, in two, for both RV 555 and RV 558 boast 11 virtuoso parts: RV 555 in C, for violin, two violas, two flutes, oboe, cor anglais (or, more likely, a low oboe), two trumpets, two harpsichords, and string band; RV 558 in C, for two flutes, two salmoè, two violins in tromba marina, two mandolins, two theorboes, cello and string band.

John McCabe's 'Mini-Concerto' (1966) has more solo players but they are hardly of the 'virtuoso' variety: 485 penny whistles, with percussion and organ accompaniment.

The first piano concerto to include human voices was **Daniel Steibelt's** Concerto No 8 in E flat (1820), which concludes with a 'Bacchanalian Rondo' for chorus with piano and orchestra. Better-known is **Busoni's** Concerto No 2, Op 39 (1904), a massive five-movement composition, the finale of which includes a male choir singing a text by the Danish poet A.G. Oehlenschläger. **Mondonville** wrote a concerto for violin and voice (1747) and another for violin, voice, orchestra and choir (1752).

In the early 18th century **Vivaldi, Albinoni** and some others wrote concerti for string group without any soloist at all; these are proto-symphonies which were given the name 'concerti' because of the vague terminology of

Antonio Vivaldi surrounded himself with soloists. Eleven virtuoso parts were allocated in two of his concerti. (Royal College of Music)

the period. More notable are a small number of concerti for soloists without orchestra:

Alkan: Concerto, Op 39/8–10 (1857) for piano; Concerto, Op 74 (*c.*1872) for piano
Bach: 'Italian' Concerto, BWV 971, for harpsichord
Schumann: Concerto for Piano Without Orchestra, also called Sonata No 4 in F minor, Op 14 (1836).

The Danish composer **Carl Nielsen** composed three concerti. The first, for violin, is unremarkable, but the later two introduce additional and unexpected soloists. In the Clarinet Concerto (1928) a side drum takes a major role in the musical development, while a bass trombone joins the main soloist in the Flute Concerto (1926), its coarse-grained character complementing the sensitive nature of the flute.

The Polish composer **Barbara Buczek** (b. 1940) seemed to hark back to the 16th century when she composed a concerto for 12 voices unaccompanied in 1969; and **Hans Werner Henze's** Violin Concerto No 2 (1971) includes the reading of a poem by Hans Magnus Enzensberger, together with voices and taped effects, and the soloist is required to perform exaggerated gestures and movements in addition to getting his notes right.

THE MUSIC OF FRIENDS

This is just one of the descriptions given to the intimate musical activity usually known by the anachronistic name 'chamber music'. It gives a good impression of the nature of this art form: a small group of artists who must be friends if their long hours of practice and discussion are to result in fine performances, playing music to a relatively small audience. Boccherini was amongst the most prolific of chamber music composers so one would expect him to understand: he called some of his works 'conversations', while Charles Ives titled two movements of his String Quartet No 2 'Discussions' and 'Arguments'.

Just what is the music of friends? We may take an arbitrary figure of 10 for the maximum number of artists involved, although some legitimate chamber works require more and some symphonies could be performed with less. The lower figure may be set at two, but it is surely possible to admit solo works into the realm of intimate music played in a chamber. How treacherous and misleading are such labels! But who would deny that the string quartet is the kernel of the chamber music repertoire? Answer: Verdi, for one. His string quartet sounds much better on a full string orchestra. Boulez for another: his *Livre pour quatuor* (1949) was transformed two decades later into the *Livre pour cordes*, for 60 string players.

This is not the place to examine the history and evolution of the many chamber music genres; nor is it necessary even to mention all of them. Indeed, we may note only some of the milestones along the way and glance at the odder examples which crave admittance to the hallowed chamber.

Nonets to Quintets

There is by no means an established constitution for chamber works, but some composers would seem to have exceeded the bounds of acceptance and credibility. Ives's *Scherzo: Over the Pavements* (1913) calls for piccolo, clarinet, bassoon, trumpet, three trombones, piano, cymbal and drum, while Vladimir Stcherbatchev's *Nonet* has a string quartet joined by piano, harp, violin, dance and light. Ives and others agreed with Stcherbatchev that the string quartet needs some kind of support. His String Quartet No 1 (1896) includes flute, piano and double bass; three composers have added a soprano soloist (Schoenberg's No 2, 1908; Milhaud's No 3, 1916; and Rochberg's No 2, 1961), while Jan Kapr's Quartet No 6 (1963) adds a baritone solo. Robert Simpson (for a bet or a dare or a commission?) composed a Quintet in 1981 for a grotesque combination: clarinet, bass clarinet and three double basses; but Mauricio Kagel dismissed both instruments and players for his *Ornithologica multiplicata* of 1968. He merely attached microphones to two occupied bird cages and expected his audience to listen to the result.

Kagel had prepared his listeners for the unexpected three years earlier with his *Pas de cinq*, a quintet like no other. The performers' instruments are walking sticks, and their actions are precisely-controlled perambulations up ramps and steps, the whole action set within a pentagon. The 'music' comes from the tapping of canes and the thump of footsteps; the fascination, if any, comes from the mind-numbing experience of watching responsible human beings carrying out these ludicrous actions.

Quartets

The string quartet, without additions, is probably the most perfect vehicle for conveying the composer's deepest emotions to his public. No-one knows who wrote the first. Undoubtedly the violin I, violin II, viola, cello combination was hit upon by some experimenter, perhaps **Telemann** or someone earlier — **Vivaldi**, **A. Scarlatti**, **Biagio Marini** who died in 1663, and even **Giovanni Gabrieli** in the *Canzoni* of 1608 have been suggested. But the true string quartet written specifically for those instruments and no others, and not requiring a continuo line, did not appear until *c.*1750–5. Its early history is bound so closely to that of the emerging symphony by **Sammartini**, **Richter**, and **Tartini** that there can be no incontrovertible answer, but **Haydn** is usually credited with establishing its distinct character sometime around 1760. Even after this, the quartet continued to be called variously *sinfonia*, *sonata* or *divertimento*, and, although the phrase *quatuor pour cordes* was a frequent description on publications originating in France, it was not until about the second decade of the 19th century that the phrase 'string quartet' became common.

By far the most prolific string quartet composer was **Cambini**, with a total of at least 174 (Cambini, incidentally, invented the wind quintet — for flute, oboe, clarinet, bassoon and horn — in about 1795 as a by-product of the *sinfonie concertant*). Next comes **Boccherini** with 91, but Boccherini is better known as the probable inventor and certainly the most prolific composer of the string *quintet* for two violins with one or two violas and one or two cellos, of which he wrote 137.

The second number, 'Excentrique', of **Stravinsky's** *Three Pieces for String Quartet* (1914) was indeed eccentric enough to incur sad head-shakings from wise old critics, for it is a representation in sound of the antics of the clown Little Tich, whom Stravinsky had laughed at in London. The clown's acrobatic drollery is faithfully echoed by the instruments, but what really offended the traditionalists was the direction that the second violin and the viola should play their instruments upside-down in the manner of the cello. No such tomfoolery invaded **Milhaud's** quartets Nos 14 (1948) and 15 (1949) except that each makes sense when played separately, as do they both when played simultaneously.

Why call a string quartet a string quartet? **Xenakis** had a better idea in 1962: he called his *ST/4–1, 080263*. This is not a telex number but a simple code meaning *St*ring Quartet No *1*, written on 8 February 1962.

Caged-bird and walking-stick fancier **Mauricio Kagel** is full of novel effects. His String Quartet of 1967 must be played as part of a normal chamber recital, its two movements separated by an interval or by a 'conventional' work. For the quartet itself cannot be described as conventional. The players are instructed to sit in positions remote from one another and to walk about, and they play with various items (paper clips, matches, etc.) wedged between or attached to the strings, and sometimes they must lay aside their bows and rake their valuable instruments with notched sticks or hit them with the hand. **Heinz Holliger** (b. 1939) showed more consideration — eventually — for his players. His Quartet (1973) is of such surpassing strenuousness for the players (the listeners being left to cope with it as best they may) that the composer writes fatigue into the score, fatigue which manifests itself in the tone (shaky bow, tense, halting bowing, etc). As Paul Griffiths has remarked, 'the work descends . . . from manic activity to tremulous grey pianissimos and silence'.

Of similar strenuousness is **Robert Simpson's** String Quartet No 9 (1982) which, far from ending in consideration for the artists, calls on them to play a mighty closing fugue. The Quartet consists of 32 variations on a theme of Haydn. Each variation follows Haydn's example by being a perfect palindrome, travelling to a central point and then returning note for note to the beginning.

The string quartet's instrumentation, having been established firmly in the mid-18th century, is today by no means inviolable. The English composer **Bernard van Dieren** (1887–1936) replaced the cello with a double bass in his Quartet Op 22. Two quartets by an unknown author (both have been attributed to Haydn, one to Benjamin Franklin, the other to Ferandini, Roller, Martinez and Pleyel) changed the rules almost as soon as they had been formulated, for they are written in such a way that the *three* violins and cello were mistuned and played without stopping the strings. Possibly these oddities were intended for practice purposes.

SONATAS

The word's derivation is not obvious. It arose during the 13th century to indicate a new concept in 'art' music: a piece for instruments alone which was important enough to merit its own generic category. The word *sonada* occurs in France, Spain and Germany, denoting various types of instrumental pieces, and by the 16th century the Italian version *sonata* (= 'something played') was being used as the antithesis of *cantata* (= 'something sung'). Shakespeare (d. 1616) used 'sennet' as a stage direction for a trumpet signal. However, the sonata did not acquire its present meaning until the mid- to late-18th century, when the concept of tonal conflict between two or more themes resulted in the term 'sonata-form', which is now applied to instrumental pieces which exploit this conflict in an established way.

By 1700 (see p 177) the sonata was well established and was to remain the favourite chamber form for small groups. Some composers became exceptionally prolific: **Tartini** wrote more violin sonatas (191) than anyone else, and **Johann Joachim Quantz** wrote 204 flute sonatas, mostly for the use of his employer King Frederick the Great of Prussia. The king himself managed to contribute a further 120 of his own.

Joseph Haydn. (Mary Evans Picture Library)

History of the Sonata

The early history of the sonata is hazy but the following landmarks stand out.

1597 G. Gabrieli's sonatas for multiple choirs.
1605 First organ sonatas: Adriano Banchieri (1568–1634), written for use in church services between hymns and lessons.
1610 First solo sonatas (instrument unspecified) with continuo, and first trio sonatas (violin, cornett and continuo): Giovanni Paolo Cima (*fl.* 1600–22).
1613 First two-violin sonatas: Biagio Marini (*c.*1587–1663).
1638 First sonatas for two unaccompanied trumpets: Girolamo Fantini (*fl.* 1630–38).
1641 First harpsichord sonatas (with

alternative use for organ): Gioanpietro Del Buono (dates unknown).
1645 First sonatas for a low instrument: the *Compositioni musicali* by Giovanni Antonio Bertoli (died *c.*1645 or later) for dulcian (an early bassoon); but, mindful of their limited appeal, Bertoli suggested that other instruments, or perhaps even singers, might perform them.
1664 First sonatas for unaccompanied violin: H.I.F. Biber (1644–1704).
1680s First cello sonatas: Domenico Gabrieli (1651–90).
1688 First sonatas for viola da gamba and continuo: Johannes Schenk (1660–1712).
*c.***1703** First sonatas for two harpsichords: Bernardo Pasquini (1637–1710).

Most of the earlier sonatas required the continuo support of harpsichord (and often of low stringed instruments), but the emancipation of the harpsichord gradually occurred, a process that was complete by the time of **Domenico Scarlatti**. His is the largest corpus of sonatas by one composer in the history of music. There are at least 555 harpsichord sonatas, the majority of which are single-movement pieces which exploit and extend the accepted abilities of the instrument. The English composer **John White** (b. 1936) has, according to recent information, written 98 piano sonatas.

The first true piano sonatas were written by **Lodovico Maria Giustini** (1685–1743), whose Op 1 published in 1732 contains 12 works. But the high point of the classical solo keyboard sonata (all often played on pianoforte, but earlier examples are more effective on harpsichord, clavichord or fortepiano) ended in 1831. The output of these four composers has not been surpassed in quality:

Giuseppe Tartini, composer of 191 violin sonatas. (Politikens Forlag, Denmark)

Franz Joseph Haydn (1732–1809): 47 sonatas between *c.*1760 and *c.*1795.
Wolfgang Amadeus Mozart (1756–91): 28 sonatas between 1766 and 1787
Ludwig van Beethoven (1770–1827): 35 sonatas between 1783 and 1822
Muzio Clementi (1752–1832): 79 sonatas and 9 duets between 1765 and 1831.

B. Audran Sculp.
LE CONCERT CHAMPÊTRE
Gravé d'Apres le Tableau original peint par Watteau haut de 1 pied 10 pouces et large de 1 pied 7 pouces.
CONCENTUS AGRESTIS
Sculptus juxta Exemplar a Watteavo depictum cujus altitudo 1 pedem cum 10 unciis et latitudo 1 pedem cum 7 continet.

(Mary Evans Picture Library)

VIII
At the Concert

A concert is an organized performance of music given before an audience. History does not record when the first was given, but it was certainly not of the type suggested by the above simple description: a disciplined, penguin-suited body of musicians conducted by a tail-coated gentleman standing on a raised platform and calmly beating time with a stick, his back to a politely attentive audience. On the contrary, the earliest 'concerts' evolved slowly from virtual chaos as small bunches of players gradually attracted non-players who were content to sit and listen. Concerts have existed since the earliest days of humanity; it is merely references to them that are lacking.

Pictorial evidence of group music-making in Ancient Egypt shows lutes, lyres, pipes, drums and other percussion in use at least 2000 years before Christ, and musical instruments of similar types were known (and doubtless used in concert) in Ancient Greece. Musical discipline is likely to have been slack due to the primitive methods of indicating pitches and, probably, the difficulty of conveying rhythm other than practically. Much as in a jazz jam session, a group of musicians in ancient times would have taken a rhythmic lead from a drummer and improvized one after the other according to a pre-arranged rota.

The earliest concert for which direct evidence exists took place in the 6th century BC in Babylon, according to Daniel 3: 5, 7, 10, 15. Nebuchadnezzar's orchestra comprised *quarnā* (horn or trumpet), *mašroquīta* (pipe), *qatros* (lyre), *sabka* (horizontal angular harp), and *psantrîn* (vertical angular harp), . . . *sūmponiah* . . . (. . . which sound together . . .), . . . *zmārâ* (. . . against a percussion group).

The following is an attempt at a chronology of important moments in concert history to illustrate its spread and increasing popularity.

*c.*309 BC Evidence of a musical group is implied by a report of its exceptional absence: the Greek Aristos in Rome brought his players out on strike in a dispute connected with meal breaks. Thereafter, firm evidence of musical groups is sparse until:

8th century AD A touring orchestra of 40 Arabian females made frequent pilgrimages to Mecca under their leader Jarmila.

1482 The first Accademie, set up primarily for musical instruction, discussion and performance, were held in Bologna. A similar Accademia was established in Milan in 1484.

1570 The Académie Baïf was set up by Jean Antoine Baïf at the court of Charles IX. Although inspired by the Italian examples, these French meetings were less formal, consisting mainly of musical settings of poems written by members of the Académie.

1571 Beginning on 25 March, waits (musicians employed by a town to perform on certain occasions) sang and played shawms, sackbuts, violins, viols and lutes from the turret of the Royal Exchange in London for the sole object of bringing pleasure to people living nearby. This friendly practice was continued every Sunday (until stopped by Charles I in 1642) and holiday evenings from Lady Day to Michaelmas (until Pentecost in 1572).

*c.***1576** Orchestras of organs, lutes, viols, recorders, and pandoras, together with voices, would entertain the audience for an hour before and half an hour after a play at theatres such as that at Blackfriars, London. The practice was widespread by the early 17th century.

1580–*c.*90 Nicholas Yonge gave private musical parties at his home in the City of London every day. Mostly these consisted of Italian (and English imitation) madrigals.

1672 30 September was an important date.

At The Concert

For the first time people were asked to pay to listen to music. The musical performances before and after plays were not strictly what the audience had paid to hear; therefore, all musical performances up to that date had been free. John Bannister (or Banister) was the world's first musical impresario. He was one of the 24 violinists of King Charles II's 'Musick', who saw a way to supplement his income. At his music school near the George Tavern, Whitefriars, London, every day at 4pm were held concerts at which the performers, both instrumental and vocal, were placed out of sight behind a curtain. The public was allowed to listen upon payment of 1s (5p) per head. In 1675 the organization moved to Covent Garden, and later to Lincoln's Inn Fields, and finally to Essex Street, off the Strand.

1678 Thomas Britton, a coal-dealer, converted his Clerkenwell coal cellar into a concert-house and there, until his death in 1714, gave a series of concerts which started as diversions for his friends but quickly grew famous among the gentry. Visitors are said to have included Handel and other famous musicians. At first, entrance was free, but as numbers increased Britton was compelled to impose a fee of 1s (5p) per concert or 10s (50p) per year.

1693 The first Scottish concert was organized in Edinburgh by Beck, a German music teacher active in Fife.

1710 Jean Loeillet gave concerts of mainly Italian music for the flute at his London home.

1714 Hickford, the dancing master, gave over his room to concert-giving, first at James Street, Piccadilly, and, from about 1738, in Brewer Street, Soho, until 1779.

*c.***1720** The Academy of Ancient Music was formed to give concerts at the Crown and Anchor Tavern in the Strand. These continued until 1792.

1724 The Castle Society, another organization centred upon a local inn, did likewise at the Castle Tavern, Paternoster Row, and later elsewhere.

While these and many other organizations flourished in London, the practice of concerts was developing in the courts and residences of Germany and other European countries, growing out of the Collegia Musica, which themselves had evolved from the Italian Accademie. In France another development of lasting importance took place:

1725 Anne Philidor (Danican) founded the Concert Spirituel series in Paris. These, the first true public concerts in France, were held at the Salle des Cent Suisses in the Château des Tuileries until 1784 and were extremely popular and influential, attracting the attention of composers from many other countries. For instance, Haydn wrote for the Concert Spirituel a set of six 'Paris' Symphonies. Even after the series ceased in 1791 there were attempts to revive the name (in 1805 and 1830).

1731 The earliest known American secular concert was given on 16 December in Boston, Mass. Announced as a 'Concert of Music on sundry instruments at Mr Pelham's Great Room', it began at 6pm and tickets were 5s (25p) each. In the same year concerts began in Charles Town (later Charleston), South Carolina.

1736 The first concerts in New York began on 21 January at the house of the vintner Robert Todd, next to Fraunces' Tavern. New York quickly became the centre of American musical activity, for more concerts were given there between 1736 and 1775 (a total of 46) than in any other American centre.

1743 The First modern symphony orchestra was established at the Court of the Elector Palatine, Duke Karl Theodor, at Mannheim. In the same year the oldest symphony orchestra still in existence, the Leipzig Gewandhaus Orchestra, at first known as the Grosses Concert and, from 1763, the 'Liebhaber-Concerte', came into existence. The name 'Gewandhaus Orchestra' dates from 1781, when a new room specially built for the activities of this group of players was erected in the Gewandhaus ('Cloth Merchants' House'). A new Gewandhaus was completed in 1884, designed purely for music while yet retaining the traditional 'cloth-house' name.

1760–75 Three famous concert houses were opened in London: Mrs Cornelys's Carlisle House in Soho Square (1760–80); The Pantheon in Oxford Street (1772–1814); and the Hanover Square Rooms (1775–1874).

1776 The Concerts of Ancient Music commenced. They became known as the 'King's Concerts' from 1785 because of the regular attendance of George II, and they continued until 1848.

1783 The Professional Concerts were founded in London by Clementi, Wilhelm Cramer and J.P. Salomon and gave concerts in the Hanover Square Rooms until 1793.

1828 The Société des Concerts du Conservatoire were established in Paris by F.A. Habeneck, the composer and violinist who gave French audiences their first opportunity to hear Beethoven's symphonies. The orchestra gave its first concert on 9 March.

1837 The first promenade concerts were launched in Paris, conducted by Henri Justin

Valentine, but they were not well attended and ceased after one short season.

1839 Promenade Concerts à la Valentine were opened at the Crown and Anchor Tavern in the Strand, London. The same year saw the launch of the Original Promenade Concerts à la Musard at the English Opera House.

1840–1 During this winter season there were three separate promenade concert series running in London, all well patronized, but after many years this division of effort was channelled into one driving force — see below, at 1895.

1840 The Liverpool Philharmonic gave its first concert on 12 March under the direction of John Russell. Philharmonic Hall was built for the orchestra in 1849 but was destroyed by fire in 1933.

1842 The Vienna Philharmonic gave its first concert on 28 March, conducted by Karl Otto Nicolai. On 7 December of the same year the New York Philharmonic gave its first concert in the Apollo Rooms, the conductor being Ureli Corelli Hill, its co-founder with William Scharfenberg and Henry Christian Timm. The orchestra joined with the New York Symphony in 1928 to become the New York Philharmonic Symphony.

1858 The Hallé Orchestra, Manchester, grew out of the Gentlemen's Concerts, Sir Charles Hallé taking them over on 1 January, 1850. The first Hallé concerts were a subscription series started on 30 January 1858 at the Free Trade Hall, Manchester.

1864 The Moscow Philharmonic Orchestra was launched under the directorship of Nikolai Rubinstein.

1878 The New York Symphony, founded by Walter Damrosch, merged with the New York Philharmonic in 1928.

1881 Henry L. Higginson founded the Boston Symphony. Symphony Hall was built in 1900.

1881 Charles Lamoureux founded the Lamoureux Orchestra in Paris.

1882 The Amsterdam Concertgebouw Orchestra founded. Its first concert, in the newly-built Concertgebouw ('Concert House') was held on 11 April 1888, at which the conductor was Henri Viotta.

1882 The Berlin Philharmonic was formed, a corporate body derived from an orchestra led by Benjamin Bilse. Its first concert was given on 17 October 1882. Hans von Bülow was conductor from 21 October 1887 to 13 March 1893, and he conducted the orchestra's first concert in Philharmonic Hall on 5 October 1888.

1891 The Chicago Symphony founded by Theodor Thomas. The first concert held in Orchestra Hall was given on 14 December 1904.

Symphony Hall, Boston, built to house the famous orchestra. (Photo: John Brook)

1893 Cincinnati Symphony founded; its first conductor was Frank van der Stucken. In Munich Franz Kaim established the Munich Philharmonic in the same year.

1894 The Czech Philharmonic was formed as a society. Its first concert, of music by Dvořák conducted by the composer, was given on 4 January 1896.

1895 The first Henry Wood Promenade Concert was held on 8 August. Henry (Sir Henry from 1911) Wood was manager and principle conductor from that date until his death in 1944. They were held in the Queen's Hall until its destruction in 1941, after which they transferred to the Royal Albert Hall, where they continue to this day.

1895 San Francisco Symphony founded.

1896 Los Angeles Symphony founded.

1899 Pittsburg Symphony founded.

Ernest Ansermet, founder of the Suisse Romande Orchestra and its conductor for 50 years. (Decca Record Co. Ltd)

1900 Philadelphia Orchestra established by Fritz Scheel.
1901 Warsaw Philharmonic founded under the protection of Prince Lubomirski and Count Zamoyski.
1903 Minneapolis Symphony founded.
1904 London Symphony formed as a cooperative organization.
1907 St Louis Symphony founded.
1913 Hague Residentie founded by Henri Viotta.
1916 City of Birmingham Symphony founded.
1918 Cleveland Symphony founded. In the same year the Orchestre da la Suisse Romande was founded by Ernest Ansermet, who remained its chief conductor until his death in 1968.
1919 Los Angeles Philharmonic founded.
1930 BBC Symphony founded by its principle conductor Sir Adrian Boult.
1932 London Philharmonic founded by Sir Thomas Beecham; the orchestra became autonomous in 1939.
1945 Philharmonia Orchestra founded by Walter Legge.
1964 New Philharmonia formed as a company out of the members of the Philharmonia Orchestra, which was wound up only a few days earlier in March 1964. The component 'New' was discarded in 1977.
1967 Orchestre de Paris founded by its principle conductor Charles Munch.
1984 Philharmonic Symphony Orchestra established in London by the Argentinian conductor Carlos Païta.

At The Concert

Sir Henry Wood as seen by Bernard Partridge in a 1926 Punch *caricature. (Mary Evans Picture Library)*

What's in a Name?
Music-lovers exasperated or perplexed by references to 'the Beethoven B flat' or 'the Mozart G minor' will approve of the habit of identifying major works by names rather than numbers. How forgettable is 'String Quartet in D, Op 50, No 6'; how memorable is 'the Frog Quartet'. Literally hundreds of works have been given nicknames by their composers or by publishers, and a selection of the best known is given here — sufficient, it is hoped, to satisfy the curiosity of the regular concert-goer and record-buyer.

Edward Downes, conductor of Prokofiev's War and Peace *(in his own English translation) at the opening of the Sydney Opera House, 28 September 1973. (Ingpen and Williams, Ltd)*

THE CONCERT-GOER/RECORD BUYER'S GUIDE TO NICKNAMES

Nickname	Work	Composer	Remarks
Adélaide	Violin Concerto in D, KA 294a (*c.*1775?)	?Mozart	Supposedly dedicated to the eldest daughter of Louis XV, Mme Adélaide de France. The dedication may have strayed from another work; the concerto is probably spurious.
Alla Rustica	Concerto in G for strings, RV 151	Vivaldi	Written in 'rustic' style.
Alleluja	Symphony No 30 in C (1765)	Haydn	Uses a Gregorian Alleluja theme.
American	String Quartet in F, Op 96 (1893)	Dvořák	Written at Spillville, Iowa, and based partly on Black American themes.

Nickname	Work	Composer	Remarks
Antar	Symphony No 2, Op 9 (1868)	Rimsky-Korsakov	Antar was a 7th-century Russian poet.
Antartica	Symphony No 7 (1953)	Vaughan Williams	Based on the composer's film music for *Scott of the Antarctic* (1948).
Appassionata	Piano Sonata in F minor, Op 57 (1806)	Beethoven	A publisher's title referring to the passionate nature of the music.
Archduke	Piano Trio in B flat, Op 97 (1811)	Beethoven	Dedicated to the Archduke Rudolf.
Babi Yar	Symphony No 13, Op 113 (1962)	Shostakovich	Commemorates the Jewish cemetery at Babi Yar, Kiev.
Battle of Vittoria	Symphony (1813)	Beethoven	Also known as Wellington's Victory; a pictorial celebration in music.
Bear	Symphony No 82 in C (1786)	Haydn	A title added by French audiences (*L'Ours*) to characterize the growling start of the finale.
Bell	Symphony No 2 (1943)	Khachaturian	The opening is said to be bell-like.
Bells of Zlonice	Symphony No 1 in C minor, Op 3 (1865)	Dvořák	The young composer lived at Zlonice and is said to have incorporated the motifs of the town's bells into the work.
Bird	String Quartet in C, Op 33, No 3 (1781)	Haydn	The first movement incorporates bird impressions.
Caccia	Violin Concerto in B flat, Op 8, No 10 (*c.*1725)	Vivaldi	One of several Vivaldi concerti depicting a hunting scene.
Capricieuse	Symphony No 3 in D (1842)	Berwald	An imaginative and appropriate title for a capricious work.
Chasse	Symphony No 73 in D (1781)	Haydn	An authentic title referring to the character of the finale, originally the overture to an opera setting the scene of sylvan blood-lust.

At The Concert

Nickname	Work	Composer	Remarks
Choral	Symphony No 9 in D minor (1823)	Beethoven	Chorus and soloists appear in the finale.
Classical	Symphony No 1 in D, Op 25 (1917)	Prokofiev	Written in the style of classical composers.
Clock	Symphony No 101 in D (1794)	Haydn	So-called because of the 'tick-tock' rhythm of the slow movement.
Colloredo	Serenade in D, K 203 (1774)	Mozart	Used, but probably not written, for the name-day of the Archbishop Colloredo.
Coronation	Piano Concerto in D, K 537 (1788)	Mozart	Possibly played during the festivities surrounding the coronation in Frankfurt of Leopold II.
Creation Mass	Mass No 11 in B flat (1801)	Haydn	The Gloria introduces a theme already famous from the oratorio *The Creation* of 1798.
Dance	Symphony (1929)	Copland	Adapted from the ballet *Grohg*.
Death and the Maiden	String Quartet in D minor, D 810 (1826)	Schubert	The second movement uses the theme of the song of that name.
Dissonance	String Quartet in C, K 456 (1785)	Mozart	Remarkable for the harsh dissonances in the first movement.
Distratto	Symphony No 60 in C (1774)	Haydn	A symphony reconstructed from music for the play *Der Zerstreute* = the absent-minded one.
Dream	String Quartet in F, Op 50, No 5 (1787)	Haydn	The second movement has a dream-like quality.
Drum Mass	Mass No 7 (1796)	Haydn	Written as Napoleon's army approached Vienna; there is a prominent drum part in the *Dona nobis pacem*.
Drum Roll	Symphony No 103 in E flat (1795)	Haydn	Refers to the arresting solo drum-roll at the start of the work.

At The Concert

Nickname	Work	Composer	Remarks
Dumky	Piano Trio in E minor, Op 90 (1891)	Dvořák	Based on the Czech dance of that name.
Ebony	Clarinet concerto (1945)	Stravinsky	Written for Woody Herman's clarinet, made presumably of ebony.
Eco in Lontano	Two-Violin Concerto in A, RV 552 (1740)	Vivaldi	'Echo in the Distance'; one of several 'Echo Concerti' by this composer.
Eine Kleine Nachtmusik	Serenade in G, K 525 (1788)	Mozart	Mozart's own name for his most popular work.
Emperor	Piano Concerto No 5 in E flat (1809)	Beethoven	A title used in English-speaking countries only; there is no authority for the name.
Emperor	String Quartet in C, Op 76, No 3 (1799)	Haydn	The famous theme of the slow movement was said to have been inspired by the English national anthem which Haydn heard in England. Haydn's donation to Austria is far greater.
Eroica	Symphony No 3 in E flat (1802)	Beethoven	At first the name was attached to the symphony 'in memory of a hero' (Napoleon), but was later forcibly removed by the composer.
Espansiva	Symphony No 3 (1910–11)	Nielsen	Suggests the expansive mood of the music.
Eyeglass	Duo in E flat	Beethoven	In full: 'with the obbligato for two eyeglasses'. Nicolaus Zmeskall, cello, and Beethoven, viola, both wore spectacles.
Fantasia	String Quartet in E flat, Op 76, No 6 (1799)	Haydn	A mnemonic title recalling the slow movement, a Fantasia in B major.
Farewell	Symphony No 45 in F sharp minor (1772)	Haydn	This symphony is the source of the oft-told tale of dissension in the ranks of Haydn's orchestra: desire for an overdue holiday is reflected in the instrumentalists' departures in the finale.

Nickname	Work	Composer	Remarks
Favorito	Violin Concerto in E minor, RV 277	Vivaldi	A favourite in its day, but now eclipsed by the *Four Seasons*.
Festive	Symphony in E (1854)	Smetana	Also 'Triumphal Symphony'. The finale ends with an extended presentation of Haydn's 'Emperor's Hymn'.
Fiery Angel	Symphony No 3 in C minor (1928)	Prokofiev	Based on material from the opera of that name.
Fifths	String Quartet in D minor, Op 76, No 2 (1799)	Haydn	Name taken from the opening motif, which is based on a falling fifth.
Fire	Symphony No 59 in A (*c.*1766–8)	Haydn	The movements were used apparently between or during the acts of the opera *Die Feuersbrunst* ('The Burning House').
Four Temperaments	Symphony No 2 (1902)	Nielsen	Based on the medieval description of the 'humours' of man: 'Four Humours reign within our bodies wholly, and these compared to four elements, The Sanguine, Choler, Flegeme and Melancholy.'
Frei aber Einsam	Sonata for violin and piano (1855)	Brahms; Schumann; Dietrich	A 'joint' composition, each composer contributing one movement. The title translates as 'Free but Lonely'.
Frog	String Quartet in D, Op 50, No 6 (1787)	Haydn	Exhibits a curious croaking effect in the finale, produced by the bariolage technique.
From My Life	String Quartet No 1 in E minor (1876)	Smetana	An autobiographical work.
From the New World	Symphony No 9 in E minor (1893)	Dvořák	Written during the composer's visit to the American continent.
Ghost	Piano Trio in D, Op 70, No 1 (1808)	Beethoven	Named from the eerie character of the second movement.

At The Concert

Nickname	Work	Composer	Remarks
Great	Symphony No 9 in C major (1825)	Schubert	So named to differentiate it from the 'Little' Symphony in the same key.
Great Organ Mass	Mass No 2 (*c*.1766)	Haydn	There are concertante organ parts in the Kyrie and Benedictus.
Haffner	Symphony No 35 in D, K 385 (1782)	Mozart	Written for the Salzburg Haffner family. An earlier Serenade (K 250, 1776) was composed for the same family.
Hallelujah	Organ Concerto in B flat, Op 7, No 3	Handel	Incorporates a motif from the famous chorus in *Messiah*.
Hammerklavier	Piano Sonata in B flat, Op 106 (1818)	Beethoven	Written to be played on the 'hammered klavier' rather than the plucked harpsichord.
Harmonie Mass	Mass No 12 in B flat (1802)	Haydn	'Harmonie' = a group of wind players. This mass freely employs a large wind group.
Harmonious Blacksmith	Harpsichord Suite No 5 in E	Handel	A fanciful name; supposedly a Stanmore blacksmith's actions inspired Handel.
Harp	String Quartet in E flat, Op 74 (1809)	Beethoven	A name suggested by the pizzicato passages in the first movement.
Heiligmesse	Mass No 8 (1796)	Haydn	A German mnemonic title referring to the use in the Sanctus of an old hymn, 'Holy, holy'.
Hen	Symphony No 83 in G minor (1785)	Haydn	The second subject in the first movement, and parts of the Andante, are supposed to cluck.
Hoffmeister	String Quartet in D, K 499 (1786)	Mozart	Published by Hoffmeister in Vienna; a meaningless title.
Hornsignal	Symphony No 31 in D (1765)	Haydn	Refers to the hunting-horn fanfares in the outer movements.

At The Concert

Nickname	Work	Composer	Remarks
Hunt	String Quartet in B flat, K 458 (1784)	Mozart	The finale suggests a hunting scene.
Hymn of Praise	Symphony No 2 in B flat (1840)	Mendelssohn	The choral finale is in the style of a hymn of praise.
Ilya Murometz	Symphony No 3 (1911)	Glière	Ilya Murometz was a hero of Russian legend.
Imperial	Symphony No 53 in D (*c.*1777)	Haydn	Refers to the ceremonial style of the first movement.
Inextinguishable	Symphony No 4 (1916)	Nielsen	Expresses the indomitability of the human spirit.
Inquietudine	Violin Concerto in D, RV 234	Vivaldi	Possesses a restless mood.
Intimate Pages	String Quartet No 2 (1928)	Janáček	An autobiographical work dealing with the composer's feelings for a young woman, Kamila Stösslová.
Italian	Solo harpsichord Concerto (1735)	Bach	A rare example of a concerto without orchestra; it is in the Italian format of three movements, fast-slow-fast.
Italian	Symphony No 4 in A (1833)	Mendelssohn	A musical picture of the composer's impressions of Italy.
Jeunehomme	Piano Concerto in E flat, K 271	Mozart	Possibly written for Mlle Jeunehomme on her (disputed) Salzburg visit in 1776.
Joke	String Quartet in E flat, Op 33, No 3 (1781)	Haydn	The last movement stops and starts several times, keeping the audience guessing as to when to applaud.
Jupiter	Symphony No 41 in C, K 551 (1788)	Mozart	A name, coined possibly as late as 1819, to suggest the stature of the work.
Kaffeeklatsch	Piece for flute clock	Haydn	Suggests the gossiping of customers in a coffee shop.
Kegelstadt	Trio in E flat, K 498 (1786)	Mozart	'Skittle-alley Trio', said to have been planned in the composer's head during a game of skittles.

Nickname	Work	Composer	Remarks
Kreutzer	Violin Sonata in A, Op 47 (1803)	Beethoven	Dedicated to the French composer/violinist Rodolphe Kreutzer
Lamentatione	Symphony No 26 in D minor (*c.*1768)	Haydn	The name reflects the religious intensity of the music.
Lark	String Quartet in D, Op 64, No 5 (1790)	Haydn	Describes the ascent of the violin at the start of the work.
Laudon (sic)	Symphony No 69 in C (*c.*1778)	Haydn	Dedicated to the Austrian field-marshal Ernest Gideon, Freiherr von Loudon.
Leningrad	Symphony No 7 in C (1941)	Shostakovich	Composed while the composer endured the siege of Leningrad.
Linz	Symphony No 36 in C, K 425 (1783)	Mozart	Composed in the Austrian city of Linz.
Little	Symphony No 6 in C major, D 589 (1818)	Schubert	So called simply to distinguish it from the 'Great' Symphony, No 9, in the same key.
Little Organ Mass	Mass No 5 in B flat (*c.*1775)	Haydn	An organ appears in the Benedictus. The name distinguishes the work from the 'Great Organ Mass', qv.
Little Russian	Symphony No 2 in C minor (1872)	Tchaikovsky	The finale used the folk-song 'The Crane' from Little Russia (i.e. the Ukraine).
Liturgique	Symphony No 3 (1945–6)	Honegger	A work of religious character; the movements are *Dies irae; De profundis clamavi; Dona nobis pacem.*
London	Symphony No 104 in D (1795)	Haydn	One of 12 symphonies written for the English capital; therefore, a meaningless title.

Nickname	Work	Composer	Remarks
Maria Theresia	Symphony No 48 in C (1769?)	Haydn	Originally thought to have been written for the visit of the empress to Esterháza in 1773; the name should perhaps more correctly be attached to Symphony No 50 in the same key.
Mariazellermesse	Mass No 6 in C (1782)	Haydn	Written for the Austrian monastery of Mariazell
Matin	Symphony No 6 in D (1761)	Haydn	First of three symphonies representing the times of day. See *Midi* and *Soir*.
May Day	Symphony No 3 in E flat (1930)	Shostakovich	Written to commemorate the national holiday of the working class.
Mercury	Symphony No 43 in E flat (*c*.1771)	Haydn	May refer to the mercurial passagework in the outer movements.
Midi	Symphony No 7 in C	Haydn	See *Matin*.
Military	Symphony No 100 in G (1794)	Haydn	Turkish military insruments appear in the slow movement and finale.
Miracle	Symphony No 96 in D (1791)	Haydn	Another migrating nickname (see *Maria Theresia*). A chandelier fell during the performance, miraculously hurting no-one; but it fell during No 102, not No 96.
Moonlight	Piano Sonata in C sharp minor (1801)	Beethoven	An imaginative title which has nothing to do with Beethoven.
Musikalischer Spass	Serenade in F, K 522 (1787)	Mozart	This musical joke is on everyone from Mozart's contemporaries to the modern listener.
Nelson Mass	Mass No 9 in D minor (1798)	Haydn	Performed at a time of rejoicing over Nelson's victory at Ab'ukir.
New World	see *From the New World*		

Dimitri Shostakovich (1962). (BBC Hulton Picture Library)

Camille Saint-Saëns, composer of a stirring 'Organ Symphony'. (The Mansell Collection)

Nickname	Work	Composer	Remarks
1905	Symphony No 11 in G minor (1957)	Shostakovich	Commemorates the abortive revolution of that year.
1917	Symphony No 12 in D minor (1961)	Shostakovich	Celebrates the successful Bolshevik Revolution of October 1917.
Nullte	Symphony in D minor (1864, rev. 1869)	Bruckner	'Symphony No 0', an early work, pre-No 1.
October	Symphony No 2 in C (1927)	Shostakovich	Commemorates the October Revolution. See also *1917*.
Organ Symphony	Symphony No 3 in C minor (1886)	Saint-Saëns	An organ is prominent in parts of the work.
Overture in the Italian Style	Symphony No 32 in G, K 318 (1779)	Mozart	A one-movement work with a slow central section. The *form* may be Italian; the *style* is pure Mannheim!
Oxford	Symphony No 92 in G (1789)	Haydn	Played there on the occasion of the composer receiving an honorary Doctorate in 1791.
Paris	Symphony No 31 in D, K 297 (1778)	Mozart	Mozart wrote the work specifically for the French capital.
Passione	Symphony No 49 in F minor (1768)	Haydn	A reference to the sombre nature of the music
Pastoral	Symphony No 6 in F (1806)	Beethoven	A work in the fashionable rural temper of the time. Beethoven's Piano Sonata in D, Op 28 (1801) bears the same title.
Pathètique	Piano Sonata in C minor, Op 13 (1798)	Beethoven	Refers to the affecting nature of the music.
Pathètique	Symphony No 6 in B minor (1893)	Tchaikovsky	The composer's sad farewell. See p 224.
Philosopher	Symphony No 22 in E flat (1764)	Haydn	Refers to the brooding character of the first movement.
Polish	Symphony No 3 in D (1875)	Tchaikovsky	The main theme of the finale is in the rhythm of a polacca.

Nickname	Work	Composer	Remarks
Post-Horn	Serenade in D, K 320 (1778)	Mozart	A solo post-horn figures in the second trio of the sixth movement.
Prague	Symphony No 38 in D, K 504 (1786)	Mozart	Written for performance in that city.
Prodigal Son	Symphony No 4 in C (1930, rev. 1947)	Prokofiev	Based partly on the music of the ballet of that name.
Razor	String Quartet in F minor, Op 55, No 2 (1788)	Haydn	Haydn, having difficulty in shaving, said 'My best quartet for a new razor'. The publisher Bland rushed out, bought a razor, and clinched the deal.
Razumovsky	String Quartets Op 59, Nos 1–3 (1806)	Beethoven	Dedicated to Count Razumovsky.
Reformation	Symphony No 5 in D minor (1830)	Mendelssohn	Written to commemorate the 300th anniversary of the Augsburg Confession.
Reine de France	Symphony No 85 in B flat (1785–6)	Haydn	Said to have been a favourite of Queen Marie-Antoinette.
Rhenish	Symphony No 3 in E flat (1850)	Schumann	Evokes the composer's feelings about life in the Rheinland.
Rider	String Quartet in G minor, Op 74, No 3 (1793)	Haydn	The motion of a horse-rider is suggested by the rhythms of the outer movements.
Romantic	Symphony No 4 in E flat (1874, rev. 1878 and 1880)	Bruckner	The work originally possessed a 'programme' in the romantic manner which the composer later suppressed.
Roxelane	Symphony No 63 in C (1777?)	Haydn	The slow movement is a set of variations on an aria of La Roselane in the play *Soliman II.*
St Anthony	Divertimento in B flat (pub. 1780)	attrib. Haydn	The second and last movements are based on the old *St Anthony Chorale*.

Nickname	Work	Composer	Remarks
Schoolmaster	Symphony No 55 in E flat (1774)	Haydn	The rhythm of the Adagio suggests the slow plod of an ageing schoolmaster.
Scottish	Symphony No 3 in A minor (1829–42)	Mendelssohn	Reflects the composer's impressions of his Scottish visit.
Sea	Symphony No 1	Vaughan Williams	Based on the sea poems of Walt Whitman.
Semplice	Symphony No 6 (1924–6)	Nielsen	Perhaps a deliberately misleading name given by the composer to a complex work.
Sérieuse	Symphony No 2 in G minor (1842)	Berwald	An unhelpful composer's title, for the work is no more serious than his others.
Simple	Symphony (1934)	Britten	Written for the young. The movements are: *Boisterous Bourée; Playful Pizzicato; Sentimental Sarabande; Frolicsome Finale.*
Singulière	Symphony No 4 in C (1845)	Berwald	The composer's title; again (see *Sérieuse*), it is not noticeably more 'uncommon' than his other symphonies.
Soir	Symphony No 8 in G	Haydn	see *Matin.*
Sospetto	Violin Concerto in C minor, RV 199	Vivaldi	'The Suspicious One', perhaps the title of a stage work with which the concerto was associated.
Storm at Sea	Violin Concerto in E flat, RV 253	Vivaldi	This, and another Concerto, RV 344, depict in gentle terms the chaos of a drama at sea.
Study	Symphony in F minor (1863)	Bruckner	Meant as a mere exercise, this Symphony has now established itself as a worthy work.

Nickname	Work	Composer	Remarks
Sunrise	String Quartet in B flat, Op 76, No 4 (1799)	Haydn	At the beginning the first violin gradually emerges from the harmonies like a rising sun from mist.
Surprise	Symphony No 94 in G (1791)	Haydn	After a quiet opening the Andante is punctuated by a heavy orchestral chord.
Tempest	Piano Sonata in D minor, Op 31, No 1 (1802)	Beethoven	An unauthentic name which nevertheless accurately describes the nature of the music.
Theresia Mass	Mass No 10 in B flat (1799)	Haydn	Thought to have been written for the Empress Marie Therese (wife of Franz II) but now known to have been for Princess Maria Hermenegild.
Titan	Symphony No 1 in D (1888)	Mahler	Thus named by the composer after the novel by Jean Paul.
Tragic	Symphony No 4 in C minor, D 417 (1816)	Schubert	Title added later by Schubert himself.
Trauer	Symphony No 44 in E minor (*c.*1771)	Haydn	Haydn requested that the slow movement be played at his funeral.
Trout	Piano Quintet in A, D 667 (1819)	Schubert	The fourth movement is a set of variations on his song *Die Forelle* (*The Trout*).
Unfinished	Symphony No 8 in B minor, D 759 (1822)	Schubert	Long thought to consist of only two movements this work is now considered to be partly lost, rather than unfinished.
Voces Intimae	String Quartet in D minor (1909)	Sibelius	An authentic title suggested by the nature of the third movement.
Wagner	Symphony No 3 in D minor (1873, rev. 1878, 1889, 1890)	Bruckner	Dedicated to that composer.
Waldstein	Piano Sonata in C, Op 53 (1803–4)	Beethoven	Dedicated to Count Waldstein.

Nickname	Work	Composer	Remarks
Wanderer	Fantasia in C, D 760 (1822)	Schubert	The second movement is based on the song of that name.
Winter Daydreams	Symphony No 1 in G minor (1866)	Tchaikovsky	Taken from the title of the first movement: 'Daydreams on a Wintry Road'.

A Symphony called 'Fred'

The concert-goer may occasionally encounter works where the nickname has done little to enhance popularity. Some even given a false impression.

For instance, Honegger's *Di tre re* Symphony is not a celebration of the biblical three kings but a reference to the note D (re) that closes each of its three movements; and Koechlin's *Seven Stars* Symphony of 1933 is not a re-write of Holst's *The Planets* Suite but a series of personal impressions of favourite film stars of the day: Douglas Fairbanks, Lilian Harvey, Greta Garbo, Clara Bow, Marlene Dietrich, Emil Jannings and Charlie Chaplin.

Which music-lover has not invented his own names for pieces of music? The authors could suggest worthy recipients for titles such as the *Interminable* or the *Maudlin*, the *Objectionable* or the *Farcical*, but really there is no need, for genuine titles abound, and they can be as pretentious, melodramatic and depressing as anyone could wish. There are, for example, eight *Dramatic* Symphonies by various composers, Kósa's *Man and Universe* Symphony, Valen's modestly-titled Piano Sonata No 2 called *The Sound of Heaven*, Porrino's *Sonata Drammatica*, and the *Apocalyptic* symphonies of Weigl and Waltershausen, not forgetting Langgaard's Symphony No 6, *Heaven-Tearing*, and Stankovich's defiant Symphony No 3, *I Assert Myself*.

For further mental elevation one may turn to Leonard Bernstein's Symphony No 2, *The Age of Anxiety*, Schreiber's Symphony No 7, *Death and Eternity*, or Nejedly's Symphony No 2, *Poverty and Death*. On the other hand, lighter entertainment is offered by Alexander's *Clockwork* Symphony, Reznièek's Symphony No 4, *Ironic*, *Silly* Symphonies by Moortel and Moross, and Don Gillis's Symphony No 5½, *A Symphony for Fun*.

There is no copyright on nicknames. Schubert's *Tragic* Symphony (No 4) is echoed in like-named symphonies by Antheil, Axman (an inveterate title thief!), Berger, Bergh, Chisholm, MacDowell, Reznicek and Saikkola, and a *Tragic* Trio by Tovey. There are *Appassionata* sonatas by Axman and Paganini as well as by Beethoven, *Eroica* symphonies by Axman, Schulhoff and Sulek and a *Czech Eroica* by Vomáčka, plus *Heroic* symphonies by Clapp, Golubev, Huber, Kiladze, and *Heroic* piano concerti by Hubeau and Rodrigo. One can discover half a dozen works called *Pathètique* and 20 called *Pastoral*, in addition to the expected ones.

Just as Hallnäs seems anxious not to detain us too long with *A Quite Small Symphony*, so others are reluctant to bore us, for our research has uncovered 200 works titled *Short, Brief, Little, Mini, Piccolo* and so on in various languages.

While we must confess ignorance of the import of some names such as Bajoras's string symphony *Stalactites*, Williams's Symphony No 9, *Tadpoles*, Ashley's *Crazy Horse* Symphony and Wheeler's First Symphony, appealingly titled *Fred*, we can throw light on other enigmatic names. Janáček's sonata bears the date *1.X.1905* as a title, this being the death date of an innocent Czech worker at the hands of German troops at a demonstration in Brno; while Onslow's *Bullet* Quintet commemorates the day he was out hunting and when he stopped to jot down a theme he stopped also a stray bullet which put him into hospital, where he completed the quintet. It is possible to guess what Szelényi's Symphony and Field's Piano Concerto represent from their titles: respectively, *Factory* and *Conflagration During the Storm*; less obvious are Ronald Binge's *Saturday* Symphony, McDonald's *Cakewalk* Symphony, Kasschau's *Candlelight* Concerto, Haubenstock-Ramati's Symphony No 2 called simply *K*, Gregor's No 3 called *Dizziness*, and Zimmermann's Trumpet Concerto *Nobody Knows de Trouble I See*.

Who shall judge whether Harold Farberman's Piano Concerto really is *Paramount* or Henry Cowell's String Quartet No 1 *Pedantic*? In what way is Kósa's String Quartet a *Self-Portrait*, and how many packets did Vačkář demolish while writing his Piano Sonata and Third Symphony, both called *Smoking*? If we hear Argenta's Concerto for oboe, violin, horn and orchestra called *Bravo Mozart*! shall we say 'Bravo Argento!'? And what is the intriguing story behind Podešva's Symphony No 3, whose title runs: *Culmination — The Pearl at the Bottom*?

What's Missing?

Concert-goers have a right to expect an orchestra of reasonable size unless their taste is for 'enlarged' chamber groups of exclusively strings or exclusively wind. No concert promoter today would dare resort to the penny-pinching tactics offered by the busy pruning shears of Emile Tavan (1849–1930), whose speciality was arranging and modifying concert favourites for orchestras much smaller in size than the composers envisaged. Peter Racine Fricker's *Waltz for Restricted Orchestra* (1958) goes even further by depriving the wind players of their instruments: they must produce sound with their mouthpieces only. Such antics kept the audience amused at the Hoffnung Interplanetary Music Festival in that year. It is doubtful whether this masterpiece has been performed since.

A small group of works of more serious intent are scored for a normal orchestra, with choir (Brahms's *Requiem*), or for strings only, but *without violins*.

Bach: Brandenburg Concerto No 6 in B flat (1708–10)

Brahms: *Ein Deutsches Requiem:* 1st section (1868); Serenade No 2 in A (1859)

Garcia, José Maurício Nunes: (1767–1830) *Missa pastoril para a noite de Natal* ('Christmas Mass') (1811)

Hartmann, K.A.: Symphony No 5, 'Concertante' (1950)

Hummel: Piano Concerto in B minor, Op 89, with four horns and low strings (original version, *c.*1821)

Méhul: *Uthal* Overture (1806)

Morthenson, Jan: (b. 1940) Sinfonia da Camera, Op 1 (1960)

Mozart, L. *Sinfonia burlesca* in G; Symphony in F (before 1751); both the above for two violas, two cellos and bass
Symphony in C (before 1751), for viola, two cellos, two horns and bass

Inverted Commas

By no means all music one hears at concerts is wholly original. Ignoring the sets of variations based on other composers' themes, and works which draw almost exclusively on the music of another (e.g. Respighi's *La boutique fantasque*, which is ballet music made up from Rossini's music), we are left with a huge list of pieces that, for a special effect or out of just plain wickedness, take often quite extensive excerpts from pre-existing music. Elgar at least had the grace to insert inverted commas in the score round his Mendelssohn quote in the *Enigma Variations* but others have been less scrupulous. This list excludes works 'in the style of' another composer, whether or not acknowledged as such (Schubert's 'Overtures in the Italian Style', based on Rossini's formula, and Kreisler's mock-18th century violin pieces, for instance). Even within its own confines the list is far from complete: Ives's borrowings alone, and Handel's, would take a sizeable share of this book if exhaustively treated.

Alwyn, William. The second movement, Adagio e poco rubato, of his *Sinfonietta* for strings (1970) quotes a few bars from Act 1 of Berg's Lulu, the allusion being to Mosco Carner, British musicologist, critic and dedicatee of Alwyn's work, who at that time was working on a study of Berg's music.

Asafiev, Boris. His ballet *The Flame of Paris* (1932) quotes the *Marseillaise* and music by Cherubini, Gluck, Gossec, Grétry, Lesueur, Lully and Méhul, and the following year his ballet *The Fountain of Bakhchisarai* used the song *The Fountain of the Bakhchisarai Court* by Aleksander Gurilev and a nocturne by John Field as *leitmotivs*.

Bartók, Béla. The *Concerto for Orchestra* (1945) parodies Shostakovich's 'popular' style by quoting the oft-repeated theme of the first movement of the *Leningrad* Symphony.

Beethoven, Ludwig van, introduced some elements from the first three movements of his *Choral* Symphony into the fourth, a device which has since been used by others.

Berio, Luciano. His *Sinfonia* (1968) quotes a great number of composers but notably the third movement of Mahler's Symphony No 2. Berio writes: 'The Mahler movement is treated like a container within whose framework a large number of references are proliferated, interrelated and integrated into the flowing structure of the original work itself. The references range from Bach, Schönberg (*sic*), Debussy, Ravel, Strauss, Berlioz, Brahms, Berg, Hindemith, Beethoven, Wagner and Stravinsky to Boulez, Stockhausen, Globokar, Pousseur, Ives, myself and beyond.'

Berlioz, Hector. In the finale of his *Harold in Italy* Symphony there are self-quotations from earlier movements.

Bizet, Georges, based the *Habañera* in *Carmen* on a song by Yradier.

Blake, David, composed his Chamber Symphony, Op 7 (1966) in memory of Hans Eisler and used quotes from Eisler's own Chamber Symphony.

Boucourechliev, André, based his *Ombres* for 11 strings, also called *Hommage à Beethoven* (1970, Beethoven's bicentenary), on aspects of the late quartets.

Branscombe, Gena, set the main theme of the finale of Brahms's Symphony No 1 as a choral and orchestral work, 'The Lord is our Fortress' (1948).

Brian, Havergal. The finale of the English Suite No 1, Op 12 (1904) quotes *God Save the King*. In his opera *The Tigers* (1918) Brian quotes from Strauss's *Ein Heldenleben*, Wagner's *Ride of the Valkyrie*, etc.

Brott, Alexander, uses *God Save the Queen* and *Yankee Doodle* in his *Profundum praedictum* (1964), for double bass, violin, cello and strings.

Brouwer, Leo, in his *Sonata pian'e forte* (1970), quotes not only from Gabrieli but also from Beethoven, Scriabin and Szymanowsky.

Butterley, Nigel, quotes the *Song of the Volga Boatmen* in *The Four Elements* (1971, revised 1974).

Carr, Benjamin, includes the *Marseillaise*, *Yankee Doodle* and *O Dear, What Can the Matter Be?* in his *Federal Overture* (1794).

Delius, Frederick, caused much ill-feeling in the country concerned when he incorporated the Norwegian National Anthem into his *Norwegian Suite* (1897).

Dickinson, Peter, quotes from the first *Gnossienne* of Satie in *Transformations (Hommage à Erik Satie)* (1970).

Dvořák, Antonín. His overture cycle 'Nature-Life-Love' (*Amid Nature, Carnival,* and *Othello*, 1891) uses a theme which appears in all three in the manner of a linking self-quotation.

Elgar, Sir Edward, quotes Mendelssohn's Overture *Calm Sea and Prosperous Voyage* in his *Enigma Variations* at variation XIII, called simply ★★★. The asterisks conceal the name Lady Mary Trefusis, who was on a sea voyage when the music was being composed. Elgar

Georges Bizet. Not all of the famous Carmen *was original. (Mary Evans Picture Library)*

Sir Edward Elgar. (Portrait in oils by Talbot-Hughs). (Royal College of Music)

also suggested the slow movement of Beethoven's *Pathètique* Sonata at the start of variation IX, 'Nimrod'. In the Overture *Polonia* (1915) he introduces Jósef Nikorowicz's patriotic Polish song *Z dymem pozarów* ('With the Smoke of Fires'); to make matters even he quotes *Rule, Britannia!* in his choral ode *The Music Makers* (1912).

Gardiner, William, wrote an oratorio, *Judah* (1821) which quotes extensively from the masses of Haydn, Mozart and Beethoven.

German, Edward, quotes *Men of Harlech* in his *Welsh Rhapsody* (1904).

Grainger, Percy, took Stephen Foster's 'Camptown Races' in his *Tribute to Foster* (1914) and turned it into an elaborate piece in which he presages Nielsen's Fifth Symphony (1922) by asking individual instruments to play in tempi different from that of the orchestra, and fading out with clarinet and sidedrum playing apparently independently of each other.

Harper, Edward, takes the main theme of Elgar's Cello Concerto as a basis for his *Meditation* for viola and percussion (1980).

Harvey, Jonathan. In *Four Images after Yeats* (1969) for piano, the fourth image represents Yeats' belief in a purgatorial stage after death by a mixture of his own music with fragments of keyboard music by Schumann, Bach and others.

Haydn, Joseph, quotes the opening of his own Symphony No 45, 'Farewell' in the first movements of his symphonies Nos 60 (1774) and 85 (*c.*1785).

Haynes, Stanley, quotes several popular 19th-century violin concerti in his *Rendezvous.*

Heinrich, Anthony Philip, quotes *God Save the King* in his orchestral Fantasy *Pushmataha* (1831).

Henze, Hans Werner, completely rewrote Paisiello's 1769 opera *Don Quixote* in 1976. Henze requires two members of the audience (who will presumably have their ticket money refunded) to join the action by identifying with Quixote and Sancho Panza.

Hewitt, James, incorporated *Washington's March* and *Yankee Doodle* in his *Battle of Trenton* (1797).

Ibert, Jacques, quotes Mendelssohn's *Wedding March* (from *A Midsummer Night's Dream*) in the second movement, *Cortège*, of his *Divertissement* (1930).

Ireland, John, quotes the *Internationale* in *These Things Shall Be* (1937).

Ives, Charles, is indubitably the world's most enthusiastic musical borrower. A few examples are given; no prizes are offered to any reader who can quadruple the length of this list.

Golden Slippers (minstrel song), and *Cleansing Fountain* (hymn tune played to the words 'Are you washed in the blood of the Lamb?') both quoted in the song *General William Booth Enters into Heaven* (1914). *The Battle Hymn of the Republic, Hail! Columbia, The Red, White and Blue, The Star-Spangled Banner, America* (alias *God Save the King*), and *The Battle Cry of Freedom,* all quoted in *Lincoln, the Great Commoner* (1912). The Violin Sonata No 4 (1916) is based entirely on hymn tunes.

The opening notes of Beethoven's Fifth Symphony are repeatedly referred to in the Piano Sonata No 2, *Concord, Mass, 1840–60* (1915).

Marching Through Georgia, Jingle Bells, Boys and Girls Come out to Play, My Old Kentucky Home, In the Sweet Bye and Bye, and *Rock of Ages* all occur in the Piano Trio (1904).

Arkansaw Traveller, Marching Through Georgia, The British Grenadiers, Semper fidelis, and many other references occur in *Three Places in New England* (1914).

Old Black Joe, Masa's in de Cold, Cold Ground, Bringing in the Sheaves, I hear thy Welcome Voice, and *In the Sweet Bye and Bye* appear in *Orchestral Set No 2* (1915).

Oh, What a Friend We Have in Jesus, There is a Fountain Filled With Blood, and *Just as I am Without One Plea*, are in Symphony No 3 (1904).

Jarre, Maurice, used ideas from the first movement of Shostakovich's Symphony No 7, *Leningrad*, in his music for the film *Is Paris Burning?* (1967).

Kraus, Joseph Martin, quotes the *Sailors' Hornpipe* in his *Anglois* in G in the ballet *Fiskarena* ('The Fishermen') (1789).

Lanner, Joseph, composed *Die Mozartisten*, Op 196 (1842), which drags in many popular Mozart works and arranges them in waltz time.

Liszt, Franz, included extensive extracts from the slow movement of Beethoven's *Archduke* Trio in his *Festival Cantata*, written for the unveiling of the Beethoven monument in Bonn on 13 August 1845.

Litolff, Henry, quotes *La Marseillaise* in his Overture *Robespierre* (1856).

Lundsten, Ralph, quotes both Mendelssohn's and Wagner's *Wedding Marches* in his electronic *Nordic Nature* Symphony No 2, *Johannes och Huldran* (1975), third movement: 'The merry games of Love'.

McCabe, John, based the slow movement of his Symphony No 3, *Hommages* (1978) on the corresponding movement of Haydn's String Quartet in E flat, Op 76, No 6.

Musgrave, Thea, quotes from a Beethoven *Ecossaise* and from the *Pastoral* Symphony in *Memento vitae: Concerto in Homage to Beethoven*, written for the 1970 bicentenary; and in *Orfeo II* for flute and tape (later for flute and 15 solo strings), written for James Galway in 1976, she quotes *What is Life?* and *Dance of the Blessed Spirits* from Gluck's opera *Orfeo*.

Penderecki, Krzysztof, includes *Silent Night* in his Symphony No 2, *Christmas*, completed at Yuletide 1980.

Rand, Bernard, quotes Debussy's *Clair de Lune* in *Canti lunatici* (1984).

Rees, Howard. *Mr Vivaldi's Winter* (1974) is said by the composer to maintain the chord sequence and musical structure of the original, but in much of this ultra-modern paraphrase the link is, at best, tenuous.

Rimsky-Korsakov, Nikolai, quotes (appropriately) from Mozart's *Requiem* in his opera *Mozart and Salieri* (1897).

Saeverud, Harald, concocted a mixture of national songs — *Yankee Doodle, La Marseillaise, Waltzing Matilda* and others — in the movement called *Blandet selskap* ('Mixed Company') in his music for *Peer Gynt* (1947).

Saint-Saëns, Camille, appropriated the *Can-Can* from Offenbach's *Orpheus in the Underworld* and slowed it enormously to depict tortoises in his *Carnival of the Animals* (1886).

Satie, Erik, quotes *España* (see Waldteufel, below) in *Españaña* from *Croquis et egaceries d'un gros bonhomme en bois* (1913). Satie was in the habit of quoting instantly recognizable folk songs and popular pieces by other composers, rarely giving acknowledgement. When he did identify the source, as in *Edriophthalma* from *Embryons desséchés* (1913), he called Chopin's *Funeral March* 'Schubert's famous Mazurka'.

Schumann, Robert, incorporated *La Marseillaise* into the first movement of his *Faschingschwank aus Wien* (1840).

Telemann, Georg Philipp, quotes from, and converts to French style, the finale of Corelli's Concerto Grosso Op 6, No 7 in his *Corellisante Sonate* No 6 (1735).

Tippett, Sir Michael, quotes the opening bars of the finale of Beethoven's Symphony No 9, *Choral*, in his Symphony No 2 (1957); and 36 bars of Gibbons's *Fantasia* occur in the Symphony No 4 (1977).

Vainberg, Moisei, the Soviet composer, introduces into his Trumpet Concerto, Op 94 (1967) a final movement called *Fanfares*. The fanfares, however, are not his own: he borrowed them from Mendelssohn (the *Wedding March* in a minor-keyed version), Rimsky-Korsakov (the crowing from *Le Coq d'Or*), and Stravinsky (*Petrushka*).

Waldteufel, Emile, paraphrased Chabrier's *España* (1883) in his Waltz titled *España* (1886). See also Satie, above.

Wieniawski, Henryk, used two songs by Alexander Varlamov, *The Red Sarafan* and *I Saddle the Horse*, in his *Souvenir de Moscou* (1853).

GIGANTISM

The 19th and 20th centuries have seen an expansion in the size of musical forces used by composers, although economic factors have sometimes produced the effect of extreme economy during times of depression. But public interest is always aroused by the massive, and the first part of this century saw that interest satisfied by three works whose sheer sizes have yet to be surpassed. First came Schoenberg's *Gurre-Lieder* in 1901, and Mahler's Symphony No 8, *The Symphony of a Thousand*, followed in 1907. Biggest of all is Havergal Brian's *Gothic Symphony*, which grew in his mind from 1919

Havergal Brian in 1966, composer of the largest concert work ever written. (Photo: G. MacDomnic)

to 1927. In a radio interview Brian admitted: 'It was never intended for performance. I expanded myself on something which might be regarded as impossible.' The impossibility was removed in 1961, when Bryan Fairfax conducted a partly-amateur first performance in the Westminster Hall in London, The first fully professional performance took place on 30 October 1966 under Sir Adrian Boult. (See also p165).

In this work 126 instruments are specified (Schoenberg 66, Mahler 61) *in addition to* the full string band. In the chart the three composers' requirements for their works are listed.

Musical requirements	**Schoen-berg**	**Mahler**	**Brian**
Vocal soloists	5	8	4
Choruses	4	3	3
Piccolos	4	1	2
Flutes	4	4	7
Oboes	3	4	8
Cors anglais	2	1	2
Clarinets	4	5	9
Basset horns	—	—	2
Bassoons	5	5	5
Horns	10	8	16
Trumpets	7	8	17
Cornets	—	—	2
Trombones	7	7	14
Tubas	1	1	10
Euphoniums	—	—	2
Piano	—	1	—
Organ	—	1	1
Celesta	1	1	1
Glockenspiel	1	1	1
Harmonium	—	1	—
Timpani	6 sets	3 sets	6 sets
Sidedrums	1	—	2
Bass drums	1	1	2
Tenor drum	1	—	—
African drum	—	—	1
Tambourines	—	—	2
Cymbals (pair)	1	1	6
Triangles	1	1	2
Gong	1	1	1
Xylophone	1	—	1
Tubular bells (set)	—	1	1
Thunder machine	—	—	1
Chimes	—	1	1
Bird scare	—	—	1
Chains	large	—	small
Harps	4	2	—
Mandolin	—	1	—

IX
Musical Notes

Without the facility of rendering on to the written or printed page a precise indication of what music sounds like, the entire art would rely for its continuity on improvization and memory. Performances of large-scale works would be impossible, and instrumental groups would have to invent anew each time they performed. There would be no such thing as a 'standard classic' because nothing would be standard for more than a few performances, and no single piece of music would be given the opportunity to become a classic; its spread would be restricted to a local audience, temporally and geographically.

This is one aspect of 'written music'. The literature of music goes much wider than this, however, into the realms of musical dictionaries, encyclopaedias, biographies, periodicals, criticism and musicology — all, be it noted, impossible if precise indications of the sound of music were not able to be transferred to paper.

The birth and evolution of music notation is described in Section III (pp 81–2), with special reference to the crucial role of Guido d'Arezzo, an 11th-century Italian monk and singing teacher. The written language of musical composition has made possible the whole apparatus of history, biography and criticism described here.

Guido d'Arezzo, inventor in c. 1020 of the beginnings of the present system of musical notation. (Royal College of Music)

Modern Notation

Explanations of some familiar symbols:

Clef = **key**, i.e. indication of the register

 = **G clef.** A representation of a medieval letter G, the focal point of which indicates the line G.

 = **F clef.** A relic of the medieval letter F, centred on the F line.

= **C clef.** Its centre point, which may be fixed on any line, indicates the position of middle C.

♭ = **Flat.** This sign flattens all the notes of the pitch indicated which follows it in the bar.

♯ = **Sharp.** This sign sharpens all the notes of the pitch indicated which follow it in the bar.

♮ = **Natural.** Indicating that a previously flattened or sharpened note is to return to its natural pitch.

= **Repeat** (or da capo). This sign instructs the player(s) to return to the beginning of the movement or piece, or to the sign: 𝄋

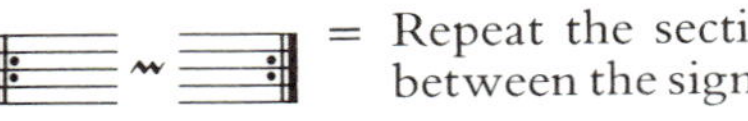

= Repeat the section shown between the signs.

NOTE LENGTHS AND THEIR EQUIVALENT RESTS

In the early days of musical notation there were four note lengths: the double long (a black rectangle with a tail), the long (a black square with a tail), the breve, i.e. 'short' (a black square without a tail), and the semibreve, i.e. 'half-short' (a black diamond). A diminution of values has occurred since then so that we have today reached a situation in which the very longest note ever to be encountered is called 'short', and the longest generally-used note is called 'half-short'.

Note	*Rest*	*Names*	*Meaning*
		breve (double whole note)	short
		semibreve (whole note)	half-short
		minim (half-note)	shortest (i.e. minimum)
		crotchet (quarter-note)	hook or crook from its old appearance
		quaver (eighth-note)	to trill, or quaver (quiver) in very short notes
		semiquaver (sixteenth-note)	half-quaver
		demisemiquaver (thirty-second-note)	half of half a quaver
		hemidemisemiquaver (sixty-fourth-note)	half of half of half a quaver
		semihemidemisemiquaver (hundred-and-twenty-eighth-note)	half of half of half of half a quaver

TIME SIGNATURES

3/4 = three quarter-notes (crotchets) to the bar

4/4 or C = four quarter-notes to the bar

3/8 = three eighth-notes to the bar.

Other time signature meanings may be inferred from these examples.

During the present century composers have felt the need to extend all the above symbols and meanings in order to bring ever-more strict specifications of their requirements to the notice of their performers. One of the simplest extensions was made by the Romanian-born Greek composer Xenakis who, in order to reduce the difficulty in reading many leger lines (additional lines above or below the staves to carry higher or lower notes), adopted the practice where necessary of adding a continuous line to represent the note B above the B above the treble clef, and another line to represent the D below the D below the bass clef, thus:

BAR LINES

Known more accurately in American as 'measures', bars divide the music into given periods to assist rhythmic stability, but in the 18th century C.P.E. Bach sometimes encouraged expressive rhythmic freedom by dispensing with bar lines, a device taken up later by Beethoven, Stravinsky, and Satie. Federico Mompou developed a technique, *Primitivista*, in the second decade of the present century in which both bar lines and key signatures are dispensed with.

MUSIC IN PRINT

The earliest printed music is a book of plainsong issued in Esslingen, near Stuttgart, Germany, in 1473. It is Johannes Gerson's *Collectorium super Magnificat*, printed by Conrad Fyner. The earliest English printed music was in Ranulf Higden's book *Policronicon*, which appeared in 1482, printed by Caxton, but the musical example itself had to be impressed on each copy by hand and some copies escaped the process. For the reprint in 1495 Wynken de Worde ingeniously contrived to incorporate the example in print by using the square bottoms of ordinary type to represent notes.

The earliest publishing house devoted almost entirely to music-printing was established in Venice in 1501 by Ottaviano dei Petrucci (1466–1539).

The oldest American printed music appeared in the ninth edition of *The Bay Psalm Book* in 1698 (its earlier editions, the first in 1640, were without music; its last edition of more than 70 was published in 1773). A direct-to-print song, bypassing the usual manuscript stage, was 'Marching Through Georgia' by the composer and music compositor Henry Clay Work. He commemorated General Sherman's march of 1864 by setting the song directly into print.

MUSICAL DICTIONARIES

One of the most useful branches of musical literature is the section which contains works which explain and clarify the terms, often obscure and usually foreign, for the benefit of the non-specialist reader. While usually fulfilling this function admirably, it should not be overlooked that, except for the most basic, these volumes are of prime value to the professional musician as a depository of facts necessary to his work. Such works of reference have a long and noble history.

The first musical dictionary is the *Terminorum Musicae Diffinitorium*, compiled by Johannes Tinctoris and published at Treviso about 1498. It defines 291 terms related to Renaissance musical practice and theory, and has been considered so vital to the correct understanding of this period that it has been translated into German (1863), French (1951), English (1963), and Italian (1965).

The first combined musical dictionary and collection of musical biographies was Johann Gottfried Walther's *Musikalisches Lexicon, oder musikalische Bibliothek*, first published in Berlin in 1732 and reprinted by Bärenreiter in 1953.

The first biographical music dictionary was *Grundlage einer Ehren-Pforte . . .*, by Johann Mattheson who also published the first music criticism (see below) in 1740. The majority of the biographies were first-hand contributions by the subjects themselves.

MODERN MUSIC ENCYCLOPAEDIAS

The latest, and the largest, musical encyclopaedias come from Germany and England.

Die Musik in Geschichte und Gegenwart. Allgemeine Enzyklopädie der Musik, edited by Friedrich Blume and published by Bärenreiter. Volume I appeared in 1949. Written throughout in German but giving a world-wide coverage, it seeks to incorporate the very latest in musical research in its composer biographies and comprehensive lists of works, but since the first volume was issued so many years ago it is clear that musicology has outrun the entries in the early part of the alphabet. Nevertheless, it is an unrivalled source-book of information containing often greatly extended articles of intricate detail.

Grove's Dictionary of Music and Musicians, founded by Sir George Grove. Multi-volume reference work in English, covering much the same ground as *Die Musik . . .* above, but with less attention paid to lesser composers, particularly in the matter of their composition lists. Six editions have been published, each one greater and more extensive than the last:

- I Edited by Sir George Grove: 4 volumes, 1878–89.
- II Edited by J.A. Fuller-Maitland: 5 volumes, 1904–10.
- III Edited by H.C. Colles: 5 volumes, 1927–8.
- IV Edited by H.C. Coles: 5 volumes, plus supplement to the third edition, 1940.
- V Edited by Eric Blom: 9 volumes, 1954 plus Supplement 1961.
- VI Edited by Stanley Sadie: 20 volumes, 1980.

Mention should also be made of the American *Harvard Dictionary of Music*, edited by Willi Apel with A.T. Davison.

In addition to these long-lasting reference works there is a healthy business in musical magazines in all the musically aware countries of the world. Essentially journalistic, these publications nevertheless carry a vast amount of information which fails to find a place between hard covers: many of the articles, particularly those dealing with musicological subjects by some of the most eminent writers in the field, should achieve a more secure permanency. Fortunately, Detroit Information Service Inc. publishes its own periodical which is devoted to indexing the material in others, thereby preventing this valuable material from being buried unknown in library basements.

Journals

The first musical journal was *Musica Critica*, edited by Johann Mattheson. The first number was published in Hamburg in 1722; it contained the first published music criticisms.

After this date the useful if not always responsible practice of musical criticism was slow to spread.

The first French musical journal, *Journal de Musique Française et Italienne*, appeared in 1764.

The first British musical journal, *The New Musical and Universal Magazine*, appeared in 1774.

The first American musical journal, *American Musical Magazine*, appeared in 1786.

By the end of the 18th century the art of criticism was well established, particularly in Germany, where the really serious business of discussing the art of music in scientific detail was begun by the *Allgemeine Musikalische Zeitung*, first published in Leipzig in 1798.

The oldest still-existing British musical magazine is *The Musical Times*, which first appeared in 1844 as *The Musical Times and Singing Class Circular*. It was based on *Mainzer's Musical Times and Singing Circular*, founded by the German musician Joseph Mainzer in 1842.

The first Czech language music periodical was *Cecilia*, founded by Josef Krejčí in 1848.

Musical Criticism

We have already noted, above, the first printed musical criticisms (in Mattheson's *Musica Critica*) in 1722.

The first English music criticism of any consequence appeared in 1752, when Charles Avison published his *Essay on Musical Expression*.

The first French music criticism appeared in a pamphlet *Letter on French Music*, written by Jean-Jacques Rousseau and published in 1753. It was written specifically to attack the French operatic school and to praise the Italian. A sharp divide had been caused in Parisian taste by the performance the previous year of an old opera by Destouches, very much in the old-fashioned French style, and the rival appearance of Italian artists in Pergolesi's *La Serva Padrona* (1733). This led to one of the first musical hoaxes: the performance of an opera said to be by an Italian composer living in Vienna but actually, as was later revealed, by the Frenchman Dauvergne. After this opera, *Les Trocqueurs* (1753) written in imitation of the Italian style, Dauvergne reverted to the French method, feeling perhaps that he had won the day by having an Italian-style French opera acclaimed and that he could now return to the serious matter of making real French operas.

The first American music criticism did not appear until *Dwight's Journal of Music*, published in Boston in 1852.

Programme Notes

The earliest programme notes appear to have been prepared by the French Prime Minister Cardinal Mazarin to apprise the audience of events in a performance of Rossi's Italian opera *Orfeo*, given in Paris in 1647.

The Composer as Author

Below is a selection of books, both autobiographical and otherwise, written by composers, giving insight into the backgrounds, philosophies, intentions, and aspirations of the composers concerned. Dates are those of publication unless otherwise stated. English translations of foreign works are listed where known. Predominantly didactic books (e.g.: Aaron Copland's *What to Listen for in Music*) are excluded.

Antheil, G: *Bad Boy of Music* (1945)

Arditi, L: *My Reminiscences* (1896)

Musical Notes

Bax, A: *Farewell My Youth* (1944)

Berlioz, H: *Mémoires de Berlioz* (1870; Eng trans 1912: *Memoirs*; 1932: *Memoirs from 1803 to 1865*)

Berners, A: *First Childhood* (1934)
A Distant Prospect (1945)

Cage, J: *Silence* (1961)
A Year from Monday (1969)
Empty Words: Writings '73–'78 (1980)

Copland, A: *Copland on Music* (1960)

Cornelius, P: *Autobiographie* (1874)

Czerny, K: *Erinnerungen aus meinem Leben* (*c.*1860, reprinted 1968)

Dittersdorf, K: *Lebensbeschreibung* (completed 1799, two days before his death; Eng trans 1896)

Doráti, A: *Notes of Seven Decades* (1979)

Foote, A: *An Autobiography* (1946)

Gyrowetz, A: *Biographie* (1874; new edition edited by Alfred Einstein, 1915)

Hindemith, P: *A Composer's World* (1952)

Honegger, A: *Je suis compositeur* (1951: Eng trans: *I Am a Composer*, 1966)

Ives, C: *Essays Before a Sonata, The Majority, and other Writings by Charles Ives* (Ed Boatwright, 1970)
Autobiographical Memos (Ed Kirkpatrick, 1971)

Jackson, W of Exeter: *Observations on the Present State of Music in London* (1791)

Kelly, M: *Reminiscences* (2 vols, actually written by Theodore Hook, 1826)

Mackenzie, A: *A Musician's Narrative* (1927)

Martin, F: *Un compositeur médite sur son art (Écrits et pensées recueillis par sa femme)* (1978)

Mason, D G: *Music in My Time and other Reminiscences* (1938)

Mason, W: *Memories of a Musical Life* (1901)

Milhaud, D: *Notes sans musique* (1949; Eng trans: *Notes Without Music*, 1952)

Nielsen, C: *My Childhood in Funen* (1927; Eng trans 1953)
Living Music (1929; Eng trans 1953)

Partch, H: *Genesis of a Music* (1949)

Prokofiev, S: *Autobiography, Articles, Reminiscences* (a collection published in English in Moscow, 1954?)
Notes from Childhood (Eng trans: *Prokofiev by Prokofiev: a Composer's Memoir*, 1979)

Quantz, J J: Autobiography in *Selbstbiographien deutscher Musiker*, 1948; extracts in Eng trans in Paul Nettl's *Forgotten Musicians*, 1951

Rimsky-Korsakov, B: *My Musical Life* (1876–1906; Eng trans 1942)

Rubinstein, A: *Autobiography* (1889; Eng trans 1890)
Recollections of 50 Years (1892; Ger trans 1895)

Satie, E: *Mémoires d'un Amnésique* (1953)

Scott, C: *My Years of Indiscretion* (1924)
Bone of Contention (1969)

Sessions, R: *The Musical Experience of Composer, Performer, Listener* (1951)

Shostakovich, D: *Testimony: The Memoirs of Shostakovich* as related to and edited by Solomon Volkov (1979)

Smetana, B: *Smetana ve vzpomínkáck a dopisech* (1939); Eng trans: *Smetana — Letters and Reminiscences* 1953)

Smythe, E: *Impressions that Remained* (2 vols, 1919)
Streaks of Life (1921)
As Time Went On (1935)
What Happened Next (1940)

Sousa, J P: *Marching Along: Recollections of Men, Women and Music* (1928)

Spohr, L: *Selbstbiographie* (1861; Eng trans 1865; 1878)

Stanford, C V: *Pages from an Unwritten Diary* (1914)

Strauss, R: *Betrachtungen und Erinnerungen* (Ed Schuh, 1949; Eng trans: *Recollections and Reflections*, 1953)

Stravinsky, I: *Chroniques de ma vie* (2 vols 1935; Eng trans: *Chronicles of My Life*, 1936; 1975)
Also to be noted are:
The Poetics of Music (1947)
Themes and Conclusions (1972)
and a series of volumes by Stravinsky and Robert Craft:
Conversations with Stravinksy (1959)
Memories and Commentaries (1960)
Expositions and Developments (1962)
Dialogues and a Diary (1968)
Selected Correspondence (3 vols, 1980–85)

Telemann, G P: Autobiography included in a collection of biographies published by Johann Mattheson in 1740: *Grundlage einer Ehrenpforte* (modern ed, Berlin 1910; Eng trans by Rachel Orr: *The Memoirs of Telemann*, 1982)

Thomson, V: *The State of Music* (1939)
The Musical Scene (1945)
Virgil Thomson (1966)

Tippett, M: *Moving into Aquarius* (1959)

Tomášek, J V: Autobiography in periodical *Libuše* (1845 *et seq*; Eng trans: *Excerpts from the Memoirs of J V Tomášek*, in *Musical Quarterly*, 1946)

Vaughan Williams, R: *Some Thoughts on Beethoven's Choral Symphony, with writings on other musical subjects* (1953)

Wagner, R: *Mein Leben* (1911; Eng trans: *My Life*, 1911)

Weingartner, P: *Lebenserinnerungen* (2nd ed, 1928; Eng trans: *Buffets and Rewards*, 1937)

Musicology

This activity may be described as the study in depth of subjects peripheral to the practice and performance of music; alternatively, the pursuit of information on all aspects of music and musicians except that of actual performance. The value of such study is not always evident at first, but the gradual building up of a large body of facts surrounding music is useful in establishing other facts directly concerning the music, even though the usefulness of this peripheral information might not become apparent for many years after its publication. To take an example, it is well known that Brahms liked to smoke strong cigars. The actual make of these cigars can be of little interest to future generations since the cigars themselves no longer exist and Brahms was foremost a composer not a cigar-smoker. However, if it can be proved that, in order to obtain his favourite make of cigar, Brahms travelled to another town on a given date, that much more is known about his life, and his appearance in that town on a certain date may assist in establishing the date of a piece of music. This imaginary example can be paralleled by real ones. For instance, the records of doctors who attended Schumann prove that his hand injury was not caused by his invention and use of a mechanical device to strengthen the third finger: there was already a deterioration in his hand action brought about by mercury poisoning (due to the then accepted treatment for syphilis) which led to his trying to strengthen the hand mechanically (see Eric Sam's closely reasoned article in *The Musical Times*, December 1971).

The most obviously useful musicological study is into the background of the actual music of a composer, and one of the most obvious benefits to come from this kind of study is the thematic catalogue (see below).

The first stirrings of musicology were published in 1798 in the Leipzig magazine *Allgemeine Musikalische Zeitung*. The magazine *Cäcilia*, printed in Mainz by Schott from 1824 to 1850, went into musicological subjects even more deeply, and the contemporary *Neue Zeitschrift für Musik*, edited by Schumann, appeared in Leipzig from 1835. It dealt almost exclusively with the then modern movements in music.

The first use of the term 'musicology', or the German equivalent *Musikwissenschaft*, was in 1863, when Friedrich Chrysander published his periodical *Jahrbuch für musikalische Wissenschaft*.

The ultimate in musicology may be said to have been reached with the private publication of volume I of the *Life of Wagner* in 1898. It was assembled from a huge collection of manuscripts, letters, and other paraphernalia, by Mary Burrell, a life-long admirer of the composer's music and was engraved in script, with countless reproductions and photographs included. This first volume was 3in (7.5cm) thick, 30in (76cm) tall, and 21in (53cm) wide, and covered merely the first 21 years of Wagner's life. (A copy sold for £209 at Sotheby's, London, on 9 February 1976). The planned succeeding volumes did not appear, due no doubt to the removal of the driving force with the death of Miss Burrell in 1898, but much of the material she so assiduously collected was made available to the public in *Letters of Richard Wagner*, published in America in 1950.

Italian Musical Indications

A few words might be said in explanation of those Italian musical terms which, because of their frequent appearance on concert programmes and record sleeves, have become part of the English language.

That Italian is by tradition the language of music is understandable since virtually all the important forms of music (the only notable exceptions being the symphonic, or tone, poem, and serial music) had their origins in that country. The convention is so well established world-wide that even Russian programme notes printed in Cyrillic revert to the Roman

Musical Notes

type when words such as 'andante' appear in the text. During concert intervals in England it is not uncommon for these directions to merge into the conversation, to the complete understanding of all parties no doubt, in criticisms such as 'I don't think his finale was as cantabile as it might have been.

It is entertaining to compare the musical meanings, as accepted for centuries, with the common Italian usage. Where there is no significant difference between the two, the latter has been omitted, and only the most common terms are included. The less common directions will be found in reference books of a more specialist nature than the present volume. Abbreviations, where commonly recognized, are given in brackets.

Direction	*Musical use*	*Common Italian use*
A Capella	in the style of church music (i.e. voices without instruments)	at chapel
Accelerando	increasing the tempo gradually	making haste
Acciaccatura	a short grace-note	something crushed
Adagietto	a short (small) adagio	–
Adagio (Ad^{o})	slow; faster than largo and grave	slowly; at leisure
Affettuoso	tender, affectionate, pathetic	–
Allegretto (All^{tto})	light, cheerful; in tempo between allegro and andante	diminutive of allegro
Allegro (All*o*)	lively, briskly	gay, cheerful, merry
Amoroso	tenderly, gently, affectionately	lover; loving
Andante (And^{te})	moving easily; flowing; at a walking pace	going, current, flowing; (a) fair (price)
Andantino (And^{tino})	slightly slower than andante	diminutive of andante
Appassionato	passionate, intense	eager, enthusiastic
Appoggiatura	long grace-note	something which leans
Aria	tune, song, usually for a single voice	air, wind, song
Assai	very, more, extremely	much, copiously
Attacca	commence the next movement immediately	attack
Brillante	bright, sparkling, brilliant	–
Brio	fire, vigour	fire, vivacity
Cadenza	a solo showpiece usually near the end of a piece	–
Cantabile	in the singing style	–
Canzona	a graceful and elaborate song	ballad, song
Capriccio(so)	a capricious or fanciful composition	caprice, whim
Coda	an ending piece	end, queue, tail
Col	with the	–
Comodo	with ease, comfortably	convenience, ease, leisure
Con	with	by, with
Crescendo	with a gradually increasing tone	growing
Decrescendo	opposite of crescendo	–
Diminuendo	decrease of power	abatement
Dolce	sweetly, softly, gently	dessert, sweet, soft
Dolente	sorrowful, pathetic	–
Energ(et)ico	energetic, emphatic	energetic, powerful
Espressivo	expressively	–

Musical Notes

Direction	Musical use	Common Italian use
Fantasia	fancy, caprice	–
Finale	final section or movement	–
Forte (*f*)	loud	forcible, heavy, high, loud, strong
Fortissimo (*ff*)	very loud	augmentative of forte
Fuga	a strict contrapuntal work	escape, flight
Fugato	in fugal style	–
Fuoco	fire, energy, passion	fire
Garbo	simplicity, grace, elegance	courtesy, grace, politeness
Gentile	noble, pleasing, graceful	courteous, kind, polite
Giocoso	humorous, merry	facetious, jocose
Grave	majestical, serious, slow	heavy, serious
Grazia	grace, elegance	favour, grace, mercy
Grazioso	graceful, smooth, elegant	dainty, gracious, pretty
Intermezzo	an interlude	–
Lamentoso	lamenting, mournful	–
Larghetto	slow, but not as slow as largo	
Largo	slow, broad, solemn	breadth, width, room
Legato	smooth, slurred	tied, connected
Lento	slow	loose, slow, sluggish
Maestoso	majestically, dignified	–
Marcato	strongly marked emphasized	–
Mesto	melancholy	–
Mezzo	middle (mezzo *f*=half loud)	–
Moderato (Mod[to])	moderately quick	–
Molto	much	–
Moto	movement	agitation, exercise, impulse, motion
Obbligato	necessary, obligatory	–
Pesante	weighty, heavy, ponderous	–
Pianissimo (*pp*)	very quiet	augmentative of piano
Piano (*p*)	quiet	–
Più	more (più forte=louder)	–
Pizzicato (pizz)	the strings are to be plucked instead of bowed	pinched
Poco	little	–
Pomposo	stately, grand	pompous
Prestissimo	very quickly	augmentative of presto
Presto (P[o])	quickly, rapidly	soon, quick
Quasi	like, as it were	–
Ralentando (ral)	a gradual slowing of the tempo	–
Ricercare	any musical work employing novelty in design	to enquire into; seek, research into
Risoluto	resolutely, boldly	–
Ritardando (rit; ritard)	a gradual slowing of the tempo	–
Ritenuto (rit)[1]	a sudden slowing of the tempo	–
Scherzo	jest, a lively piece	freak, jest, trick
Sempre	always	–

[1] Because of the common abbreviation of 'rit' for both 'ritardando' and 'ritenuto' it is better to use 'ralentando' instead of the former to avoid error.

Direction	Musical use	Common Italian use
Senza	without	–
Sforzando	forced, greatly stressed	–
Sordino	a mute, muted	–
Sostenuto	sustained, sonorous	–
Sotto voce	with half the voice	in an undertone
Spiccato	very detached, bouncing the bow	to stand out, be prominent
Spirito	energy, spirit	courage, ghost, spirit, wit
Spiritoso	energy, spirit	alcoholic, witty
Staccato	pointed, distinctly separated	–
Tanto	so much, as much	–
Tosto	quick, swift	hard
Tranquillo	tranquilly, quiet	–
Tutti	all, the entire group	–
Vivace	lively, briskly	bright, sprightly

Some Extremes

The slowest tempo indication is 'Adagio molto assai'. This is rarely used, 'Adagio assai' usually sufficing.

The fastest would be some such combination as 'Prestissimo assai possible' (literally, 'as extremely very fast as possible').

The quietest indication was *pppppp* (literally *più più più più piano* or 'more more more more more quiet') in the first movement of Tchaikovsky's Symphony No 6 (1893), and in bar 37 of the duet for Otello and Desdemona in Act I of Verdi's *Otello* (1887), but it is assumed that this direction has been surpassed in more recent music, in which no extreme seems too extraordinary.

The ultimate in quiet music must be silence itself. Silence has been used as an integral part of music from the earliest days: one thinks of the effective use of pauses towards the end of certain Bach fugues, and the dramatic silences in many of Haydn's works (the first movements of Symphonies 39 in G minor (*c.*1768), and 80 in D minor (*c.*1783/4) are particularly effective examples).

The present century has seen many extensions of this use of silence. György Ligeti's Chamber Concerto (1969) ends with two whole bars of silence, carefully conducted, presumably to avoid the destruction of the effect of the close by the sudden, and aurally shattering, intrusion of applause.

It is when silence is used, not as an adjunct to music, but instead of it, that one must question the validity of certain pieces of so-called 'music'. John Cage, in 1952, 'wrote' a work entitled *4′ 33″*, this being the length of, to quote the composer, 'a piece in three movements during which no sounds are intentionally produced'. Any group of instruments, and presumably singers, may join in provided only that they make no musical sound for the duration of the three 'movements'. Cage's contention is that there is always something to hear so long as one is alive and has ears to hear it. He has a valid point there, but as far as the writer is aware he has not explained why, in order to hear this silence, one has to pay to sit watching motionless artists; nor does it explain the presence of those artists. Cage has written also works entitled *26′ 1.1499* for string player (1955) and *34′ 46.776* for piano (1954) and similarly named pieces.

The loudest indication will coincide with the occasion on which a composer tires of writing the letter *f*. Indications such as *ffff* are quite common in modern music, sometimes with the addition of *fz* to add force to the power: *fffffz*. The addition or subtraction of one *f* in such indications makes no difference in actual performance because, by the time the players reach *fff* they are playing as loud as they know how anyway. It becomes a matter of degree, and of judgement by the conductor: if he sees a piece of music with *fff*, building up to a final *fffz*, it is up to him to ensure that the players are not stretched to the utmost for the *fff*, and that something has been left in reserve for the additional z.

The longest indication (and perhaps the most ambivalent) is that for the *Kyrie* of Beethoven's Mass in C, Op 86 (1808): *Andante con moto assai vivace, quasi Allegretto, ma non Troppo.*

The first dynamic indications are possibly those (*forte, piano*) used in 1639 by Domenico Mazzochi.

The first accelerando in music occurs in Haydn's Symphony No 60 in C, *Il Distratto* (1774). At the end of the fifth movement (Adagio) a repeated phrase occurs four times, over the third of which Haydn writes 'Allegro'. It is evident from the nature of the music and the character of the symphony as a whole that Haydn intended some bizarre effect here, and although he did not specify 'accelerando' it is safe to assume that that is what he meant. However, as early as 1591 William Byrd indicated by the use of progressively shorter note lengths that he intended an accelerando at the end of his descriptive keyboard work *The Battell*.

As with accelerando, we may conjecture that the first crescendo in music was not marked as such but its existence is indicated unmistakably in the music.

Rossini earned the nickname 'Signor Crescendo' because of his striking use of the effect (known irreverently as 'the Rossini steamroller'), not least in his popular overtures. However, the invention of the device is credited to Johann Simon Mayr (1763–1845), who constructed greatly extended crescendi lasting over a number of bars and built up by successive entries of instruments. The true origin of the crescendo dates back much further than this in fact. The Mannheim orchestra under Jan Vačlav Stamic (1717–57) employed the effect frequently as part of its internationally famous virtuosity while the operas of Nicolo Jommelli (1714–74) also incorporated it as a structural entity. Many passages of repeated figuration in the earlier Italians such as Vivaldi (1678–1741) and Albinoni (1671–1745) invite this swelling treatment without actually calling for it in the music. It may be assumed that performances would include the effect as a matter of course (it is difficult to imagine a completely deadpan rendering of some of Vivaldi's symphonies, for instance) so the composers saw little point in stating the obvious in the scores. The dynamic succession *f, più f, ff* (literally 'loud', 'more loud', 'very loud') appears occasionally in Vivaldi's music, but the concept of a gradual tonal increase was doubtless well known before then in choral music, in which grades dynamics were required for expressive purposes.

The first 'hairpins' < > indicating minute crescendi and diminuendi are found in the violin sonatas of Giovanni Antonio Piani (*c.*1690–1760+), published in 1712.

Opus

Opus is an Italian noun meaning 'work' or 'piece' and is related to *opera* in that an opera is a 'work' with music for the stage. (Italian for 'opera' is *dramma per musica*). An opus number should identify the approximate chronology of a composer's work, but it is a far from infallible guide. For instance, in the cases of Beethoven and Schubert the highest numbers are often attached to early works because they were published posthumously.

The highest opus number, 798, appears to have been achieved by Karl Czerny who, nonetheless, composed over 1000 works, some of them large collections.

Thematic Catalogues

In appearance there are few less musical of music publications than a thematic catalogue. For the most part it consists of a series of musical staves, each giving the beginning of a piece of music (the *incipit*, or 'beginning') interspersed with virtually unreadable lines of abbreviations indicating sources. Careful reading of the introduction and foreword, and a valiant effort to memorize the list of abbreviations will help to unravel some of the meanings of these supposedly elucidatory lines of letters and numbers, but the production as a whole is likely to remain daunting in the extreme to the ordinary music-lover.

In fact, the thematic catalogue is one of the most vitally useful tools the musicologist has in his perpetual struggle to classify and codify the formidable quantity of music since the first pieces were written down (see the beginning of this Section). It lists, in some kind of logical order, the contents of a group of works by one composer or a group of composers, and it identifies each work in a way as near foolproof as possible: by actually quoting the start of each piece of music. The opening theme or incipit of a piece of music is almost as unique to that work as is a person's fingerprint – it is extremely rare to find two pieces of music in which the opening two or three bars are alike in every particular, and the longer the quoted incipit the less likely even that remote circumstance becomes. To illustrate this point, let us take the example of Haydn's Symphony No 70, which was used as model for a Symphony in D by the Polish composer Karol Pietrowsky. A listener knowing one of these works and then coming afresh to the other would be struck by the extraordinary resemblances between the music of the works' respective first and last movements, but an examination of the incipits of each, although indicating a resemblance, unfailingly identifies the two pieces of music as absolutely distinct. The incipits quoted are of the first violin part only, and the examples are limited to the first three bars of each movement.

Haydn: Symphony 70: first movement:

Pietrowsky: Symphony in D: first movement:

Haydn: Symphony 70: last movement:

Pietrowsky: Symphony in D: last movement:

Once the uniqueness of each piece of music is recognized it will be seen how useful a thematic catalogue can be.

Another example: Beethoven's symphonies. In referring to the Symphony in A, we can mean only Symphony No 7, since that is the only symphony he wrote in that key; similarly, all the other symphonies may be identified explicitly by key only, except Nos 6 and 8, which are both in F major. In this case, however, No 6 is known as the 'Pastoral' Symphony whereas No 8 has no subtitle, thus confusion is again avoided.

When turning to Vivaldi's concertos we are faced with a completely different and inherently defeating situation in which there are more than 20 Violin Concertos in C, only two of them with subtitles. Of the remainder, 16 are in the standard three-movement form of fast-slow-fast, and eight of these have the identical movement markings of Allegro; Largo; Allegro. Of these, several are without even the notoriously misleading opus numbers. Clearly, some method of visual identification is required to distinguish between these works, and between the similar potential confusions among Vivaldi's concertos in G, D, A, etc. The thematic catalogue rescues us from this confusion, and by referring to the numerical position of the work in the standard thematic catalogue of Vivaldi's concertos it is possible to pinpoint which work is meant with unmistakable accurancy.

It is only during the present century that the value of the thematic catalogue has been widely appreciated, but it is so well established as a research implement today that any deep research into a composer of the past loses much of its usefulness without one. The following examination of the field will illustrate just how widely accepted is the thematic catalogue, not only in the dusty corridors of music research, but also in the general identification requirements of concert programmes and the catalogues of music-publishers and record companies.

The first thematic catalogue is a single-page list giving 22 Psalm themes, published as part of *The Book of Psalms in Metre* in London in 1645.

The largest thematic catalogue is that issued in parts and supplements over a quarter of a century from 1762 to 1787 by the Leipzig music-publisher Johann Gottlob Immanuel Breitkopf (1719–94). In total, the catalogue contains some 14 000 incipits of music ranging in form from song to symphony, and its 888 pages include the identification of music by over 1000 composers. Breitkopf's catalogue was intended to advertise the manuscript and printed music for sale at his Leipzig premises; he was not to know that it was to prove an almost priceless source of information for researchers into the musical scene of the 18th century, and that its value is considered to be so great today that the entire catalogue and supplements were republished in fascimile by Dover in New York in 1966, under the guiding influence of Professor Barry S. Brook of the City University of New York.

A much larger thematic catalogue is in preparation in New York by Professor Jan la Rue, who has been collecting material for a Union Thematic Catalogue of 18th-century Symphonies and Concertos for more than 25 years. In order to cross-reference this data efficiently, assistance is being sought of electronic data-processing techniques. The future holds promise of a thematic catalogue of potentially infinite proportions (see RISM p. 218).

The best-known thematic catalogue is the *Chronologisch-thematisches Verzeichniss sämmtlicher Tonwerke W.A. Mozart's* by Ludwig Ritter von Köchel, the first edition of which was published by Brietkopf and Härtel in Leipzig in 1862 (just 100 years after the beginning of Breitkopf's own thematic house catalogue, see above). The latest edition of more than 1000 pages (nearly double the page-count of the original) incorporates the work put in on the catalogue in 1937 by Alfred Einstein and was published in 1964 under the editorship of Franz Geigling, Alexander Weinmann, and Gerd Sievers, but it is still referred to as 'The Köchel Catalogue', or just 'K'. For years it has been known by the concert-going public that, whereas most composers' music is identified by 'opus', Mozart's are known by the letter 'K' and a number. These numbers have become so identified with the works to which they attach that it is common in musical circles to hear comments such as 'What do you think of Klemperer's K 550?'

The thematic catalogue with the most beautiful title-page is the first of the two catalogues prepared in about 1785 for the music collection of the Comte d'Ogny (1757–90). This first catalogue lists orchestral and instrumental music (the second is devoted to vocal works) and it was written anonymously by someone who had a better eye for calligraphic excellence than for musicological detail. The hand-painted title-page is a production of extreme beauty.

A List of Thematic Catalogues

In the following chart are listed the most important published thematic catalogues which give all or a major part of the works of their chosen composers. The numbers in these publications are generally more reliable than opus identifications, which are usually only publishers' references. It is relevant to note that the opus numbers originally appended to Mozart's works are nowadays never encountered, and those by which Schubert's music is identified have almost entirely given way to 'D' numbers.

There are four basic types of catalogue:

1. Chronological, in which the composer's works are arranged in their proved or surmised order of composition (often by reference only to the opus numbers), regardless of genre.
2. Genre, in which the works are grouped according to type and regardless of chronology.
3. Chronological within genre.
4. Tonality within genre.

Composer	*Symbol*	*Compiler*	*Type*
Abel*	Kn	Walter Knape, 1971	2
Albinoni*†	Gia	Remo Giazotto, 1945	2
Albrechtsberger	Som	László Somfai, 1961–7	3
C.P.E. Bach	Wq	Alfred Wotquenne, 1905 (reprint, 1964)	3
J.C. Bach*	Terry	Charles Sanford Terry, 1929 (reprint, 1967)	3
J.S. Bach	BWV or S	Wolfgang Schmieder, 1950 (BWV = *Bach-Werke-Verzeichnis*)	2
W.F. Bach	F	Martin Falck, 1913	4
Beethoven*†	Kinsky	Georg Kinsky and Hans Halm, 1955	1
Boccherini*	Gér	Yves Gérard, 1969	3
Camerloher	Z	Benno Ziegler, 1919	2
Chopin*†	Fr	E.W. Fritsch, 1870	2
	Brown	Maurice J.E. Brown, 1960	1
Clementi*	Allorto	Riccardo Allorto, 1959	1
	Tyson	Alan Tyson, 1967	1
F. Couperin	Cauchie	Maurice Cauchie, 1949	1
Dittersdorf	Kr	Carl Krebs, 1900	3
F.X. Dušek	Sýkora	Václav Jan Sýkora, 1958	2
Dvořák*	Sourek	Otakar Sourek, 1917	1
Field	Hop	Cecil Hopkinson, 1961	1
Franck	Mohr	Wilhelm Mohr, 1969	2
Fux	Köchel	Ludwig Ritter von Köchel, 1872	2
G. Gabrieli	Kenton	Egon Kenton, 1967	1
Gluck	Wq	Alfred Wotquenne, 1904	1

Musical Notes

Composer	*Symbol*	*Compiler*	*Type*
J.G. Graun	M	Carl H. Mennicke, 1906	4
K.H. Graun	M	Carl H. Mennicke, 1906	4
Handel	B	Berend Baselt, 1974	3
Hasse	M	Carl H. Mennicke, 1906	4
F.J. Haydn*	Hob	Anthony van Hoboken, Vol I: Instrumental music, 1957 Vol II: Vocal music, 1971	3
J.M. Haydn	Perger	Lothar Perger, 1907 (instrumental)	2
	Klafsky	Anton Klafsky, 1925 (church)	2
Hoffstetter* (J.U.A. and R.)	Gottron	Adam Gottron, Alan Tyson, and Hubert Unvericht, 1968	2
L. Koželuh	Post	Milan Poštolka, 1964	3
Locatelli*†	Koole	Arend Koole, 1949	1
J.-B. Loeillet*	Priestman	Brian Priestman, 1952	1
J. Loeillet*	Priestman	Brian Priestman, 1952	1
Mahler	Martner	Knud Martner, in preparation	1
Martinů	Saf	Miloš Safranek, 1961	1
Monteverdi	Zimm	Franklin B. Zimmerman, in preparation	2
L. Mozart	DTBIX/2	Max Seiffert, 1908 (included in a volume of *Denkmäler der Tonkunst in Bayern*)	2
W.A. Mozart	K, or KV	Ludwig Ritter von Köchel, 1862 (reprinted and revised 1964)	1
Offenbach	Al	Antonio de Almeida, 1974	1
Pugnani	Zsch	Elsa M. Zschinsky-Troxler, 1939	2
Purcell	Zimm	Franklin B. Zimmerman, 1963	2
Roman	Bengtsson	Ingmar Bengtsson, 1955	2
Rosetti	Kaul	Oskar Kaul, 1912	2
	Schmid	Hans Schmid, 1968	2
D. Scarlatti	Longo	Alessandro Longo, 1937	4
	Kk	Ralph Kirkpatrick, 1970	1
Schubert*	D	Otto Erich Deutsch, 1951, 2nd Ed, 1978	1
Sibelius*†	T	Ernst Tanzberger, 1962	2
Soler	M	Frederick Marvin, 1963–?	4
	R	Father Samuel Rubio, 1960–?	2
J. Strauss*	S/R	Max Schönherr and Karl Reinöhl, 1954	3
R. Strauss	MvA	Erich H. Müller von Asow, 1955–68	1
Tartini	Dounias	Minos Dounias, 1935	4
Tchaikovsky*†	J	Boris Jurgenson, 1897	2
Telemann‡	SS	Käthe Schaefer-Schmuck, 1932 (keyboard works)	2
	Hörner	Hans Hörner, 1933 (Passion music)	2/3
	Hoff	Adolf Hoffmann, 1969 (orchestral suites)	4
	Kross	Siegfried Kross, 1969 (concertos)	2
Ruhnke	Ruhnke	Martin Ruhnke, 1984 (chamber music)	2
Torelli*	Gie	Franz Giegling, 1949	2
Viotti*	Pou	Arthur Pougin, 1888	2
	Gia	Remo Giazotto, 1956	1
Vivaldi*	RV	Peter Ryom, 1974	2/4
	Fanna	Antonio Fanna, 1968	2
Wagenseil	Mich	Helga Michelitsch, 1966 (keyboard works) 1973 (orchestral and chamber works)	2
Wagner	Kast	Emerich Kastner, 1878	1
Weber*	J	Friedrich Wilhelm Jähns, 1871	1+2
Zach	Komma	Karl Michael Komma, 1938	2

*The established opus numbers are misleading and should be disregarded in favour of information in the thematic listing.
†The established opus numbers give a good idea of chronology.
‡A complete catalogue of Telemann's music, incorporating the above catalogues in revised form and to be known as TWV – *Telemann-Werke-Verzeichnis* – is in preparation by Bärenreiter Verlag of Kassel.

'Omnibus' Catalogues

The following thematic catalogues each dealing with the works of more than one composer should also be mentioned as being of particular value to the music-researcher. It should be noted, however, that once again it has proved necessary to be arbitrarily selective since there is now such an enormous literature of thematic catalogues available to the specialist that nothing less than a separate book would do justice to the subject. Such a book exists: *Thematic Catalogues in Music* by Barry S. Brook (1972; an updated edition is in preparation). It may come as a surprise to those with an awareness in this field only of Köchel's Mozart catalogue that Professor Brook's bibliography contains no less than 1444 annotated entries, a total certain to be greatly increased in the forthcoming second edition.

Basel University Library: list of manuscript music of the 18th century (1957).

Breitkopf: see p. 216.

Brook, Barry S: *Catalogue of French Symphonies* (and associated works; also of some foreign symphonies published in France) *of the second half of the 18th century* (1962).

Duckles and Elmer: *Thematic catalogue of a manuscript collection of 18th-century Italian instrumental music in the University of California, Berkeley Music Library* (1963). Although mainly of Italian music, other countries' composers are not entirely excluded.

Dunwalt: a manuscript catalogue compiled by, or under the direction of, Gottfried Dunwalt in 1770. It lists over 500 orchestral and instrumental works in Dunwalt's possession at that time. The catalogue is preserved in the British Museum.

Garland Publishing: the Reference Volume of *The Symphony 1720–1840*, containing 184 totally new thematic indexes of early symphonic works (1986).

Hummel: a publisher's catalogue with six supplements (a seventh was announced but apparently not issued) of music published between 1754 and 1774. The catalogue and the known supplements were published in facsimile with an introduction by Cari Johansson in 1973.

Kade, Otto: a catalogue with supplements of the music libraries of Duke Friedrich Franz III and the Mecklenburg-Schwerin Collections (1893–1908).

Karlsruhe: four manuscript catalogues of the collections of early music in the Badische Landesbibliothek at Karlsruhe.

Mannheim: a list of the symphonies written in the 18th century by composers of the Mannheim School.

d'Ogny: two manuscript catalogues of instrumental and vocal music in the collection of Comte d'Ogny (1757–90). The catalogues were prepared about 1785 with the utmost attention to beauty of presentation, and the first catalogue (of orchestral and instrumental music) was graced with a finely executed title-page (see above).

RISM: the initials stand for 'Répertoire International des Sources Musicales'. This organization's ambition is to collect for international availability a thematic listing of nothing less than the entire musical printed and manuscript holdings of all the sources (libraries, museums, etc.) of the world. An international project of this magnitude, requiring the goodwill and funds of many separate institutions, will require very many years of patience and tenacity before beginning to approach useful completion, and the number of incipits to be included will run into millions. The Czechoslovakian affiliate has reported that cataloguing has been completed for 186 000 works, and the holdings of other collections still awaiting thematic cataloguing is formidable: East Germany: 53 000; West Germany: 88 000; Hungary: 20 000, etc.

Music Appreciation

The first step towards the establishment of music appreciation as a regular subject in school curriculae could be said to be an article written by Agnes Mary Langdale in 1908, published that year in *The Crucible*.

The first broadcast music appreciation courses were begun by Walter Damrosch over the American NBC Network in 1928.

The most powerful forces in the widening of musical appreciation were the writings of Sir Donald Francis Tovey, whose carefully argued and imaginative writings on music were originally used as programme notes mostly for the Reid Concerts Orchestra in Edinburgh earlier this century.

As Essays in Musical Analysis, they were first published in hardback form by the Oxford University Press in 1935 and have achieved enormous and totally justified popularity, serving as an unattainable standard for later writers.

X

Whoopee in D major

Madness in great ones must not unwatched go.

Hamlet III:i

What is music? Readers who have got this far may be taken by surprise by this question. Surely the earlier pages have answered it adequately?

The American composer Henry Brant chose the title *Whoopee in D major* for an orchestral piece he wrote in 1938. It is a thought-provoking name, for it embodies an apparent contradiction: a spontaneous cry of joy that is yet constrained by the strict rules of harmony. An exuberant exclamation subjected to technical discipline. It has been said that music begins where words end, and Brant illustrates by his title that even so exultant a word as 'whoopee' is sharpened by being given the straight-jacket of a key. The primary purpose of music is to accentuate and intensify human emotions. Carlyle's description of music as 'the speech of angels' implies more than some ethereal message performed by a heavenly choir; it implies that music can 'say' far more than mere words and is therefore on a far higher plane.

We know, then, that music exists to stimulate emotion. Contrary to rumour, the modern composer writes music for the same purpose, though the increasing intellectuality of much of today's music creates a barrier for many listeners. Early this century the great American musical experimenter Charles Ives was sickened by the lily-livered conservatism of the average listener. A work by his friend Carl Ruggles provoked a gentleman in the audience to shout indignant abuse at the performers. Infuriated, Ives rose and faced the offender: 'Stop being such a goddamned sissy. Stand up and use your ears like a man!'

Experimental Music

The problem is not new. François Campion (*c.*1686–1748), a noted lute and guitar player at the Académie Royale de Musique, found 'modern' music intolerable. What *had* he been listening to? In his average lifetime he had seen music intelligible to him give way to something more advanced, showing that even then composers were straining the musical tolerance of trained musicians. But 'modern' music has always had a bad press. Haydn was said by his contemporaries to be scandalously noisy; Beethoven, according to Weber, should be incarcerated in an asylum for writing his Seventh Symphony; and the audience turned to physical assault at the first performance of Stravinsky's *The Rite of Spring*. Yet Haydn, Beethoven and Stravinsky were amongst music's most imaginative and successful experimenters.

Today the situation is more extreme. Composers consistently write 'ahead' of their audiences and have done so for most of this century, but in so doing they have found it necessary increasingly to expand the bounds of music by introducing ever more bizarre instruments and effects into their ensembles, and violating the rules of harmony, counterpoint, rhythm and structure by ever more severe excesses. Ask a composer today 'what is music?' and your answer is likely to be 'music is what I choose it to be', or 'music is in the ear of the listener'.

Only a small proportion of musical experiments lead anywhere. Undoubtedly the most successful experimenter was Beethoven, who took established classical principles and drove them by emotional, dramatic and technical means, into the Romantic era. Some believe that Arnold Schoenberg (d. 1951) was as successful (see p. 151); but even he yields to some

Edgar Varèse in the 1950s. Composer or metallurgist? (Philips Records Ltd)

of the insane things perpetrated by recent composers.

BY ANY OTHER NAME

Having written a piece of music, what should a composer call it? Clearly, these days, 'violin concerto', 'string quartet', or other titles indicating the number of artists used and, more or less, the sort of music the audience can expect to hear, are prosaic and out of date. But it still might be desirable to indicate the number of players involved, as did Tristram Cary in 1961 when he called his concerto grosso *Three Threes and One Make Ten*, from which it is a simple matter to deduce that it is for five winds and five strings. John Cage's *Cartridge Music* (1960) also tells you what to expect: they are gramophone cartridges (pick-up heads) attached to amplifiers. Szalonek's *1+1+1+1* (1969) is of course for four strings, and Varèse's *Density 21.5* (1936) is self-evidently a piece for solo flute, because, as everyone knows, that is the density of platinum, the metal from which the instrument is constructed. Josef Alexander's *4 for 5* (1958) is clearly four movements for five brass instruments, but from *Three Acts for Four Sinners* (1961) by Alexander Brott it is not immediately identifiable that the guilty ones are saxophonists.

In *Action for Four Strolling Musicians* (1969) Goeyvaerts allows his artists to choose any instruments they like as long as they are all different, while in *MP5* (1967) by Hrisanide the instruments are specified: tenor sax (doubling clarinet), violin, viola, cello and piano. The title, incidentally, simply means *Musique Pour 5* (Players). *Music for a Five and Dime Store* (1931) by Henry Brant, the composer whose work gave this section its name, uses a selection of culinary instruments collected, no doubt, in such a Depression-era store; but an American lady by the name of Lucia Dlugoszewski specifies not the maker of the music but the receiver and its location in a series of works during the 1950s and 1960s: *Music for Left Ear in a Small Room*, for piano (1959) and for violin (1965), and so on, while her *Concert of Man Rooms and Moving Space* (1960) is for flute, clarinet, timbre piano (her own invention, along with about 100 other percussion instruments) and four unsheltered rattles in various locations. The previous year she wrote *Delicate Accidents in Space* for unsheltered rattle quintet.

Number-and-letter titles have attracted composers, too. Earle Brown's *25 Pages* (1953) is just that. The pages of music may be played in any order, right-way-up or upside-down. Also obvious, when you know, is the meaning of Claudio Spies's *LXXXV, 8s and 5s* for clarinet and strings. Its date of 1967 gives a clue: it was written to honour Stravinsky's 85th birthday. Charles K. Hoag wrote *ZZZZ!* for 30 string players in 1969; Kenneth Gaburo retaliated with *The Flow of* $((i))^2$ for assorted 'phenomena' in 1970.

Some titles tell a story, or promise to do so. David Bedford's *18 Bricks Left on April 21st* for two electric guitars (1967) comes in this category as (perhaps) does *Pounding Silk Floss* (1966) for 12 percussionists by Brian Dennis. A story told unexpectedly by an American, David Rosenboom, is *How Much Better if Plymouth Rock Had Landed on the Pilgrims* (1971). Harrison Birtwistle's 1976 piece for six percussionists, *For O, for O, the Hobbyhorse is Forgot* draws its title in fact from one of the world's great stories, Hamlet (III:ii); *What Next?* asked Yori Aki Matsutiara with soprano and two noise makers in 1967, but the question had already been answered in 1958 by chorus and instruments in *0 0 0 0 That Shakespeherian Rag* by Salvatore Martirano. There is a story behind one of the strangest of all titles, David Bedford's *A Horse, his name was Hunry Fencewaver Walkins* (1977) but you may be relieved to learn that its telling is not a part of the music. It seems that Bedford was reading a poem by Kenneth Patchen when his wife asked him if he had chosen a title for his new piece of music. At that moment Bedford had reached the line that became the title.

Eh?? asked Folke Rabe in 1967, using one, two, or four-track tape; and if Rabe's title is one of the shortest, he might well have used it to query one of the longest. It is La Monte Young's *The Obsidian Ocelot, the Sawmill, and the Blue Sawtooth High-Tension Line Stepdown Transformer Refracting the Legend of the Dream of the Tortoise Traversing the 189/98 Lost Ancestral Lake Region Illuminating Quotients from the Black Tiger Tapestries of the Drone of the Holy Numbers* (1965), which is one part of a work for voices, instruments and electronics. The longest single word in a title comes in Jani Christou's 1968 piece for baritone, viola and ensemble: *Anaparastasis I: astronkatidhanyteronomighyrin* (= 'I have become familiar with the assembly of the stars of the night' – Aeschylus).

Could there be something to be said for 'violin concerto' after all?

David Bedford. Composer or bricklayer? (Universal Edition (London) Ltd)

CLOSE YOUR EYES, JUST LISTEN

Close your eyes, just listen
Live completely alone for four days
without food,
in complete silence, without much movement,
Sleep as little as necessary,
think as little as possible.
After four days, late at night,
without conversation beforehand,
play single sounds.
WITHOUT THINKING what you are playing
close your eyes,
just listen.

These are Stockhausen's instructions to the unfortunate performers who undertake to play his *Goldstaub* ('Gold dust'), and they are symptomatic of the lengths to which composers will go in their search for new means of musical expression. Richard Orton's 12 brass players in *Brass Phase* (1978) are to sit on revolving stools, and Gilberto Ambrosio Garcís Mendes, in *Son et Lumière* (1968), calls for piano, tapes, photographic flashes and 'a very beautiful woman pianist who walks like a mannequin' instead of playing the piano. Donatoni's two pianists, however, *are* required to play in *Black and White*, but they receive little help from the composer: they are told which fingers to use but not which notes to play, nor for how long each note is to sound.

Orchestral players have to have extraordinary skills to meet modern composers' demands, as in Varèse's *Déserts* (1954), where they must imitate the sounds coming from a tape of prerecorded electronic music as it is interpolated into the performance. Players also have to develop immunity to isolation, vertigo and disorientation if they are to perform Henry Brant's music composed since 1953. *Antiphony I* of that year employs five distinct orchestras spacially separated, while *Voyage 4* of 1963 disperses groups of performers vertically up the walls and even under the floor. The brass and percussion in *Millennium* 2 (1954) entirely surround the audience.

Orchestral managers and concert organizers also have to be virtuosi in their fields. Assuming a tap dancer can be booked to perform Morton Gould's concerto of 1952, and an actor can be persuaded to appear in Bolcom's 1970 creation titled *Theatre of the Absurd* along with its tape, piano, wind quintet and mechanized eyeballs, it may be predicted that some of Ferde Grofé's unusual effects may present problems. He demands a typewriter in *Tabloid* (a machine to be found, perhaps, in a corner, covered in dust after the most recent performance of Satie's *Parade*), sirens and drills in *Symphony of Steel*, a bicycle pump in *Free Air*, foghorns (appropriately) in *San Francisco*, and a carpenter to hammer scenery and a director to do the shouting in *Hollywood Suite*.

Gilberto Mendes set out to chill the blood of the concert organizer with the last word of his line-up for *Cidade cité city* (1964), for after listing 'three voices, percussion, piano, double bass, three phonographs, dust catcher, floor polisher and television set' he added the infinitely menacing abbreviation 'etc.' Eight years later he demanded an electric fan and an electric shaver in *O objeto musical*, and coffee cups, spoons and a medicine dropper in *Pausa e menopausa*. Domestic appliances were first used musically at the Hoffnung Music Festival in London in 1956, when vacuum cleaners were solemnly cued in and out during Malcolm Arnold's *A grand grand overture*, and by 1965 the craze had spread as far as Chile, where Miguel Aguilar-Ahumada required balloons, glasses containing liquid, and cow-sounds on tape for his *Composicién con 3 sonidos*.

While in South America the would-be concert organizer would do well to seek some native instruments if he would mount Chavez's 1940 work *Xochipilli-Macuilxochitl*: its five-member wind group is joined by a glittering array of percussion in the hands of six players with the following responsibilities:

1 Small teponaxtle; omichicahauxtli
2 Large teponaxtle; small copper rattles
3 Small and medium Indian drums; clay rattle
4 Small huehuetl; smooth rattle
5 Medium huehuetl; clay rattle; large copper rattle
6 Large huehuetl; omichicahuaxtli

Other composers have been less demanding. Peter Michael Braun affably advises that his *Spuren* (completed in 1970) may be performed by *any* instruments or voices, and John Cage is equally easy-going for *O' O"* since it is a piece 'to be performed in any way to anyone'; how John Cage himself once performed it may be learnt on p 114. Paolo Castaldi's *Tema* (1968) also presents few problems: it is a piece for silent reading.

Possibly the only work to call for a tuning fork in the actual performance is *Tsi* (1970) by Tona Scherchen-Hsiao, in which it is supported by a gong and 16 vocalists. More homely still is the sound of cuckoo clock and musical box in *Time Structures II* for orchestra and tape (1974) by the

Modern 'musical' instruments. (Artwork: Peter Harris)

South African contemporary composer Peter James Leonard Klatzow. Earlier we met a work whose title informed us that there were 18 bricks left on 21 April; one of them has strayed into Gustavo Becerra-Schmidt's *Juegos* (1966), where it is joined by piano, ping-pong balls and tape. Of a less exotic hue, uncharacteristically, is John Cage's *Cheap Imitation* (1972) which comes in three sizes: for 24 or 59 or 95 players, with or without conductor. But the conductor cannot be so easily dismissed in Dieter Schnebel's *Nostalgie (Visible Music II)* of 1962, for the conductor's gestures are the only 'music' present. And as if to reassure the poor conductor once and for all of the necessity of his existence, Jan Bark's *Missa Bassa* (1964) for orchestra and six vocalists calls for seven conductors.

It was inevitable that music would be invaded by machines in our highly mechanized age. Varèse's *Poeme Electronique*, written to be heard in the Philips Pavilion at the Brussels World Fair in 1958, was intentionally interrupted by the sound of passing jet aircraft as it thundered down from 400 speakers, and George Antheil's *Ballet Mechanique* (1925) introduced (too often) the sound of a piston-engined aeroplane along with its eight pianos, player-piano, four xylophones, tam tam, four bass drums and siren. Naim June Paik, in *Hommage à john cage* (1959) added a motor cycle to the weird collection of three tape recorders, projectors, 'live actions involving eggs and toy cars', and two pianos (which are destroyed during the performance); and an internal combustion engine is included in Franco Casavola's ballet *La danza dell'elica* (1924). Presumably the road vehicles in these works would need to be controlled by the two red traffic lights operated from a keyboard in the wings during John Alden Carpenter's *Skyscrapers* (1924).

The most ambitious motor-musical happening was Robert Moran's *39 Minutes for 39 Autos*, an event that involved the whole of San Francisco on 29 August 1969, when car horns and lights, a Moog synthesizer, tape recorders and broadcasting facilities, both radio and TV, were 'conducted' by Moran. Even home and office lights were turned off and on by the audience acting on broadcast cues. Not for the city's electricians the advice 'close your eyes, just listen' as surges set power station dials spinning.

Despair in C Minor

Music has been responsible for some grotesque tales. One concerns the strange power it can have on sensitive people, and the powerful nature attributed to some keys — see p 152. Could music, for instance, kill?

It is reputed to have killed Joseph Keller. He was a Budapest cobbler who committed suicide in 1936 leaving a note which quoted the lyrics of the song *Szomorú Vasárnap* by Seress Reszó. The title translates as 'Gloomy Sunday', and Reszó's music is set in the unrelieved melancholia of C minor. Keller's death was treated merely as a bizarre incident until it was found that a further 17 suicides in Hungary might be in some way connected with the song. A ban on performance followed. Within a year or so the song, preceded no doubt by a certain amount of ballyhoo, hit America. The Hungarian lyrics by László Jávor were translated into such uplifting phrases as:

Gloomy Sunday, midst shadows I spend it all.
My heart and I have decided to end it all.
and
Death is no dream, for in death I'm caressing you.
With the last breath of my soul I'll be blessing you.

Artie Shaw and others recorded it, and the records became best-sellers on both sides of the Atlantic. The BBC, however, feeling that the morale of the British public should be protected from the down-beat mood of the song, banned all broadcasts of it.

Music may have caused suicides (some music-lovers claim that it is a positive force in preventing them), but the strain of writing music has certainly produced an unbearable burden on some composers. The adjacent list gives only a selection of unhappy composers who have been driven over the brink, but the most famous composer of all to commit suicide was forced into it by others.

When a lad, the sensitive Tchaikovsky was separated from his deeply-loved mother and sent to a law school in St Petersburg. Four years later his mother died and Tchaikovsky was apparently driven to express his strong emotional nature in another way. Unfortunately, his law school was a male-dominated environment.

Many years later he faced an accusation by an aristocrat that there had been a homosexual relationship between the composer and the aristocrat's nephew. The lawyers, by now middle-aged, held a meeting at which it was decided, with reluctance, that the profession could not abide a scandal, and the composer was 'sentenced' to die by his own hand. His death on

6 November 1893, for so long blamed on cholera, was caused apparently by self-administered arsenic.

Composers who Committed Suicide

Antoni, Antonio d' (1801–59), Italian operatic composer and conductor, took his own life in Trieste.

Carey, Henry (*c.*1689–1743), English song-writer, poet, and composer of a number of operas and pantomimes, hanged himself at his east London home because of business worries.

Clarke, Jeremiah, (*c.*1674–1707), English composer and organist at St Paul's Cathedral, London, was the true composer of *Trumpet Voluntary*, for long attributed to Purcell. Being unlucky in love, Clarke shot himself.

Distler, Hugo (1908–42), German composer and organist who killed himself because he was unable to tolerate the terrors of wartime Germany.

Maxfield, Richard Vance (1927–69), American modernist composer and pupil of Roger Sessions, committed suicide at the age of 42.

Milford, Robin Humphrey (1903–59), prolific English composer whose sincere music quite simply went out of fashion. This, and the death of his 6-year-old son, drove him to take an overdose of aspirin.

Moorehead, John (?–1804), Irish violinist and theatre composer, went insane and was imprisoned in London in 1802. Upon release he joined the navy, but hanged himself soon afterwards in Kent.

Nedbal, Oskar (1874–1930), Bohemian operetta composer. Long-standing financial worries wore him down until he reached breaking-point at Christmas 1930 and committed suicide.

Pedrotti, Carlo (1817–93), Italian composer, drowned himself in the River Adige at Verona during an attack of nervous depression.

Powell, Felix (1879–1942), Welsh composer of the popular World War I song 'Pack up your troubles in your old kit-bag', was unable to take the advice of his brother (the lyric writer), and escaped through suicide.

Warlock, Peter (1894–1930), writer, composer and editor of old English music. The mystery of his death has never been satisfactorily resolved.

Zimmermann, Bernd Alois (1918–70), German composer of, *inter alia*, the cantata *In Praise of Stupidity*, shot himself.

Back from the Dead

A composer's death, however caused, does not necessarily mean the end of his composing activities. When the young 19th-century violin virtuoso Florizel became known for introducing into his programmes previously unknown works by Paganini, audiences became suspicious, for Paganini had been dead for some years. Florizel's mother answered these questions by asserting that these 'new' compositions had been discovered during research in Genoa, Paganini's native city. Then she came clean, and the 'truth' proved to be even less believable.

When Florizel was seven his mother had bought him an old guitar in a little Parisian curio shop, the dealer having spun a line about its having once belonged to Paganini. That evening Florizel had a dream in which Paganini's father visited him and hummed him a tune which Florizel committed to memory. More dreams followed. In one, Paganini's father told him that there was an unknown Paganini composition hidden in a panel in the guitar, and after a search next morning Florizel and his mother found it. Subsequent dreams provided further works (transmitted by either Paganini himself or his father) which Florizel memorized while asleep, wrote down upon waking, and included in his concerts.

There is not an atom of proof that this colourful story is anything other than a romantic publicity stunt.

The well-documented case of Rosemary Brown is somewhat different, for not one but a whole crowd of composers are 'coming through', and the 'receiver' is not a musical virtuoso capable, at a pinch, of forging music, but a south London housewife with only slight knowledge and limited ability in music.

Rosemary Brown (b. 1917) tells us that it all began when she was a girl. An elderly gentleman 'appeared' to her and told her he was a famous composer who would return in later years to give her music. This was Liszt, who, when he appeared again in the early 1960s (as a much younger man), dictated a number of piano pieces to Mrs Brown — or, rather, 'wore her hands like gloves' and played passages

Franz Liszt, after the portrait by Lenbach. Liszt was the first composer to 'come through' to Rosemary Brown from 'the other side'. (Corvina Press)

several times which she then wrote down. Other composers joined Liszt: Schubert (who dictates *Lieder* as well as piano music — 'but he hasn't got a very good voice', though 'he communicates very easily'), Rachmaninoff ('. . . he's a very patient, kindly sort of person'), Beethoven ('. . . seems to be about 35. He looks very fine — he hasn't got that crabby look'), Debussy ('. . . he does much more painting than music now'), Bach, Mozart, Chopin and others. There is a great deal of posthumous music from these composers now, not just piano pieces (some of which have been recorded by Howard Shelley, Peter Katin and Mrs Brown herself) but string quartets and at least two symphonies by Beethoven. These last, one of them a Choral Symphony, were begun during the late 1960s but have not yet been offered to the public. Presumably the delay is due to the difficulty of a composer dictating such a complex score to a receiver of limited technique.

So the friendly spirits would do well to try other outlets. Apparently Handel has dictated a new oratorio, *Beyond the Veil*, to Clifford Enticknap (b. 1920), who lives in Buckinghamshire, and there have been other claims of similar contacts. The authors reserve the right to be sceptical because absolute proof is lacking — yet it could be so easily arranged.

In a communication dictated to Mrs Brown by Sir Donald Francis Tovey, who died in 1940 but 'came through' 30 years later, we are assured of

Rosemary Brown.

an afterlife and are told that these musicians are attempting to prove its existence by transmitting music which musicians of this world are expected to identify as genuine. Some of it does sound genuine; much does not. But no matter how authentic the music *sounds*, one cannot avoid the suspicion that some clever fraud is being perpetrated. If only one of these spirit composers would simply tell us of the whereabouts of a lost genuine work composed during their earlier existence — the whereabouts of a manuscript that could be examined by musicologists in the light of today's forensic and stylistic testing procedures — it would not only provide the world, one hopes, with a work of great value but also give incontrovertible proof that 'the other side' is in contact with us. That might be the occasion for whoopees in all sorts of keys.

Bibliography

To mention all the sources consulted in the preparation of this book the bibliography would have to be many times its size. For example, more than a hundred thematic catalogues and countless scores have been examined, many contributing little or nothing directly to the text other than to confirm, deny or clarify some small point. Acknowledgement is made to these and to the many periodicals and specialist studies which have assisted in the information-gathering process over the years.

Bird, J. *Percy Grainger: the Man and the Music*, London, 1976

Brook, Barry S. *Thematic Catalogues in Music*, New York, 1972

Charroux, R. *The Mysterious Past*, London, 1974

Clemencic, R. *Old Musical Instruments*, London, 1973

Cohen, A.I. *International Discography of Women Composers*, Westport and London, 1984

Cohen, A.I. *International Encyclopedia of Women Composers*, New York and London, 1981

Cowell, H. and S. *Charles Ives and his Music*, London, 1955

Dent, E.J. *Opera*, Middlesex, 1940

Geiringer, K. *Musical Instruments, Their History in Western Culture from the Stone Age to the Present Day*, London, 1943

Harding, J. *Erik Satie*, London, 1975

Headington, C. *The Bodley Head History of Western Music*, London, 1974

Hitchcock, H.W. *Music in the United States: A Historical Introduction*, New Jersey, 1969

Jenkins, J. *Eighteenth Century Musical Instruments: France and Britain*, London, 1973

Jenkins, J. *Musical Instruments (preserved in) The Horniman Museum*, London, 1970

Loewenberg, A. *Annals of Opera 1597–1940*, Geneva, 1942; 1955

Mellers, W. *Music in a New Found Land*, London, 1964

New Grove Dictionary of Music and Musicians (20 volumes), London, 1980

Nyman, M. *Experimental Music, Cage and Beyond*, London, 1974

Pleasants, H. *The Great Singers*, London, 1967

Rushmore, R. *The Singing Voice*, London, 1971

Scholes, P.A. *The Oxford Companion to Music*, London, 1956

Vinton, J. *Dictionary of 20th century Music*, London, 1974

Warwick, A.R. *A Noise of Music*, London, 1968

Weinstock, H. *Rossini: a Biography*, New York, 1968

Index

Subjects, names and instruments are gathered together in one index. Important personalities are indexed fully but it has been considered unnecessary to list every personality mentioned in the book on the premise that readers are more likely to be searching for subjects than for often obscure names. To this end the subject listing has been made as comprehensive as practicable.

The lists of works by key (pp 155–162) and by nicknames (pp 184–198) are not individually indexed.

Page numbers in *italics* denote illustrations.

Index

C

D

E

F

G

N

O

P

Q

R

X

Y

Z